THE CROSS-CULTURAL PROCESS
IN CHRISTIAN HISTORY

THE CROSS-CULTURAL PROCESS IN CHRISTIAN HISTORY

*Studies in the Transmission and
Appropriation of Faith*

Andrew F. Walls

Orbis Books
Maryknoll, New York

T&T Clark
Edinburgh

Founded in 1970, Orbis Books endeavors to publish works that enlighten the mind, nourish the spirit, and challenge the conscience. The publishing arm of the Maryknoll Fathers and Brothers, Orbis seeks to explore the global dimensions of the Christian faith and mission, to invite dialogue with diverse cultures and religious traditions, and to serve the cause of reconciliation and peace. The books published reflect the views of their authors and do not represent the official position of the Maryknoll Society.

To learn more about Maryknoll and Orbis Books, please visit our website at www.maryknoll.com.

Library of Congress Cataloging-in-Publication Data

Walls, Andrew F. (Andrew Finlay)
    The cross-cultural process in Christian history: studies in the transmission and appropriation of faith / Andrew F. Walls.
      p. cm.
    Includes bibliographical references and index.
    ISBN 1-57075-373-3 (pbk.)
    1. Missions—History. I. Title.

BV2100. W257 2001
270—dc21

                                  2001041425

British Library Cataloguing-in-Publication Data is available from the British Library.

T&T Clark/ISBN 0 567 08869 3

FOR CHRISTINE AND ALAN AND ANDREW

Hereditas Domini Corona Senum

Contents

Preface

A popular panel game on BBC radio required contestants to speak on one topic for one minute without hesitation, deviation, or repetition. The qualities needed for that exercise are, alas, missing in this book. Hesitations and deviations are here a-plenty; and the degree of repetition that occurs in essays on related themes originally prepared for different audiences may well seem excessive.

There is repetition in another sense. Many of the pieces have appeared before, and I am grateful to the editors and publishers of the works in which they previously appeared. Revision in these cases has been minimal, though sometimes remarks belonging to the original location have been omitted or modified. The tripartite structure of the volume follows that of an earlier collection, *The Missionary Movement in Christian History* (Orbis, 1996). First come essays on recurrent themes of Christian history, and of Christian historiography, viewed intercontinentally. Then follow studies of the transmission and appropriation of the Christian faith in two specific fields, Africa and the modern missionary movement from the West. These illustrate themes identified in the first section. The view of the nature and process of Christian conversion set out in the early essays suggests that African Christianity can be viewed both as a Christian chapter in the history of African religion and as an African chapter in the history of Christianity. The theme of cross-cultural diffusion as the lifeblood of historic Christianity is illustrated in the final section, which centers on the Western missionary movement as one example of that process of diffusion. The missionary movement is a major factor in bringing about that cultural and demographic transformation of Christianity which was its leading characteristic in the twentieth century. It also has exemplary significance as the learning experience of Western Christianity.

A justifiable complaint was made of the earlier collection that its subtitle spoke only of the transmission of faith while the subject matter also dealt with its appropriation. I gladly acknowledge that transmission and appropriation are equally aspects of diffusion, and I hope that this is reflected both in the contents of the present work and in its title.

Anything of value in the present volume owes a great deal to other people. These include the friends and colleagues whose conversation over the years has stimulated ideas; among these I am especially grateful to Lamin Sanneh, Kwame Bediako, Richard Elphick, and Moonjang Lee. Members of various audiences who heard the original papers helped to clarify, moderate, and inform the presentation. My students at the University of Edinburgh, at Princeton Theological Seminary (where I have spent more than four happy years as guest professor), at Harvard Divinity School (during my brief tenure of the Monrad Family Visiting Chair of World Christianity), and at the Akrofi-Christaller Memorial Centre in Akropong, Ghana, have probably been the most formative influence of all.

Bill Burrows, managing editor of Orbis Books, has been a valued guide and remembrancer; his admonitions have served the purposes achieved in a former age by keeping a skull in one's closet as a *memento mori.* To him, to other thoughtful and efficient members of the Orbis staff, and to the copy editor, Robert Maccini, I offer sincere thanks. Anne Fernon and Ruth Scott at Edinburgh, and Joan Blyth at Princeton, performed feats of virtuosity in the preparation of the typescripts. My wife, Doreen, has been consistent in her support. In going over the manuscripts she has identified many flaws and faults otherwise unnoticed, and in other respects—to use words applied by Jane Austen to one of her more admirable characters—has softened, humored, or concealed those of the author.

Andrew F. Walls
Princeton
May 2001

Part One

THE TRANSMISSION
OF CHRISTIAN FAITH

1

A History of the Expansion of Christianity **Reconsidered**

Assessing Christian Progress and Decline

A library, as Victor Hugo pointed out long ago, is an act of faith. It is a commitment to an unseen future. In the first lecture of the Day Library Associates, given in the course of the first meeting of the Yale-Edinburgh Group on the History of the Missionary Movement, Dr. Stephen Peterson celebrated the vision of George E. Day.[1] As a student at Yale, Day met the *Amistad* captives, whose arrival in New Haven initiated American missions to West Africa. As professor of Hebrew, he assembled at Yale a specialist collection of publications on missions. Peterson's lecture showed that Day's was an Abrahamic journey, in which future generations were blessed. The bibliological acorn he planted produced in time a mighty oak. In taking up the high privilege of delivering another lecture in the Day Library Associates series, I must, as a member of the University of Edinburgh, rejoice to be doing so during another meeting of the Yale-Edinburgh Group. And for the topic, it seems appropriate to turn to a work of scholarship that rests squarely on the provisions of the library that Day founded, and that is, perhaps, its most remarkable monument to date.

The first volume of *A History of the Expansion of Christianity*, by Kenneth Scott Latourette, appeared in 1937; the seventh and final volume in 1945, a half century ago. I speak as one of the many who have derived refreshment and resource from Latourette's writings, and especially from the seven volumes of the *Expansion*. Mine was the first student generation to have access

The Day Missions Library Associates Lecture for 1995, delivered at Yale University Divinity School Library. Published as Occasional Publication Number 8 of the Yale Divinity School Library, 1996. Reprinted with permission.

[1] S. L. Peterson, The Day Missions Library Centennial, Yale Divinity School Library Occasional Publication No. 2 (New Haven: Yale Divinity School Library, 1993).

to the whole work—not that my student generation was falling over itself to do so. Significantly, it was not from any of my teachers that I learned of its existence, but from a visiting preacher, the dashing bishop of Tirunelveli, Stephen Neill, during a university mission. The range of the book, its profusion of information, captivated me. In time its central theme gripped me and helped to shape my own work; but long before that, as a teacher in Africa, embarking on serious study of the then scarcely regarded field of African Christian history, I discovered the surprising richness of Latourette's bibliographies. They were about as comprehensive and as full as anyone could get during that period. I did not yet know the secret of their source, though Latourette himself reveals it at the very beginning of volume 1:

> For more than a quarter of a century the author has had the privilege of living with much of the pertinent literature. During most of that time he has had constant access to one of the world's richest collections of printed material related to the subject, in the libraries of Yale University and especially the Day Missions Library.[2]

In due course, I was able to visit the quarry from whence the *Expansion* was hewn, and, indeed, the Day Missions Library became a regular part of my life. This chapter, however unworthy in itself, is offered in celebration of the achievement of K. S. Latourette by taking up themes dear to him, often with reference to his own words and conclusions. This chapter also acknowledges a personal debt to a wonderful library and to a succession of librarians, curators, and library staff whose effectiveness and helpfulness are, in my experience, unparalleled. Librarians as a race are the salt of the earth. Those connected with the Day Library exemplify the traditional uses of salt in superlative measure; they preserve the food of scholarship, and they enhance its flavour.

Latourette's *Expansion* as a Monumental Work

Nothing like Latourette's *Expansion* had appeared before, and so far it has no obvious successor. Its scope, for a single-author work, is extraordinary. It describes and documents, so far as the resources then available allowed, the story of the Christian faith in every century and in every part of the world. Such exhaustive coverage can produce sentences of almost comic intensity. Thus, summarizing religious developments region by region over the period 1914–44, the author tells us, "Of Greenland . . . little need be said." This solemn statement is then given solemn justification.[3]

[2] K. S. Latourette, *A History of the Expansion of Christianity*, vol. 1 (New York and London: Harper, 1937), xv. Subsequent note references to this work will use the abbreviation *HEC*.
[3] *HEC* 7:162.

Latourette did not forget even remote islands. I once had an enquiry from a lady in England concerning a Scottish ancestor claimed by family tradition as the first Baptist missionary to St. Helena. I was surprised to hear of any Baptist mission in that bastion of Anglican rectitude in the South Atlantic, let alone a Scottish one. But a quick reference to *Expansion* revealed that such was the case, and even better, Latourette had provided a reference.[4] It was to a book published in New York in 1852 describing how a Scot who had developed Baptist views betook himself to South Africa on his own initiative, and, after an interim ministry to convicts, mutinous sailors, and guano lifters found a niche in St. Helena. And, of course, the book was in the Day Library, where Latourette himself had found it, and its subject's descendant was able, to her delight, to get a photo copy.

Latourette's ecumenical vision is as remarkable for this period as his geographical range. Indeed, it is identified as his distinguishing feature by the author of a recent study of Latourette, who describes his theme as "unity of all Christians in love and mission."[5] Latourette seeks to describe Christian expansion in such a way as to include all those who have borne Christ's name; and he did this long before mutual recognition between Catholics, Protestants, and Orthodox was at all widespread. It represented more than conventional courtesy for this evangelical Baptist to begin volume 6 with a tribute to John J. Considine, of what he calls "the goodly fellowship"[6] of Maryknoll, for helping to initiate him into the ambience of Catholic missions.

But Latourette's vision has deeper springs than a desire for evenhandedness between the confessions. He is not writing church history, but *Christian* history. Church history writing requires ecclesiological choice; it assumes, consciously or unconsciously, a specific identification of the church, or at least a particular manifestation of it. The various models of church history teaching that have been adopted as classical in the West are produced by accumulations of essentially local factors, which lead to certain selections of themes and certain proportions in their treatment. Even volumes on "the history of the early church" do not always mean what those words, taken literally, might imply. What they usually give is a selection of themes from early Christianity that are relevant to a particular body of Christians with a particular geographical and confessional location today. (Note how in Western curricula the Eastern church progressively tapers off after the christological controversies). The local nature of

---

[4]*HEC* 5:317.

[5]Juhani Lindgren, *Unity of All Christians in Love and Mission: The Ecumenical Method of Kenneth Scott Latourette*, Annales Academiae Scientiarum Fennicae Dissertationes Humanarum Litterarum 54 (Helsinki: Suomalainen Tiedeakatemia, 1990).

[6]*HEC* 6:ix. Latourette also acknowledges a debt to Considine in his autobiography, *Beyond the Ranges* (Grand Rapids: Eerdmans, 1967), 78–79. III.

these models is revealed when—as, alas, is too commonly the case—they are absorbed unchanged into curricula intended for Africa or Asia. What then often happens is that material about African and Asian church history is simply stitched on the end of material originally conceived for a Western purpose. Study of church history in Africa and Asia requires a process of thorough reconception and reselection. There is no fixed normative corpus of church history to which additions and updatings can be made. The end shapes the beginning. If the end is to understand the place of Christianity in modern India or Nigeria or Uruguay, or even in a global society involving all these places, the whole of the study of the church even in its early phases has to be rethought.

Latourette seems to have recognized this principle. Because he wished to study the Christian faith in relation to human history as a whole, he reconceived its historical framework in a quite different way from that in which Christian history hitherto had been presented. The contrast with the usual view of early church history is manifest in his opening volume, covering the first five centuries. The average study of early Christianity is concerned almost entirely with Christianity in the Roman Empire. Latourette, of course, is also concerned with the significant expanse of early Christianity outside the Roman Empire, in the Middle East, in Central and Southern Asia, in Eastern and Nilotic Africa. But he does more than widen the geographical scope of the traditional history of the early church. He puts matters in perspective by pointing out how comparatively small a proportion of the world's population was comprehended within the Roman Empire, and by carefully introducing the two other contemporary political units with which it bore comparison. He points to the Persian Empire, with a different and highly complex Christian story, and the Han Empire of China. Here, as elsewhere, Latourette's short service in China gave proportion to his account of other themes, just as his work as a professor of Asian history intertwines with his work as a professor of missions. He talks, for instance, as few Western historians of his day would, in terms of a single Euro-Asiatic continent, of which western Europe (the focus of so much study of Christian history) forms only the far tip. He interprets the emergence of the characteristic forms of Western Christianity in relation to its distance from the Mongol and Turkish incursions, the fact that the Scandinavians were the last major invaders from the land mass eastward. Perhaps the concept of China as the Middle Kingdom influenced him more than he knew.

Still more interesting is his treatment of the subject matter of early church history. No area of early Christian history has received more attention than that of Gnosticism, and perceptions of it have been radically revised by the remarkable discoveries that have taken place since the *Expansion* was published. But when Latourette treats Gnosticism, he does so in relation to his central theme of Christian expansion. This means that the crucial question that he asks about Gnosticism is, To what extent did the heavily acculturated forms of Christianity that make up what is today called Gnosticism draw people in Hellenistic society towards faith in Christ? Were they more or less successful than the less heavily acculturated forms usually called "catholic"? His answer, as usual, is not straightforward; it is sometimes more and sometimes less. Gnostic, Arian, Montanist, Donatist, Nestorian, Jacobite, as well as those forms of Christianity denominated orthodox, are all examined in terms of their missionary significance and effect.[7] The only generalization Latourette allows himself is that it was those groups that most clearly maintained the centrality and ultimate significance of Jesus Christ that had the most durable effect. The same principles applied to later centuries ensure that he gives equal attention, so far as the available resources allow him ("of Slavic languages [I have] used only Russian,"[8] he admits modestly), to Catholic, Protestant, and Orthodox activity in Christian expansion. He does not ignore the Reformation, but he treats it in a quite different way from the standard church histories, whether Catholic or Protestant, of the period. His viewpoint is indicated in the explanatory rubric attached to chapter 1 of volume 3, where the Reformation period is described as "The Revival in Western Christianity expressing itself through the rise of Protestantism and the Roman Catholic Reformation."[9] The language is significant, for, as we shall see, he did not interpret expansion in terms of crude statistical increase. How Latourette would have revelled in the materials that would have been open to him today, in the multitudinous indigenous churches of Africa, the base ecclesial communities of Latin America, the extrachurch and nonchurch movements of Asia, the diverse embodiments of Christianity in his beloved China, the house churches of the West, and the explosion of evangelical charismatic and Pentecostal communities everywhere. But he lived in an age when everyone assumed that Christianity existed in three distinct modes: Catholic, Protestant, Orthodox. In our day we are realizing not only that there are substantial companies of Christians who do not fall into any of these categories, but also that the terms themselves, reflecting as they do the religious and cultural history of the West, are increasingly unhelpful as terms of description or analysis, even if they retain significance in terms of connexion and organization.

Historiography since Latourette

It goes without saying that the researches of fifty years have transformed the possibilities for the study of Christian expansion. The transfor-

---

[7]In his autobiography (*Beyond the Ranges*, 108), he describes with relish how at the inaugural meeting of the World Council of Churches in Amsterdam in 1948, where he was a consultant, he insisted that "reunion" was a misnomer. Even in New Testament times, Christians had never been united.

[8]*HEC* 1:xvi.

[9]*HEC* 3:1.

mation is particularly marked with regard to what Latourette called "The Great Century," the nineteenth, to which he devoted three of his volumes, and to the first half of the twentieth century, subject of part of his seventh volume. For these periods Latourette had to rely largely on printed mission sources. Since his time, much fundamental research has been conducted on the primary sources, oral and written, and new perspectives have been taken up in which Africans, Asians, and Latin Americans figure as the principal agents of Christian expansion. Such resources were not available to Latourette, and he is untroubled by the questions about the relationship of missionary history and church history that his successors have to face. Nevertheless, he is aware of other basic issues in the philosophy of history, and he is conscious of a tension in dealing with them. As a Christian, he believes in a divine purpose for the world behind history. He is also by instinct and training a post-Enlightenment Western historian, for whom such factors should play no part in historical discourse.[10] Latourette never resolves this tension. He meets it by openly confessing his Christian faith while in his historical analysis conscientiously trying to act as a post-Enlightenment historian. The nature of his subject, however, from time to time calls him to make generalizations about Christian history, and thus to comment on the nature of Christianity as displayed in its history. Such statements fail to be examined by historians and theologians alike, and I suspect that Latourette's generalizations have barely satisfied either group. He made no claim to being a theologian, and his theological language sometimes sounds naive as well as dated; and theologians, for whom teleological questions about history are primary, have not taken him particularly seriously. In this chapter I want to treat *Expansion* not simply as a chronicle with bibliographies, but as a work of generalization and synthesis about the Christian faith. I wish to suggest that the theological implications of the account that Latourette gives need to be taken much more seriously than his sometimes simplistic theological language might suggest.

Three Tests of Christian Expansion

One way of approaching the topic is to examine just what is meant by the *expansion* of Christianity. I have noted that Latourette eschews any ecclesiological or institutional definition of Christianity; he will not identify it with any particular church or group of churches. At the same time, he attempts no definition of the type that might be used in the phenomenol-

---

[10]See *HEC* 1:xviif., and note Latourette's conviction that a synthesis is possible if the Christian interpretation is accepted, but not otherwise. He gave his presidential address to the American Historical Association on the theme "the Christian understanding of history." It was politely received, but some auditors evidently indicated that if they wanted a talk on that subject, they would go to church. See Latourette, *Beyond the Ranges*, 115.

ogy of religion. At one point he seems to paraphrase his title as "the spread of the influence of Jesus,"[11] bringing down the wrath of Reinhold Niebuhr, who detected in *Expansion* an underlying secular liberal view of progress and a tendency to appropriate to the influence of Christ what were really the products of secular influences.[12] But Latourette's paraphrase has certain helpful features. In the first place, it reminds us of the distinctive character of Christian faith: Christianity is about Christ. In the second place, it implicitly distinguishes Christ from the community that bears his name. The witness of the Christian community to Christ is, as Niebuhr himself insisted, constantly ambiguous. Vital as the church may be as a vehicle of Christ's influence, it is stultifying to identify its influence with his. No one is saved through Christianity—though it may be possible to be damned through it.

But Latourette later becomes more specific, proposing a threefold means for measuring the influence of Christ—that influence which is the source of Christian expansion.[13] The first is the spread of Christian profession in particular areas. The second is the number and strength of new movements owing their origin to Christ. The third is what he calls "the effect of Christianity on mankind as a whole." One English reviewer of *Expansion* describes these as "non-ecclesiastical, undogmatic tests, of a kind rather uncongenial to the main tradition of Western Christendom,"[14] which I take to be an Oxford way of saying that they are more or less what one might expect from an American. In fact, I suggest, on close examination, each of these tests of Christian expansion is seen to be highly theological, with implications that can be clustered around a series of New Testament themes. I do not presume to interpret Latourette's mind here, nor is what follows to be seen as attributable to him, even when it arises out of his words. It is tempting to add to his threefold analysis a further dimension of expansion: the expansion of the Christian faith by its inter-

---

[11]K. S. Latourette, *The Unquenchable Light* (London: Eyre and Spottiswoode, 1948) ix, 131; cf. HEC 1:ix, and frequently in his contribution to the discussion "Christ the hope of the world" (see n. 12, below). It may be worth recalling the sharp words of one of his contemporaries: "The Christian faith has just as little to do with the influence of Jesus on the history of the world as it has to do with his historical personality" (E. Brunner, *The Mediator* [London: Lutterworth, 1934], 81).

[12]See the discussion by Latourette, Niebuhr, and F. E. Stoefflen, "Christ the Hope of the World. What Has History to Say?" *Religion in Life* 23, no. 3 (1954): 323–51. Latourette's contribution occupies pp. 323–33, Niebuhr's 334–40.

[13]*HEC* 7:417f.

[14]E. A. Payne, "The Modern Expansion of the Church: Some Reflections on Dr. Latourette's Conclusions," *Journal of Theological Studies* 47, no. 2 (1946): 143–55. Lest a wrong impression be given of this perceptive and prescient article, another of its comments on perspective may be cited. Latourette may appear to a European, Payne says, a product of American optimism. But might not a work on the same topic by a European scholar appear to American readers a characteristic product of European pessimism?

action with different cultures and even languages, so that by cross-cultural diffusion it becomes a progressively richer entity. This process has been exemplified abundantly since Latourette's day, for over that time Christianity has passed from being a mainly Western to a mainly non-Western religion. But such a theme needs fuller treatment than can be given here, and it seems prudent to restrict discussion to Latourette's own three stated criteria.

The Church Test

The first of these, it will be remembered, is the spread of Christian profession in particular areas. This is the easiest of the three to apply, for in principle, if not always in practice, it relates to something that can be counted. In our own day, David Barrett's *World Christian Encyclopedia* represents the most thoroughgoing attempt at counting Christians yet undertaken.[15]

It is clear that there are times and places when large numbers of people newly profess allegiance to Jesus Christ and form new Christian communities. And it is equally clear that at other times and in other places this process stagnates or goes into reverse, where those newly professing allegiance to Christ are few and where the communities of his worshippers dwindle and die away. This theme is fundamental to Latourette's construction, his pattern of Christian advance and recession.

This first mark of Christian expansion should not lightly be dismissed as a "non-ecclesiastical, undogmatic" category, even by the most exacting theologian, for it leads directly to the New Testament theme of the church, the whole people of God. The first sign of the expansion of the influence of Christ is the presence of a community of people who willingly bear his name, an "Israel" that maintains his worship. The other tests themselves presuppose this one, the existence of a statistically identifiable, geographically locatable Christian community, however small.

In considering the primacy of the church factor, it is worth remembering that the first effect of Christian expansion is not the production of saved or enlightened individuals, but of congregations. Unless it be the Ethiopian eunuch (and even he must have had some institutional form of worship of the God of Israel back home, or what motivated his journey?), it is doubtful whether the New Testament provides a single example of an individual convert, a "saved individual," left to plough his lonely furrow without family or congregation. The influence of Jesus not only produces group response; it works by means of groups, and is expressed in groups.

---

[15]David Barrett, ed., *World Christian Encyclopedia: A Comparative Study of Churches and Religions in the Modern World, A.D. 1900–2000.* (Nairobi: Oxford University Press, 1982).

The influence of Jesus, that is, operates in terms of social relations.

The early days of the modern missionary movement soon revealed the impossible position of the individual convert. *The Missionary Register* for July 1820, for instance, publishes the following letter, addressed to the assistant secretary of the Church Missionary Society:

Dear Reverend Brother-

I am just told I going to leave you, day after tomorrow. I will therefore write you,

Dear Sir

I go home tell my countrymen, that Jesus is the true God. Atua is false—no God, all nonsense.

I tell my countrymen, Englishmen no hang his self, not eat a man—no tattooing—no fall cutting his self. My countrymen will say to me, "Why Englishman no cut himself?" I tell them Book of Books say, "No cut—no hang—no tattoo" I tell them "Jesus say all they that do so go to hell." I tell them they sin—they do wrong. I know that Jesus Christ's blood cleanseth all sin. I tell my poor countrymen so. He no find out the way to Heaven—poor fellow! Jesus our Lord, He found a way to Heaven for all who know Him . . . I tell my countrymen, Christians no fight, no use war club, no spear—they read Book of Books—all true! says, No fight, all love . . .

I get home to New Zealand, and I go tell my countrymen, "Come countrymen, into House of Worship, where true God is worshiped."

I hope you farewell. Good bye.

Your affect friend
Thomas Tooi[16]

Tui was a Maori of some significance in his home community. Like many of his seafaring contemporaries, he had travelled, and in the course of his journeys reached Australia. There he came to the notice of the Rev. Samuel Marsden, colonial chaplain and zealous promoter of missions, whose high hopes of the Christian potential of the Polynesian peoples contrasted with his despair over Australian Aboriginals. Tui stayed two years with Marsden, fully confirming all the latter's hopes of a breakthrough for the gospel in New Zealand, and resulting in Marsden arranging with the Church Missionary Society for Tui to spend a further year in England. Tui's evident conviction and general demeanour during his stay

---

[16]*The Missionary Register for MDCCCXX*, 309.

delighted the friends of missions. The edifying letter was written on the eve of his return to New Zealand, and many must have been waiting eagerly for the effect of his testimony among his compatriots.

Tui returned with Marsden. But a week after his return, he was telling Marsden that he could not stand his ground unless a European joined him. The only way he knew of being a Christian was the European way he had met in Australia and England. There were no other Christians in his community; the only way he could support a Christian life was by maintaining a European lifestyle—a "civil life," Marsden called it, effectively outside his community. It is hardly surprising that his attempt soon broke down. In a few months, all that was left of the profession of Christian faith and the years of Christian training was a blue jacket. The glimpses we get of Tui's later life in written records indicate prowess as a warrior ("the greatest profligate and savage on the coast," according to one European visitor), and the last mention of all refers to an attempted deal by Tui with a French sea captain: tattooed head in exchange for a keg of gunpowder.[17] There are plenty such examples of the tragedy of the lone convert. Not the convert, but the congregation is the first sign of the influence of Christ.

The first test of the expansion, then, is the church test: the emergence of a worshipping congregation. But in employing it, it is necessary to take its fragility into account. It is manifest that the expansion of Christianity does not plant churches that endure for ever. The first centre of Christianity, and one that saw rapid statistical growth, was Jerusalem. The homelands of Tertullian and Augustine no longer burgeon with Christian scholars and political leaders. In many once Christian countries, former churches have become mosques; in my own they have become garages and sometimes nightclubs. The Christian story—and this, too, is fundamental to Latourette's view—is not a steady, triumphant progression. It is a story of advance and recession.

Latourette's whole arrangement of Christian history is based on this theme of advance and recession; the history of expansion includes within itself a history of contraction. The rhetoric in which Latourette was raised was one of Christian triumph from age to age; the leaders of the missionary movement to which he himself belonged had been in a hurry to bring it to completion. But Latourette the historian knew that the history did not match the rhetoric; and, in a section near the end of volume 7,[18] he shows that he is aware that Islamic experience has been different.

---

[17]Tui appears intermittently in Marsden's New Zealand journals; see John Rawson Elder, ed., *The Letters and Journal of Samuel Marsden, 1765–1838* (Dunedin, New Zealand: Coulls, Somerville, Wilkie and A. H. Reed for Otago University Council, 1932). On his later career, see Harrison M. Wright, *New Zealand 1769–1840: Early Years of Western Contact*. (Cambridge: Harvard University Press, 1959).

[18]*HEC* 7:469–73.

Islam can point to a steady geographical progression from its birthplace and from its earliest years. And over all these years it has hitherto not had many territorial losses to record. Whereas the Jerusalem of the apostles has fallen, the Mecca of the prophet remains inviolate. When it comes to sustaining congregations of the faithful, Christianity does not appear to possess the same resilience as Islam. It decays and withers in its very heartlands, in the areas where it appears to have had the profoundest cultural effects. Crossing cultural boundaries, it then takes root anew on the margins of those areas, and beyond. Islamic expansion is progressive; Christian expansion is serial.

Do the resiliency of Islam and the vulnerability of Christianity reflect something of the inherent nature of the two faiths? Does the very freedom of response inherent in the Christian gospel leave it open to ultimate rejection? Is the Christian impact durable only when there is sustained, unceasing penetration of the host culture? Christianity has no culturally fixed element, as is provided by the Qur'an fixed in heaven, closed traditions on earth, perfection of law in *shari'a*, single shrine in Mecca, and true word everywhere in Arabic. If the acts of cultural translation by which the Christians of any community make their faith substantial within that community cease—if (if one may use such language) the Word ceases to be made flesh within that community—the Christian group within that community is likely to lose, not just its effectiveness, but its powers of resistance. Most cultures are in frequent change or encounter with others, so the process of translation is endless.

It is not profitable to moralize on the fate of vanished churches; to do so is like claiming to know that those on whom the Siloam tower fell were Jerusalem's chief sinners. We do not, cannot, know why the candlestick is taken from its place. But the New Testament is clear that God can dispense even with self-important Christian communities, and that God depends on no single instrument.

The church test of Christian expansion is therefore a provisional one. New churches, or churches in new areas, are not gains to be plotted on the map. That is an Islamic, not a Christian, view of expansion. Such churches are simply positions through which the influence of Jesus Christ may come to bear on people and communities.

The Kingdom Test

There are other reasons why the church test on its own is not a satisfactory measure of the influence of Christ. There may be many elements in the actual local expression of Christianity at any one time that cannot be remotely traced to him. And yet, within the same community that bears the Christian name may be groups of believers striving to respond to him, trying to find a way of life that more nearly reflects his, to bring his life and teaching to bear more radically upon their church and society.

This brings us to Latourette's second test of Christian expansion: the numbers and strength of new movements owing their origin to Jesus Christ. This was his rough and ready way of measuring the *depth* of Christian expansion at any one time in any given area. Clearly, he thought that the test of the local strength of Christianity was whether it was radical and innovative. Once more, I suggest, the simplistic appearance of his criterion is deceptive; and, though the criterion may seem at first sight to be a sociological one, it is highly theological.

Latourette's second test in fact is a kingdom test; it stands for the signs of the kingdom of God. The kingdom shines in the church and exerts its energy within and beyond it, yet cannot be identified with it. The kingdom of God, the Gospels tell us, is sprouting seed, growing in secret and suddenly bursting into flower. The kingdom of God is fermenting yeast that stirs things up so that a little of it transforms three whole measures of meal. The kingdom of God is declared when demons are cast out by the finger of God. The kingdom of God has drawn near in the presence of Christ with his acts of mercy and power.

Kingdom signs like these mark the innovative new movements that reflect true Christian expansion. Because, like the kingdom, they sprout and stir up, they produce a more radical Christian discipleship. Because, like the kingdom, they can transform the whole basin of meal into yeasty bread, they bring the Spirit of Christ to bear more widely within their society—penetrating that society's culture more deeply, translating Christ into that society more perfectly, making the Word flesh within it. Because, like the kingdom, they stand for the casting out of demons, and because the demons that blight our world are legion, they have a multitude of specific objects and effects.

The archetype of the movements that the kingdom test reveals as the agents of Christian expansion is the great prophet of the kingdom, John the Baptist, with his call to God's people for a change of heart, for radical righteousness, his revealing of a day of crisis and decision. It is probable that John did not invent the rite that gave him his nickname. The new thing he did was to take the ceremony that marked the entrance of a pagan convert into Israel and insist that it applied also to the birthright people of God. The people of God needed repentance as much as anyone in the pagan world. "You must be born again," says Jesus, taking up the same theme.[19] "You" is plural here—not so much, surely, Nicodemus personally, as "you people," the leadership of the congregation of God's people that Nicodemus represented. You must start again, with repentance for the past and God's Spirit for the future, if you are to begin to know the kingdom and what it really means to be what you claim to be, the people of God.

---

[19]John 3:7.

Kingdom movements call the church to repentance and to alertness to the presence of Christ within. The presence of the church—the first test of Christian expansion—is no guarantee of the continuing influence of Christ. The church without the signs of the kingdom becomes a counter-sign of the kingdom, hiding Christ instead of revealing him to the world. It is for creative minorities, like the righteous remnant in old Israel, to reveal a better way and to make it possible for the wider church to move towards it.

Among the kingdom movements may be counted many movements of reformation, renewal, and revival. (It will be recalled that Latourette noted a "revival in Western Christianity expressing itself through the rise of Protestantism and the Roman Catholic Reformation.") Many movements for the propagation of the faith may also be so counted as well as many movements seeking a righteous society, struggling against manifest evil, seeking to cast out demons. Kingdom movements are infinitely diverse. For one thing, there are legions of demons to cast out. For another, those who seek the kingdom find it where they are, and they stand in very different places, their perceptions and relationships formed by different histories.

Kingdom movements, then, are not in themselves the kingdom, any more than the church is the kingdom. They are *signs* of the kingdom, reminders that the kingdom seed is growing, the kingdom yeast fermenting; reminders of the triumph of God and the assured defeat of evil.

The movements may or may not take an institutional expression; in complex societies it is usual for such institutional expression to emerge. But in either case, we must beware of confusing movement and institution. Even the most unmistakable signs of the kingdom in human expression can pass over into counter-signs.

It will be helpful to illustrate the second test of Christian expansion by references to examples that are very well known.

Monasticism was born of the desire for wholehearted discipleship, in repentance from a development in Christian history that had enabled affluent people to combine piety and self-indulgence. "Sell all that you have and give to the poor," was the word of the Lord heard by Antony the Copt. The same desire for radical discipleship was to seize many more in the very different setting of early West European Christianity. Had not Jesus said, "If any want to follow me, let them say no to themselves and take up the cross"? And had he not promised that those who gave up family and lands would find sisters and brothers and houses and lands in plenty? All over Christendom, therefore, men and women covenanted to live under discipline, resigning personal rights and private property, avoiding relationships that would force them to put the interest of their own kin, or of their feudal superior, before the welfare of their brothers, sisters, or the poor. The monastic movement produced many a mobile missionary task force, not least for the harshest and most uninviting environments. It established permanent mission stations, which were also centres of learning, hospitals, shelters for travellers, sources of immediate relief for the down and out. One has only to visualize the bleakness of life in early medieval Europe, the miserable hovels of the little settlements, the constant destruction of crops as raiders and rivals fought across fields, the arbitrary claims of lord upon vassal and of kin upon kin, to guess the significance of these centres of worship, peace, and charity. Many motives brought people to the monastic life, and by no means always the highest; but in their origins, and at their highest, monasteries were a culturally coherent way for those who wished to be radically Christian to imitate the lifestyle of Jesus and his apostles. Further, they were alternative communities for those who saw no way of living a consistent Christian life amid the demands of kinship and vassalage and the pressures of a violent society. "Will many be saved?" someone once asked St. Anselm. "No," replied the archbishop, who knew the ways of the king's court and the habits of the Christian nobility. "And most of those who are saved will be monks."

Long a potential sign of the kingdom, the monasteries over time became counter-sign of the kingdom. Within Anselm's old domain of England, following processes in themselves natural and intelligible, the corporate followers of the one who had nowhere to lay his head became over time collectively the major holders of real estate, the directors of the most profitable export business, and a comfortable class of rentiers. The conditions that had made the monasteries so crucial to the societal context passed away. And what was meant for selfless service to the poor became—without any set intention, any planned change of direction or deliberate revision of aims—self-regarding. Sign turned to counter-sign.

The process of renewal and reformation did not, of course, die, even in the worst of times; and in the sixteenth century it became a ferment. To realize the multiplicity of forms that the kingdom signs take, it is worth pausing a moment longer on the monasteries. The Catholic reformation sought to restore them to their original form and motivation, with a heightened sense of the monastic life as vocation, a call to perfection. The Protestant reformers abandoned them, arguing that family life and active participation in society could be just as holy as life within the monastery walls, and life within them as sinful and self-centred as life outside. The radical reformers, often called Anabaptist, went further. For them the local church was a covenanted community of dedicated people—a monastery, in effect. The gathered church congregation is the fully Protestant version of the monastery, with husbands, wives, and children all committed to a Christian style of life.

The second example of a dynamic and innovative movement may be taken from the Protestant world: the missionary society. Missionary societies came into being by what William Carey called "use of means" to spread the good news of Christ in the non-Christian world—that is, from the point of view of their founders, in the greater part of the world. Commonplace as the concept of societies for specific purposes is now, in Carey's day it was still quite novel. The conditions under which people could freely associate, adopt programmes, raise and apply funds, were quite recent. The Protestant missionary movement that arose became possible only by means of these new structures. Small groups of people—lay people, very often, and when clergy, not generally the most significant leaders of their denomination—made their own arrangements for preaching the gospel and establishing new churches overseas. They gathered networks of local supporters, most of whom contributed from modest incomes, and fed those networks with regular and detailed literature, creating a circle of concerned, informed, giving, praying people. They did all this with little reference to, and still less assistance from, the formal structures of their churches. Indeed, it soon became clear that those structures, the product of another period of Western and Christian history, simply had no way of coping with the task of evangelism overseas. The voluntary society took on that task, and many other tasks, both at home and abroad, until the network of voluntary societies subverted the whole organization of European Protestantism. It was in the voluntary societies that women began to play an organizational role in church life. In all sorts of ways these societies did more than has perhaps been realized to establish Christian agendas for the nineteenth century, and raised and applied the resources to maintain them.

The missionary societies not only performed a vital role in mobilizing and sustaining a missionary task force (there is a parallel story in the Catholic church with the missionary orders); they also became the natural channel of communication between Western Christians and the new Christians of Africa and Asia. In a Christian world transformed out of all recognition from that of William Carey, the images held by too many Western Christians of the non-Western world are formed from the legacy of the—often now attenuated—mission societies. And one can envisage a time when some missions, like some monasteries, come to divert and obscure rather than to act as channels of the concerns of the kingdom. In using the kingdom test of Christian expansion, we must give no final and absolute value to even the radical and innovative movements, or to the dearest to ourselves.

A third example comes from a development hidden from Latourette's view. One of the most noticed features of modern Christian history in Africa has been the emergence of churches that owe little to Western models of how a church should operate, and much to African readings of Scripture, for which the conditions of African life often provide a hall of echoes. Studies of these "spiritual" churches have rightly stressed their closeness to traditional African worldviews, and their involvement in the problems that concern large numbers of people in modern African society. Stress is often laid on the syncretistic aspects of these churches, which tends to obscure the extent to which they are also radical, innovative, and revolutionary movements. Certainly the charismatic healer whose ministry forms the point of attraction to the church may use techniques found also among African diviners; but he (or she) will almost certainly do so in the name of the God of the Scriptures, and justify his use of them by biblical examples. And if he insists that the deliverance he proclaims comes from the God of the Scriptures, and associates it with Christ or the Holy Spirit, then he has broken the ring of the local powers who lie at the heart of most traditional religious systems. The interview with the person seeking healing may follow a pattern similar to those conducted by traditional diviners, but the effects may be startlingly different. The seeker of healing admits to wearing a curative charm, and throws it away; or to having buried something at home, and goes shamefacedly away to dig it up in order to secure healing. Even the seeker who confesses to witchcraft or sorcery is not necessarily responding to psychological pressure to admit an imaginary offence; what is emerging is the acknowledgement of deepest hatreds, jealousy, and envy that corrode relationships, poison the personality, and produce the very antithesis of health. There are signs of the kingdom here for many Christians who attend church regularly, while in trouble resorting to the traditional diviner—but at night, and with a bad conscience. They do not wish to turn back from the Christian faith, but they are unable to trust wholly, for nothing in the (essentially Western) model of the church as they know it offers defence against the worst features of the world as they know it. Many such have seen the kingdom signs in such "spiritual" churches.

In recent years a new wave of churches has appeared in many African countries proclaiming the visible immediacy of Christ's salvation and the overcoming power of the Holy Spirit in the face of all the omnipresent ills of modern Africa. It is noticeable that they rarely embrace the "spiritual" churches as allies; rather, they see them as bastions of occultism and immorality. This is not the place to discuss developments and relationships of considerable complexity; but it is appropriate to reflect again how readily the kingdom sign embodied within human movements passes into counter-sign.

The Gospel Test

It is now time to consider Latourette's third test of Christian expansion, and on any reading the hardest to apply. He called it "the effect of Christianity upon mankind as a whole"[20] or, more specifically, "the effect of Jesus on individual lives and civilizations." Had he been writing today, he might have spoken rather of the effect of Christ on people and on cultures. And the capital difficulty of making this into any sort of principle of

---

[20]*HEC* 7:418.

judgment is that the influence may be direct and acknowledged, or direct and unacknowledged, or indirect and even unconscious.

Whatever difficulties of measurement this brings, it appears that once again Latourette has fixed upon a *theological* principle, and one further reaching in its implications than he claims. I propose to denominate it the "gospel test," and to link it with the New Testament theme of good news. The term "good news" seems to have been more popular with Paul and the other early Christian missionaries to the non-Jewish world than even the word "kingdom," which featured so prominently in the preaching of Jesus himself. The adoption of a gospel test is intended to argue that there is a dimension of Christian expansion beyond those that we have already examined, those that issue in the planting of the church and the development of radical corporate discipleship.

When Paul sums up the gospel as he preached it, he emphasizes two elements: Christ died for our sins according to the Scriptures, and he rose again according to the Scriptures.[21] Elsewhere in the epistles the death and resurrection of Christ is presented as a Roman triumph in which the cross forms a victor's chariot for the conquering hero, while the principalities and powers trail behind like the captives of a Roman general publicly exhibited to the crowds at his homecoming.[22] It matters little whether we see the principalities and powers here as demonic forces, or like some interpreters, as political (or as we might say today, structural) world rulers. Either way they are powerful spiritual entities that oppose God and spoil the world. They seek to destroy truth, goodness, and love as manifested in Christ. And the gospel as Paul declared it proclaims that in the resurrection of Christ something completely new happened, and history took on a new dimension. Christ defeated— *spoiled* is the word—the principalities and powers and put them to public humiliation.

We cannot do justice to such themes by throwing all their significance into an eschatological consummation still to come. The whole point is that the resurrection makes a difference in the here and now. And if the death and resurrection of Christ is related to the reconciling of all things to God, then we have to recognize a world already bought back by God, a world in which the principalities and powers are already defeated.

The scope of the principalities and powers and their corrupting rule is immense. That rule poisons the environment and sends a virus through society. It soils every dimension of life and every level of the personality. The scope of the good news that proclaims Christ's victory over them is

---

[21]1 Cor. 15:3–4.

[22]Col. 2:15. Other interpretations of this text have been suggested, but this seems the natural sense, and is excellently supported. A recent discussion is Roy Yates, "Christ Triumphant," *New Testament Studies* 37 (1991): 573–79. I am grateful to my colleague Professor J. C. O'Neill for this reference.

correspondingly immense. It extends through environment and society and reaches the depths of the individual personality.

In the view of Christianity that I believe underlies Latourette's work—though again I must insist that he bears no responsibility for the theological extrapolation that I have made from it—there are not different gospels for individuals and for society. There is no question of there being an option of which to proclaim, or of balancing the claims of one against another. Nor are there different gospels for different kinds of people, or for different situations. There is only one good news of salvation through Jesus Christ, resting on one event, the death and resurrection of the divine Son. But the *scope* of that event, and of the gospel on which it rests, is beyond the most comprehensive description of it as experienced by any person or by any part of the redeemed creation. The spoiling of the principalities and powers proclaims the victory of God at every level of creation. By the same token, the proclamation of the good news, which is the witness of the church to the cross and resurrection, also extends to all the various reaches of their domain. It should not be surprising if different walls and redoubts of the demonic kingdom collapse at different times as Christ is uplifted in the proclamation of the good news. And, since the application of the good news is greater than anyone's experience of it, we may well proclaim the good news in anticipation of a response reflecting our own experience; we find others responding in quite another way, but nevertheless hearing good news. For at every level at which the good news is heard, it corresponds with reality, with a real victory secured by Christ over the forces of evil and death.

This is the basis on which I would justify Latourette's third test of Christian expansion, and why I think it may be called the gospel test. It will help to proceed with a couple of examples.

We have already noted the discouraging nature of the beginnings of missionary work in New Zealand. It took five years to get a mission settlement established at all, fifteen before there was a single baptism, three years more before the next. That takes us to 1827. But by 1840 there were thirty thousand Maori associated with the missions and regularly hearing Christian teaching. Four hundred were baptized in six months. By 1845 nearly two-thirds of the population were attached to the Anglican, Methodist, or Roman Catholic mission, and a New Testament in Maori was circulating for every two of the total population.[23] Yet the missionar-

---

[23]The interpretation of the New Zealand story followed here owes much to Harrison M. Wright, *New Zealand 1769–1840*. For other versions, see, e.g., J. M. R. Owens, *Prophets in the Wilderness: The Wesleyan Mission to New Zealand 1819–27:* (Auckland: Auckland University Press, 1974), and his essay in Christopher Nichol and James Veitch, eds., *Religion in New Zealand* (Wellington: Victoria University, 1980), 5–52; and Allan K. Davidson, *Christianity in Aotearoa* (Wellington: New Zealand Education for Ministry Board, 1991).

ies—certainly those of the Church Missionary Society—were far from ecstatic about what was happening.

One reason for their reaction lay deep in their own experience. They had themselves known evangelical conversion, in which an oppressive sense of guilt had been succeeded by a happy consciousness of guilt removed through Christ. Their framework of thought distinguished the "real" Christianity, to which these experiences were the prelude or early stages, from the formal Christianity accepted by the bulk of society who understood neither the seriousness of sin nor the effect of the work of Christ. It was natural to assume that if the Maori were to become Christians, it would be by the gate of conviction of sin and subsequent sense of divine forgiveness, the marks of genuine conversion and the gateway to "real," as distinct from formal, Christianity. The missionaries also believed (though they would have regarded this as belonging to a lower order of conviction) that British education, technology, and civil polity—what they called "civilization"—were closely associated with Christianity. They were perhaps not fully agreed among themselves as to whether "civilization" was a fruit of receiving the gospel or an attractive and helpful preparation for it.

The Maori were not remotely interested in Christianity and not very interested in civilization; they were reasonably satisfied with the style of life they already had. What they did recognize was that some aspects of that lifestyle could be enhanced by certain metal goods that could be obtained only from Europeans; and the missions were useful, being permanently resident sources of such items. For many years, therefore, the missionaries had to live on that basis. They could stay only on the Maori terms, tolerated as convenient suppliers of metal goods, subject to endless badgering, and essentially insecure. For twenty years of proclamation of the evangelical gospel there was only one unmistakable achievement: the missionaries had proved that it was possible to live with the Maori without being killed and eaten. And the fruits of that achievement were, to say the least, ambiguous. Encouraged by missionary durability, other Europeans came in, with more liberal policies on trading in firearms, and the honest commerce, which in the original visions was to ease the path to wholesome "civilization," spawned violence, prostitution, and, above all, arms trading. For muskets soon were the most desirable iron goods in New Zealand. Ritualized warfare was endemic in New Zealand, and the traditional code of honour enforced obligations of satisfaction and revenge effected through networks of kinship. For the prosecution of such, firearms proved more efficient than the traditional spears and clubs. "This people are in the Gall of bitterness and the bond of iniquity," wrote one weary missionary. "Every man's hand seems to be against his brother."[24]

---

[24]The writer is Henry Williams, leader of the missionaries of the Church Missionary Society, who left extensive journals.

No one seemed to heed their message. "There is not one native on the Island," said the same missionary, "in whom it can be said that the work of grace is begun." As for cannibalism or human sacrifice, there was not a trace of compunction, let alone guilt, about such practices.

But the introduction of Western firearms into the Maori patterns of ritual combat and satisfaction was well nigh disastrous. Under its impact Maori society was no longer satisfied and confident, no longer finding the powerful new weaponry delightful. A weariness and depression settled on the once enthusiastic warriors as they realized they were in danger of wiping one another out. Some wished for flight to a distant island, or talked of going to Australia with the missionaries. And they began to feel themselves trapped in a tyrannous circle of events they could no longer control. "They said it was all very good what we had told them," records the same missionary commentator, "but as other Natives would not let them alone, they stood greatly in need of muskets and powder in order to defend themselves." Maori society now longed for peace, but with the concurrence of musketry and the traditional code of satisfaction, despaired of achieving it. Some things the missionaries had been saying these many years began to sound, for the first time, attractive, things about the good news of peace, and their constant deprecation of Maori violence. Occasions arose when these outsiders who had invited themselves in could be useful—for instance, in arranging peace at a point when tradition would have demanded a fight to the finish. Alas, that was the problem; the Maori could not give up the practices that were destroying their society without also giving up a code that for centuries had been crucial to their way of life. The pattern of satisfaction and revenge had all the sacredness of ancestral tradition. Not to avenge harm done to one's kin brought unalterable shame and diminished a person to negligibility. The only way to get rid of self-destructive war was to give up the system under which it was conducted, and the only viable way of doing that was to take up a new way of life. The Maori began to do so with enthusiasm. They came forward in companies to learn to read the Bible, and manifestly sought to follow its teachings. They brought in their neighbours and took the message to the peoples living in districts beyond. They formed regular congregations of their own.

The missionaries did not fall over themselves to sweep in new converts. All their understanding of the surgery of the soul made them anxious about offering inducements or accepting too ready and superficial response. They could not deny the evident sincerity of the movement that now almost overwhelmed them. They had to accept what was happening as a work of God. And yet where was the mourning for sin, and the rejoicing in forgiveness, which should mark a *real* conversion?

From the viewpoint of a later time, it may be easier to recognize what happened in New Zealand as a genuine response to the gospel, a genuine hearing of it, a genuine demonstration of the victory of the cross over the power of evil. In the Christian movement the self-destructive forces in Maori society were bound as nothing else could have bound them. But the Maori responded to the gospel, not to the missionaries' experience of the gospel. They did not misunderstand the good news preached to them, even if they did not fully understand it (who does so, ever?). And even if they did not respond in the terms anticipated by the missionaries, one can still trace in their response an evangelical paradigm that the missionaries themselves might have recognized as valid. There was repentance, a clean break with the past, a turning toward the God of the Scriptures. There was a step of faith, for in turning to the way of peace they risked much: the wrath of the *Atua* (local spiritual powers), humiliation by enemies in their newly chosen defencelessness, and the disorientation of abandoning the known ways. And if not delivered from guilt (and how could they feel guilt for following the ways ordained by the fathers?), they were certainly delivered from shame, from the shame involved in not avenging wrongs done against oneself or one's clan. They turned to Christ when they had come to an end of themselves and of the resources of their society.[25] That too is in tune with the evangelical paradigm, and recalls the theme that the gospel can be heard, and responded to, at various levels of experience.

In this example of the application of the gospel test of Christian expansion, a new Christian community was born. In other words, Christian expansion took place by the church test also. Is it possible, however, to speak meaningfully of Christian expansion, in the sense of the spread of the influence of Christ, where no such sign of church expansion takes place?

Our second example, then, is from India. *Sati*, the burning of widows on the funeral pyres of their husbands, was a custom traditional in some parts of Hindu society. Christian missionaries caused the custom to be well known in the West, portraying it as perhaps the worst horror to be encountered in India. They felt particular outrage that it occurred undisturbed in areas under British rule, a rule exercised by the East India Company. The Company's essential purpose was commercial; its declared policy was to avoid interference in social and religious matters, and its general ethos was resistant to missionary influence. In 1829 *sati* was prohibited by order of the governor general. The violent Hindu outcry and reaction that many had predicted did not take place.

Three different groups of people may be seen as in some way responsible for the abolition of *sati*. First, the missionaries, who described what happened, placed the facts before the public that their writings could reach, denouncing from the Scriptures both the practice and the attitudes that tolerated it. But on their own, the influence of missionaries would not

---

[25]This is not, of course, the end of the story of the Maori and Christianity. Some of the chapters to follow were very distressing, but we cannot pursue them here.

have moved government. There were many other issues in which the missions, and the section of the British public that supported them, were out of tune with the conventional wisdom of the British governance of India, and their impact was limited. Second, there was a group of East India Company officials, and especially, the governor general himself, Lord William Bentinck. The revulsion that this rather radically minded aristocrat felt for *sati* came from ideas of natural justice and humanitarian conviction, which themselves had come to him in Christian forms—the evangelicalism of his wife's family may have sharpened them. But even a strong governor general—and Bentinck had had his fingers burnt before—could not have brought about the end of *sati* in the face of determined resistance. Earlier governors had hated the practice but felt powerless to stop it. What enabled Bentinck to act was the work of a third group of people, Hindu reformers who detested the burning of widows as a corruption of true religion and a blot on India's honour. Without the influence of Rammohun Roy and those like him, no influence of missionaries or of the governor general would have availed.

But what had made Roy a reformer was the effect of his encounter with Jesus through the New Testament. While the New Zealand missionaries were plodding through their dark days, Roy was writing a book that appeared under the title *The Precepts of Jesus the Guide to Peace and Happiness*.[26] The book did not find favour with Christian missionaries in India. It confined itself to the teaching of Christ, omitted the Gospel miracles (Indians had heard of bigger ones, said Roy, and so were not impressed), and did not deal with the issue of his person. Missionaries felt obliged to go on producing refutations of this remarkable work in the name of Christian orthodoxy. Nevertheless, Roy believed that "no other religion can produce anything that may stand in competition with the Precepts of Jesus—much less that can be pretended to be superior to them." This conviction gave point to his very active life, which was devoted to the abolition of customs such as *sati*, the regeneration of Hindu society by the stripping away of its overlying corruptions, and the recovery of what Roy believed was the genuine, monotheistic, faith of India.

If we use the gospel test, we may thus argue that the abolition of *sati* was a result of the spreading influence of Jesus. There was a hearing of, and response to, good news, even though no expansion of the church resulted from it. But the difficulty goes deeper. The abolition of *sati* was not a matter of a single, isolated institution; it was part of a wider story of the emergence of a reformed and reformulated Hinduism. Not for nothing has Roy been called "the father of modern India"; nor was he the last of

---

[26]*The Precepts of Jesus the Guide to Peace and Happiness, Extracted from the Books of the New Testament Ascribed to the Four Evangelists.* The first Indian edition was published anonymously in 1820: bearing Roy's name, the first London edition was published in 1824, with a second edition coming in 1834.

the line of devout Hindus who encountered Christ in the Scriptures and were moved by him. From Roy to Gandhi and beyond there stretches a line of those who sought to purge their land of evil things, and their faith from misconceived things under the guidance of a Christ they knew from the Scriptures. Sometimes they brought to light the radical nature of that teaching in a way that Christians had forgotten. "God uses many instruments," said E. Stanley Jones, "and he has used Mahatma Gandhi to help christianize unchristian Christianity."[27]

The paradox of the gospel test goes further still. It is possible that the reforms we have seen as an expression of the influence of Christ by the gospel test actually hindered the expansion of Christianity in India as measured by the church test. There was a period when the missionary Alexander Duff, whose work was made possible by Rammohun Roy's endorsement of the school he operated, was making a substantial impact on young Hindu intellectuals. Then, without any obvious change in method or direction, the stream of such converts stopped. Reformed Hinduism increasingly became resistant Hinduism. Duff's young men came from the very stream in Hindu society that had no place for customs such as *sati*, who felt oppressed by traditional society's refusal to embrace new learning and ideas, and hemmed in by the corruption of much contemporary religion. Perhaps it was the effectiveness of the movements for purity and reform, themselves inspired in part by the teachings of Christ, that stifled in such people the revulsion that once might have left open a path to open Christian discipleship. It is a question we must leave with God. But can we look at the total history of India over the past two centuries and say that even the indirect and unacknowledged influence of Christ is not a response to good news? Or dare to say that it is outside of God's saving purpose for the world God redeemed?

Conclusion

A reconsideration of the seven volumes of the *History of the Expansion of Christianity*, then, finds it possible to invest Latourette's three criteria of Christian expansion with more theological significance than perhaps he realized. There is the sign of the Church: the emergence of communities of people who worship God, acknowledge Christ, and confess his ultimacy. There is the sign of the Kingdom: the impact within the church as the remnant principle operates afresh, and movements of reformation, renewal, and devotion spring up to challenge it and channel Christ's influence to the world. And there is the sign of the gospel: people respond, directly or

---

[27]E. Stanley Jones, *Mahatma Gandhi: An Interpretation* (London: Hodder and Stoughton, 1948), 102. The missionary involvement in the *sati* controversy, without reference to Roy, is discussed by Kenneth Ingham, *Reformers in India, 1793–1833* (Cambridge: Cambridge University Press, 1956), chapter 3.

indirectly, to Christ's victory over evil through his cross and resurrection. The consequences and availability of this victory reach as widely as the vitiating effects of evil; that is, to every level of personality, society, and environment. There are many factors determining which echoes of that victory particular people hear from where they are standing. But every echo corresponds to reality, and it is good news.

But there is built-in fragility in each of the tests. The fragility of the church sign is obvious; and the kingdom sign passes all too readily into counter-sign. So also with the gospel sign; the responses to the gospel that we have noted by its aid are not complete and final. Indeed, none of the tests for Christian expansion enable us to mark up gains on the map of the world, or chart progress towards the final goal. Such ideas do not belong to a Christian understanding of expansion; they are closer to the essentially secular optimism with which some of Latourette's critics (inappropriately) charged him. Latourette saw that advance and recession, not irreversible progress, was the pattern of Christian expansion; just as Bunyan saw that there was a way to hell even from the gate of heaven. But there is a more fundamental fact still underlying Christian expansion, and it seems appropriate to close this reconsideration by repeating the words with which the monumental work closes:

> The Christian is certain that Jesus is central in human history. His confident faith is that in those who give themselves to God as they see Him in Jesus there is working the power of endless life and that from them God will build, to be consummated beyond time, the heavenly city, the ideal community, in which will be realized fully the possibilities of the children of God. The eternal life and this ideal community are, in the last analysis, not the fruit of man's striving, but the gift of a love which man does not deserve, and are from the unmerited grace of God.[28]

---

[28]*HEC* 7:505.

2

Christianity in the Non-Western World

A Study in the Serial Nature of Christian Expansion

The central figure in the story we turn to in this chapter is that of Alexander Duff, the first missionary formally commissioned by the Church of Scotland and the best-known India missionary after William Carey. In 1866, then retired from missionary service, he urged upon the General Assembly of the Free Church of Scotland the creation in New College of a new chair in what he called "evangelistic theology."

This is not the place to consider Duff's argument or the details of his specification for the chair (Myklebust 1955), except to note that Duff regarded its remit as central to the whole theological curriculum, as relevant to those whose ministry would lie in Scotland and to those who would go to the mission field, and as interdisciplinary and ecumenical in its scope. The concerns of the new chair would penetrate all the traditional aspects of the theological curriculum—biblical, dogmatic, historical, and practical—and by involving the study of faiths and thought patterns other than the Christian, go well beyond the traditional curriculum. But Duff wanted much more than this. He saw the chair as only a first stage of academic provision. He envisaged an institute that would address the questions arising from the Christian encounter with other cultures. This institute would develop the study of what Duff called "the geography, history, ethnology, mythology, habits, manners and practices of unevangelized peoples and nations" (Duff 1866). It would promote the study of Asian and African languages. It would address the condition of the Scottish cities, review the religious situation of the European continent, concern itself with the Jewish community, and consider how to provide for the hundreds of Scottish families now annually emigrating to Canada, South Africa, and the Antipodes. Duff, a Protestant of firm, not to say crustacean, convic-

First published in *Studies in World Christianity* 1 (No. 1, 1995): 1–25. Reprinted with permission. A lecture for the opening session of the Faculty of Divinity, University of Edinburgh, in New College.

tions, found inspiration here in Rome—in the Catholic insight of missionary zeal as one of the marks of the authenticity of church, and its scholarly
institutional expression in the Urban University and the library of the Pro-
paganda Fide. He noticed also the Feast of Languages held in Rome at
Epiphany time, when the mighty works of God were recited in languages
from all over the world. This reflection of Pentecost exhibited an aspect of
the church still at that time hidden from most Western Protestants.

For Catholics, 1492 marked the start of a new missionary era. The fifth
centenary of Columbus's landfall in the Americas was widely, if con-
tentiously, commemorated in 1992. For our present purposes we need to
recognize that it marks an event of immense importance for the history of
the Christian faith, because from that time onwards, a Christianity that
had become thoroughly identified with and conditioned by the lands and
life and thought of Europe had to extend its consciousness, its vision, and
eventually its theology to cope with the realities of the world beyond Europe. These included some items outside all previous Christian experience. The chapter of intra-European difficulties that we call the Reformation to some extent distracted attention from this even more fundamental
reformulation of the Christian view of the world, and has continued to
distract the attention of historians of Christianity since. The bicentenary of
the publication of William Carey's *Enquiry into the Obligation of Christians
to Use Means for the Propagation of the Gospel among the Heathens* and the
formation of his missionary society was less of a media event than the
Columbus anniversary, but in some quarters it was celebrated as marking
the birth of the modern missionary movement. How one identifies that
movement's origins is a matter of perspective, but 1792 is at least as good
a date for it as several others. That same year also saw the arrival in Sierra
Leone of some 1,100 people of African birth or descent, bringing with
them from North America their own churches and preachers, to form the
first church in tropical Africa in modern times.

Taken together, 1492 and 1792 stand for the two great cycles of activity
that make up the missionary movement from the West. The first, largely
Catholic in composition, though with a small, vital Protestant component,
began in the late fifteenth century and was nearing exhaustion by the
eighteenth. The second, beginning in the late eighteenth century, was
largely Protestant in its origins, but by the nineteenth was enjoying the
support of every sector of European Christianity. But the landfall in Sierra
Leone has its significance as well as that in the Carribbean islands. The
first church in tropical Africa in modern times was not a Western missionary creation, but an African one, an African creation marked by the experiences of America. Columbus and Carey stand for Western activity, and
in their different ways they stand also for Western Christianity; but the
peoples of the new worlds beyond Europe were not passive in the encounter either with Europe or with its faith. After the meeting with the
Americas, Africa, and Asia instituted in the fifteenth century, Europe was

never the same again. It is the submission of this chapter that the meeting with the Americas, Africa, and Asia has been equally transformative of the Christian faith, marking a new and decisive period in its history. It is a further submission that such periodic transformations are entirely characteristic of Christian history and belong to the nature of the faith, being rooted ultimately in the central Christian affirmation that the Word became flesh and dwelt among us.

The history of the expansion of the two great missionary faiths, Christianity and Islam, suggests a contrast. While each has spread across vast areas of the world and each claims the allegiance of very diverse peoples, Islam seems, as noted in chapter 1, thus far to have been markedly more successful in retaining that allegiance. With relatively few (though admittedly important) exceptions, the areas and peoples that accepted Islam have remained Islamic ever since. Arabia, for example, seems now so immutably Islamic that it is hard to remember that it once had Jewish tribes and Christian towns, as well as the shrines of gods and goddesses to which the bulk of its population gave homage. Contrast the position with that of Jerusalem, the first major centre of Christianity; or of Egypt and Syria, once almost as axiomatically Christian as Arabia is now Islamic; or of the cities once stirred by the preaching of John Knox or John Wesley, now full of unwanted churches doing duty as furniture stores or night clubs. It is as though there is some inherent fragility, some built-in vulnerability, in Christianity, considered as a popular profession, that is not to the same extent a feature of Islam. This vulnerability is engraved into the Christian foundational documents themselves, with their recurrent theme of the impending rejection of apostate Israel, and their warnings to early Christian churches of the possible removal of their candlestick. Neither of these eventualities are seen as jeopardizing the saving activity of God for humanity. I have argued elsewhere that this vulnerability is also linked with the essentially vernacular nature of Christian faith, which rests on a massive act of translation, the Word made flesh, God translated into a specific segment of social reality as Christ is received there (Walls 1990: 24–39). Christian faith must go on being translated, must continuously enter into vernacular culture and interact with it, or it withers and fades. Islamic absolutes are fixed in a particular language, and in the conditions of a particular period of human history. The divine Word is the Qur'an, fixed in heaven forever in Arabic, the language of original revelation. For Christians, however, the divine Word is translatable, infinitely translatable. The very words of Christ himself were transmitted in translated form in the earliest documents we have, a fact surely inseparable from the conviction that in Christ, God's own self was translated into human form. Much misunderstanding between Christians and Muslims has arisen from the assumption that the Qur'an is for Muslims what the Bible is for Christians. It would be truer to say that the Qur'an is for Muslims what *Christ* is for Christians.

It is quite in line with fundamental Islamic convictions that Islamic expansion has been progressive in concept and, to a large extent, in experience also. Mecca, the original theatre of the revelation, retains its cosmic significance for all the faithful, demonstrated in the *qiblah*, the direction to which they turn in prayer. And the missionary preaching that calls all humankind to surrender to Allah has produced a progressive, generally continuous, and remarkably durable geographical expansion. The rhetoric of Christian expansion has often been similarly progressive; images of the triumphant host streaming out from Christendom to bring the whole world into it come to mind readily enough. But the actual experience of Christian expansion has been different. As its most comprehensive historian, K. S. Latourette, noted long ago, recession is a feature of Christian history as well as advance (Latourette 1945: esp. vol. 7, ch. 16). He might have gone on to note that the recessions typically take place in the Christian heartlands, in the areas of greatest Christian strength and influence—its Arabias, as one might say—while the advances typically take place at or beyond its periphery.

This feature means that Christian faith is repeatedly coming into creative interaction with new cultures, with different systems of thought and different patterns of tradition; that (again in contrast to Islam, whose Arabic absolutes provide cultural norms applying throughout the Islamic world) its profoundest expressions are often local and vernacular. It also means that the demographic and geographical centre of gravity of Christianity is subject to periodic shifts. Christians have no abiding city, no permanent sacred sites, no earthly Mecca; their new Jerusalem comes down out of heaven at the last day. Meanwhile, Christian history has been one of successive penetration of diverse cultures. Islamic expansion is progressive; Christian expansion is serial.

The first change in the centre of gravity of the Christian world, entirely representative of what was to follow, took place within the first century of the Christian era, and its pathway is marked within the New Testament itself. Within a remarkably short time, Christianity ceased to be a demographically Jewish phenomenon centred in Jewish Palestine and expressed in terms of the fulfilment of God's promises to Israel. It moved towards a new expression as a demographically and culturally Hellenistic one, dispersed across the Eastern Mediterranean, and then beyond it. The Gentile mission, initially a mere by-product of the messianic movement centred in Jerusalem, sparked by the forced removal from the city of many of the leading activists (Acts 8:1), turned out to be the means of the movement's very survival. The crux was the fall of Jerusalem in A.D. 70 and the accompanying destruction of the Jewish state. With that state, the original Jewish model of Christianity typified by James the Just—the righteous, deeply observant Jew who was the very brother of the Lord—was swept away forever. That Christianity itself was not swept away was due to the cross-cultural diffusion that had already begun, and the consequent emergence of a new Hellenistic model of Christian expression.

The Hellenistic-Roman model of Christianity was by the fourth century quite as secure in its identity and its place in the world as the now vanished elders and apostles at Jerusalem had been in their vision. The Hellenistic-Roman model had a by-product, too, that proved crucial for the future: the movement or series of movements that transmitted the faith, no doubt in partly assimilated forms, to the peoples beyond the imperial frontiers whom the Hellenistic-Roman world called barbarians and feared as the likely destroyers of civilization. The significance of this process of transmission became evident only when the overextended frontiers of the Western Empire collapsed under the weight of the barbarians in a sequence of fierce and nasty little wars, and when the provinces of the Eastern Empire, which could point to the tombs of the most glorious martyrs and to the brightest treasures of Christian spirituality and scholarship, took on a new existence as Islamic states. Once again the survival of the Christian faith as a major force in the world depended on its having crossed a cultural frontier. Against all expectations, the future of Christianity lay with the barbarians. The Christian heartlands moved from the urban centres of Mediterranean civilization, with their advanced technology and developed literary tradition, to a new setting among peasant cultivators and semisettled raiders. A new model of Christianity developed among the Celtic and Germanic peoples between the Atlantic and the Carpathians, and another took its most distinctive shape among the Slavic peoples.

But the serial process of recession and advance, of withering heartland and emergence within a new cultural setting, can be seen in much more recent times. I would not wish to go to the stake for the figures given in the *World Christian Encyclopedia,* but I am sure that the direction that they indicate, the situation that can be extrapolated from them, is broadly correct. On this basis one can reckon that in the year 1800 well over 90 percent of the world's professing Christians lived in Europe or North America. Today, something like 60 percent of them live in Africa, Asia, Latin America, or the Pacific, and that proportion is rising year by year. Still more strikingly, there were as recently as 1900 perhaps ten million professing Christians in the African continent. An educated guess today might put the figure at something over 300 million, and that figure, too, is rising (Barrett 1982: 4)

In other words, the period bounded by the two anniversaries of 1492 and 1792, and substantially the period since the second of them, has seen the Christian centre of gravity steadily move away from the West and towards the southern continents. That movement has accelerated in the twentieth century, and is now in spate. The last hundred years have seen the most considerable recession from the Christian faith to occur since the early expansion of Islam, and the area most affected has been Europe. A rather longer period has seen the most substantial accession to the Christian faith for at least a millennium; and that accession has taken place in the southern continents, especially in Africa, Latin America, and the Pacific. Always predicted by gloomy prophets, the pace of Christian recession in the West has probably been faster than even the gloomiest expected. If the first open sign of recession came when Holy Russia embraced an officially atheistic ideology, it eventually became clear that it bit most deeply within the open, liberal regimes of the West. And the accession of Christians in the southern continents, so often regarded as the marginal effect of a misdirected missionary activity that largely failed, has been such as would have startled the most sanguine of the missionary fathers of 1792. When the delegates of the World Missionary Conference gathered in the Assembly Hall at New College in 1910, they did so with a view to organizing the resources of the Christian West to bring the Christian gospel to the rest of the world. A symbolic handful of Indian, Chinese, and Japanese Christians pointed to the future of the church; there was not a single African present. Today, the signs suggest that what the Christianity of the twenty-first century will be like, in its theology, its worship, its effect on society, its penetration of new areas, whether geographically or culturally, will depend on what happens in Africa, in Latin America, and in some parts of Asia.

There is a significant feature of each of these demographic and cultural shifts of the Christian centre of gravity. In each case a threatened eclipse of Christianity was averted by its cross-cultural diffusion. Crossing cultural boundaries has been the life blood of historic Christianity. It is also noteworthy that most of the energy for the frontier crossing has come from the periphery rather than from the centre. The book of Acts suggests that it was not the apostles who were responsible for the breakthrough of Antioch, whereby Greek-speaking pagans heard of the Jewish messiah as the Lord Jesus, but quite unknown Jewish believers from Cyprus and Greece (Acts 11:19–20). The same book indicates that, for Christians who lived there, the real centre of the church was always Jerusalem. It was Jerusalem that sent out commissions to decide whether the conversion movements among Samarians and Antiochene Gentiles were really acceptable; it was Jerusalem that had to settle the question of how far non-Jewish believers in Jesus must conform to Jewish cultural norms (Acts 8:14ff.; 11:22ff.; 15:1–2). And when Paul tried to tell Jerusalem believers of the success of the good news about Jesus in Asia, Acts reveals that he was told to look at the still more spectacular successes among Jerusalem Jews who were zealous for the law, and invited to vindicate his own Jewish credentials (Acts 21:20–25). The whole Gentile mission of Paul and his colleagues must have seemed a sideline in comparison with the work in Zion, where the words of the prophets were daily fulfilled, where the Lord's own brother was in regular attendance at the temple of God among the covenant people of God at the place where the Lord would return. But the day came when there was no temple, no sign of the nation, no brother of the Lord, and no Jerusalem church, no dominant community of the believing circumcised. It was at this point that the real significance of the apostle to the Gentiles and his colleagues became plain. So did the significance of those unnamed people from Cyprus and Cyrene who decided that Jesus had something to do with their Greek-speaking pagan neighbours in Antioch.

In the same way, we can read the substantial writings of the great theologians of the fourth and fifth and sixth centuries, or follow the accounts of the ecumenical councils, establishing with infinite pains acceptable formulations of the doctrines of Trinity and incarnation. Or if we choose, we may look at the same period, and many of the same events, in terms of the power struggles within church and state, or between metropolitan centre and outlying provinces. Whichever focus we adopt, we are dealing with central concerns of Hellenistic-Roman Christianity. But those concerns might today be no more than chapters in Greek intellectual history or late imperial politics had it not been for a peripheral development within Hellenistic-Roman Christianity that gave the outcome of those concerns significance for a later time. That development is the beginning of the transmission of Christianity from the imperial to the barbarian setting. Its symbolic figures are people like Wulfila, the son of Christian prisoners brought up among the Goths, a man whose Christology was formed in the wrong place, away from the influences eventually determined as orthodox, who became the pioneer of Gothic Christianity; or Patrick, another prisoner of war a generation or so later, brought up on the crumbling British fringes of imperial influence, who had no Greek and was apologetic about his Latin, yet is crucial in the Irish Christian story.

What of the more recent development that has produced a transforming change in the centre of gravity of Christianity within the last century? There is much about this development, as I hope to show, that has nothing to do with the West at all; but at the same time it is impossible to ignore the presence of the missionary movement from the West as the detonator of a considerable explosion. But that movement was for most of its life a peripheral and minority concern within Western Christianity. One can work through great monuments of historical scholarship about the nineteenth-century church with hardly a glimpse of it. Neither Owen Chadwick's *The Victorian Church* nor Sydney Ahlstrom's *History of Religion in America* gives even a chapter to the missionary movement; the former, indeed, though its distinguished author knows a great deal about the missionary movement, has only incidental references to it. This is not due to carelessness; it reflects reality, or at least the sort of reality that these historians are recording. The missionary movement, though for much of the nineteenth century widely applauded, was never more than a marginal concern of Western Christians. Alexander Duff, in his speech in which he argued for his missionary chair and institute, claimed that the entire Scottish missions could be sustained and increased from the resources of Aberdeen or Dundee alone, were their church people really concerned about such things. Andrew Ross has shown how the common belief in a significant Scottish missionary response to the news of the death of David Livingstone has little foundation in fact (Ross 1972: 52–72). The tragic end of the visionary Scottish traveller (who was, incidentally, a member of neither of the great Scottish churches, and frequently called himself an Englishman) brought no great stirrings of liberality or flood of offers of missionary service from the parishes of Scotland. Until well on in the nineteenth century, a majority of missionaries did not even reflect Western Christianity in its most developed expressions; for at least two generations, a high proportion of Anglican missionaries would not have met the requirements for ordination in England. As in the early church of Jerusalem, so in the churches of the West, charity began at home, and it was only the few who lifted their active vision beyond it. From the standpoint of posterity, the sideline of the Gentile mission looks like the single most important development in Palestinian, that is, New Testament, Christianity. In terms of total Christian history, the missionary movement may prove to be the single most important development in modern Western Christianity.

The missionary movement is a connecting terminal between Western Christianity and Christianity in the non-Western world. I propose now, in the most tentative way, to explore the relationship between the two, using three hypotheses.

The first is that the history and outlook of Western Christians right up to the present time has been shaped by the peculiar circumstances in which the northern and western barbarians received the Christian faith, which led to the idea of a Christendom, a conception in which Christianity was essentially linked to territory and the possession of territory.

The second is that the gap we now recognize between the idea of Christendom and the realities of the contemporary religious situation in the post-Christian West should be seen in the context of the mode of contact that the Western world established with the non-Western world. I do not wish to belittle the elements indigenous to the West that have eroded Christendom, but I do want to suggest that one of its major solvents has been colonialism.

The third is that in keeping with the serial nature of Christian expansion that seems so characteristic of the Christian faith, the dissolution of Christendom made possible a cultural diffusion of Christianity that is now in process of transforming it. The process should be seen as analogous in significance to the shift whereby the urban centres of the Eastern Mediterranean replaced Jerusalem as the workshop of the Christian world, or that whereby the new Christians of Western lands found themselves in situations once held by the likes of Athanasius and Augustine. The new Christian heartlands in Africa and Asia—and, it is now becoming curiously evident, even in Latin America—are neither extensions nor replicas of Christendom. Christendom is dead, and Christianity is alive and well without it.

The Origins of Christendom

The best writers on the process by which Christianity was brought to northern Europe, writers such as Gregory of Tours and Bede, reflect a cool realism about it. They show clearly how the peoples of the north and west responded to the Christian proclamation in terms of traditional expectations and goals. A single example will suffice from the many at hand: Bede's well-known account of the conversion of the kingdom of Northumbria. In this the king, Edwin, has a Christian wife, a princess from an allied kingdom southward. Struck by her chaplain's preaching, the king is personally well-disposed to Christianity, but he knows that he cannot move in that direction without the support of his military elite. He therefore calls a council, and the first to speak is a priest of the old religion. He gives his vote in favour of a change to Christianity, provided due procedures of investigation have been carried out. The reason for this was that he had himself shown unfailing devotion to the gods, and yet many people stood higher than he did in the king's favour. It was plain, therefore, that devout service of the gods conferred no advantages. When at length the council voted in favour of the new worship, that same cult priest led the public profanation of the altars of the gods who had so signally let down their faithful servant. Then, Bede tells us, "The king, with all the nobility of the nation, and a large number of the common sort, received the faith, and the washing of regeneration" (Bede 2,13–14). Bede, himself a seeker for wholehearted Christian obedience, recognizes that the people of his own country initially responded to the proclamation of Christianity in terms of the expectations of their old religion and in terms of traditional goals. It could hardly be otherwise: it is hardly possible to take in a new idea except in terms of ideas we already have. And in societies of this type, religion could not be a matter for individual decision—even the individual decision of a strong ruler such as Edwin. It was about essentially communal matters: ancestral custom, acceptable modes of life within the community, and the sanctions governing both. It was therefore a matter for corporate discussion and consensual action. In earlier Christian history, in the Christianity of the old Roman Empire, conversion, sealed by baptism, marked a person's entrance into a new community. In the experience of northern and western Europe, Christian conversion led rather to a symbolic reordering of the community already existing.

This is the birthplace of territorial Christianity, the origin of the idea of the Christian nation. Not Constantine, not Theodosius, could have envisaged the form of the territorial Christianity that developed in the north. The Roman Empire that they ruled had too much diversity, too many interest groups, too much inbuilt pluralism, to sustain anything of the kind. But the northern peoples, with no easy way of dividing sacred and profane custom, produced territorial Christianity by their need to have a single body of custom. A single people must follow a single code.

To this extent, territorial Christianity reflected the continuation of a principle inherent in the primal cultures of the north. But it also transcended these cultures in a variety of ways. One of the most important and far-reaching in its effects was the introduction of an element arising out of the Christian past in the Roman imperial world. This was the idea of universality, of catholicity, transcending the various kinship groups and tributary relationships. In the West this was particularly potent by virtue of the special position of Rome, its only assured link with the apostolic age. In a sense the church continued the Roman Empire; if Rome had lost imperial political significance, it was still the seat of the Empire of Christ, even when a Holy Roman Emperor sat elsewhere. The role of the Christian church in maintaining and transmitting, in residual form, the cultural legacy of Rome strengthened the conception. In entering the Christian faith the peoples of the north and west entered a wider universe, recognized wider kinships, than they had done before: a single assembly of Christian princes and peoples, a single church, a single sacred language, a single tradition of learning. Anyone who could read, whether in Ireland, France, Hungary, or Poland, could read the same books in the same language. A single civilization fused elements from the Celtic and Germanic cultures with what it could absorb from the Roman Empire, and preserved that empire's language for the purposes of learning, worship, and wider communication after it had ceased to be anyone's vernacular. To be Christian was to share in a civilization rooted in ancient Rome. Not for nothing does Gregory of Tours preface his *History of the Franks* by demonstrating how the dioceses of Tours and Clermont Ferrand can be linked to the biblical story of salvation via Roman history. Later writers, in territories with much less historical connexion with the Roman Empire than his, maintained a similar sense of solidarity with a Roman past. To be Christian was to share a special history and literary tradition, as it were by adoption. To be Christian was also to belong to specific territory—Christian lands, the entire contiguous lands from Ireland to the Carpathians, states and peoples subject to princes subject to Christ, hearing the voice of Christ's apostle from the Eternal City that antedated them all.

English has two words: "Christianity," suggesting a concept, a religious system, a term that can be used in forms of discussion as the formal parallel of other religious systems such as Hinduism or Buddhism, and "Christendom," suggesting an entity with temporal dimensions, something that can be plotted on a map. Many European languages have only one word for both. The Christendom idea, the territorial principle of Christianity, latched to the idea of a single inherited civilization, was brought into Christian history by the "barbarian" model of Christianity, much as the Hellenistic model of Christianity had introduced the principle of orthodoxy. Both were the natural outcome of the interaction of Christian faith and tradition with the dominant cultural norms. The Christendom idea has been extremely resilient. It survived the sixteenth-century Reformation practically unscathed. The Protestant Reformation resulted in the division of Christendom, but not in the abandonment of the idea. The Protestant reformers held to it as firmly as any Catholic. What they sought was a *reformed* Christendom; they did not recognize the possibility of opting out of that reformed community. As in the Latin church, the Christian prince or magistrate had his proper duty: he stood in the place of Hezekiah or Josiah, the royal reformers of old Judah. There were certainly more radical reformers, such as those of the Anabaptist tradition, whose theology did undermine the Christendom concept; their persecution by Catholic and Protestant alike shows how seriously the threat was taken. Yet when radical reformers went over to New England, they could not resist, at least for a brief period, setting up Christendom all over again, a pure and godly commonwealth, uncorrupted by the tired old iniquities of Europe.

With infinite travail, the various components of Christendom devised their church settlements. Many of these settlements contained compromises, forced by recalcitrance rather than conceded out of charity. But these were only qualifications of a continuing principle: a state ruled according to Christian norms expressed through a single recognized channel. Modern Europe wrestled with new formulations of the old principle of its barbarian forebears: a single code of sacred custom for a single people. A study of liberalism and democracy (Parry 1986) illustrates the effect in British politics as late as the last quarter of the nineteenth century. Whether the nominal issue on the agenda was education, or the relief of poverty, or the government of Ireland, the questions that divided people were about how a state dedicated to Christian norms related to the now various manifestations of the Christian church. The Christendom tradition still maintained its vigour, but it was now complicated by the accumulated developments of individualism and pluralism, which were forcing religion increasingly into the sphere of private judgment.

The effect of European individualism and pluralism on the erosion of Christendom lies outside our present scope. There was a further solvent of the Christendom idea deriving from the pressures brought by western Europe's encounter with the non-Western world, and in particular by Western hegemony, or the attempt to establish hegemony, over it. And Christianity, when transmitted to the non-Western world, proved to have a dynamic of its own, and took a course quite different from that of the West.

The first of the anniversaries with which this study began, Columbus's landfall of 1492, marks a supremely confident time for Christendom. The last pagan peoples, in Finland and the Baltic states, had been brought within Latin Christendom. Still more strikingly, Muslim power had been broken in southern Spain; the Muslims, after centuries of presence there, had been driven out or forced to accept incorporation into the church. Christian theology could be described as virtually complete; it appeared that every important question had been canvassed and settled. There was a secure tradition of literature and a flourishing tradition of art, which owed their canons to Bible and church. It was sacred art that set the artistic norms and provided the register of symbols and conventions.

And just at this point of assurance, Europe came, by means of the expansion of the Iberian powers, into massive contact with the non-Western world. With Christianity essentially territorial in concept, all recent experience pointed to crusade as the natural mode of relationship.

The earliest colonialism was conceived in crusading zeal. As early as 1415 the Portuguese conquered part of Morocco—a blow for Christendom against Islam. (It may be noted that the principal experience western Europe had hitherto of the world beyond Christendom tended to heighten the identification of faith with territory.) A telling passage in a near contemporary account describes how Prince Henry the Navigator of Portugal wrote to all the kings of Christendom inviting their help in discovery and conquest for "the service of our Lord" and on the basis of shared profits. They all sent apologies for absence, which Henry collected and sent to the Pope (da Silva Rego 1959: 14). The reply was all that he wanted. It was to be formalized in the course of the next century in the Padroado or Patonato by which the pope not only gave to the monarchs of Portugal and Spain monopoly powers of rule and trade in the new worlds that they were now meeting, but committed to them the oversight of the church in those lands. The latter provision marks the first reflex action of colonialism upon Christendom, and perhaps marks the first step in its secularization.

The Iberian voyages, with the French, Dutch, and English ones that followed, and their results in settlement and conquest altered the whole map of European and Christian knowledge. J. H. Elliot (1970: ch. 1) has pointed out that the maps and the reference books did not immediately alter; it took contemporaries some time to take in the new discoveries. It is often the way: discoveries that remove the old landmarks and undermine accepted concepts of the world are ignored as long as possible.

The natural objective was to incorporate the new lands within Christendom. The only known model of Christianity was territorial; and the precedent of crusade, so recently blessed with prosperity in the restoration of Granada to the rule of Christ, seemed to authorize the use of the sword to bring about that extension. Conversion would be the fruit of conquest.

At first it seemed to work. In Mexico and Peru the Spaniards destroyed Amerindian cult, proscribed traditional rites, baptized whole populations. It was not long, however, before the difficulties such methods created were apparent. A century afterwards one earnest priest was lamenting that because of the work of destruction he knew little of the old culture; and, because of his ignorance "they can practise idolatry before our very eyes."

Such an utterance marks the beginning of self-doubt. Destruction of cult was easy; trying to comprehend a society so different from the norm of Christendom exposed the gaps in European intellectual and, indeed, theological equipment. The only tools at hand lay in the pre-Christian Latin classics; the only "pagans" of whom European Christians now know anything were to be met there. The irrelevance of Ovid and Virgil to the understanding of the Quechua and Aymara of the Andes was soon manifest. The issue was of no great moment from a strictly colonial point of view; it might be urged that understanding was not formally necessary—it was enough to compel. But as the heartcry of the priest already quoted indicates, it was at the pastoral level that compulsion broke down. Similarly, from a colonial point of view, the use of indigenous language was hardly an issue, for the Castilian language of the conquerors could be imposed. From the point of view of European theologians, this might be welcome, for the European controversies of the sixteenth century had set a premium on accurate definition. A range of doctrines and liturgical practices was being more precisely formulated that ever before, and the official formulations were in Latin. But for pastoral practice, this was of little help; how could an Andean peasant make a confession to salvation without understanding? The only way forward was to grapple with understanding the Andean vernaculars and attempt to explain Christian doctrine in indigenous terms. Both European-based theologians and the local guardians of colonial safety in church and state took fright at this. The Andean languages did not, they argued, have the words or concepts to safeguard saving truth, or were so riddled with false concepts of the divine as to make their use dangerous. European experience also suggested the easy connexion between vernacular translation and heresy. Official policy thus suggested the employment of loanwords from Latin or Spanish for all important concepts. But the use of loanwords, of course, solves nothing; if confession is to be made from the heart, loanwords have to be understood in the vernacular. A two-way traffic between Christian theology and the Andean worldview opened up, and new ideas were once more apprehended in terms of ideas already there. As William Mitchell puts it, "The option for the vernacular means that one can speak of the Christianization of the Andes in the early colonial period only if one speaks of the Andeanization of Christianity."

Meanwhile, the brutality and rapacity of the representatives of Christendom, taken as a whole, called into question the moral, and thus the Christian, status of the Spanish mission. The story of Bartolomé de Las Casas, and in particular his passionate debates with Sepúlveda, show how the affairs of America forced new questions onto the theological agenda—questions about the constitution of humanity, about the place of ccmpulsion in religion, about the conditions of the just war. Already America was showing the limitations of that apparently assured encyclopedia of theology developed over the centuries of Christian Europe. An observer attentive to the issues facing the missionaries in Peru and Mexico, even those arising out of the catechism itself, might decide that the task of theology was far from complete. The wider question of the extent to which Andean Christianity was developing a life of its own did not become apparent until the twentieth century.

The success of the Spanish project to incorporate its new world into Christendom was thus more apparent than real. More important for the future of Christendom, however, than the apparent success of the Spanish was the fact that the Portuguese found the task impossible. The Spanish presence was concentrated in America and the Philippines; the Portuguese presence stretched like a thread along the coasts of Africa, along the Persian Gulf and across the Indian Ocean, into South India and Sri Lanka and the coasts and islands of Southeast Asia, to offshore China and on to Japan—not to mention Brazil. Much of this area was not so much an empire as a system of trade monopolies staffed by little companies of merchants, soldiers, and priests. And Portugal was a small country with a standing army never above ten thousand men. Portugal began its empire with joyful acceptance of the task of expanding Christendom. But its resources were slender, its hold often precarious, and even in the territories it occupied, resistant Islam, and resistant Hinduism, and resistant Buddhism refused to lie down.

The result was important for Christianity. It was in the Portuguese territories, and still more in the powerful states on which the Portuguese presence in India and China depended, that the conditions appeared that called forth the modern missionary movement. In the Spanish territories the task was to teach the faith to people already obliged to receive it. The Portuguese experience allowed only limited scope for this. It did, however, make necessary the creation of a new body of people who did not have the power of coercion, whose function was to commend, persuade, demonstrate, and discuss; and who in order to perform these tasks needed to understand and enter into the life of other societies. The original conception of the expansion of Christendom involved laying down terms for other people; its development in the missionary movement involved preparedness to live on terms set by other people. The Jesuits first arrived at the court of the Mughal emperor Akbar the Great by invitation; they arrived at the court of the Chinese emperor by perseverance. Once there, in either case, their ways of working were circumscribed by the interests of those monarchs. They had to conduct themselves in accordance with local custom and to find a niche within local society. Some sought a high degree of identification and cultural transfer, the most famous early example being Roberto de Nobili, with his adoption of the lifestyle of a Brahmin sannyasi and his refusal to be classed as Portuguese (the only locally known form of European). Sometimes the approach to another culture was less dramatic but equally remarkable in its cultural achievement; the missionary Giuseppe Beschi, for instance, is a seminal figure in Tamil literature. In this strange way, interfaith dialogue was born of frustrated colonialism. Putting it another way: in the mercy of God, the king of Portugal never had enough servants to go out into the highways and byways and compel them to come in.

The fundamental missionary experience is to live on terms set by others. This was true in a literal sense for a high proportion of missionaries between the middle of the sixteenth century and the middle of the nineteenth, who were subject to the conditions laid down by the sovereign rulers of the territories in which they lived, or were able to carry on their missionary work only because the leaders of the society found them useful for something else. In the case of the early Scottish mission in Calabar, it was commercial interest, to boost their international trading advantage; in many another African situation it was an intermediary with the whites, or a contact for commerce; in the early New Zealand mission it was a regular source of iron goods. The colonial advance, of course, and especially the high imperial period between 1880 and 1920, altered a great deal of this by creating another power structure of which missionaries were part. Even with these conditions, however, missionaries as a class, and not always by their own desire, had to take note of others' terms more than most Europeans of the colonial period. The need to speak someone else's language, the consciousness of doing it badly or even laughably, being unsure of etiquette, constant fear of giving unintended offence, realization of the vast depth and complexity of another community's traditions and history, and thus identity—all this was part of the daily experience of thousands. It led to some herculean efforts of understanding and sympathy, and to the collection and systematization of knowledge. The primary missionary aim was to enter the minds and hearts of other people, since that was the only way they could effectively talk about Christ. In the process they altered the map of Western learning more than any other group of Western residents in the non-Western world.

Scholars today (though in practice it is more the custom of the popularizers and media exponents) can afford to be snide or patronizing about the missionary movement, but many branches of Western learning now exist because of it. Scientific anthropology became possible as a result of the missionary movement. It is instructive to follow the correspondence of Max Müller, or J. G. Frazer, or A. C. Haddon with missionaries; not because these luminaries could identify with missionary aims, but because they were aware of no other group of Western people so regularly engaged at such a fundamental level with the languages and cultures of the non-Western world. If some of the results now seem absurd or offensive, it is well to remember that we are all subject to the principle enunciated earlier: it is only possible to take in a new idea in terms of ideas we already have.

The science of comparative African linguistics was the almost single-handed creation of Sigismund Wilhelm Koelle, a lonely, eccentric, and rather cantankerous German missionary in Sierra Leone. The significance of tone and the devisal of a system of marking it were due to the insistence of the African missionary Samuel Ajayi Crowther, the most important influence in the production of the Bible in his mother tongue, Yoruba, and pioneer of the substantial literature in that language. The most important single figure in the Western understanding of the Chinese classics is probably the Scottish missionary James Legge, whose first aim was to understand China, and who from that understanding concluded that Christian theology could be regarded as continuous with the ancient religion of China now obscured by modern accretions. Another Aberdonian, John Nicol Farquhar, produced the fullest comprehensive compendium of information on Indian religious literature, still in print in India. Indeed, one is tempted to suggest that the missionary movement affected every department of scholarship—except theology. Even for missionaries, theology generally remained a "given"; it is the postmissionary era of the non-Western churches that has shown that they opened both new issues and new directions in theology. It is part of the prescience of Alexander Duff, Edinburgh's founder of modern mission studies, that he realized that the Brahmo Samaj and Keshub Chunder Sen were raising theological issues in India that had not been discussed in Western theology; and that the Xhosa cattle killing in South Africa was a religious event for which Western experience had no analogy and therefore no tools for understanding.

Perhaps part of the significance of the missionary movement is the very converse of the cultural imperialism with which it is often quite justifiably charged. The missionary movement arose from the need to live on someone else's terms, to make Christian affirmations within the constraints of someone else's language. The missionary movement is the learning experience of Western Christianity. But it is far more, since, in the process of introducing Christian affirmations in other languages, it set them free to move within new systems of thought and discourse. Lamin Sanneh has shown how in many parts of Africa missionary activity acted as a means of cultural renewal by its use of vernaculars, and, in the production of vernacular worshipping communities and the creation of vernacular literatures, hymnody, and liturgy, provided resistance to eroding influences from outside. He draws attention to the fact that his own people, who have been Muslim for centuries, have forgotten their own name for God; whereas in almost all areas of West Africa where Christian influence has predominated, the God and Father of the Lord Jesus Christ has a vernacular name (Sanneh 1990). The Western theological process starts from the fact that the northern and western barbarians abandoned their old pantheons and took in God from the outside, envisaged in terms of Yahweh of Hosts, the God of Israel, merged with the highest Good of the Greek philosophical tradition. African theology starts at a different point. God has a vernacular name. As Olorun, Nyame, Ngewo, God is there in the African, indeed, in the Yoruba, the Akan, the Mende past. From one point of view, the Western missionary movement can be seen as the last flourish of Christendom. From another, it represents a departure from Christendom or perhaps an Abrahamic journey out of it.

The missionary movement had another effect on Christendom not envisaged in its origins. The establishment of a body of European Christians working, however inconsistently, on a different set of terms from the "official" colonial presence gradually introduced a principle of separation between the religion of Christendom and its political, military, and economic power. The wedge was narrow to begin with, but it is visible in de Nobili's vigorous rejection of the Portuguese name, and in the demeanour and activities of many other early missionaries who did not come from the lands that held the Padroado. The later colonialisms witnessed a thickening of the wedge. The Dutch, who succeeded the Portuguese in so much of their empire, broadly retained Portuguese religious policy, simply substituting Reformed for Catholic worship. But the Dutch had no missionary orders, and the predikants of the East and West India Companies were inevitably limited in their effect on communities outside the church. Planters of Protestant origin in the British Caribbean colonies frequently feared missionary activity among the slave population lest it make slaves ungovernable. The Honourable East India Company, the mode of British administration in India down to 1858, for a long time ostentatiously dissociated itself from Christianity, and even after 1813, when evangelical pressure in Parliament secured the insertion of "pious clauses" into its charter, maintained a more than discreet distance.

Missionaries, whether Protestant or Catholic, had grown up in the Christendom concept, and, taken as a group, they had no quarrel with it. The first evangelical missionary project for British India envisaged what would in effect have been a state mission. What better gift could Britain give to the territories over whom Providence had set it than the gospel of Christ? What greater treason could it commit than to hide that gospel? Even after the cataclysm of 1857, evangelicals were demanding that Britain identify itself in India as the Christian nation it was. Britain is the first conqueror of India, said John Clark Marshman to a meeting at Exeter Hall, who has not let it be known what his religion is (*Christianity in India* 1858: 22).

But they spoke in vain, and great was their scandal to find the British government the official guardian by treaty of the Temple of the Tooth in Kandy, and legally responsible for the appointment of Buddhist priests (de Silva 1965). Nor did Catholic missionary spokesmen fare better. Cardinal Lavigerie saw in Algeria the possibility of an Arab Catholic peasantry that would be the mirror image of Brittany; the French government legislated against the conversion of Muslims, and were prepared to prosecute any who tried to leave Islam (de Montclos 1965).

By the end of the nineteenth century there is a clear note of embattlement in missionary literature, a sense of betrayal by the Christian state. At the beginning of that century the great Islamic power had been the sultan of Turkey; by the end it was the British Empire, with the Royal Republic of the Netherlands in second place. The missionary interest was lamenting that Britain kept missionaries out of the emirates of northern Nigeria, that Britain was encouraging the Islamization of the Sudan. Furthermore, the British did these things more efficiently than the sultan ever did. In the twentieth century it appeared that the most considerable religious effects of imperial rule were the renovation and reformulation of a Hinduism that had seemed to be disintegrating at the time British rule was established, and a quite unprecedented spread of Islam. Colonial rule did more for Islam in Africa than all the jihads together.

Colonialism, in fact, helped to transform the Christian position in the world by forcing a distinction between Christianity and Christendom. Colonial experience undermined the identification of Christianity with territory and immobilized the idea of crusade. It introduced new theological and moral questions, for the issues argued in one century by Las Casas and in another by Buxton and Philip go to the heart of religion; fundamentally they are questions about salvation. It opened the way for Christian understanding and interpretation of other religions and cultures for which the conditions of Western Christianity provided no space. It undermined that pillar of Christendom, church establishment, because the principles of establishment could so rarely be maintained abroad.

It is usual, and entirely correct, in describing the colonial period to point to the connexions between Christian missionaries and the colonial states. Perhaps the reverse, however, is equally true: it is the colonial period that marks the divergence of interest between Christianity and the Western powers, the separation of the religion of the West from its political and economic interests. If several generations of missionaries once felt betrayed when a state nominally Christian refused to offer the support they felt due, we now may be humbly grateful that God is kinder than to answer all the prayers of his people.

Paradoxically, and in sharp contrast to its first vision, colonialism helped to ensure that new Christendoms did not arise. The pattern of colonial rule prevented the development of the relationship of throne and altar that developed in the northern lands. The nearest approach to a new Christendom has come in some Pacific island communities—Samoa, Tonga, Fiji—where entire populations with their rulers moved towards Christianity during the nineteenth century and where until quite recently a single church predominated in each state. Even there, however, it was often colonial overrule that produced arrangements incompatible with the Christendom pattern, as with the introduction of a substantial Indian population to work the sugar plantations of Fiji. Latin America, scene of the earliest colonial attempts to extend Christendom (and, as we saw, with initial apparent success), has progressively departed from the Christendom model since the end of the colonial era. The new republics could not encourage the immigration they needed without liberalizing their religious policy, and the evangelical explosion of the past half century has complicated the situation still further. And what of sub-Saharan Africa, the most remarkable theatre of Christian accession in the modern world? It would be easy to draw African parallels, in the last two centuries, with the stories from Gregory and Bede with which we began. That the two movements of conversion did not have the same issue is due at least in part to colonialism. Colonial rule brought together diverse peoples of different religious affiliation in units dictated by administrative convenience. The present states of sub-Saharan Africa are virtually all colonial constructs, based on colonial frontiers. This makes them of their nature religiously as well as ethnically plural, a natural home of the secular state among incorrigibly religious people.

The new chapter of Christian history, then, seems to relate to a Christianity without Christendom, a Christianity more and more determined by the southern continents. The closing remarks will relate to a few of its features.

Christianity without Christendom

1. The missionary movement from the West is only an episode in African, Asian, and Pacific Christian history—a vital episode, but for many churches an episode long closed. Missionary enterprise continues, but its Western, and especially its original European, component is crumbling. The great missionary nation is now Korea; in every continent there are Korean missionaries by the hundreds, and in coming years we can expect hundreds more, preaching from Tashkent to Timbuktu, and reaching where Westerners have long been unable to tread. In a more modest way, Brazil is now a major sending country. The eventual effect of such transformation in the sending structures can hardly be calculated.

2. The 1792 anniversary reminds us that the first church in tropical Africa was an African, not a missionary, creation. Most Africans have always heard the gospel from Africans, and virtually all the great movements towards the Christian faith in Africa have been African led.

3. The Christian communities of the southern continents are not struggling infants, but mature churches with substantial Christian histories behind them. Theology is always a hazardous business, "an act of adoration fraught with the risk of blasphemy." It grows and develops in situations of crisis and urgency. The churches of Africa and Asia have abundant experience of crisis and urgency. No Western church has ever had to beat a way to survival in the way the church in China has; yet in its period of isolation, the Chinese church has not only survived but multiplied. We talk of theologies of poverty and options for the poor; African churches routinely face hunger, oppression, extortion, plague, endemic war, and pandemic AIDS. What this does for life and thought and liturgy and preaching is manifest in preaching in Kenya, where Deuteronomy and Amos

became contemporaries, or the remarkable songs of suffering of Dinka Christians uprooted from their soil and largely ignored by the world.

4. Such experiences have produced a greater degree of theological development than has often been recognized. Such development has been needed, for the churches of Africa and Asia are being forced to work out some sort of Christian response to situations where Western theology has no answers because it has no questions or any relevant experience. Kwame Bediako has shown the parallels between the quest of Hellenistic theologians of the second and third centuries coping with their own identity as Christian heirs of a tradition of culture and literature, and a whole generation of African theologians seeking at once to be Christian and African (Bediako 1992). Cyril Okorocha shows how conversion has different significance and takes on different expressions at different points of the religious itinerary of an African people (Okorocha 1987). Christian theology is expanding as it comes into contact with new areas of human experience, new accumulations of knowledge, relationship, and activity. Themes are being recognized in the Scriptures that the West had never noticed.

5. In the process, new theological methods will be developed. Western theology has evolved, in comparatively recent times and from within its own resources, a particular approach to the Bible and its exegesis. There are quite different approaches to the Bible in large areas of the Christian world. These are not necessarily the products of naiveté or obscurantism, but of different approaches to sacred and classical texts, rooted in a cultural and religious tradition much older than the Western. Those who have noted the polite boredom of Eastern Orthodox colleagues with some of the questions raised by Western scholarship about the New Testament and patristic literature will already be alerted to the need to take account of other approaches.

6. The Christianity of the southern continents has been visited by remarkable religious movements that have put down deep roots. Pentecostalism is a worldwide phenomenon. It must not be forgotten that even in the West it was originally a product of black Christian activity. In the West, Pentecostalism, though growing in importance, has generally remained marginal to church life; in Latin America it has become central, not least because its rationale makes such clear Christian sense within some local worldviews. West Africa has seen Pentecostalism move into a new phase that has unsettled the studies of twenty years ago. A Pentecostal woman singer produces beautiful and moving hymns to Christ, combining biblical allusion with the formal structure and imagery of Ashanti kings (Kuma 1981). It is a bestseller. A recent study of popular literature in Africa concluded that the popular religion of Ghana was virtually all religious. Then there is also the remarkable and essentially African phenomenon of the East African revival, which after well over half a century stubbornly refuses to go away.

7. Many strands are woven into the Christianity of the non-Western world. Some Western theologians—and let us rejoice at it—are seeking serious encounter with the religious traditions of South and East Asia, and are showing deep veneration for some of their features. It is instructive to read the passionate reaction of Indian Christians of Dalit origin, the traditionally oppressed communities, for whom those same features are symbols of their oppression and rationalizations of it. It will hardly be possible for the West to enter serious dialogue with Eastern religions without the help of Indian Christians.

Perhaps the most striking single feature of Christianity today is the fact that the church now looks more like that great multitude whom none can number, drawn from all tribes and kindreds, people and tongues, than ever before in its history. Its diversity and history leads to a great variety of starting points for its theology and reflects varied bodies of experience. The study of Christian history and theology will increasingly need to operate from the position where most Christians are, and that will increasingly be the lands and islands of Africa, Asia, Latin America, and the Pacific. Shared reading of the Scriptures and shared theological reflection will be to the benefit of all, but the oxygen-starved Christianity of the West will have most to gain.

Bibliography

Barrett, David. 1982. *World Christian Encyclopedia: A Comparative Study of Church and Religions in the Modern World, A.D. 1900–2000.* Nairobi.

Bede. *Ecclesiastical History.*

Bediako, K. 1992. *Theology and Identity: The Impact of Culture upon Christian Thought in the Second Century and in Modern Africa.* Oxford.

Christianity in India. Proceedings of a Public Meeting Held at Exeter Hall, January 5th, to Consider the Future Relations of the British Government to Religion in India. 1858. London.

da Silva Rego, A. 1959. *Portuguese Colonization in the Sixteenth Century: A Study of the Royal Ordinance (Regimentos).* Johannesburg.

de Montclos, X. 1965. *Lavigerie, le Saint-Siège de l'avènement de Pie IX à l'avènement de Lèon XIII.* Paris.

de Silva, K. M. 1965. *Social Policy and Missionary Organizations in Ceylon, 1840–1855.* London.

Duff, Alexander. 1866. *Foreign Missions: Being the Substance of an Address Delivered before the General Assembly of the Free Church of Scotland on Friday Evening, June 1, 1866.* Edinburgh.

Elliott, J. H. 1970. *The Old World and the New, 1492–1650.* Cambridge.

Kuma, Afua. 1981. *Jesus of the Deep Forest.* Accral.

Latourette, K. S. 1937–45 *A History of the Expansion of Christianity.* 7 vols. London.

Mitchell, William. 1991. "The Appropriation of the Quechua Language by the Church and the Christianization of Peru in the Sixteenth and Early Seventeenth Centuries." Ph.D. diss., University of Edinburgh.

Myklebust, O. G. 1955. *The Study of Missions in Theological Education: An Historial Enquiry into the Place of World Evangelisation in Western Protestant Ministerial Training with Particular Reference to Alexander Duff's Chair of Evangelistic Theology.* Oslo.

Okorocha, C. C. 1987. *The Meaning of Religious Conversion in Africa: The Case of the Igbo of Nigeria.* Aldershot.

Parry, J. P. 1986. *Democracy and Religion: Gladstone and the Liberal Party, 1867–1875*. Cambridge.

Ross, A. C. 1972. "Scottish Missionary Concern, 1874–1914: A Golden Era?" *Scottish Historical Review* 51: 151–52.

Sanneh, Lamin. 1990. *Translating the Message: The Missionary Impact on Culture*. New York.

Walls, A. F. 1990. "The Translation Principle in Christian History," in P. C. Stine, ed., *Bible Translation and the Spread of the Church*. Leiden. Reprinted in *The Missionary Movement in Christian History*. Maryknoll, N.Y. 1996: 26–42.

3

From Christendom to World Christianity

*Missions and the Demographic Transformation
of the Church*

The history of Western Christian missions is a single story, at least from the early sixteenth century. The Reformation complicates the story of missions, but it does not determine it. The roots of the work of the most adamantly Protestant missionaries lie in the work of Francis Xavier and Matteo Ricci and Pedro de Gante. In the non-Western world the attribute that first identifies Western missionaries is not that they are Catholic or Protestant, but that they are Western. The viewpoint even in the Eastern churches is well expressed by the remark of the Russian theologian Khomiakov that the pope was the first Protestant.

At the beginning of this story Christianity appeared to be a Western religion. Appearances were deceptive; there was nearly a millennium and a half of active and expansive Christianity in Asia before the first Western missionary arrived there. Equally, there were Christian communities in Africa that could claim a continuous history from subapostolic or early patristic times. But by around 1500, the time when a long-isolated Europe at last found itself in contact with the non-Western world, circumstances dictated that Christianity became more European than it had ever been before, and did so just at the point when Europe became more Christian than it had ever been before. Events so welded Christianity and the West together, and the domestication of Christianity in the West was so complete, the process of acculturation there so successful, that the faith seemed inseparable from the categories of European life and thought. Nor did that perception change quickly. By the end of our story, however, it was the Western world that was giving up on Christianity, with the proportion of Europeans and North

Lecture One in the Students' Mission Lecture Series for 2001, Princeton Theological Seminary.

Americans in the Christian body declining year by year, and the cultural contexts and worldviews of Africa and Asia and the rest of the non-Western world that were beginning to remake Christian living and thinking.

This demographic transformation of the church, and especially its rapid acceleration in the twentieth century, can be illustrated by a visit to two locations that provide rich materials for viewing the missionary situation a century ago, as it looked to some of the wisest and best-informed people in the Protestant world. The two locations are Princeton and Edinburgh.

The reason for choosing Princeton is the delivery of the first series of the Students' Lectures on Missions at Princeton Theological Seminary in 1893. The lecturer was the Rev. Dr. James S. Dennis, then of the American Presbyterian Mission in Beirut, and the series was entitled "Foreign Missions after a Century." The lectures were published the same year under the same title.[1] The copy I have been using carries the bookplate of B. B. Warfield.

This fairly modest volume—368 pages with generous margins—was the acorn of a mighty oak. The Princeton lecture series was expanded into three large volumes entitled *Christian Missions and Social Progress*.[2] This book, which appeared between 1897 and 1906, is one of the landmark undertakings in the study of missions. It was soon followed by a fourth volume that formed a statistical appendix—the fullest body of statistical data on missions that had hitherto been collected.[3]

Dennis delivered his lectures at the very height of the missionary movement, in the period when the number of missionaries from the Western to the non-Western world was reaching its peak. But he believed that there was work for many more. The newly instituted lecture series, the Students' Lectures on Missions was set up to appeal to students, because students were to be the primary source of the missionary multitude, the source not only of recruits but also of drive and enthusiasm. "The establishment of lectureships on missions in our prominent theological seminaries," says Dennis, "is timely and in touch with the leadings of the Spirit of God in our day." "The marvelous development of missions" was, in fact, "manifestly one of the foremost movements of Providence in the religious history of our century."[4]

The underlying assumption in Dennis's title is that in 1893 the missionary movement was about a hundred years old—old enough, that is, to have acquired wisdom and experience, young enough still to have vast

---

[1] James S. Dennis, *Foreign Missions after a Century*, Students' Lectures on Missions, Princeton Theological Seminary, 1893 (New York: Revell, 1893).

[2] James S. Dennis, *Christian Missions and Social Progress: A Sociological Study of Foreign Missions*, 3 vols. (New York: Revell, 1897–1906).

[3] James S. Dennis, *Centennial Survey of Foreign Missions: A Statistical Supplement to "Christian Missions and Social Progress," Being a Conspectus of the Achievements and Results of Evangelical Missions in All Lands at the Close of the Nineteenth Century* (New York: Revell, 1902).

[4] Dennis, *Foreign Missions*, 3f. (Hereafter, numbers in parentheses are page references to Dennis's *Foreign Missions*.)

resources of energy and stamina. It had emerged out of apathy and hostility, survived the era of infant mortality, and overcome the perils of infancy and adolescence; it now seemed unstoppable. Everything was in its favor: the march of technology that ensured rapid communications, the organisation of the world that placed power in the safe and predictable hands of the civilised nations. "When," he asks, "in the history of the Church has it been so easy to send our missionaries to the ends of the earth and extend to them adequate protection and support and sympathy?" (p. 28). Modern methods of travel, postal services, international comity, financial exchange, telegraphic communications—all are in favor of mission work. "International comity" in this context implies, of course, Western hegemony over the rest of the world; a little later, Dennis will refer to the "strong, firm, and just rule" of the British raj exercising its "benign sway" over the "vast, restless, and turbulent races" of India (p. 98). There is not a glimmer of expectation that these conditions will ever change.

Dennis's analysis of the world situation both in terms of church growth and the beneficent social results of that growth is almost unfailingly upbeat. The analysis begins with Japan, where political, social, commercial, educational, literary, and religious change had occurred since Commodore Perry opened the country to foreign influence "on a scale unprecedented in the history of any other nation" (p. 66). Japan—already influencing China in helpful directions—was the key to the Orient. If the church of Christ would seize the present opportunity, Japan would be the "grandest trophy of modern missions" (p. 71). In China, the present church growth rate extended for the next thirty-five years would produce twenty-six million Protestant communicants. China is destined to be a land of Pentecosts, and needs only the religion of Christ to become one of the dominant powers of the earth (p. 85). For India, Dennis produces dramatic statistics from the conversions in the mass movements going on at the time. He acknowledges how long, even at a rapid rate of conversion, the evangelisation of such a vast population would take; nonetheless, he sees in the developments of the past century the possibility that the empire of India will soon be in the hands of Christian converts (p. 105). By contrast, Korea, a land where there were currently only 177 Protestant church members, gets only a brief mention (pp. 72–76). And on Africa, "a whole continent of forgotten humanity," he is less buoyant. His summary view is that mission history there has less of discouragement than would naturally be expected (pp. 115–17).

Dennis's own missionary service was in the Middle East. He is dismissive of the ancient Christian churches of the East (Coptic, Syrian, and Armenian), and derides the Anglican mission that was trying to work with the old church in Mesopotamia. "God has chosen American Christians to be the saviors of Christianity in the East" (pp. 126f.), regenerating it so that it may aggressively commend Christ to Muslims. Similarly, South America is "as destitute of spiritual, saving Christianity as those who have never heard the Gospel message of salvation" (p. 139).

Africa, South America, and the Middle East are in fact the chief reminders of the long, hard labor still lying before the missionary movement. By contrast, he sees eastern and southern Asia as, from a Christian point of view, full of bright hope. It is easy to misunderstand Dennis here. His rosy portraits of the Christian future of India, China, and Japan are not prophecies, they are pointers to what *could* happen if the church—an essentially Western church—were to perform its duty. It is for the students of Princeton and their peers to rise to their responsibilities. There is nothing to impede them; they live in a politically stable world, marked almost everywhere by evidence of what Dennis calls social progress. The Asian powers, with Japan in the lead, are now in transformation, and that transformation will make them world powers. There is no sense of threat in this, or indeed in anything in the world that Dennis describes. There is much darkness in it, but it is residual darkness; there is no sight of the Mystery of Iniquity manufacturing destruction.

The interest in statistics that was later to find expression in the supplementary fourth volume of *Christian Missions and Social Progress* and later in the *Statistical Atlas of Christian Missions* is evident already in *Foreign Missions after a Century*. The very smell of a statistic can send Dennis into an orgy of calculation. He tells us that the Indian post office deals with 320 million letters a year. He knows how many miles of telegraph wire India has, and how many elementary schools there are in Japan. He calculates how long it would take the inhabitants of China to sign their names, allowing four signatures a minute for twelve hours a day, and how long the line would be while they were waiting their turn. He notes that twenty thousand people a day die in China, and that this rate of mortality would finish off New York in a month (p. 77).

But his most interesting statistics are those comparing growth of church membership in the United States with that in various parts of the non-Western world. As he puts it, "It is only when we compare results in the foreign field with corresponding results in the home field that many minds succeed in recognising the significance of the facts" (p. 47). And the facts were that the churches of Asia and Africa in 1892 were in general growing faster than those of the United States. The past year's statistics for the Presbyterian Church in the United States showed that only fourteen congregations in the whole country had exceeded the growth rate of the Presbyterian Church in Tripoli in Syria. Only eight presbyteries—and those the rich, big city ones of New York, Chicago, and Philadelphia—had admitted as many communicants as the presbytery of Shandong in China. And not a single American presbytery could come anywhere near the rate of growth of the presbytery of Laos. Laos was the "banner presbytery of the whole Presbyterian church" (p. 45). Dennis has noted the surprising development that the church overseas was increasing at a rate faster than that in the expansive, confident America from which its missionaries were coming.

And this fact moves our tale from Princeton to Edinburgh. In the building that currently houses the Scottish Parliament, and which has hitherto been the Assembly Hall of the Church of Scotland, a conference took place in 1910 to survey the issues that Dennis had presented in his Princeton lectures. Dennis, by this time recognised as the master statistician of the missionary movement, was called in to assist in one of its preparatory documents.

The World Missionary Conference, Edinburgh 1910, has passed into Christian legend. It was a landmark in the history of mission; the starting point of the modern theology of mission; the high point of the Western missionary movement and the point from which it declined; the launch-pad of the modern ecumenical movement; the point at which Christians first began to glimpse something of what a world church would be like.

The crucial events of Christian history have often taken place through obscure people. The missionary movement itself, in both its Catholic and Protestant phases, has usually been a peripheral activity of the church. It would be hard to guess from the average volume on the history of the church in the nineteenth century that events that were to transform the church altogether were going on in Africa and Asia, for these events are likely to occupy a few pages in the volume at most. So we need not be surprised to find that the origins of the World Missionary Conference lie among obscure people and in mundane circumstances. John R. Mott, the dynamic and unanimous choice for Conference chairman, though internationally known before the Conference began, was not directly involved in its origins. J. H. Oldham, the Conference secretary, became involved in an executive capacity almost accidentally. (Two more senior churchmen were originally appointed to organize the Conference. One fell ill, the other was appointed principal of the Scots College in Calcutta. Oldham, until then little known outside the Student Volunteer movement, was called in to fill a sudden gap.)[5]

The affairs of Malawi started the process that led to the World Missionary Conference. A secretary of the Livingstonia Mission Committee— the Rev. John Fairley Daly, his name not widely known then and still less since—had attended the Ecumenical Missionary Conference of 1900 in New York. In the course of a letter to the secretary of the American Presbyterian Mission Board, he asked when such another conference would be convened. Robert E. Speer responded warmly, and got it on to the agenda of the next meeting of the secretaries of the main American mission boards. That meeting agreed that it was desirable to hold another

---

[5]A "public" account of the Conference and its preparation is given in *World Missionary Conference 1910*, vol. 9, *The History and Records of the Conference Together with Addresses Delivered at the Evening Meetings* (Edinburgh: Oliphant, Anderson and Ferrier; New York: Revell, 1910). See also W. Richey Hogg, *Ecumenical Foundations: A History of the International Missionary Council and Its Nineteenth-Century Background* (New York: Harper, 1952), ch. 3; C. H. Hopkins, *John R. Mott, 1865–1955: A Biography* (Geneva: World Council of Churches; Grand Rapids: Eerdmans, 1979), ch. 7.

conference ten years after the New York meeting of 1900, and added that it would be appropriate for it to be organised in Britain.

There was nothing particularly new about the idea of a general missionary conference in itself. The idea goes back at least to the early years of the nineteenth century. In 1806, William Carey proposed an intercontinental meeting of missionaries. Perspectives were different in those days. It would never have occurred to Carey, who never returned to Britain in the course of his long Indian service, to hold a missionary conference in Edinburgh. He assumed that such a conference would take place where missionaries were actually working, and suggested the Cape of Good Hope as a suitably central location. His proposal was dismissed as the "pleasing dream" of an "enlarged mind."[6] The first missionary conference actually to take place is probably that which occurred in New York in 1854. The occasion was the visit of Alexander Duff, missionary in India of the Free Church of Scotland, to the United States. Duff was already celebrated not only as an eminent missionary but also as the spokesman for the systematic study of missions, a cause that he constantly brought to the attention of his church. In the next decade he was to persuade it to establish in New College, Edinburgh, the first chair of mission studies (evangelistic theology, as he called it) anywhere in the world, and he saw this as only the first step towards a Christian institute of languages and cultures such as existed elsewhere only in Rome.[7] In America, Duff had a triumphal progress, and the first international missionary conference was hurriedly erected around his visit.[8] The better-known Conference on Mission held in Liverpool in 1860 was a British initiative, and overwhelmingly British in composition. There was just one participant from Asia, the Rev. Behari Lal Singh, an Indian minister of the Free Church of Scotland. His interventions were substantial and lively, notably in his insistence that Hindu and Muslim scholarship posed intellectual challenges that Christians ignored at their peril.[9] A larger conference took place in London in 1878, and a really big one, the so-called Centenary Conference, in 1888.[10] Then there was the Ecumenical Missionary Conference, already re-

---

[6]See Hogg, *Ecumenical Foundations,* 17; see also Ruth Rouse, "William Carey's 'Pleasing Dream'," *International Review of Missions* 38 (1949): 186–92.

[7]The fullest account is by O. G. Myklebust, *The Study of Missions in Theological Education: An Historical Enquiry into the Place of World Evangelisation in Western Ministerial Education with Particular Reference to Alexander Duff's Chair of Evangelistic Theology* (Oslo: Egede Institute, 1955).

[8]See Hogg, *Ecumenical Foundations,* 37f.

[9]*Conference on Missions Held in 1860,* edited by the Secretaries to the Conference (London: Nisbet, 1860). Singh's interventions on missionary education (p. 129) and on native agency (p. 216) are particularly noteworthy.

[10]It was held at Exeter Hall, "the ark and sanctuary of the Evangelical party." Before 1910 it had been "surrendered to a firm of caterers." See G. W. E. Russell, *A Pocketful of Sixpences* (London: Nelson, n.d.), ch. 20.

ferred to, in New York in 1900. "This Conference is called ecumenical," said one of its organizers,

> not because all portions of the Christian Church are to be represented in it by delegates, but because the plan of campaign it proposes covers the whole area of the inhabited globe. Blot out of the map the desert and waste places, the Arctic and the Antarctic zones, and what you have left is the ecumenical world.[11]

Add to these the conferences of the Student Volunteer Missionary Union, with their batteries of eminent speakers and published proceedings, and it is clear that Edinburgh 1910 was far from being the first major international missionary conference. It was not even the biggest; over three hundred more delegates attended the London Centenary Conference of 1888 than came to Edinburgh twenty-two years later. Yet that meeting and most of the others are now largely forgotten.[12] Something about Edinburgh 1910 makes it the best-remembered conference of all, better even than its successor meetings in Jerusalem and Tambaram. So it is worth considering some of the ways in which it differed from its predecessors.

First, it differed in composition. It attempted to maintain a balance between the missions so as to produce a microcosm of the actual mission situation overseas. The intended outcome was that the Conference would also reflect the proportionate involvement of the various parts of the missionised world in the work of evangelising the nonmissionised or partly missionised. (In this respect it differed greatly from the Centenary Conference, whose large body of delegates was dominated by the host country, Britain.) At Edinburgh there were five hundred delegates from Britain, five hundred from North America, 170 from continental Europe, and twenty-six from "the colonies" (that is, the white populations of Australia, New Zealand, and South Africa). This may have slightly underrepresented North America, but it gave a generally fair picture of the relative strengths of missionary forces.

Representation, curiously as it may seem today, was proportional to financial outlay. Missions got one delegate for the first £2,000 a year they spent on overseas work, and another for each £4,000 thereafter. In the long run this correlated fairly well with their deployment of personnel and relative scale of operations.

Even more importantly, the conference sought to be comprehensive in confession, tradition, and ethos. There was at this date no possibility, of

---

[11] See *Ecumenical Missionary Conference New York 1910* (London: RTS; New York: American Tract Society, 1910), 10.

[12] See, however, the interesting series of articles by Thomas A. Askew, notably, "The New York 1900 Ecumenical Conference: A Centennial Reflection," *International Bulletin of Missionary Research* 24 (2000): 146–54.

course, of including Catholic or Orthodox Christians, and for Christians of those traditions, 1910 is not a particularly significant date. But the aim at Edinburgh of bringing together the whole Christian world other than the Roman Catholic and the Greek was remarkable in its day, and the degree of its achievement is equally remarkable. It is safe to say that in 1910 no theological concern other than missions could have brought together such a comprehensive gathering. Even the Centenary Conference had been unable to secure the participation of the oldest British missionary societies, the Society for Promoting Christian Knowledge (SPCK) and the Society for the Propagation of the Gospel (SPG) or of other Anglican societies that drew on a largely High Church constituency.[13] The gap was significant; not only did the SPCK and the SPG contain important doctrinal and ecclesiological strands in Anglicanism not otherwise represented at the conference, but also they represented something like the official expression of the English national church. Ecclesiastical and doctrinal divisions in England were still sharp in 1910, and potentially explosive in the political field; that Anglicans of every hue were represented at Edinburgh was extraordinary. There was an SPG contingent of thirty-five, and among the "special delegates" who accepted invitations to participate were the archbishops of Canterbury and York, and seven other English bishops—Charles Gore as well as Handley Moule—and the primus of the Scottish Episcopal Church.[14] It had taken a good deal of Scottish and American diplomacy to secure this participation. One factor that undoubtedly helped was the knowledge that High Church Anglicans were now joining the Student Missionary Volunteers.[15]

It is significant that it was High Church Anglicans, not principled Evangelicals, who found it difficult to join in concert with those of other views. In 1910 it was still possible to recognise a common purpose in the task of mission. The cleavages over the definition of mission lay in the future, even though the methods and priorities of contemporary missionaries differed greatly. Some of the ardent young people who went out as missionary volunteers were motivated by the thought of millions entering a Christless eternity; others wanted to bring relief, healing, or reconstruction in Christ's name to deprived societies overseas. These different styles had not yet been polarised into different and exclusive theologies of mission.

Nevertheless, there was a price to pay to achieve consensus. A self-denying ordinance was accepted by delegates not to raise "any matter of faith or policy on which those participating in the Conference differ

---

[13]J. Johnston, ed., *Report of the Centenary Conference on the Protestant Missions of the World* (London: Nisbet, 1889), x–xi.

[14]Delegates are listed in *History and Records*, 35ff.

[15]See Eleanor M. Jackson, *Red Tape and the Gospel: A Study of the Significance of the Ecumenical Missionary Struggle of William Patton, 1886–1943* (Birmingham, Ala.: Phlogiston Publishing and Selly Oak Colleges, 1980), 46.

among themselves."[16] The most important result of this was that in the Conference programme one major area of the world, Latin America, was quietly ignored. Edinburgh's silence was deliberate. The whole construction of contemporary missionary thought was territorial; there were missionised lands and there were nonmissionised lands. Some members of the Conference would have judged that Latin America belonged to the nonmissionised lands and others would not. As a result, Edinburgh 1910 was a World Missionary Conference without Latin America.[17]

Confessional comprehensiveness is one thing; ethnic, cultural, and geographical comprehensiveness another. We have seen that the Liverpool Conference on Missions in 1860 had a single representative from the southern continents. The report of the Centenary Conference of 1888 has a section headed "Races Represented,"[18] but this is not what it may seem. It observes that the Conference brought out "the great extent to which the work of the evangelisation of the world is taken up by, or thrown upon, the Saxon race"—in other words, the British and the Americans, with the assistance of "our noble brethren, the Saxons of Germany" and "our honoured cousins of Scandinavian blood." The only other race mentioned is "the Latin race," in manifest decline since its subjection to Rome, despite the noble efforts of a few small missionary societies originating in Belgium, France, and Switzerland. The Centenary Conference comes as nearly as possible to thanking God that the British are not as other people are.

Far more participants at Edinburgh came from the new churches arising from the missionary movement than had attended any earlier conference. There were delegates from Burma, Ceylon, China, India, Japan, and Korea. Among them were people of status not simply in their churches but in their nations. Two were among fourteen recipients of honorary degrees awarded by the University of Edinburgh on the occasion of the Conference: the Rev. K. C. Chatterji, and President Tosuku Harada of Doshisha University. The Conference organisers had hoped for more Asian participation, and were partly frustrated by the mission boards' priorities. But when one reads the conference reports now, it is striking how

---

[16]Standing Orders of the Conference, Number XI *History and Records,* 74.

[17]There were, however, delegates present from the South American Missionary Society, and "Indians and Orientals in South America," and "Indians in Central America" are included in the survey of the non-Christian world in *World Missionary Conference: Report of Commission I. Carrying the Gospel to All the Non-Christian World with Supplement* (1910), 246–50, 252f. Groups like these, which were in no sense of the word evangelised, were not controversial. It is interesting to find these pages including the words "South America may still well be called the Neglected Continent" (ibid., 249; a phrase quoted also by Dennis, *Foreign Missions,* 133).

[18]Johnston, *Report of the Centenary Conference,* xv–xvi.

little is made of the significance of that small but eminent and articulate group of Asian Christians.

There is no sign of recognition that they heralded the greatest demographic change within the Christian faith since the conversion of the Western barbarians, which would render the patronising language of the Centenary Conference about "the races" simply laughable. The presence of the Asian contingent is mentioned in the official report as demonstrating the universal nature of Christian faith, and as reflecting the way in which the assembly's purpose transcended race and colour. But there is no sign that these delegates were expected to have a *distinctive* or original contribution to the conference. The key lies in the repeated use of the phrase "the infant churches." (In at least one paper, infancy was modified to adolescence.[19]) Of course, no one suggested that these distinguished Asians were in any sense infants; but their churches were still thought of as infant, not likely to take steps (safely, at any rate) independently of their parents. The churches of the south were, in fact, still seen mainly as extensions of the missionary movement, incorporations into a church still overwhelmingly Western in location and tradition. Edinburgh 1910 was itself to provide a basis for a new vision of the Christian reality.

There was not a single African present—and no one seems to have thought that strange. When the organizers specifically mention that they would have welcomed the involvement of more Asians, they do not mention the absence of any African participation at all. The immense Christian significance of Africa was still not visible. In no way has the demographic shift within the Christian church been so dramatic as in the emergence of Africa as a continent of the Christian heartlands. The most important single transforming feature of twentieth-century Christian history was unpredictable even to the best-informed at the end of that century's first decade.

The purpose of the Conference was consultative rather than educative; it was not simply to be a shop window for missions, as the Centenary and Ecumenical Conferences had been. Nevertheless, much effort was devoted to bringing mission issues into the consciousness of the Western churches and into the life of the church as a whole. It was not a conference of *churches;* that would have been impossible in 1910. It was a meeting of mission agencies, some related directly, with more or less formality, to the structures of various churches, others purely voluntary societies. But as one tries to relive the World Missionary Conference, one can see that during its course the missions became almost a surrogate church. Delegates were experiencing a sense of common purpose that they recognized as belonging to the nature of the church, or as a foretaste of what the church could be.

---

[19]The China-based American bishop L. H. Roots, "The Problem of Co-operation between Foreign and Native Workers," in *History and Records,* 289.

John R. Mott described the Conference as "the first attempt at a systematic and careful study of the missionary problems of the world." The important word here is "systematic." There had never before been such a systematic conference as Edinburgh, at least not in the English-speaking world. The "steady stream of facts and truths poured in upon heart and brain"[20] were meant to issue in clear-headed appraisal and appropriate action. Edinburgh sought to survey and assimilate the accumulated experience of the interaction of the Christian and non-Christian worlds with a view to bringing the encounter to a new stage.

This was reflected in the Conference organization itself. There were no announcements; Oldham saw that all necessary information was delivered on paper to each delegate at breakfast time each day. Contemporaries were also struck by the brevity of the speeches. In an age when pulpit oratory counted for much, no one, other than those presenting commission reports, was allowed more than seven minutes. It was observed that this cut out conventional pieties and inhibited any tendency of speakers to talk about themselves. It all heightened the sense of urgency, of business, of active engagement. The very shape of the General Assembly Hall furthered the sense of a participatory conference, not a series of orations to an audience.[21]

Still more important was the method by which the Conference worked. Well in advance of the Conference eight major topics were identified as arising from the experience of the world missionary movement. Each of these topics was remitted to an international commission with a mandate to consult on a worldwide basis and bring a printed report for discussion to the Conference. These printed reports of the Commissions (the discussions, in small type, form supplements) fill eight of the nine Edinburgh Conference volumes.

For no previous conference had such a quantity of preliminary work been done; perhaps nothing like so much was ever done again. Some commissions did more than others by way of consultation. Commission I, "Carrying the Gospel to All the Non-Christian World" endorsed the production of a supplementary volume of information much larger than its report. Commission IV, "The Missionary Message in Relation to Non-

---

[20]John R. Mott, Closing Address, History and Records, p. 349.

[21]New College, on the Mound in the centre of Edinburgh, was established following the Scottish Disruption as the Theological Faculty of the Free Church of Scotland, and the Church's Assembly Hall was part of the same complex of buildings. The union of the Free Church with the United Presbyterian Church in 1900 made a larger hall desirable, and the Conference was using the reconstructed building. Its arrangement permitted a speaker from the body of the hall to address the whole gathering from his or her place. The college buildings formed an adjunct to the Conference. The hall is now the General Assembly Hall of the Church of Scotland and New College, the location of the Faculty of Divinity of Edinburgh University; at the time of writing, it is serving as the debating chamber of the Scottish Parliament.

Christian Religions," produced a particularly careful analysis and exposition based on detailed questionnaires sent around the world.

This procedure differed from that later adopted at Tambaram, for instance, where one person, Hendrik Kraemer, wrote a major contribution, a substantial book, in fact, on the theme that had occupied Commission IV at Edinburgh, for others to react to. It differed still more from that of some more recent conferences where preparation seems to be mainly directed to group dynamics. The concern at Edinburgh was with the whole missionary operation of the church and the preparation of suitable instruments for it. Thus, the supplement to the report of Commission I (held by the Commission to be essential for the study of the report itself) was a *Statistical Atlas of Christian Missions* (the statistics compiled, naturally, by Dennis, the atlas by Harlan P. Beach of Yale). The work caused some pre-Conference tension—its perspectives were too manifestly those of American Protestantism for some Anglican tastes, and Oldham had to make a hurried transatlantic journey to sort out the trouble—but the *Statistical Atlas* is a landmark in the process of understanding how the Christian world was changing. It is the true ancestor of Barrett's *World Christian Encyclopedia*.

The full title of Edinburgh 1910 was "World Missionary Conference to Consider Missionary Problems in Relation to the non-Christian World." The effect of concentration on the non-Christian world was a new understanding of the Christian world.

The place of the World Missionary Conference in the history of the ecumenical movement is so well documented as to require no further commentary. The lineal connexion between Edinburgh 1910 and Amsterdam 1948 is clear.[22] The World Council of Churches is a direct descendant of the World Missionary Conference and the International Missionary Council. All aspects of its work—in mission and evangelism, in faith and order, and in service to the world—can claim to have their background in the Edinburgh meeting. Western Christianity understood itself only when the missionary movement brought it into encounter, first with non-Christian faiths and cultures and then with the new Christianities forged by the gospel within those cultures.

But the World Council of Churches is not the same thing as the ecumenical movement, and the Council is only one of the children of the World Missionary Conference. The determinant factors in twentieth-century Christianity include worldwide presence, consequent cultural diversity, and the growth of conciliarity. And conciliarity is not restricted to the World Council of Churches. Since Vatican II it has been part of Catholic structures through the synod of bishops and the regional bishops' confer-

---

[22]See, for example, Ruth Rouse and S. C. Neill, eds., *A History of the Ecumenical Movement, 1517–1948*, vol. 1 (London: SPCK, 1967); H. E. Fey, ed., *A History of the Ecumenical Movement, 1948–1968*, vol. 2 (London: SPCK, 1970).

ences, and it has become part of Evangelical Christianity, even in those sections of it that have stood aloof from the World Council of Churches. The Lausanne movement for world evangelisation is essentially conciliar in structure, and the crucial interventions of African, Asian, and Latin American participants at its Lausanne and Manila conferences show just how effective its conciliarism can be. To describe the Edinburgh conference, therefore, as a landmark in the ecumenical movement is to indicate its connexion with one of the outstanding features of twentieth-century Christianity as a whole. It was at Edinburgh that Western Christianity, at least Protestant Western Christianity, first caught a clear sight of a church that would be bigger than itself.

Edinburgh developed instruments for mission, both new structures and new studies. At earlier conferences the desirability had been asserted of further meetings, but not until Edinburgh 1910 was effective machinery for international cooperation put in place. In the late sessions of the Conference, a Continuation Committee was established with a minimum of fuss, with Mott as chairman and Oldham as full-time secretary. The First World War rudely shocked and might have wrecked it, but it survived to be the seed of the International Missionary Council.[23] These structural developments are so well known that they have overshadowed the impulse Edinburgh gave to the development of instruments of another kind. It marked, if not the birth, a genuine renaissance of mission studies. We have already noted the significance of the *Statistical Atlas of Christian Missions*, a pioneering Christian survey of the world Christian situation that has had many successors. It was only one of a range of new instruments forged from scholarly application that can trace their origin to Edinburgh. Another was the first general international ecumenical missiological journal, the *International Review of Missions*. It began in 1912, and included from the beginning a quarterly bibliography of mission studies, originally edited by Oldham. Another major journal appeared in 1912, the fruit of the labours of another Student Volunteer movement activist, Samuel Marinus Zwemer, with eminent international assistance. It was called *The Moslem World*. The first issue acknowledges its origins in the interest in the Islamic world manifested at the World Missionary Conference. Its opening editorial calls it "a quarterly review of current events, literature, and thought among Mohammedans, and the progress of Christian missions in Moslem lands." It was intended to represent "no faction or fraction of the Church" but "all who hold the unity faith in the bond of peace and righteousness of life"—authentic Edinburgh sentiments. The importance and scholarly status ever since of *The Muslim World* (as its title now is) needs no affirmation.

---

[23]*History and Records*, 19.

There are aspects of ambiguity and uncertainty about some aspects of the Edinburgh legacy, and these deserve more investigation than they have so far received. For instance, how far did Edinburgh begin the movement that has made English the language of ecumenical theology? In the Conference report it is noted with pleasure that, with only two exceptions, every contribution to the debates was made in English; and of the exceptions, one speaker, a Japanese, afterwards made a speech in excellent English. But that is only part of the story. The continental battery of delegates, 170 strong, while by no means contemptible in numbers, must have been overwhelmed by a thousand Anglo-Americans. And they could have claimed that of the serious theological effort devoted to the cause of mission up to that time, more had been conducted in German or Dutch than in English. It is well known that Gustav Warneck, the German doyen of all missiologists, had serious reservations about the way the missionary movement was now going, and that his attempt to have them expressed at Edinburgh was only partly successful.[24] It may be argued that in 1910, English set out on its career as the successor to Latin as the international language of theology. The full implications of this for the world church remain to be faced.

A still more obscure area is how far Edinburgh marks the bifurcation of the missionary movement, with an American-led section of Western Evangelicalism taking an independent path. We have seen that at Edinburgh the task of mission brought together people of diverse theological and ecclesiological priorities. Does the divide that has emerged between "ecumenical" and "evangelical" have its origins in the outcome of the Conference? It is certainly safe to say that if the World Missionary Conference had not met in 1910, it would have been impossible to convene it on the same basis in 1930, and the history of the International Missionary Council would have been quite different. It is equally true that both "ecumenical" and "evangelical" today have their roots in Edinburgh 1910. If each will go back to the pit whence both were dug, each may understand both themselves and the other better.

The Conference ended on a note of high optimism, justifiably in view of the purposeful way the deliberations had gone. It set up machinery for international cooperation in the task of bringing the whole gospel to the whole world, from the fully missionised lands (that is, Europe and North America with Australia and New Zealand) to the lands not yet fully missionised (for practical purposes, the rest of the world). With sober assessment of the resources available and careful planning to maximize those resources, the evangelisation of the world seemed possible. "The end of the Conference is the beginning of the conquest," were Mott's stirring words at the close of the Conference. "The end of the planning is the beginning of the doing."[25]

---

[24]Hogg, *Ecumenical Foundations*, chs. 4 and 5.
[25]John R. Mott, "Closing Address," in *History and Records*, 347.

The most prescient of the delegates could not have guessed what was to follow. One by one all their assumptions about how the evangelisation of the world could be effected crumbled away. They had identified cooperation between the missionary-sending nations, so cheeringly realisable in the conference itself, as a key to world evangelisation. Within a few years of the conference, the nations that were to cooperate were at war with one another, and fellow missionaries in the field were being interned as enemy aliens. Deep were the wounds, and bitter the feelings that followed. Another assumption had been that the flood of young missionaries, people like the student volunteers Dennis had sought from Princeton, would continue to flood to the mission field. But much of that young life drained away into the trenches of France and Flanders, and in the postwar world that sat licking its wounds, people spoke less confidently of the evangelisation of the world, on whatever schedule. The missionary movement in 1910 was riding the tide of Atlantic prosperity; the depression that followed the First World War cut deeply into its economic base, and after the 1920s things were never the same again. The Second World War followed, bringing with it the first use of weapons that hinted at the possibility of the destruction of the planet. Many, perhaps most, of the delegates at Edinburgh were looking to the Western empires to provide the stable conditions under which Western missions could do their work effectively (remember Dennis on the firm, just rule of Britain over turbulent India). In the years that followed the Second World War, those empires melted away. But the most fundamental assumption of all, that there were fully missionised lands that would continue to form the base for the evangelisation of those not yet missionised, proved fallible. Christendom itself crumbled. The first sign was the dissolution of Holy Russia during the First World War; within a decade of the end of the Second, a great recession from Christianity was manifest throughout the liberal democracies of western Europe. It has proved one of the largest and fastest movements away from the Christian faith ever to have taken place—much faster, for instance, than that in the Middle East which followed the rise of Islam.

The whole basis on which the thinking and planning of Edinburgh had been predicated had been swept away; so had the world of J. S. Dennis and of the Princeton students who heard the first series under this lectureship. Dennis, looking out in 1893 over boundless social progress, never glimpsed the Mystery of Iniquity lurking in the background. We who lived in or through the twentieth century saw it again and again—an abomination of desolation, standing where it ought not. Perhaps no century in all human history has been more violent. Even now, when we survey the world continent by continent, as Dennis did in 1893, we sense the presence of the Angel of Death.

But if the world is different, the church is still more different. In the period from the Edinbugh Conference until now (that is, a period roughly equivalent to the period from the beginning of Christ's ministry to the end of the apostolic age), the period that has seen this great recession from the Christian faith in the West, there has been an equally massive accession to that faith in the non-Western world. When Dennis spoke at Princeton, well over 80 percent of those who professed Christianity lived in Europe or North America. Now, approaching 60 percent live in the southern continents of Africa, Asia, Latin America, and the Pacific, and that proportion grows annually. Christianity began the twentieth century as a Western religion, and indeed, *the* Western religion; it ended the century as a non-Western religion, on track to become progressively more so.

Many of the trends that Dennis identified in his world survey have since either receded or washed past us. But one of the most significant points in his analysis is his observation that even at a time when the great churches of America were still growing fast, the churches of the mission field were growing faster. It was not clear at that time which contemporary developments would do most to shape the future church. Like most of his contemporaries, and like the delegates at Edinburgh, Dennis looked with most hope at Japan, at China, at India. In each of these cases the twentieth century brought deep disappointments; and the trauma of the midcentury events in China did more than anything else to change the direction of mission thinking. By contrast, Korea, which Dennis passes over so quickly, has become the missionary phenomenon of the century, with a place in world Christian witness that is all its own. Latin America, which Dennis called a forgotten continent and which Edinburgh avoided discussing, is home to a religious and theological ferment such as Europe has hardly known since the sixteenth century. And strangest of all, Africa, which had no representative at Edinburgh, and not much more than ten million professing Christians at the time, has now some three hundred million or more who profess the faith of Christ, one of the largest concentrations of Christians anywhere. A century ago there were hardly any Christians among the aboriginal peoples of northeast India, and Nepal was a land closed to Christianity even fifty years ago; now, a vast belt of actively Christian peoples extends from Nepal and northeast India into southwest China, Myanmar, and Thailand—a great, unnoticed Asian Christian constituency. Kenneth Scott Latourette described the nineteenth century as the "great century of missions," and devoted three of his seven volumes of the *History of the Expansion of Christianity* to it; but the most remarkable century in the history of the expansion of Christianity has been the twentieth.

As a result of missions, the centre of gravity of the church has shifted substantially during a single lifetime. Europe, so long the Christian heartland, the matrix of such formative Christian movements as the sixteenth-century Reformations, has seen quiet but insistent Christian erosion. There are now far more Muslims in England than there are Presbyterians in Scotland. It is not for me to make prophecies about North America, or indeed anywhere else; I will say only that many signs are visible in the United States now that marked Europe when its own rapid retreat from Christianity began. Yet, globally, Christianity is not in decline. Africa has quietly slipped into the place once occupied by Europe; and the third Christian millennium begins with the likelihood that the West will matter less and less in Christian affairs as the faith becomes more and more associated with, and more and more marked by, the thought and life of Africa and Latin America and Asia.

All this could not have happened without the missionary movement. Not that missionaries have been the sole agency. The twentieth-century evangelisation of Africa, for instance, has been carried out mainly by Africans. There have been times when the expansion of the church has taken place in the absence of the missions, perhaps because of that absence. The number of missionaries was drastically curtailed during the First World War, and that seemed grievous at the time; in Ghana and Malawi the withdrawal led to a notable expansion of the church as Africans took responsibility for it. Missionaries were expelled from Myanmar in 1961; since then, on some estimates, the Christian population has trebled. We have noted the trauma inflicted on missions around 1950 by the forced abandonment of a century of missionary investment in China. Estimates of the number of Christians in China today differ widely, not to say wildly; but all agree that there are many, many more than when the missionaries left. Few would have predicted this in 1910, still less in 1970.

Missions have not been the sole agency, then, in the demographic transformation of the Christian church; but they formed the detonator of the vast explosion that brought it about. This must make the missionary movement one of the most important developments in the entire history of Western Christianity. Yet it has been little studied by church historians, and is still little understood. It would be interesting, for instance, to discuss how far missions were a lay movement, developing in spite of church structures rather than because of them, and constantly subversive of church order and diversionary to concerns that seemed consumingly important at home. Equally, one could pursue the question of to what extent missions were a women's movement, sustained by women through times when male church leaders thought other issues more important, and taken over by women when the men got tired. One way and another, there is a case for approaching the history of the missionary movement in terms of the now-fashionable genre of subaltern history.

The demographic transformation of the church brought about by the missionary movement faces us with twin challenges: a post-Christian West and a post-Western Christianity. As J. S. Dennis saw the world in 1893, Korean Christianity barely existed, Latin America was a neglected continent where little in the way of vital religion was noticeable, and even an inveterate optimist like myself could describe the results of mission work in Africa only as less discouraging than might have been expected.

By contrast today, we can look back on a century of recession in the West from the Christian faith, washing over the Christian base in western Europe that in 1893 was still producing the majority of the world's missionaries. Meanwhile, a parallel accession to the faith in other parts of the world has left Christianity a predominantly non-Western religion, with Africa and Latin America as outstanding Christian heartlands, and with important Christian communities in Asia, among which Korea is particularly noteworthy. In other words, there has been a century-long process of cross-cultural diffusion of Christianity with the Western missionary as a connecting terminal (and the most curious feature of the process period in which the Christian faith crossed cultural frontiers into African and Asian communities is that it lost its hold on much of the West).

This is far from being an unprecedented event; such movements have been a recurrent feature of Christian history. The process by which Christianity spreads is not progressive, but serial. Long ago, Kenneth Scott Latourette pointed out that the history of Christianity has not been one of steady progress, let alone of unresisted triumph. There have been periods of advance, but also periods of recession, or falling back, of withering and decay. Islam can make a much better claim than Christianity for progressive expansion, for steady numerical increase and geographical growth. Generally speaking—there are some exceptions—lands that became Islamic have so far remained Islamic. The Arab lands seem now so inalienably Muslim that it is hard to remember that Yemen was once Christian territory. Contrast Jerusalem, home of the first Christian church, or Syria and Egypt and Asia Minor and North Africa, which once provided the brightest examples of Christian devotion, scholarship, and witness. Or take my own country, where John Knox and John Wesley once preached, now full of unwanted churches turned into furniture stores, garages, or nightclubs.

In each of these latter cases, a place that had been a Christian heartland, a shining center of Christian devotion and activity, ceased to have this function; the light burned down or burned out, and the candlestick was taken out of its place. But in none of these cases did this decline mean the disappearance of the Christian faith or the end of Christian witness—rather the reverse. By the time the Jerusalem church was scattered to the winds, the gospel had taken hold in the Hellenistic world of the eastern Mediterranean. When the literate civilization of the Roman Empire broke up, the gospel was making its way among the barbarians north and east of that empire. And as the modern recession began to accelerate in Europe and to wash into North America, the churches of Africa, Asia, and Latin America have begun to come into their own. The Christian story is serial; its center moves from place to place. No one church or place or culture owns it. At different times, different peoples and places have become its heartlands, its chief representatives. Then the baton passes on to others. Christian progress is never final, never a set of gains to be plotted on the map. The rhetoric of some of our hymns, and many of our sermons, about the triumphant host streaming out to conquer the world is more Islamic than Christian. Christian history reveals the faith often withering in its heartlands, in its centers of seeming strength and importance, to establish itself on or beyond its margins. It has vulnerability, a certain fragility, at its heart—the vulnerability of the cross, the fragility of the earthen vessel.

In other words, cross-cultural diffusion has been necessary to Christianity. It has been its life's blood, and without it the faith could not have survived. It does not, like so many of the religions of India, belong to a particular soil; nor does it, like Islam, produce a distinctive and immediately recognisable form of civilization. The missionary movement from the West, therefore, seen in the context of the total history of Christianity, is one of a series of major cross-cultural diffusions. The first recorded is in Acts 11, which tells how some Jewish believers in Jesus who had been driven out of Jerusalem decided that their Messiah had something to say to the Greek pagans by whom they were surrounded in Antioch.

The process of cross-cultural diffusion thus initiated means that since the first century, the church has in principle been not only multiracial, but also multicultural. The earliest believers were devout, observant Jews, maintaining circumcision, delighting in the Torah, devoted to the worship of the temple, and understanding Jesus and his work in terms of Jewish history, Jewish destiny, and the salvation of the nation of Israel. The new Antiochene believers were not circumcised, did not keep the Torah, probably could not (for the most part) keep the Sabbath, ate pork, maintained social relations with their pagan neighbors, were excluded from the temple, and—so far as we know—did not dwell on the political destiny of Israel. In order that they should come to faith in Christ, Christ had been presented to them in a way wholly different from that in which he had been presented as Messiah among Jews; in order that they should maintain that faith, they had to develop a totally new style of life adapted to Hellenistic social and family conditions. But this had to take place within a church of old-style believers retaining the Torah-keeping way of devotion to the Messiah that had been characteristic of the Jerusalem church.

Issues of culture are at the heart of Christian faith, because Christianity is about conversion. Conversion means turning. Conversion to Christ is turning towards him. Before the time of Christ, Jews had designed ways of welcoming Gentiles who recognised the God of Israel and wanted to serve him in the community of Israel. Proselytes were circumcised, and baptised (thus symbolically washing away the dirt of the heathen world), and they entered the life of Israel by seeking to obey the Torah. It would have been very natural for that first, entirely Jewish, community of believers in Jesus to maintain this system. But the great council described in Acts 15, which considered how Gentiles who believed in Jesus should be introduced into the community, deliberately rejected the time-honored model of the proselyte. It was an astonishing decision. Hitherto, all believers in Jesus had been circumcised and kept the Torah, just like the Lord himself. It was the standard lifestyle for believers. But the early church decided that Gentile believers in Jesus—although ex-pagans without the lifelong training in doctrine and morality that Jews had—should not be circumcised, should not keep the Torah, and should be left to find a Christian lifestyle of their own within Hellenistic society under the guidance of the Holy Spirit. They were not to be proselytes, but converts.

This distinction between convert and proselyte is of fundamental importance. If the first Gentile believers had become proselytes, living exactly the style of life of those who brought them to Christ, they might have become very devout believers, but they would have had virtually no impact on their society; they would effectively have been taken out of that society. In fact, it was their task as converts to convert their society; convert it in the sense that they had to learn to keep turning their ways of thinking and doing things—which, of course, were Greek ways of thinking and doing things—towards Christ, opening them up to his influence. In this way a truly Greek, truly Hellenistic, type of Christianity was able to emerge. Not only so, but that Hellenistic Christianity was able to penetrate the Hellenistic intellectual and social heritage. Hellenistic thought, Hellenistic social and family life, and Hellenistic civic organization were challenged, purged, modified, and put to new uses—but from the inside, by people whose own inheritance they were. The fact that cross-cultural diffusion is so characteristic of Christian history leaves the Christian faith with tensions that may be creative or destructive. Cultural diversity is built into the church; so is the ecumenical sharing of its diverse cultural communities. The greatest problems of the church are therefore often ecumenical. The New Testament makes plain that even after the council of Jerusalem appeared to settle the matter, some of the Jerusalem believers in Jesus were still sure that a form of faith that did not include the precious traditional items of Torah and circumcision must be defective. It has been a recurrent problem. Those who have brought others to Christian faith have quite frequently insisted that the new Christians should exactly follow the way of life of their teachers, in effect should adopt their Torah and circumcision. Of all the heresies in Christian history, it is Judaizing that has been the most persistent.

One of the few things that are predictable about third-millennium Christianity is that it will be more culturally diverse than Christianity has ever been before, and thus have more capacity for blessing, and more capability for disaster, than any previous era. We need to reflect on the implications of Africa and Latin America and Asia becoming the home of representative Christianity, that is, mainstream, norm-setting Christianity.

The late Lesslie Newbigin spoke in 1984 of what he called "missionary encounter with our own culture"—that is, the post-Christian culture of the West. Among the priorities for that engagement, Newbigin identified the assistance of Christians from the non-Western world.

We need their witness to correct ours, as indeed they need ours to correct theirs. At this moment our need is greater, for they have been far more aware of the danger of syncretism, of an illegitimate alliance with false elements in their culture, than we have been. But . . . we imperatively need one another if we are to be faithful witnesses to Christ.[26]

Western Christians, Newbigin argued, need African and Asian and Hispanic Christians to help them make a Christian analysis of Western culture. Syncretism is a greater peril for Western than for African or Indian Christians, and less often recognizable for what it is.

The demographic transformation of the church brought about by the missionary movement opens the possibility of testing our Christian witness by that of others, of experiencing one another's gifts and sharing our combined resources. Equally, it opens the prospect of a score of local Christianities operating independently without interest or concern in one another. Either of these processes is possible; only one of them reflects the New Testament view of the church or the Spirit of Christ.

The great issues of twenty-first-century Christianity are likely to be ecumenical. The most urgent issues of ecumenism no longer relate to confessional and denominational issues. The World Missionary Conference of 1910 gave a glimpse of a church in which these were overcome, but in our own day this has become an essentially Western and rather parochial matter. The great ecumenical issues will be about how African and Indian and Chinese and Korean and Hispanic and North American and European Christians can together make real the life of the body of Christ. The principal Christian significance of the United States may now be in the fact that—thanks to the immigration law of the 1960s—nearly all the main Christian discourses have functioning congregations there. More than in any other nation in the world, the body of Christ could be realized—or fractured—in the United States.

In Edinburgh in 1910, Europe and America sat down together to settle the missionary problems of the world, acknowledging benignly the presence of a score or so of Asians without fully understanding their significance. From now on, Europe and America will preside at the world table no longer. Whatever may happen in the political or economic sphere, the key events in the Christian sphere will increasingly be those taking place in Africa, Asia, and Latin America. At Edinburgh and over the years that followed, representatives of the missionary movement from the West gave the best they had to fulfill the dazzling vision that beckoned there,

---

[26]Lesslie Newbigin, *Foolishness to the Greeks: The Gospel and Western Culture* (Grand Rapids: Eerdmans, 1986).

the bringing of the gospel of Christ in its fulness to the entire world. The time seemed ripe, the instruments at hand. But they were not in control of the time or the instruments. Time and again their assumptions were undermined, their hopes shattered. The church of the West at large abandoned the vision, and concentrated on other things. Yet the vision was achieved all the same. The goal that the Edinburgh participants sought— the transmission of the gospel to the non-Western world and its appropriation there—was achieved, though not in the ways, or by the means, or at the times, or even in the places that they expected, and so quietly that the Western church, caught up in its own affairs, has still not noticed that it has taken place.

Indeed, a vision beyond what most of the best visionaries of 1910 could see has been fulfilled. They still saw the churches founded through mission endeavours as infants learning to walk. During the conference, and still more afterwards as people reflected on what happened there, glimpses occurred of a world church of mutual sharing. One of the Asian delegates, the South Indian priest V. S. Azariah, was deputed to speak on cooperation between native and foreign workers. His closing words have become the most famous uttered at Edinburgh:

> Through all the ages to come the Indian church will rise up in gratitude to attest the heroism and self-denying labours of the missionary body. You have given your goods to feed the poor. You have given your bodies to be burned. We also ask for love. Give us FRIENDS![27]

It was a bombshell. While missions were busy planning the evangelisation of the world, the first desire of the so-called infant churches was not for leadership, not for more workers, not for more funds, but for friendship.

Friendship implies equality and mutual respect. These churches were not prattling infants, and over the years since Edinburgh 1910, they have gone through the fires. What church in history has gone through what the church in China has over the last fifty years and then emerged as it has? What churches in history have had to cope routinely with such persistent horrors of devastation, war, displacement, and genocide than those of central Africa and the Sudan? Which have survived a more testing religious environment than that of southern Asia? Which have been required more urgently to give moral leadership to their nation than those of South Africa, or to speak for the poor and needy than those of Latin America, or have ever more thoroughly devoted themselves to the spread of the Christian gospel than those of Korea? It is now the churches of the non-

---

[27]*History and Records*, 315.

Western world that have the accumulated and ripened experience of God's salvation.

The church of Christ on earth has an altogether different face and an altogether different shape as a result of the events of the twentieth century. Missions have taken the history of Christianity in a new direction. They did not do it all themselves, of course; the labour on the ground was done by hosts of people of many nations, mostly unknown and some not even formally connected with missions. But it all happened because missions were there. When the servants of God offer their faith and love in service in Christ's name, God does not spurn them, nor mock them when a wise providence exceeds their utmost understanding.

4

The Ephesian Moment

At a Crossroads in Christian History

Christian salvation depends on a historical event: Christ suffered under Pontius Pilate. But that event can only be understood as part of a historical process. Had it been otherwise, the incarnation might have immediately followed the fall, in a single saving action. As it is, we can only understand who Christ is, and why he is so called, by reference to a story covering many centuries. That story includes the emigration of one small clan out of Mesopotamia, the growth and diversification of that clan into tribes in Palestine and Egypt, the gradual solidifying of those tribes into a nation and eventually into a kingdom, the rise and fall and fall and rise of that kingdom and its eventual collapse. According to the early Christian commentary on this history that we know as the Epistle to the Hebrews, God's self-revelation proceeded over the whole of this period "many times and in many ways," here one aspect of the divine being and activity, there another, until "at the end of these times" God spoke by the Son. That act brought together in visible, personal form all the scattered revelations that had come fragmentarily, "many times and in many ways" (Heb. 1:1–2). God was in no hurry over the incarnation; when the Word became flesh, that event crowned a historical process of redemption that had lasted not just centuries but millennia.

But in crowning the process, God did not wind it up, even if some of those who knew Christ best expected the two events to take place in quick succession. In fact, the historical process of redemption was not finished; and it has so far run for another twenty centuries, and we do not know even now whether we are living in the last days or in the days of the early church. A glimpse of the significance of the process since the incarnation is provided by that same early commentator, the writer to the Hebrews. After summarizing the achievements and the sufferings of the key figures

First publication of this lecture is in this volume.

in the story of Israel, all illustrating his theme of faith as the mainstay of the Christian life, he says,

> What a record all of these have won by their faith! Yet they did not receive what God had promised, because God had decided on an even better plan for us. His purpose was that only in company with us would they be made perfect. (Heb. 11:39–40).

The significance of Abraham's faith, and the promised reward of that faith, were not clear in Abraham's lifetime. They were not even made clear in the incarnation, when God "spoke" by a Son. They were delayed until they could be shared with "us." By "us" the writer means, of course, that miscellaneous group of early believers in Christ, Jewish and Gentile, to whom he was writing. They were tied into Abraham's story, and Abraham into theirs. *Abraham was waiting for them.* The point about the long catalog of the saints of Israel that makes up Hebrews 11 is that it tells a story that had not finished. The greatest of the heroes of faith would not be "made perfect" until certain events had taken place long after their death. The history of salvation is not completed in any of its exemplary figures, even the greatest of them. The story of Abraham or of Moses is incomplete in itself; even such great figures cannot be complete, "made perfect," without those who follow them.

The same principles must surely apply to the two millennia that have ensued since the letter to the Hebrews was written. "They"—the addressees of the letter for whom Abraham is waiting—have not yet been "made perfect," because they are waiting for us, for the later generations of faith. Abraham is waiting for us, as for them. The whole company of faith between are bound together as part of a single story, a single act of salvation. No part of the story is complete in itself, nor will it ever be. We can see, readily enough, the incompleteness of those who went before, yet we are not the final stage of Christian formation. Others will look at us and see, perhaps with wonder, our incompleteness. The work of salvation is a historical process that stretches out to the end of the age.

And, the end of the age itself is not (as it has sometimes been presented) an act unrelated to the historical process. It is not a sudden act of divine despair that abandons the process on Earth as useless. Such a view would imply that Christ's work of redemption was somehow not enough, that God needs to inaugurate a new act of salvation that involves the equivalent of a celestial sledgehammer. Equally, the end of the age is not (as presented in some other accounts) a sort of evolution in which the heavenly kingdom grows naturally out of a set of conditions achieved on Earth. It is possible instead to see the end of the age in terms of summary: the completion of the process of "summing up" the work of redemption in Christ. Thus, the Ephesian letter speaks of "the power that is working in us" (i.e., in the midst of the believing community) being the same as the "mighty strength" demonstrated in Christ's resurrection and exaltation. The exalted Christ is thus "given" to the church, and "the church is Christ's body, the completion of him who himself completes all things everywhere" (Eph. 1:19–23).

The theme of the church as Christ's body is crucial to the Ephesian letter. When we think of the church as the body of Christ, we usually think of it as comprehending different races (Jew and Gentile), different lifestyles (Hebraic and Hellenistic), or different people with different gifts and functions in the body. All these aspects are mentioned in the letter. In all these aspects, space is the medium in which the body of Christ functions; its various manifestations are contemporary one with another, representing different social realities at a single point in time. But if the church is Christ's body, then its temporal dimension also has to be taken seriously. The body functions in time as well as in space; time is also an element in which salvation is worked out: its various manifestations across time are necessary for its completion, for "the completion of him who himself completes all things everywhere." Christ takes flesh as he is received by faith in various segments of social reality at different periods, as well as in different places. And these different manifestations belong together; they are part of the same story. Salvation is complete only when all the generations of God's people are gathered together, for only then is Christ's humanity complete. By the same token, the church has to be viewed across time. No one single segment of time encapsulates it; the segments belong together. The work of salvation is cross-generational.

Time is valorized by the incarnation, by the fact that the divine Word took flesh in a datable historical setting. The fact that Christ continues to be formed in local Christian communities whose ways of life are quite different from the one in which the incarnation took place means that for Christians, "sacred time" is not confined to the period of the incarnation, but extends to the whole historical process in which the work of salvation goes on, Christ's presence being demonstrated as he is received by faith. The process may be a painful one, as the New Testament makes clear (e.g., Gal. 4:19–20); and the community's actual representation of Christ may sometimes be a misrepresentation. Nevertheless, genuine manifestations of Christ cannot be separated from specific segments of social reality that occur in time.

This creates a characteristically Christian understanding of history. For thousands of years, devout souls in India have sought deliverance from the bondage of history, to escape the continuing tyranny of time and rebirth. Even where deities enter the world for its salvation, it is only for an era; the tyranny of time is reasserted. The illumination that the Buddha received, and that all subsequent Buddhas and Bodhisattvas receive, is outside of history, independent of history, timeless. Even though Muslims share with Christians the sense of a historic revelation, they have a sense of historic closure; obedience to Allah lies in faithful reproduction of conditions that obtained at the time the Qur'an was revealed. For Christians, the historical element is never abandoned, because time is the stuff within which God's saving activity in Christ takes place. And sacred history is never closed off, because that saving activity of Christ continues until its final summing up.

Christian faith, therefore, is necessarily ancestor-conscious, aware of the previous generations of faith. It cannot divinize the ancestors, however, for their continuing significance comes only from God's activity in and towards them. The work of salvation is cross-generational, and never completed in one generation. And the generations—two millennia of them since the incarnation—are parts of a single body, and that body needs them all.

But we must return to the spatial dimension of the body of Christ. Here the different manifestations that make up the body are contemporaneous with one another, and this is the particular theme of the Epistle to the Ephesians. The rhapsodic note in this letter is unmistakable from the opening verses onwards. The "mystery"—the secret now open—is the special place of the Gentile nations in the saving purpose of God (Eph. 3:3–6). In principle, the fact that Gentiles would be saved was not very new, or very secret; Jews had always believed that the other nations would be blessed by means of Israel's Messiah. The novel element, strikingly, indeed devastatingly, demonstrated in the impact of the gospel in the wider Hellenistic Roman world, was the sheer scale of Gentile salvation, the huge significance of the Gentiles' role in the story of Israel.

To understand the rhapsody at this realization, and the stunning nature of the newly discovered "mystery," we must remember the nature of the earliest church. The original Jesus community, led by his own chosen disciples, was as wholly Jewish in their way of life as in their ethnic origin. They kept the law, and delighted in it. They worshiped in the temple, and they loved it, and saw it as their home.[1] They observed animal sacrifice and the rites of purification (see Acts 21:21–26). This was the way of life Jesus had followed, and he had said that not a jot or tittle would be deleted from the law by his agency, and he had called the temple his Father's house. It was the style of life the apostles had led, and Peter had never eaten anything common or unclean. It was the style of life splendidly demonstrated in the Lord's brother James, leader of the Jerusalem Christians, and widely known in the city as Righteous James, righteous in Jewish terms of heartfelt obedience to the Torah. These people loved God's law, and lived the law the Jesus way. This led them to radical new expressions of that law: they willingly shared their property, for instance, and they shared their meals in the enjoyment of the company of other followers of Jesus.

Then came troubled times and another new departure. Persecution drove many of them out of the city, and some, arriving at metropolitan Antioch, began to share their faith in Jesus with their Greek pagan neigh-

---

[1]Note Acts 2:42, where "the prayers" are those of the temple liturgy.

bors. And those Greek pagans responded. After study and discussion, the leaders of the Jesus community agreed that it would be wrong to apply to these people the traditional requirements for Gentiles who wished to enter the community of Israel. These traditional requirements included circumcision, the mark of God's covenant with Israel. Circumcision, however, was no longer to be the gate for believers in Jesus from a Gentile background. Nor were the food laws, or the laws of ritual purity, or the other requirements of the Torah to be enforced for them. The well-trodden way of Torah had been joyously embraced by all previous believers in Jesus, including the most senior in faith, who had been his personal disciples, and those acknowledged to be closest to his spirit. These new, raw believers, however, were left to find, under the guidance of the Holy Spirit, a way of life that expressed Jesus under the conditions of Hellenistic society. This was necessary because the new believers were to represent Jesus in Hellenistic Antiochene society. Christ's life was to be demonstrated among Antiochene Hellenistic pagans in intelligible human terms, just as it had once been demonstrated in Palestinian Jewish society. This meant developing a whole new Christian lifestyle for conditions that no previous believer had had to cope with. It meant facing a whole array of situations that simply had not arisen, and could not arise, for any Jerusalem believer—such as, what to do in a pagan friend's house if offered meat that might have been bought from a pagan temple (see 1 Cor. 8:8–13). No Jerusalem believer would be likely ever to have been at a pagan dinner table. Hellenistic former pagan believers would be living in a world that made no allowance for the Sabbath. Many of the guideposts for Christian living suddenly were removed; Torah and circumcision were gone as parameters for that living. It was necessary, nonetheless, to develop a lifestyle that could function in Hellenistic pagan society and yet display Christ recognizably there for what—and who—he is.

Traditionally, observant Jewish society and Hellenistic pagan society could be viewed as distinct entities, and the distinctiveness of each was marked by the meal table. Jews ate with Jews, Gentiles with Gentiles. The events reflected in Acts 15 produced two distinct Christian lifestyles corresponding to these ethnic and cultural divisions, the one for Jewish society, the other for Hellenistic society. One might expect as a result that these would be two Christian communities, a Jewish church and a Gentile church. The Ephesian letter has not a dream of such an outcome:

> In union with him [Christ] *you too are being built together with all*
> *the others* to a place where God lives through his Spirit. (Eph. 2:22)

Emphatically, there was to be only *one* Christian community. That community had become more diverse as it crossed the cultural frontier with the Hellenistic pagan world; and Christian obedience was tending to increase the diversity by developing parallel lifestyles that would penetrate and influence Jewish society on the one hand and pagan society on the other. But the very diversity was part of the church's unity. The church must be diverse because humanity is diverse; it must be one because Christ is one. Christ is human, and open to humanity in all its diversity; the fulness of his humanity takes in all its diverse cultural forms. The Ephesian letter is not about cultural homogeneity; cultural diversity had already been built into the church by the decision not to enforce the Torah. It is a celebration of the union of irreconcilable entities, the breaking down of the wall of partition, brought about by Christ's death (Eph. 2:13–18). Believers from the different communities are different bricks being used for the construction of a single building—a temple where the One God would live (Eph. 2:19–22).

Then comes a bold change of metaphor: they are different parts of a single body, a body of which Christ is the head, the mind, the brain, under whose control the whole body works and is held together (Eph. 4:15–16). Old believers and new believers, Jewish believers who had seen the salvation of Israel and Hellenistic ex-pagans who now worshiped *Kyrios Iēsous*, were part of a single, functioning organic life system. And this was because they were "in Christ"; and Christ, the New Adam, incorporated all human diversity and was manifested in different cultural forms as people who were formed by these cultures put faith in him, and he was formed among them. As the body of Christ is thus built up, *"we shall all come together* to that oneness of our faith and knowledge of the Son of God" (Eph. 4:13); the coming together of diverse elements from different quarters produces common convictions, a common assurance, about Christ. This in turn brings the church's maturity, "the very height of Christ's full stature" (Eph. 4:13). The very height of Christ's full stature is reached only by the coming together of the different cultural entities into the body of Christ. Only "together," not on our own, can we reach his full stature.

It is usual to see the great celebration of Ephesians 2 in terms of the reconciliation of two races, Jew and Gentile; and the words have in modern times spoken powerfully to situations of racial division. But in their own time these also stood for two cultures; and, in the church, they stood for two contrasting Christian lifestyles. Two lifestyles met at the institution that had once symbolized the ethnic and cultural division: the meal table. One of the most noticeable features of life in the Jesus community in Jerusalem had been that the followers of Jesus took every opportunity to eat together. Doubtless, the followers of Jesus took the same custom to Antioch, and beyond. But at that point, all the followers of Jesus were Jewish. What was to happen when there were also Gentile followers of Jesus, uncircumcised, following Hellenistic eating patterns? Would it still be the mark of the followers of Jesus that they ate together? The test was the meal table, and clearly, many old believers found it difficult to break the tradition of centuries and sit at table with fellow servants of the Messiah who still bore all the marks of their alien background. What could be defended on grounds of theological principle sometimes demanded great resolution in the face of peer pressure. Thus, Peter can argue from traditional premises for the liberty of Gentile believers (Acts 15:7–11), but find it more convenient not to share a table with them when there was a chance of being observed by his home constituency (Gal. 2:11–14). The shared table was the acid test. It stood for diverse humanity redeemed by Christ and sharing in him.

Each Christian lifestyle, representing a culture converted to Christ, expressed something that the whole body needed. Hellenistic Christianity was not a Torahless soft option for benighted heathen who could do no better, as some Jerusalem believers undoubtedly thought it. Nor was Judaic Christianity a system of legalistic bondage for people who had never known the benefits of a cosmopolitan culture, as some Hellenistic believers may have thought it. Nor was it the case that each was an authentic form of Christian faith complete and valid in itself, apart from the other. Each was necessary to the other, each was necessary to complete and correct the other; for each was an expression of Christ under certain specific conditions, and Christ is humanity completed.

The understanding of Christ—knowing the "full stature"—thus arises from the coming together of the fragmented understandings that occur within the diverse culture-specific segments of humanity where he becomes known. When Ephesians was written, there were only two major cultures represented in the Christian church, the Jewish (reflecting a spectrum of attitudes and accommodation to Greek thought) and the Hellenistic. They could easily have formed separate churches, but that thought does not occur to the author. Two races and two cultures historically separated by the meal table now met at table to share the knowledge of Christ.

The Ephesian moment—the social coming together of people of two cultures to experience Christ—was quite brief. Circumstances—the destruction of the Jewish state in 70 C.E., the scattering of the Jewish church, the sheer success of the mission to the Gentiles—soon made the church monocultural again; and in the eastern Mediterranean the Christian movement became as overwhelmingly Hellenistic as once it had been overwhelmingly Jewish.

But in our own day the Ephesian moment has come again, and come in a richer mode than has ever happened since the first century. Developments over several centuries, reaching a climax in the twentieth, mean that we no longer have two, but innumerable, major cultures in the church. Like the old Jerusalem Christians, Western Christians had long grown used to the idea that they were guardians of a "standard" Christianity; also like them, they find themselves in the presence of new expressions of Christianity, and new Christian lifestyles that have developed or are developing under the guidance of the Holy Spirit to display Christ under the conditions of African, Indian, Chinese, Korean, and Latin American life. And most of the world's Christians are now Africans, Asians, or Latin Americans.

There are two dangers. One lies in an instinctive desire to protect our own version of Christian faith, or even to seek to establish it as the standard, normative one. The other, and perhaps the more seductive in the present condition of Western Christianity, is the postmodern option: to decide that each of the expressions and versions is equally valid and authentic, and that we are therefore each at liberty to enjoy our own in isolation from all the others.

Neither of these approaches is the Ephesian way. The Ephesian metaphors of the temple and of the body show each of the culture-specific segments as necessary to the body but as incomplete in itself. Only in Christ does completion, fullness, dwell. And Christ's completion, as we have seen, comes from all humanity, from the translation of the life of Jesus into the lifeways of all the world's cultures and subcultures through history. None of us can reach Christ's completeness on our own. We need each other's vision to correct, enlarge, and focus our own; only together are we complete in Christ.

The return of the Ephesian moment is of special importance on two accounts: theological and economic.

The purpose of theology is to make or clarify Christian decisions. Theology is about choices; it is the attempt to think in a Christian way. And the need for choice and decision arises from specific settings in life. In this sense, the theological agenda is culturally induced; and the cross-cultural diffusion of Christian faith invariably makes creative theological activity a necessity.

The materials for theology are equally culturally conditioned. They are inevitably the materials at hand in the situation where the occasion for decision has arisen, in interaction with the biblical material. The materials at hand have to be "converted," turned towards Christ, in the process. The classical doctrines of the Trinity and the incarnation are largely constructed out of the materials of middle-period Platonism, converted in this way. (Conversion, we must constantly remind ourselves, is about turning *what is already there;* it is more about direction than about content.)

These same classical doctrines of Trinity and incarnation sprang from the need to think in a Christian way about issues that had arisen out of the cross-cultural diffusion of the faith. The first believers were Jews who saw Jesus in terms of Jewish history, tradition, and belief. But when they came to share that faith with Greek-speaking Gentile peoples, they found it was of little use to talk of Jesus as Messiah. The word meant nothing to Greeks, and needed endless explanation. They had to translate, to find a term that told something about Jesus and yet meant something to a Greek pagan. They chose the word *Kyrios,* "Lord," the title that Greek pagans used for their cult divinities (Acts 11:19–21). Jewish believers (and the action was taken by Jewish folk) had long seen the title Messiah as key to the identity of Jesus, the truest expression of his significance. It was a rich term, full of biblical allusions and echoes of the history of Israel and pointers to its ultimate destiny. The transposition of a message about the Messiah to a message about the "Lord Jesus" must have seemed an impoverishment, perhaps a downright distortion. Was it not dangerous to use language that was also used in heathen cults, and that might give the idea that Jesus was one more of the "Lords many" of the eastern Mediterranean? And should Gentile converts be deprived of knowledge about Israel's national savior?

But it turned out that the transposition was enriching without being distorting. Employing a term used of Hellenistic divinities gave a new dimension to thinking about Christ. It also raised questions, some of them awkward, that a Jewish believer, even one knowing Greek well, would be unlikely to ask. Were the question raised of the relationship of the Messiah Jesus to the One God, Jewish believers could readily use a phrase like "Jesus is at the right hand of God." The significance of that statement was well understood by the Sanhedrin: Stephen's use of it brought him to his death. But a Greek would be puzzled by such a phrase—did it really mean that the transcendent God had a right hand? What Greeks wanted to know was the relationship of that ultimately significant Christ to the Father. Thus, inevitably, the language of *ousia* and *hypostasis* enters. Were Christ and the Father of the same *ousia*? Or different as to *ousia*? Or similar in *ousia*? To find out meant a process of exploring what Christians really believed about their Lord, using the indigenous methods of Greek intellectual discourse. It was a long, painful process, but it issued in an expanded understanding of who Christ is. Christian theology moved on to a new plane when Greek questions were asked about Christ and received Greek answers, using the Greek scriptures. It was a risky, often agonizing business, but it led the church to rich discoveries about Christ that could never have been made using only Jewish categories such as Messiah. Translation did not negate the tradition, but enhanced it. The use of new materials of language and thought, and the related styles and conventions of debate, led to new discoveries about Christ that could not have been made using only the Jewish categories of messiahship. They were not incompatible with those categories. Looking back, all the signals could be seen there in the Scriptures; but only the Greek questions and consequent processes of thought made them explicit. Nor was it necessary to abandon the old Jewish categories: messiahship continues to mean all it ever did. Crossing a cultural frontier led to a creative movement in theology by which we discovered Christ was the eternally begotten Son; but it did not require the old theology to be thrown away, for the eternally begotten Son was also the Messiah of Israel.

Similar developments can be traced in later Christian theology as a result of the gospel crossing other Christian frontiers. It might be shown, for instance, how the classical doctrines of the atonement, and the very feasibility of systematic theology as an exercise, arose from the crossing of the cultural frontier between the Roman world and that of the Western barbarians. It is in this connexion that we must see the great southward shift of Christianity that has resulted in the return of the Ephesian moment. The majority of Christians now belong to Africa, Asia, and Latin America. These regions will increasingly be the places where Christian decisions and Christian choices will have to be made, where creative theology will become a necessity and where the materials for constructing that theology will be such as have not been used for that purpose before. New questions will be asked about Christ that arise from the endeavors of Christian people to express him, to think in a Christian way, and make Christian choices in settings that have been shaped by the venerable traditions of Africa and Asia. And the materials for constructing theology will be African and Asian, as surely as earlier generations used the materials of Platonism and Roman and customary law. If past experience is anything to go by, the process can only enrich the church's understanding of Christ.

The economic implications of the Ephesian moment may profitably be pondered in the light of the United Nations report on population published early in 2001. This deduces that the world's population is increasing by 1.2 percent, or seventy-seven million people, each year, with half that increase coming from six countries: India, China, Pakistan, Nigeria, Bangladesh, and Indonesia. The increase in population growth will be concentrated in countries that are least able to support it. The report projects that by 2050 Africa will have three times the population of Europe, and this despite the anticipated deaths of three hundred million Africans from AIDS by that time. On the other hand, the population in Europe and most other developed countries is projected to fall: in Germany and Japan by 14 percent, in Italy by 25 percent, in Russia and Ukraine by possibly up to 40 percent. This will require migration to maintain economic levels in the developed world; and the prime target for immigration will be the United States, which, with a million new immigrants a year, will be one of the few developed countries to increase its population. By 2050, U.S. population could rise to four hundred million, but entirely as a result of immigration.

The Ephesian moment, then, brings a church more culturally diverse than it has ever been before; potentially, therefore, nearer to that "full stature of Christ" that belongs to his summing up of humanity. The Ephesian moment also announces a church of the poor. Christianity will be mainly the religion of rather poor and very poor peoples, with few gifts to bring except the gospel itself, and the heartlands of the church will include some of the poorest countries on earth. A developed world in which Christians become less prominent will seek to protect its position against the rest. The Ephesian question at the Ephesian moment is whether or not the church in all its diversity will demonstrate its unity by the interactive participation of all its culture-specific segments, the interactive participation that is to be expected in a functioning body. Will the body of Christ be realized or fractured in this new Ephesian moment? Realization will have both theological and economic consequences. Perhaps the African and Asian and Hispanic Christian diasporas in the West have a special significance in the posing of the Ephesian question, and the United States, with its large community of indigenous believers and growing Christian communities of the diasporas, may be crucial for the answer that will be given to it.

Part Two

AFRICA IN CHRISTIAN HISTORY

5

Africa in Christian History

Retrospect and Prospect

It is widely recognised that there has occurred within the present century a demographic shift in the centre of gravity of the Christian world, which means that more than half of the world's Christians live in Africa, Asia, Latin America, or the Pacific, and that the proportion doing so grows annually. This means that we have to regard African Christianity as potentially the *representative* Christianity of the twenty-first century. The representative Christianity of the second and third and fourth centuries was shaped by events and processes at work in the Mediterranean world. In later times it was events and processes among the barbarian peoples of northern and western Europe, or in Russia, or modern western Europe, or the North Atlantic world that produced the representative Christianity of those times. The Christianity typical of the twenty-first century will be shaped by the events and processes that take place in the southern continents, and above all by those that take place in Africa.

I am not, of course, suggesting that there will not be substantial numbers of Christians outside Africa, or that what they do or what happens to them is of no importance—there have always been plenty of Christians outside the areas of representative Christianity. But the things by which people recognise and judge what Christianity is will (for good or ill) increasingly be determined in Africa. The characteristic doctrines, the liturgy, the ethical codes, the social applications of the faith will increasingly be those prominent in Africa. New agendas for theology will appear in Africa. And one of the anvils on which the Christianity of the future will be hammered out will be the question of the nation, the state, the nature of civil society.

Lecture for a forum of the Africa Theological Fellowship, meeting in Accra, Ghana, 1997. First published in *The Journal of African Christian Thought* 1 (No. 1, 1998): 2–16. Reprinted with permission.

Contemporary Africa is confronting Christians with issues relating to the nation that have not previously occurred in this form in all the long history of Christianity in the West, and where previous Christian theology therefore offers only limited guidance. But unprecedented questions about nationhood are also now beginning to break in the West, and indeed many other parts of the world. The nation-state, and the organisation of the world into nation-states, can no longer be taken for granted. A new process of nation building is taking place. This heightens the significance of African Christianity; for it suggests that Africa may be experiencing first, and in a particularly intense way, some situations that are awaiting other parts of the world. This in turn may mean that our topic is a crucial issue, not just for Africa, but far beyond. What happens about Christianity and nation building in Africa—again let us remember, whether for good or ill—may indicate whether Christians have anything of importance to say or do about civil society, or any characteristically Christian way of influencing it, anywhere in the world.

I propose therefore a swift tour of Christian history in Africa, especially in its relations with the state, followed by another through the various manifestations of the state in Africa.

A Hint from the New Testament

A special place for Africa in the history of redemption is hinted at in the New Testament itself. The fullest explicit reference to it, the story of the Ethiopian eunuch in Acts 8, is worth a moment's thought in this regard. In one sense, the story interrupts the flow of the narrative of the Acts of the Apostles. The early chapters have recounted the development of the Jerusalem church and the life of the Jewish Christians who had recognised in Jesus the Messiah of Israel. They later show the birth of Hellenistic Christianity at Antioch and the westward progress of the message about Jesus across Asia Minor over southeastern Europe to Rome. The link between the two is the story of Stephen.

So why does Luke break the chain of narrative that joins Stephen with Saul and the church of Antioch to tell us about this meeting of a government official from the Sudan with Stephen's colleague Philip on an international highway? It is not as though he tells us anything about what happened when the Ethiopian eunuch reached home; indeed, he almost goes out of his way to indicate that he does not know. The story ends with Philip being whisked away so that the Ethiopian saw him no more. But equally, Luke emphasises the providential nature of the meeting; it is no chance encounter. The whole way the story is framed is a reminder that Africa, the lands beyond the Nile, will have a Christian history too—one that is not yet charted, and one that is distinct from the story of Asia and Europe, which is the concern of the Acts of the Apostles. It is distinct, but not entirely separate; the Ethiopian is, after all, an international traveller who knows the highways of the Greco-Roman world. In the Acts story, he comes as a pilgrim, and returns as a Christian. Perhaps it is not too fanciful to take a hint that he, or his spiritual descendants, may one day travel those highways again as the representatives and bearers of the Christian gospel.[1]

What happened to the Ethiopian eunuch—an official, it would seem, of the kingdom of Meroë—we, like Luke, have no means of knowing; nor do we know much about the origins of Christianity either in Egypt or in North Africa. But it is clear that by the second century their churches could claim to be old established. Egypt and the stretch of North Africa that the Romans called "Africa" were both provinces of the Roman Empire, and so were part of the "representative" Christianity of the early centuries of the faith. Both had a notable record of suffering under the recurrent bursts of local and state persecution, in a period when martyrdom was the test of Christian authenticity. They provided much of the intellectual task force of early Christianity who developed the groundwork of Christian theology. Many, perhaps most, of the seminal theologians of the early centuries belonged to the African continent. Among them are Origen, the first Christian theologian in the modern sense of the word, the founder, one might say, of systematic theology; and the three African lawyers, Tertullian, Cyprian, and Augustine, who laid the foundations of Western theology with Roman law as the cement.

It is no accident that Western theology was first made in Africa, because the North African church pioneered the vernacular use of Latin, and was doing its theology in Latin at a time when the church in Rome was still using Greek, the language of Paul and most other missionaries. (It is worth noting that the first bishop of Rome we know of who wrote his letters in Latin is Victor, who himself came from Africa.) Indeed, one might say that the vernacular principle in Christianity was earliest exemplified in Africa; among the earliest known translations of the New Testament are the Sahidic of Lower Egypt and the Latin of Roman Africa.

Africa was also a source of Christian innovation, of new, radical, and sometimes controversial movements. Antony, an Egyptian (and a real native Copt, not a cosmopolite from Alexandria), designed the most effective challenge to the idea that Christianity could be satisfactorily combined with self-indulgence when he founded the monastic movement. That movement became both a vehicle for radical Christian living and a most successful instrument for evangelism. (I have argued that St. Antony the Copt is the first Evangelical, but it would take too long to say why.) In the same way one might describe Tertullian as the first theologian of Pentecostalism; he gave intellectual edge and coherence to the Montanist movement, which could easily have become a rustic curiosity in a Christ-

---

[1]Acts 8:26–39.

ian backwater. One might even see the African Donatists as the first liberation theologians—beginning their theology within the accepted corpus,
but insisting that theology must be tested by praxis, standing up for a deprived Numidian peasantry in the face of pressure from both the church
and state, receiving a generally bad press, and often, like their Latin
American successors, spoiling a good case by going over the top.
Whichever dimension we take, Egypt and Roman Africa must be counted
among the most fully developed centres of the Christian faith in the ancient world.

But these areas represent only one part of the early story of African
Christianity. There is, for instance, another part that began when two
young Syrian Christians were shipwrecked off the Horn of Africa, settled
in Axum, preached and practised their faith, and founded a church there.
One became a civil servant in the royal court; and in due time King Ezana,
whose religious views had already been moving in a monotheistic direction, became a Christian himself. With Axum begins the long history of
Ethiopian Christianity, which over the centuries spread over huge areas
by processes we still do not fully understand. Christianity in this part of
the world took a distinctive Ethiopian form with some observances apparently unique to it. It found a distant ancestry for itself in an ancient
connection with Israel in the days of Solomon—never absolutely cut off
from the rest of the Christian world, but generally little touched by it and
almost forgotten by it.

There were also the varied peoples of the Upper Nile Valley in what is
now Sudan, then collectively known as Nubians, who were reached by
various missions (some from the imperial strand of Christianity, some
from the distinctively Egyptian strand known as Monophysite). Here
again these long-lived churches were for a long time largely unknown to
or forgotten by the "representative" Christians to the north; it is only in
relatively recent years that archaeological expeditions (sponsored, ironically, by the former communist regime in Poland) have uncovered
enough of the Nubian churches to show how substantial, and how
durable, Nubian Christianity was.

Putting these things together, we realise that by the time the Arabs arrived in Africa bearing Islam, Christianity was already well established
and deeply rooted there. Egypt and North Africa were among the notably
Christian areas in the world; but by no means did the whole of African
Christianity lie within the Roman Empire, nor was it subordinate to the
empire.

But if these African churches beyond the Roman Empire did not
recognise any political jurisdiction from outside, they did recognise an organic link with Christians far away, brought about by their Christian allegiance. They saw themselves as part of a world community. Frumentius,
the Christian civil servant whose activity had founded the Axum church,
when at long last allowed to return home, reported on the events in Axum

to the nearest major Christian centre, which was Alexandria, where Athanasius was then patriarch. Athanasius responded by ordaining him and sending him back. The remarkable thing is that a similar process took place many times thereafter, and took place century after turbulent century, almost to the Marxist regime of the day before yesterday. The political realities changed again and again; ordinary commercial and cultural contacts often dried up; Ethiopia became a Christian empire while Alexandria was swallowed up in an Islamic one. But, time after time, when an Abyssinian *abuna* died, someone made the long, hazardous journey to Alexandria, and someone was consecrated in Alexandria for the oversight of the church in Ethiopia. That sense of an umbilical cord connecting Ethiopia with the outside world through the years of its isolation is a remarkable witness to Christian universality. That theme, that Christians in some way belong to one another across geographical, political, and ethnic frontiers, is bound to recur in the course of the present study.[2]

It is common to speak as though the early Christian story in Africa is a tale that is told. African Christian history is sometimes presented in terms of three plantings of Christianity, of which the first two, corresponding with the early church and the Portuguese appearance, were essentially failures. After all, the church of Roman Africa disappeared well over a millennium ago; it was in terminal decline before the Arabs got there; and, fairly certainly, it never brought the faith across the Sahara. The event that might have made that possible was the introduction of the camel; but when the Arabs brought the camel, they brought Islam too. Thus in due time Islam came to the Sudanic grasslands, while Christianity was eclipsed in Egypt, and Christians there reduced to a cultural island in an essentially Islamic context. The Christian world reoriented, realigned northwards; Ethiopia became isolated and Christian Nubia gradually succumbed to attrition. And so, in many accounts, ended the first planting of Christianity in Africa.

I would like to challenge this view, with its implication that the early history of Christianity in Africa has nothing to do with the contemporary

---

[2]For a general account, see W. H. C. Frend, *The Early Church*, 3rd ed. (London, 1991), and his studies of North Africa, *The Donatist Church: A Movement of Protest in Roman North Africa* (Oxford, 1985). The story of Frumentius and Aedesius is told by Rufinus. *Ecclesiastical History* 1:9–10; 10:9. There are other accounts in the histories of Socrates, Sozomen, and Theodore. On Ezana, see S. Kaplan, "Ezane's Conversion Reconsidered" *Journal of Religion in Africa*, vol. 13, fasc. 2 (1982): 101–09. On historic Ethiopian Christianity, see E. Ullendorf, *Ethiopia and the Bible* (London, 1968); and Taddesse Tamrat, *Church and State in Ethiopia 1270–1527* (Oxford, 1972). The significance of Ethiopia in the totality of African history is well identified by Adrian Hastings; *The Church in Africa 1450–1950* (Oxford, 1994). A comprehensive account of Christian Nubia is still awaited. In the meantime, see W. Y. Adams, *Nubia: A Corridor to Africa* (London, 1977); and P. L. Shinnie, "Christian Nubia," in *Cambridge History of Africa*, vol. 2 (Cambridge, 1978), ch. 9.

Christianity of Ghana and Sierra Leone and Nigeria, and its further implication that Christianity is essentially an import from the West. My reasons
derive from three factors.

The first concerns the unbroken historical continuity of the
churches of Egypt and Ethiopia of today and the ancient world. Anyone who has experienced anything of either Egyptian or Ethiopian
Christianity will bear witness to the overwhelming sense of antiquity
that they still hold. Talk with a Coptic bishop, and Athanasius does not
seem a very remote figure; he could be in the next room. And it is
worth reflecting on the organic connection of Athanasius and Axum
represented by the consecration of Frumentius and so many of his successors down to the 1960s. Ezana, king of Axum, and Athanasius, patriarch of Alexandria, belonged to the same Christian universe. Incidentally, the Christians that Muhammad thought of as representative
were Ethiopians; those who had dealings with southern Arabia, those
who sheltered his early converts when they were driven out of Mecca,
those of whom the Qur'an says, "You will find the Christians the nearest in affection to you."[3]

The second factor concerns the degree of commonalty between
northern and sub-Saharan Africa. While it would be unwise to be dogmatic about the precise skin colour of Origen or Tertullian, it is clear
that early Christianity saw northern Africa, Egypt, Ethiopia, and
Nubia as part of a single Christian universe that extended also over the
northern Mediterranean lands and the Middle East. No purely geographical factor finally divides Mediterranean Africa from tropical
Africa. There are, and were, political and cultural factors to do so, but
early Christianity transcended these. Early Christianity, irrespective of
the Roman Empire, formed and maintained organic links between
tropical and Mediterranean Africa. This is a fact worth noticing today,
when Islam maintains a similar connection, constantly drawing West
Africa into the cultural and economic orbit of North Africa. In the
modern world, as the Organisation of Africa Unity bears witness, it is
impossible to divorce sub-Saharan Africa from the lands of the Sahara
and northwards, and there are many African nations between the
North Atlantic and the Red Sea whose boundaries contain both peoples who look northwards and peoples who look southwards. For
Christians, North Africa often presents an alien, even a threatening
face; amid the tensions of nation building we may do well to remember that Africa north of Sahara and Africa of the Mediterranean have
not always been alien territory. Christian faith linked peoples of northern Africa and mediterranean Africa before either Islam or the camel
arrived there.

---

[3] Qur'an Sura 5:82.

The third factor relates to the wider use of the name Ethiopia. A century ago and more, groups of African Christians, frustrated by missionary control, established churches that would be free of missionaries. When they did so, they sometimes used the title "Ethiopian" to assert their Africanness, seizing upon the text beloved of generations of missionaries that foretells a day when Ethiopia will stretch forth its hands to God. The use of the name indicated a conviction that that day had arrived. The process has continued to this day. All over the continent and especially over its southern half, one finds churches with the word "Ethiopian" in their title. Such churches are invariably instituted by Africans, and some by people who would be hard put to say where Ethiopia is, or to indicate it on a map. But they know what it stands for. The Order of Ethiopia in South Africa, for instance, is a vigorous indigenous movement within the Anglican Church. Afro-America also has its examples of "Ethiopian" consciousness, in the names of churches and even in the Jamaican Rastafarian movement, which identifies Ras Tafari, in other words, the last emperor of Ethiopia, as its figure of hope.

I suggest that this Ethiopian consciousness should be taken seriously as representing an important instinct that many simple people have identified when more sophisticated people have missed it. Ethiopian stands for Africa indigenously Christian, Africa *primordially* Christian; for a Christianity that was established in Africa not only before the white people came, but before Islam came; for a Christianity that has been continuously in Africa for far longer than it has in Scotland, and infinitely longer than it has in the United States. African Christians today can assert their right to the *whole* history of Christianity in Africa, stretching back almost to the apostolic age.

There are important academic implications in this. Christianity in Africa cannot be treated as a colonial leftover. If it is to reflect its true place in the history of redemption, Africa must be recovered from its place in the margins of Christian thought. If Christianity is indigenous to Africa, if its continuous history in the continent is as long as that of Christianity almost anywhere else in the world, then African Christian thought belongs in the Christian mainstream; and African theology should not be satisfied with a place that reduces it to resolving local difficulties.[4]

---

[4]The distinction between "Ethiopian" and "Zionist" types of African Independent Church was drawn in the pioneer study by Bengt Sundkler, *Bantu Prophets in South Africa* (London, 1948; 2nd ed., Oxford, 1961). An early study for Nigeria is J. B. Webster, *The African Churches among the Yoruba, 1888–1922* (Oxford, 1964). On the Order of Ethiopia in South Africa, see T. D. Verryn, *A History of the Order of Ethiopia* (Cleveland, Transvaal, 1972). On Rastafarianism, see Leonard E. Barrett. *The Rastafarians: Sounds of Cultural Dissonance*, 2nd ed. (Boston, 1988); and Barry Chevannes, *Rastafari: Roots and Ideology* (Syracuse, NY, 1994).

Meeting Western Christians

We have spoken of the isolation of Ethiopia. But over much of the time it would be equally true to speak of the isolation of Europe. For centuries Europe knew nothing of the Americas, and little of Africa or Asia; Europeans thought of "Christendom" as Christian territory, roughly coterminous with Europe, and hardly thought of Christians beyond it.

Then in the late-fifteenth century, contact was established with the non-Western world, led by the Iberian powers, whose new maritime vigour was infused with religious revival and inspired by recent military success against the Muslims. There is no reason to doubt the sincerity of the Iberian quest for what one of their leaders called "gold and Christians." There seemed every reason to believe that trade could be developed, territory acquired, and Christian worship and doctrine enforced at the same time. Western Christendom was Christian *territory*; it was hard to envisage Christianity except in terms of territory, and it was natural to wish to expand the area of the world which acknowledged the King of kings. Further, the only extensive experience Europe had of interaction with non-Christians (if we except the Jews) was of crusade. The first contact of Western Christians with the New World, of which Africa was a part, was thus conceived in crusading zeal. When the Portuguese took Ceuta in Morocco from the Muslims in 1415, it was to bring it into Christendom, make it Christian territory.

But the story developed in a completely unexpected way. The theology and outlook of the Portuguese were not different from those of the Spaniards who in Mexico and Peru combined conversion and conquest; but the Portuguese experience was quite different from that of the conquistadors. Portugal, a small nation with immense commitments, was quite incapable of enforcing conversion by conquest, in Africa or elsewhere. The unintended result was the invention of the missionary movement—the establishment of a body of people whose task was to commend, convince, illustrate, and persuade, but who were unable to coerce. The Portuguese presence stretched along the coasts of west and central south and southeast Africa. Where there was a Portuguese presence there was a church presence, and the church was, by agreement, under the supervision of the king of Portugal. But those settlements became bases for a much wider missionary enterprise, for which the missionaries were not always Portuguese (frequently they were Italian), and had little reason to extend Portuguese interests for their own sake. There was not much in their own background or theology to assist the process of cross-cultural evangelisation (though probably their general worldview was closer to that of the Africans they met than was that of nineteenth and twentieth century missionaries). It was a new learning experience for Western Christians.

The results of this early Western mission work are not easy to assess. Most of it did not endure the waning of Catholic missionary activity in the eighteenth century, and the reluctance to ordain African priests may have sealed its fate. On the other hand, some aspects of it are rather impressive. One of the best-documented examples is the kingdom of Soyo, near the mouth of the Congo River. It has been common to regard the Soyo story as a piece of political opportunism that put a thin Catholic veneer over essentially unchanged African religion. In a sensitive study, Richard Gray has produced a very different interpretation, showing a genuinely African church growing in depth of understanding, and rethinking African institutions in Christian terms, though fatally flawed, once more, by the failure to ordain Africans. It is worth noticing, incidentally, that Soyo was no Portuguese puppet; it preferred non-Portuguese missionaries and insisted on trading with the Dutch (from the Portuguese point of view both interloping rivals and Protestant heretics).[5]

The Portuguese never made contact with the ancient Christianity of Africa, despite the confused stories they knew about Prester John, a great Christian prince who might join them in war against Muslims (and which may have sprung from garbled accounts of Christian Ethiopia).

The Tragic Atlantic Triangle

But the Iberian powers began one crucial connection with Africa that was to dominate the relations of Africa and the West for centuries to come: the Atlantic slave trade. By it, Africa was drawn into the commercial world of Europe and the Americas. On the basis of African labour, the economies of the Americas were reconstructed. Even Bartolomé de Las Casas, justly celebrated for his defence of the Amerindians, for a time approved the African slave trade—the stronger, more robust Africans would survive the rigours that were killing the native peoples under the new economy produced by the European conquest of the New World.

Three results of the slave trade may be mentioned. The first is the debilitating effect in Africa. African coastal peoples became middlemen in

---

[5]The outline of the story is given in K. S. Latourette. *History of the Expansion of Christianity*, vol. 3, *Three Centuries of Advance 1500–1800* (New York, 1939). For the Spanish conquest, see H. McKennie Goodpasture, *Cross and Sword: An Eyewitness History of Christianity in Latin America* (Maryknoll, N.Y. 1989). The Portuguese experience is illuminated in C. R. Boxer, *The Church Militant and Iberian Expansion, 1440–1770* (Baltimore, 1978). On the indigenous nature of Congo Christianity, see the small but important work by Richard Gray, *Black Christians and White Missionaries* (New Haven, 1990).

the trade. And in due time, endemic war became a means of keeping up the supply of slaves. Though Portuguese power declined, the slave trade did not; the Protestant powers simply took a greater share in it with equal cruelty, and less concern for the salvation of either slaves or slave holders. By the early nineteenth century, the great Muslim jihads were producing slaves for the markets of America.

The second crucial result was Afro-America—the creation of a permanent self-consciously African element in the population of North, Central, and South America. The significance of the new population appeared early; Gray shows that the papal edict against the slave trade in 1686 was secured by the initiative of a Brazilian African who was an active and influential lay member of the church. Protestants were less anxious than Catholics for slaves to receive Christian teaching, so no Protestant equivalent of Lourenço da Silva de Mendonça appears until a much later date. Nevertheless, it was Afro-America that first faced Protestant Christians with the question of Africa; and black religion in North America and the West Indies that first foreshadowed the conversion of Africa. If we are to think of the Christian faith in relation to Africa in historical perspective, and with a view to the future, we do well to consider Afro-America. Afro-America is part of the African history; it is an especially significant part of African Christian history.[6]

The third aspect of the slave trade to consider is antislavery.

The Protestant Missionary Movement in Africa—the Liberationist Phase

Antislavery is an unmistakable dimension of the early Protestant missionary movement in Africa. Protestant powers increasingly entered and often took over the Portuguese trading interests, but had neither the motivation nor the means to maintain the Portuguese missionary concern. Though Christianity was still the professed religion of powers such as Britain and the Netherlands, its extension was no active part of state policy. The one major Protestant settlement, at the Cape of Good Hope (taken over by the Dutch from the Portuguese originally as a staging post for India), was a case in point; evangelisation among the indigenous peoples or imported slaves, at least to the extent of recognising their privileges of church membership, proved incompatible with the labour market, and simply stopped.

---

[6]On slavery, see David Brion Davis, *The Problem of Slavery in Western Culture* (New York, 1988). On Las Casas, see G. Gutiérrez, *Las Casas: In Search of the Poor of Jesus Christ* (Maryknoll, N.Y. 1993). Of the huge literature on Afro-American Christianity, see especially A. J. Raboteau, *Fire in the Bones: Reflections on African-American Religious History* (Boston, 1995). On Lourenço da Silva and the papal edict against slavery, see Gray. *Black Christians.*

The birth of the missionary movement in Britain coincided with the development of the public campaign against the Atlantic slave trade. Supporters of the one movement were usually supporters of the other; and the parliamentary leaders against the slave trade were evangelical humanitarians who were mostly enthusiastic supporters of missions. They were also practical politicians who combined their moral stance against slavery with economic arguments against slavery as an economic institution.

The first African centre for the new missionary movement, Sierra Leone, was explicitly associated with the antislavery campaign. Its original basis was found in Afro-America: 1,100 people of African birth or descent who had fought and taken up arms against their masters in the American war of independence, and thereafter been transported to Nova Scotia, travelled to Sierra Leone in 1792. They took their own churches and preachers to Africa with them (the first Protestant church in tropical Africa was thus not a missionary creation, but an African one), and sang that they had passed from the house of bondage to the promised land. The church that was later formed in Sierra Leone, the first real success story of the missionary movement in Africa, was based on the conversion of slaves from slave ships intercepted at sea en route for the Americas and brought to Sierra Leone by the British navy. The "recaptive" community and its descendants provided the missionary force for much of West Africa for a long time to come. In the 1880s there was a Sierra Leonean missionary in Kenya; and Bishop Crowther planned a Sierra Leone mission to the Congo.

Missionary enterprise in Africa continued to be identified with active humanitarianism. Two figures who span the period from 1830 to 1870 encapsulate contemporary attitudes: the evangelical parliamentarian Thomas Fowell Buxton and the missionary explorer David Livingstone. The assumptions underlying Buxton's thought may be summarised thus:

1. The nominally Christian nations of the West are in debt to Africa for the extent to which, by their economic activities, they have despoiled the land and mistreated its population. Missionary and humanitarian activity must be seen in terms of reparations and accompanied by every possible measure to combat slavery and oppression.

2. Africa's redemption will be best effected by calling forth its own resources. This is true of both economic and human resources. Africa is potentially strong in world trade if it develops its products instead of wastefully exporting labour; and there are huge human resources for redeeming Africa in the active African Christian communities visible in the Caribbean and Sierra Leone.

3. The interest of Christianity and "legitimate" (i.e., nonslave) trade in Africa go together, the one easing the path for the other. Buxton's aim was

that Africa should be an equal, independent trading partner; he had no idea of a captive economy, any more than he had of annexing colonial possessions.

Such ideals were very influential among the missionaries and missionary thinkers of the middle of the century. We find the Church Missionary Society developing cotton-growing to produce an export trade for the Yoruba as an arm of missionary policy and as a discouragement to the slave trade. The Basel Mission laid the foundations of Ghana's cocoa industry. In the Cape, the only extensive European possession in Africa, Buxton's associate John Philip, of the London Missionary Society, was in continual bad odour with the white community (and some missionary colleagues) for his defence of African rights. The Scottish mission in Calabar was established at the behest of Christians not in Scotland but in Jamaica, and Africans from Jamaica were regularly among the missionaries.

Insofar as the evangelical missionary interest of this period sought to influence public policy towards Africa, it was interventionist (seeking to rouse interest and concern about violence, slavery, or the threat of it) but not usually annexationist. There were exceptions to this (Methodists in South Africa, who were associated with the pastoral care of poor white settlers, took a settler view of the Xhosa frontier); but, generally speaking, the expectation was that African governments and peoples would be steadily influenced by missionary activity and by the presence in their midst of a small but growing church. Preaching was thus directed both to conversion and to social change.

This had important implications for the missionary. Outside some special situations such as the Cape and Sierra Leone, missionaries could operate only on terms laid down by African powers. This meant that missionaries often had to acknowledge that they were welcomed or tolerated for reasons other than the one that brought them, that of preaching the gospel. The Calabar mission was originally accepted because the education it supplied would be useful in the palm oil trade that the towns controlled. The price exacted was that the mission had to keep out of the towns upriver; Calabar did not want its neighbours encroaching on its special advantages. Livingstone is scathing about sentimental talk in missionary magazines about the "spiritual hunger" of Africans. Of course they were not spiritually hungry, he says; the natural human never is. But, if one could get beyond the areas that white settlement and oppression had polluted, Christian messengers would be accepted for other benefits they could bring, and the door for the gospel be opened. In their relations with missionaries, forceful rulers like Moshoeshoe, Lobengula, and Mzilikazi were always in charge, and missionaries, however reluctantly, accepted this. Among the Basuto—Moshoeshoe's whole career was a dialogue with the Christian faith—they reaped the benefit of patience. Among the Ndebele, the missionaries paid the penalty of betraying trust or acting impatiently. It is the basic missionary experience to live on terms set by someone else; and until the 1880s, that was the missionary norm in most of Africa.[7]

The Missionary Movement in Africa in Its Colonial Phase

The significance of the colonial era is dealt with elsewhere in this chapter. Here it is enough to note some ways in which it affected the missionary enterprise. Generally speaking, missionaries welcomed the imposition of European control as likely to assist their work. (The painful experience of the early Scottish missions in Malawi in the transitional period, when they found themselves acting as a de facto government, indicated how awkward things could be when there was a power vacuum.) The result, however, was not all that they expected: in particular the missionary interest became bitterly disillusioned at the apparent readiness of colonial governments to support Islamic rule and discourage Christian activity anywhere in the neighbourhood of Muslim rulers. When the twentieth century dawned, some missionaries were complaining that when it came to Islamic interest, pagan rulers were better to deal with than the British government.

Colonial rule changed the basis of missionary life. Missionaries ceased to live so directly on terms set by Africans. They could not now be removed except by their compatriots in government, within whose framework they operated; they were part of the structures of power. The nature of their task changed. No longer was their message directed to African society as it existed; such things were now the colonial government's concern. One thing in particular was demanded of them by government; and the same thing was demanded of them by Africans responding to the new world that had been thrust upon them: Western education became the

---

[7]On the early Cape missions, see Berhard Kruger, *The Pear Tree Blossoms: A History of the Moravian Mission Stations in South Africa 1737–1869.* On the antislavery movement in Britain, see C. Bolt and S. Drescher, *Anti-slavery and Reform: Essays in Memory of Roger Anstey* (Folkstone, 1980); and Seymour Drescher, *Econocide: British Slavery in the Era of Abolition* (London, 1977). The fullest account of Sierra Leone is Christopher Fyfe, *A History of Sierra Leone* (London, 1961). Buxton's great manifesto, *The African Slave Trade and Its Remedy* (1840) was reprinted in the Cass series (London, 1967). On the mission and cotton growing in Yorubaland, see J. F. Ade Ajayi, *Christian Missions in Nigeria 1814–1841: The Making of a New Elite* (London, 1965); and S. O. Biobaku, *The Egba and Their Neighbours* (Oxford, 1957). On the Basel Mission's commercial activities, see W. J. Danker, *Profit for the Lord: Economic Activities in Moravian Missions and the Basel Mission Trading Company* (Grand Rapids, 1971). On Philip, see Andrew Ross, *John Philip (1775–1851): Missions, Race and Politics in South Africa* (Aberdeen, 1986). On Calabar, see Geoffrey Johnston, *Of God and Maxim Guns: Presbyterianism in Nigeria, 1846–1966* (Waterloo, 1988). Livingstone's views are recorded in *Livingstone's Missionary Correspondence 1841–1856*, ed. Isaac Schapera (London, 1961). On Moshoeshoe, see Leonard Thompson, *Survival in Two Worlds: Moshoeshoe of Lesotho, 1786–1870* (Oxford, 1976). On the American Presbyterian mission's experience with Mzilikazi, see E. W. Smith, *The Life and Times of Daniel Lindley* (London, 1949).

most noticeable aspect of missions in Africa. Wave after wave of new missions came in, announcing they would be caught in no such trap, that their task was only to preach the gospel—ere long they would find it was necessary to build schools, and schools that would meet government standards. Even the Salvation Army found itself operating secondary schools.

The public role of missions was reduced. Occasionally, missionaries were able to affect government policy. One of the most effective interventions was the public pressure organised in the 1890s by the London Missionary Society to prevent Bechuanaland, with its Christian high chief, Khama III, being absorbed by Cecil Rhodes's British South Africa Company. Three Tswana chiefs, with a missionary as interpreter, came to London, and impressed public and political opinion that their country would be safer in their hands than in those of the dynamic entrepreneur. That action made possible modern Botswana.

But such successes were few. Missionaries could sometimes mitigate hardships (as in the forced labour issue in East Africa) or the worst injustices (the Scottish missionary Frank Barlow in Kenya made himself an expert in Kikuyu land tenure and got much land restored that had been unjustly appropriated—including by his mission). And there were uncomfortable prophets such as the Anglican A. S. Cripps in Rhodesia. In general, however, in the high colonial period (ca. 1880–1930), missions were part of the governing system.

In 1924, the convenor of the Church of Scotland Foreign Mission Committee wrote a book entitled *Our Empire's Debt to Missions*. The chapter most concerned with Africa is called "The Civilising Work of Missions among the Child-Races of the Empire." The implication is clear: child races need a firm, patient tutor. Nothing could better indicate how far both missions and missionary language had travelled since the days of Buxton and Livingstone. Much as they believed in what they called "civilisation," that generation never saw Africans as *children*.

The language is ironical when one thinks how far it was African initiatives that shaped the Christian story in the colonial period. We have mentioned Khama, the architect of modern Botswana, who sought to turn his chiefdom into a godly commonwealth and skilfully negotiated with the colonial power. Missions in the colonial period were frequently reactive rather than proactive, struggling with small resources to meet growing demands to know about the complex ideas and activities that included the Bible, Christian faith and worship, and a new way of life. The crucial period was the First World War. The war greatly reduced the number of serving missionaries; the Germans were expelled or interned, and many of the others went off to the front. The war years saw the missions' infrastructure creaking and sometimes collapsing, but a great numerical increase in the congregations. It saw also the emergence of immensely influential African preachers who arose quite outside the mission structures, or in its humblest levels: Prophet Harris, Sampson Oppong, Simon Kimbangu, Joseph Babalola, Walter Mattita, Garrick Braide. These influenced multitudes towards the Christian faith; huge numbers came under the pastoral care of the missions as a result. But these African figures, while not usually hostile to missions, worked essentially outside the mission framework in obedience to what they recognised as a divine commission.

In the meantime, African churches were coming into being. It is suggested elsewhere that this growth was crucial in producing an alternative form of community to the traditional and the colonial forms. But it could only be so when the issue of power was resolved, and when it was clear that the churches were indeed African institutions. A nice illustration from Malawi comes in a paper from Jack Thompson, who shows that the watershed in the Livingstonia presbytery came, not simply when Africans formed a majority (they still followed the missionary lead) or even when they opposed missionary proposals (the proposals still went through), but when a missionary—it was Donald Fraser—was prepared to vote with the African members and against the all-powerful patriarch Dr. Laws.[8]

Decolonisation and the Church

Though, as indicated elsewhere, the missions and the churches contributed so substantially to making the nation-state possible, the missions were often caught unprepared by decolonisation, and the arrival of the

---

[8]On the colonialism issue, see Brian Stanley, *The Bible and the Flag: Protestant Missions and British Imperialism in the Nineteenth and Twentieth Centuries* (Leicester, 1990). On Nigeria, see, e.g., the veteran W. R. S. Miller's *Reflections of a Pioneer* (London, 1936); and Sonia F. Graham, *Government and Mission Education in Northern Nigeria 1900–1919* (Ibadan, 1966). The education question was set forward at the International Missionary Council's special conference at Le Zoute: see E. W. Smith, ed., *The Church's Mission in Africa: A Study Based on the Work of the International Conference at Le Zoute* (London, 1926). The essay by J. H. Oldham, the Council's secretary, is especially illuminating. An attack on making education central to mission was launched by Roland Allen, *Le Zoute: A Critical Review of the Christian Mission in Africa* (London, 1927). See also the summary by J. W. C. Dougall at the end of the colonial period in *Christians in the African Revolution* (Edinburgh, 1963). On Khama, see J. Mutero Chirenje, *Chief Khama and His Times c 1835–1923* (London, 1978). On Cripps, poet, priest, and Rhodesian dissident, see D. V. Steere, *God's Irregular: Arthur Shearly Cripps* (London, 1973). The author of *Our Empire's Debt to Missions* was J. N. Ogilvie (Edinburgh, 1924). Of the indigenous charismatic figures, the fullest documented are Harris (see David A. Shank, *Prophet Harris, the "Black Elijah" of West Africa*, abridged by Jocelyn Murray, (Leiden, 1994); and Kimbangu (of a large literature, see especially Marie-Louise Martin, *Kimbangu: An African Prophet and His Church* (Oxford, 1975). On Oppon(g), see G. M. Haliburton. "The Calling of a Prophet, Sampson Oppong," *Bulletin of the Society for African Church History* 2 (1965): 84–96. On Braide, see H. W. Turner, "Prophets and Politics: A Nigerian Test Case," *Bulletin of the Society for African Church History* 2 (1965): 97–118; and G. O. M. Tasie, *Christian Missionary Enterprises in the Niger Delta 1864–1918* (Leiden, 1978). The Livingstonia incident is described by T. Jack Thompson, "An Independent Church Which Never Was: The Case of Jonathan Chirwa," in Andrew Walls and W. Shenk, eds. *Exploring New Religious Movements: Essays in Honour of Harold W. Turner* (Elkhart, Ind., 1990), 107–18.

nation-state often preceded and hastened the decolonisation of church structures. There was very little time, therefore, for independent church and independent state to work out a relationship. Adrian Hastings, writing in the 1970s of the first quarter period up to 1975, notes the passivity of the churches in the face of government, the lack of a prophetic ministry, and attributes it to the absence of any such tradition under missionary direction and in the colonial period.

Since 1980 this situation has changed out of recognition. It started in Ghana, the first postcolonial state, when the Ghana Christian Council began to protest, first on religious issues, such as ritual libation, and then moved against injustices inflicted on individuals and groups. The position developed further when the government of the First Republic patently failed to co-opt the churches into its mechanisms that were meant to embrace the whole of society. More recently it has happened in many countries that churches have been left as the only functioning national corporate entities outside the government sector. This position has given them, in situations as different as Benin and Zambia, the responsibility of filling the vacuum when government has broken down, and of taking the nation on to the next stage. Something like that occurred in South Africa, where the churches became for a time the only legal opposition to government, and thereafter helped to facilitate constructive encounter. Nelson Mandela's first public statement after his release was made in Archbishop Tutu's garden. It is a situation reminiscent of that described in Europe by writers like Gregory of Tours; when the organs of the Roman state collapsed, there was nothing left but the church by which any civil society could operate. As for passivity, it was among the revival-influenced bishops of Uganda, whose own piety had forsworn all worldly entanglement, including politics, that resistance to Amin eventually developed; and Janani Luwum paid with his life.

It is instructive that we have to go back well over a millennium to find even a remote parallel in Western Christian experience to the present situation of church and state in Africa. The existing theologies of the state, cast out of Western experience, are now likely to be of very limited use or relevance. There is a high vocation for African theology, a theology of the state for the twenty-first century. Like all real theology, it will have to be lived as well as written.[9]

---

[9]On the decolonisation period, see Adrian Hastings, *History of Christianity in Africa 1950–1975* (Cambridge, 1979). Among published accounts of Ghana's story, see John S. Pobee, *Religion and Politics in Ghana* (Accra, 1991). On the churches in the "second revolution" leading to the democratization process, see Paul Gifford, ed., *The Christian Churches and the Democratisation of Africa* (Leiden, 1995). On South Africa, see John W. De Gruchy, *The Church-struggle in South Africa,* 2nd ed. (London, 1986). On Archbishop Luwum and his death, see Margaret Ford, *Janani: The Making of a Martyr* (London, 1978).

Africa and the State

The last two centuries or so have seen a multiplication in the forms of the state. The *traditional state* varied greatly in scale and organisation, but its essential cement was a sense of kinship, of shared ancestry. There are plenty of examples of large-scale state building, whether by conquest and absorption, or by consolidation for survival and growth. The Portuguese early met, and marvelled at, Monomotapa. Shaka, by skilfully developing military techniques and training and tight organisation, created the Zulu nation, incorporating conquered and displaced peoples into what had been a relatively small section of the Nguni. A decade after Shaka's death, and thousands of miles from Shaka's empire, the missionary T. B. Freeman was gazing in amazement at the quantity of gold on display at the court of the Asantehene in Kumasi. Meanwhile, Moshoeshoe, himself the son of only a minor chief, was building a new nation—to survive in essentials to this day as the kingdom of Lesotho—from refugees and leftovers from a time of endemic war, and making use of Christian missionaries for the purpose.

This is not to say that the large-scale state is the African norm; in most of the continent most of the time, the units were relatively small, based on kinship (regulated kinship, solidified by accepted patterns in which marriage alliances can take place) and territory, and reflecting a great variety of political institutions.

Across the West African grasslands and on a stretch of the East African coast, there is a long history of the *Islamic state*. Sometimes, this emerged gradually, almost imperceptibly, out of the traditional state, as the royal house and aristocracy adopted Islam, the teaching of resident Muslim clerics took root, and the peasantry adopted Islamic institutions into their mode of life. But the eighteenth century brought a turning point in the great Islamic revival associated with Sheikh 'Uthman dan Fodio. The crucial event in the revival was the unleashing of the Sword of Truth—the decision to require complete obedience to Islamic norms, which meant waging holy war on nominally Muslim rulers who were compromising with African traditional cult. If this did not produce purity of devotion in obedience to the will of Allah (and 'Uthman died bitterly disappointed at the fruits of the revival), it did produce the Fulani Empire, with its distinct emirates, incorporating various traditional states and many non-Muslim peoples. It also gave a new significance and wide currency to the Hausa language; and it locked West African savannahs into a religio-cultural system that not only crossed the Sahara and took Arabia as a cosmic centre, but also stretched unbroken from the Atlantic to the Red Sea. It seems almost comic that when British troops approached a certain town in what is now northern Nigeria, the threatened town raised the *Turkish* flag; but the gesture, however ineffective, was not an idle one. To acknowledge the caliph, the Prophet's deputy on earth, showed that a West African grassland state could define its identity in Islamic terms over against the Christian invader. In the last resort, the Islamic revival of which 'Uthman's jihads are a part is more significant for the future of Islam in Africa than the fact that in Zanzibar, East Africa had its own sultanate, originating from Arab presence, that in the Sudan in the late nineteenth century a claimant of the anointed office of Mahdi could so long and so spectacularly defy both a Muslim government and a Western military presence.

In the course of the nineteenth century, both the traditional and the Islamic state gave way to a new creation, the *Western colonial state*. In 1800, Europe knew little about Africa, and cared less; by 1880, Europe cared intensely, and by 1910, the entire continent, except for Ethiopia and Liberia (and they, too, had their predators) was divided by agreement between Britain, France, Germany, Belgium, Portugal, Italy, and Spain. The process can be traced through the volumes of Sir Edward Hertslet's *The Map of Africa by Treaty*. The title is eloquent; the boundaries of African states were determined outside Africa, on the basis of the perceived interests of European powers. The colonial period represents a very short interlude in the history of Africa, but its creation of a new type of state is a landmark in that history. The map of Africa is still in essentials the final draft of that "map of Africa by treaty" produced between about 1880 and the First World War by the jostling of a handful of European powers enforced locally by the possession of technologically based firepower.

The Islamic state, although it collided with both British and French colonial expansion, survived the transformation much better than did the traditional state. In Nigeria, the British maintained the emirates as the structures through which to rule, even though so much of the population was not Muslim. As a result, Islam spread far more effectively under colonial rule than it had ever done under the jihads. In general, the colonial powers were careful about Islamic sensibilities and did their best to avoid provocation, not least by damping down Christian missionary activity.

The traditional state faced greater problems. The new state boundaries usually took little account of ethnic considerations, or the special "belongingness" of African societies. In the case of the larger-scale traditional states, where these were a threat to the colonial state, as in the case of the Zulu, they were broken up; others like the Basuto kingdom survived as entities by accommodating the colonial power. Quite often, especially in British territories, the traditional state was retained as part of the mechanism of rule, but in attenuated form. Rulers were subject to deposition from outside, legal decisions were subject to review, and above all, the states were incorporated into wider administrative units that brought together diverse peoples who recognised neither kinship nor common interest. (Rulers like Shaka, had, of course, done the same.) There were painful reconstructions; acephalous communities were an anomaly for administrators, who created chiefs for peoples (such as the Kikuyu of Kenya) who had never had them before. Not uncommonly, colonial fiscal structures forced people into the cash economy, and to wage labour in particular, thus altering the patterns of working the land; or they demanded forced labour. (The main argument in the West against colonies had always been that they were expensive; colonial budgets accordingly were always tight, and administration was supposed to be as far as possible self-financing.) In certain parts of eastern, central and southern Africa, white agricultural settlement involved large-scale expropriation, producing landless labouring populations. The establishment of mining and industrial complexes in Southern Africa in the last quarter of the nineteenth century set up a magnet to draw population over huge areas and across state boundaries—often a male population, leaving families in the traditional areas with the traditional modes of production now no longer operable.

The missions, irrespective of their national origin, became part of the colonial state. It could not be otherwise. When power manifestly lay with whites, there was little point in distinguishing one set of white people from another. In fact, the missions had an important place in the colonial state, for they provided a high proportion of the educational and medical infrastructure. The missions were thus major agents in producing in Africa the organs of the modern state, with literacy, technology, and technologically based communications. They did so remarkably cheaply (an important factor with the constrained colonial budgets), and, on the whole, efficiently.

But if missions brought the modern world to Africa, they also offered African populations the hope of being able to cope with that world, and with the more traumatic aspects of the colonial state; and some hope of access to the baffling power concentrated in white hands. The point is forcefully made in an autobiographical aside from Jomo Kenyatta, Kenya's first president. He is writing of his boyhood, about 1907:

> I used to see tribal policemen coming to visit my father who was some kind of chief. . . . They would bring a letter pinned on a stick and after the letter had been read, I would see young people arrested . . . and sent to work for European settlers. . . .
>
> I thought, "Well, this is strange. How is it that these people bring the paper and then say that the European said so and so from Kiambu?" After they had gone I would look at the letter and listen to it and I would not hear it talking. . . . And this created in me a desire for knowledge, and I said to myself, "I must go to Thogoto to discover this miracle, how it is that a paper can talk from one who wrote it to someone else."

Thogoto was the Scottish mission. The young men who wanted to cope with the institutions of foreign rule (and ultimately to subvert and replace them) recognised that the key to the process lay with the Christian missions. A rising generation coped with life by learning to read, and that process could not be readily separated from the Christian faith. There are numbers of African languages where the word "to read" is the same as the word for "to become an inquirer, or Christian catechumen." Reading meant reading the Bible, usually the first vernacular literature available, and a vital element also even when English was the mode of instruction. The Bible, Christian teaching, and a framework that enabled the spreading of ideas through literacy provided a new world of ideas, and one to which the traditional state was not so much inimical as irrelevant.

There were other factors, too, that increased in importance as African churches developed. Like the colonial administration, church administration might bring together communities who did not recognise any traditional mutual "belongingness"; unlike the colonial state, it grounded the link in a new form of bonding, the "belongingness" of shared Christian allegiance. Church organisation also formed functioning communities that were outside both the colonial and the traditional state. Churches were also communities in which Africans could exercise leadership and have access to power and responsibility in ways not open to them elsewhere in the colonial state and not welcome in the residual traditional state. The values of the latter were increasingly conservative and its attitudes increasingly defensive. The traditional state by now posed no possible threat to the colonial state; the threat came from the climate of ideas spread far and wide through the Christian church, with the direct access to the Bible and other sources (sacred and secular), and the patterns of organisation and leadership reflected in the churches.[10]

The Nation-State

We cannot here consider the perceptions, developed following the First World War, that colonial powers were trustees acting for the benefit of the inhabitants of their colonies, and that self-government was the ultimate aim for colonies; nor the processes following the Second World War that caused all the European powers with varying degrees of alacrity or reluctance to abandon all their African colonies in little more than two decades. (Portugal, first in, was last out.) Nor can we consider the ideas

---

[10]On Shaka and the Zulu kingdom, see inter alia, Leonard Thompson, *History of South Africa* (New Haven, 1990), ch. 3. Freeman's journals have been republished: *Journals of Visits to the Kingdoms of Ashanti, Aku and Dahomi* (London, 1968). On Mosheshoe, see Thompson, *Survival in Two Worlds*. On the West African Islamic states, see J. S. Trimingham, *History of Islam in West Africa* (London, 1962). On 'Uthman dan Fodio, see Mervyn Hiskett, *The Sword of Truth: The Life and Times of the Shehu Usuman dan Fodio* (New York, 1973). On the modern outcome, see Lamin Sanneh's works cited in n. 14. Hertslet's *The Map of Africa by Treaty* was first published in London in 1894; the third edition appeared in 1909. Kenyatta tells his story in *Facing Mount Kenya* (London, 1938). Forceful use is made of the passage quoted in R. Macpherson, *The Presbyterian Church in Kenya*.

and activities that took shape in the movements for national independence and cultural renaissance in the various African colonies. We must, however, consider the outcome of these forces: *the African nation-state*.

The nineteenth century began the organisation of the world into nation-states. The redrawing of the map of Europe after World War I made it the norm; the creation of a world assembly of nation-states following each of the global conflicts of the twentieth century canonised it. And so, beginning in 1957, more than forty new African nation-states joined Ethiopia and Liberia at the United Nations table.

All the states were colonial constructs, inheriting colonial boundaries and colonial administrative divisions. They used the colonial languages— English, French, or Portuguese. They inherited the amalgamations and the divisions of ethnic groups that colonial rule had produced. The largest, Nigeria, had more linguistic, cultural, historical, and religious diversity than the whole of Europe put together: 250 language groups, several main culture areas, former Islamic states, and other communities with vigorous Christian traditions. The new states had to foster and channel a "national" consciousness transcending all nearer loyalties if they were to survive; and they had to do so while retaining the sense of kinship and "belongingness" of their various internal communities.

But neither the traditional nor the colonial state provided much rootage for *national* consciousness. The traditional state was about kinship and shared origin; the colonial state was about management and administration. Most states took over Western parliamentary institutions as part of nationhood (a few preferred eastern European style "people's democracy"), but the soil for these in the colonial period was shallow. Ironically, it was the traditional state that often had "democratic" institutions, indigenous mechanisms for securing consensus and for checking arbitrary use of power. But little use was made of these in national constitutions, and the traditional state could not readily be accommodated to the new forms of nationality.

The principal motor of the idea of nationality had been opposition to colonialism. In the quest for self-determination, in which people from various ethnic groups combined, nationality provided a platform on which all could unite; and the arena in which progress to self-determination could be measured was that of the processes and institutions that whites controlled. These lay in government, the civil service, education, finance; and it was the colonial state that provided the framework for these. True, in the nineteenth century, African aspirations were expressed in a form of pan-Africanism, with an ideal of "African" citizenship; and this stream, constantly fed from African American and Caribbean sources, has never dried up. But in terms of practical politics, it became manifest after the Second World War that the attainable target was the development of national movements in particular colonial territories, issuing in the independence of these territories.

In the emergence of these national movements, and in the subsequent erection of the African nation-states, the Christian faith had a vital influence. This was by no means always as a result of deliberate acts of the churches, still less of mission strategy. The movements depended on an elite leadership who could take on foreign pretensions in terms of the foreigners' own standards, values, and arguments, who would play the foreigners at their own game. The new states also required for their government and administration people of modern education who could make a mark in international discourse. In both respects the most likely sources were what had once been called "mission schools"—for their ethos and ideals as well as for the quality of their formal teaching.

Further, as we have seen, in the churches Africans first took leadership and managed modern institutions before such experience was widely accessible elsewhere in the colonial state. Above all, the Bible was read, and Christian teaching appropriated, and the precepts and practices of Europeans (and of missionaries) judged in this light. Christian teaching rings in the thoughts and utterances of the first generation of the leaders of the African nation-state, even those (such as Kwame Nkrumah, once a candidate for the Catholic priesthood, later the holder of a B.D. degree) who separated from the Christian church. Some steadily (Margai) or ostentatiously (Banda) identified with the particular church that had helped to form them; some (Kaunda) explicitly drew on Christian resources in enunciating a nation-building philosophy; others (Kenyatta, Azikiwe) either identified with different religious strands in turn or assumed a position above ecclesiastical differentiation, making constantly clear their acknowledgement of the potential significance of the Christian church. And large numbers of the activists of independence, the people who supplied the motive power, were Christians active in their churches. A disgruntled white resident justifiably complained, as Zambia achieved independence, "It's all the fault of the [expletive deleted] church." And certainly, whatever may have been the position earlier, once independence was clearly on the horizon, the churches seriously and self-consciously assumed for themselves a "nation building" role.

Further, as the new states were born, the churches became national institutions themselves, often with a new name and constitution to prove it. We have seen that the new states were political constructs of colonialism; they were also economic constructs of colonialism. As colonies, they had been run with modest infrastructure with an eye to avoiding expense. Externally, their trading relations had been conceived in imperial terms as part of the economy of the ruling power. (I recall a distinguished British agriculturalist describing two phases of his professional career. He had been sent to colonial Uganda to develop cotton for the sake of Lancashire. He had gone to independent Uganda for the very different task of developing it for the sake of Uganda.) Some were tightly geared to particular markets. (The possibilities of expanding cocoa drinking are finite; and when the New York cocoa market wobbled, Ghana did also.) Some had wasting assets (Sierra Leone's iron ore ran down, and new factory fibres made its piassava useless). Nigeria was unusual in having such a flexible economic counter as oil; if it wasted its opportunities, it perhaps did no worse than Britain did in the same circumstances with the same resource.[11]

The Cultural Renaissance

As nation-states, the African nations belonged to the world of modernity. The colonial state had been the matrix of modernity, with Christian missions as the midwife. But the very quest for African self-determination, made in the face of colonialism, awakened African self-consciousness. The basis for self-determination was, after all, the value (the God-given value, Christians asserted) of being African. But we are what we are because of our past; and to make a positive statement about African identity is to imply a positive statement about the African past. Along with the forces that brought the African nation-state to birth came an awakened sense of the importance of roots, of African history, of African arts, of traditional values. And this was most intense among the educated elite, who once, as the cheerleaders of modernity, had denied or denigrated so many aspects of the African heritage.

The living guardians of traditional culture were those associated with the residual traditional state, including those who had most effectively resisted the encroachments of modernity. Ritually, the traditional state was particularly important. (A not uncommon Ghanaian phenomenon is the traditional kingdom where virtually the whole population regards itself as Christian, except for the royal house and the associated priesthood. The king's relations with the church may be friendly and cooperative, but his ritual functions, necessary for the continuance of the state, debar him from baptism.) But politically, strengthening the traditional state was incompatible with strengthening nationality and central government; nor could the national state afford to lose hold of modernity. In Ghana, Kwame Nkrumah (a particularly eloquent exponent of the riches of

---

[11]On the state in Africa, see the bibliography in R. Buitenhuijs and Elly Rejnierse, *The Democratisation in Sub-Saharan Africa 1889–1992,* (Leiden, 1993), which has a section on the churches. See also Jean-François Bayart, *The State in Africa* (London, 1993), and Mahmood Mamdani, *Citizen and Subject: Contemporary Africa and the Legacy of Late Colonialism* (Princeton, N.J., 1996); and also Paul Gifford, *Christian Churches,* and now his *Christianity in Africa: Its Public Role* (London, 1998). On the nineteenth-century pan-Africanism, see the works of J. A. B. Horton, James Johnson, and E. W. Blyden. For its political aspect, see R. W. July, *The Origins of Modern African Thought* (London, 1968). Its religious aspect has not yet been studied enough. See, however, E. A. Ayandele, *Holy Johnson: Pioneer of African Nationalism, 1836–1917* (London, 1970); and Jehu J. Hanciles, "The Legacy of James Johnson," *International Bulletin of Missionary Research* 21 (1997): 162–67.

African culture) became engaged in intense conflict with the traditional states incorporated within the nation. The same happened in Uganda under Obote. The African state has simultaneously to accommodate modernity and to affirm African culture, and to espouse the latter without giving such rein to the local, territorial expressions of African culture that they disrupt national consciousness. National consciousness requires apprehension of African culture in terms that different ethnic groups can share: the assumptions and experiences that all citizens have in common.

The churches had been wrestling with a parallel question, and were doing so before the charge against the missionaries of denigrating or destroying African culture became as widespread as it has since become. When African churches were two or three generations old, the question invariably arose of the relation of Christian faith to the African past. It arose in acute form in the independence generation, when the necessity to be fully Christian and fully African was so obvious. What was God doing in Africa over all those centuries before missionaries came? Kwame Bediako, in his splendid book *Theology and Identity*, shows how similar are the quests of African theologians in this period to the struggles of the Greek theologians of the early church, and how similar are some of their conclusions too. Christian theology in Africa cannot escape the ancestors any more than political science can.[12]

Things Fall Apart

The more dismal side of the African nation-state need hardly be rehearsed. Anyone who watched the flag of a new nation go up for the first time (and perhaps prayed to be a faithful, profitable servant of that nation) will recall how moving it all was, and the euphoria and the purposiveness of those days. "Bliss was it in that dawn to be alive, but to be young was very heaven." And in general, the new nations met at first with international goodwill. (There were nasty exceptions, such as the brutality of the French withdrawal in Guinea, and international perplexities, as when the former Belgian Congo descended into chaos and the long, painful gestation of Zimbabwe.) But the goodwill did not cost much, and the honeymoon was short. Parliamentary institutions were rarely successful; some rulers declared them unsuitable for Africa and devised new structures to entrench their own power. Disillusionment with the elite leadership developed into cynicism about the whole political process that the elite represented. In nation after nation the military took over (often to popular relief and acclaim) only to fall victim to the same vices as the politicians.

---

[12]On the whole background of this section, see Kwame Bediako, *Theology and Identity: The Impact of Culture upon Christian Thought in the Second Century and in Modern Africa* (Oxford, 1992), and *Christianity in Africa: The Renewal of a Non-Western Religion* (Edinburgh and New York, 1995).

Nor did the early international goodwill lead anywhere. Though the Cold War sometimes gave the states the power of playing off one foreign power against another, the Eastern bloc countries proved unreliable aid partners for anything other than military hardware, while Western development aid schemes usually benefited the donors, the already wealthy, or nobody at all. In the international trade game, African nations were caught in forces they could not control. Crippled by foreign debt, they became net contributors to, not gainers from, the Western economies. Foreign diagnosis (physician, heal thyself) sagely recommended to the ailing economies remedies that could be enforced only by harsh repression and widespread suffering. To the crisis of rising expectations that had begun at independence was added the crisis of rising population; within twenty years of independence, states often had half their population under twenty, and all wanting education and employment, while the infrastructure of the postindependence years crumbled away. Natural disaster—drought, desertification, crop failure—was compounded by human disaster in wars of long duration and high ferocity. The majority of the world's refugees are Africans.

There are a few additional things to be said about this miserable catalogue. One is that in the light of it, the African nation-state has been surprisingly resilient. One might think that most African nations would be of eggshell fragility if only because of their ethnic composition. There were two early attempts at secession, Katanga from Zaire, Biafra from Nigeria. Each had one major economic resource and each might have made a viable state; but each failed, and failed in blood. The prospect of endless division and subdivision that secession conjures up has generally been too much for Africa to contemplate, and the colonial constructs have survived. Nor has interstate aggression been rife. Few nations anywhere had less basis for a national future than had The Gambia, especially after its internal collapse. One might expect it to have been absorbed into Senegal with hardly a murmur from the world. In fact, the Senegalese embrace was loosened well before the point of suffocation. Boundary disputes between African states have been rare; and African leaders have been restrained from fishing in their neighbours' ponds by the knowledge of how vulnerable to poaching their own ponds would be.

The second comment relates to the continuing development of Africanness, the sense of shared experience and assumptions that is part of belonging to Africa. We have seen this recognition of commonalty transcending ethnic kinship and local territory to be necessary to the nation-state. It has been recognised also as having an international dimension. Its political expression is the Africa-wide assembly of states, the Organisation of African Unity. The OAU suffers from the weaknesses of all such international bodies, compounded by the massive resource problems facing its members and the division between Anglophone and Francophone nations that reflects the colonial heritage. The interventions in African trouble spots have been few, and controversy about them is inevitable. Nevertheless, compared with international interventions elsewhere in the world involving larger and richer powers, the OAU record is enviable.

The Post-Nation-State?

One further question cannot be avoided. Granted the resilience of the nation-state in Africa, are there already signs of the *post-nation-state*?

If there are such signs, they appear at present most clearly in the Horn of Africa. Ethiopia, itself an empire that absorbed other states, also absorbed former colonial territory after the Second World War. In recent years it has proved a partial exception to the no-secession rule in Africa; the Eritrean and Tigre movements appear to have made their point, and the area to have reached equilibrium. At the time of this writing, the position of the Somali coast (including the forgotten Somaliland and Djibouti as well as the publicised Somalia) is much less clear. It is conceivable that, in Somalia at least, the basis of the nation-state may have ceased to exist, or is about to do so. All the available models of government have been tried; sometimes Western, sometimes Eastern, bloc influence has dominated; nothing has worked, nothing had any widespread basis of acceptance. Meanwhile, in the southern Sudan, an appalling war that has seen genocide committed on Christian peoples and has uprooted whole populations, takes on a tragic new dimension. No longer is it essentially about African, non-Arab, non-Islamic identity; it is also an inter-African conflict. What is undoubted, however, is that there are substantial areas of a large African country where the writ of the national government does not and cannot run. In recent years both Liberia and Sierra Leone lost the apparatus of a normal nation-state for a substantial period.

Perhaps we should be prepared to envisage the possible end of the world system of nation-states. It is not only in Africa that the tinder is present; the former Soviet Union and the Balkans have it in abundance. Large-scale foreign intervention (in effect, recolonisation) is unlikely; the West has already decided that Africa (even South Africa, to judge by recent signs) is not worth the candle.[13]

The results of the Somalia intervention have hardly been encouraging, and the world has averted its eyes from the Sudan for two decades past. But Eritrea and Somaliland, and even, for all their suffering, the areas of Sudan outside government control, demonstrate that African indigenous structures still exist, or can come into being, to support life outside the nation-state. In the light of eternity, the nation-state has no more ultimate significance than the Roman Empire, or the Assyrian.

---

[13]This was written before the visit of President Clinton of the U.S. to several African countries in 1998, which accompanied other signs of reawakening Western commercial interest in Africa; but I see no reason to alter the thrust of the argument.

Africa, the Cold War, and After

It would be idle to assume that the only geopolitical factors operating in Africa since independence have been those of the trade cycle and the African nations themselves. After decolonisation the Western presence was internationalised, with America to the fore. The new-style development experts and the new-style volunteers were new types of expatriate. In the Cold War, each side sought friends, allies, and surrogates. The present sufferings of Somalia are an indirect result. Namibian independence was deferred for years, and South African activity there and in Angola was entrenched by a U.S. policy initiative to get at Cuba by means of Angola. One of the most dramatic results of the end of the Cold War has been in South Africa. Government intransigence there was held in place by the fear of international communism; when such a threat no longer seemed realistic, there was nothing to do but to seek a settlement with the wider population.

Between Asia and the West

Africa stands between the Asian and the Western systems, and interacts with both. The principal influence from Asia has been Islamic. The Islamic impact on Africa began soon after the Prophet's death. It issued in the eclipse of Christianity in Egypt and North Africa, very heartlands of the Christian faith. It crossed the Sahara (which Christianity never did) and steadily penetrated the West Africa grasslands. It established itself on the east coast with brisk trade with Arabia and India, and a sultanate in Zanzibar that claimed to administer much of the hinterland.

One effect of the Islamic cycle of influence has been to pull the trading and cultural links of a good part of the continent northwards. It is never possible to ignore Arab Africa; too much of sub-Saharan Africa is involved in it. But much of Africa is also pulled towards the heart of the Islamic world. For a thousand years and more, African pilgrims have performed the haj at Mecca, and it is now big business for the airlines. The links with the Islamic world have made substantial financial investment possible by the combination of oil prices and international Islamic awareness. Much of this has gone into specifically Islamic institutions. Gabarone, the capital of Botswana, has a magnificent mosque from foreign money, though the Muslim community is tiny and mostly foreign. International Muslim consciousness draws African states into one or other of the networks of Islamic nations. For those African states that combine Islamic and non-Islamic communities (Nigeria, Sudan), the potential is explosive. But there are flashpoints also in countries where Muslims are a minority; part of the story of Idi Amin lies in the feelings of grievance among Ugandan Muslims of their long-standing disadvantage in a Christian dominated society.

Nor should we underestimate the appeal of the preaching of Islam, the sense of Islamic kinship, and the ideal of the Islamic state where justice is performed according to the way of God. For many poor, downtrodden people, helpless against outside forces, surrounded by corruption, and the conspicuous consumption of the wealthy, the ugly face of the Western world in the midst, the call to radical obedience to Allah brings the stirring hope of a better day that Marxism once evoked.[14]

In thinking of Asian influences, one cannot forget the long-standing Indian communities (some, but not all, Muslim) in East and South Africa. Nor should we forget the Pacific Rim countries, which have the capacity, should they develop the desire, to alter the whole pattern of African trading relations. And one, Korea, has already significantly entered the Christian missionary enterprise in Africa.

The Western cycle of influence is much later than the Asian, and has been less consistent. Its general effect has been to bring Africa into the "world" economy as envisaged in the West. Whether the results have been for Africa's weal or woe is for judgment. But the Christian story, as we have seen, antedates the beginning of Western interest; and at the start of the third millennium we view the surprising fact that Africa is one of the world's Christian heartlands, with the faith in the West in apparent recession.

What of the Future?

The concern of this chapter is with history, not prophecy. The Maori people of New Zealand speak of the future as being behind us—we cannot see it, even the part that is closest to where we are. It is the *past* that is stretched out before us, the furthest dimly visible, the closest at our feet. That seems to me quite a useful way of thinking about history and the historical process. While bearing that in mind, there may still be some things we can reasonably expect in the future, some as near certainties, others as local possibilities, and some things that fall in the category of "What if . . . ?"

First, we can be certain that there will be no exemption from the principalities and powers who work in and through every human society. Caiaphas and Pilate were pretty run-of-the-mill politicians, their actions shaped by such considerations as normally move politicians. The principalities and powers operate at the level of the nation-state, but they operate also at every level of human organisation. The principalities and powers will be at work among the multinational companies and the finance

---

[14]On the position of Christians and Muslims in modern Africa, see the works by Lamin Sanneh, *Piety and Power: Muslims and Christians in West Africa* (Maryknoll, N.Y. 1996), and *The Crown and the Turban: Muslims in West African Pluralism* (Boulder, Colo., 1997).

houses, who hold powers that no state can control; foreign exchange deal-
ers in half a dozen markets can bring the most powerful government to its
knees within days. They will be at work in the suprastate organisations,
whether the Economic Community of West African States or the European
Union; they will be at work in every level of ethnicity and nationality.

Our existing theologies of church and state were carved out of the experience of Western Christendom, and were never meant to deal with
anything as complicated as the networks of political and economic structures that will characterise the twenty-first century. I suspect there will be
a special responsibility lying upon African theologians for constructing
the new theologies of the political and economic realm that we need. One
reason is simply that the situations that theology must address are starker
and more convulsive in Africa than elsewhere. African Christian theology
has not only to face the problem of the Rwanda genocide, but also to
grasp why it happened in a country with one of the highest proportions of
Christian profession in the continent. African Christianity has daily experience of famine, drought, war, displacement of populations, of a scourge
like AIDS not as a problem of marginal people but as a pandemic affecting
populations; and because African Christianity experiences these, African
Christian theology needs to confront them. And in the great puzzles sur-
rounding national or ethnic identity, Africans have more experience than
most of the complexities that arise from the different levels of identity, of
village, clan, people, and nation. One might add that African Christians
have had more experience than most in wrestling with such problems
through experiencing them, and in measure resolving them, in the life of
the church. And in their knowledge of African realities, the realities of
most of the poor in all the continents, they have materials for evolving a
theology for the World Bank—indeed, perhaps a theology of banking—
that the whole world needs.

All these things will involve taking a theology of the state to further
and deeper reaches than it has seen before. And any theology that takes
principalities and powers seriously must also take seriously what the
New Testament says of them; they have been defeated by Christ's death
and resurrection; they are dragged behind the triumphal chariot of the
cross.

Second, this chapter has raised the possibilities of the passing away, in
some parts of the world, of the familiar apparatus of the nation-state, that
in one or two areas of Africa this may already be happening. We have also
seen over the past decade a succession of instances where in a time of national crisis, when, for instance, a long entrenched dictator fell from power,
the churches or church leaders were called on to provide leadership
through a period of transition. The reason for this, at least in some cases,
must surely be that no other form of civil society was still functioning.

In this case, there is historical precedent. When the Western Roman
Empire collapsed before the peoples the Romans called barbarians, the

whole framework of imperial organisation collapsed in centre after centre. All that was left as a functioning society was the Christian church, now uprooted from the political structure in which it had been so much at home. It was the church that eased the transition for some of the peoples of western Europe into the post-Roman polity of the barbarian kingdoms.

Such a function implies a church that can credibly demonstrate a working model of a desirable society. The mind turns to the picture in the Epistle to the Ephesians of two peoples fused into one, the middle wall of partition broken down, and the full stature of Christ's humanity attained only when both inheritances, Jewish and Greek, were brought into him. The period when this reflected a historic reality was a very brief one. The earliest church knew nothing of it, because it was a Jewish ethnic church. The second-century church knew nothing of it either, since by that time Christians were as overwhelmingly Greek as once they had been overwhelmingly Jewish. But, just for a time, first in Antioch and then in other places, a new variegated society was formed that combined both traditions. This would once have been a symbol of separation, for the two races did not eat together. Now, the table united them, and made them distinctive. A theology like that, embodied in a credible praxis, would be a beacon to Africa. But if Christians cannot produce a working model in the church, how much have they to say to the wider society?

Third, is there still stimulus and inspiration to be found in the vision of Africa of the liberationist phase of Christian mission in the middle of the nineteenth century? The vision articulated by T.F. Buxton and exemplified in a succession of African leaders, including Crowther, James Johnson, and many others, used two lenses. One showed Africa as it was—spoiled, exploited, and oppressed. The other showed Africa redeemed, as redeemed by calling out its own resources. Those resources were both economic and human; it was Christian Africans who would bring transformation to African society, a transformation springing from the understanding of the gospel. The Africans who responded to this vision had a pan-African consciousness; they saw the continent enjoying the gospel and all its fruits and taking its proper place with dignity among the nations. If their vision has anything for us today, perhaps we should remember that they saw Afro-America as part of Africa. I do not suggest that this implies what they first thought of, the return to Africa of many then in America; but it may remind us that all the ills of Africa will not be cured, nor all its resources drawn forth, if no note is taken of Afro-America.[15]

---

[15]On the general background here, compare Christopher Fyfe and Andrew Walls, eds., *African Christianity in the 1990s* (Edinburgh, 1996), and *The History of the Expansion of Christianity Reconsidered* (New Haven, 1996).

Finally, what if the gloomy prognosis of some conflict analysts is fulfilled, and the main concern of the principalities and powers in the coming century becomes to defend the lifestyles of the economically prosperous against the economically powerless? Here are words of the Harvard historian Paul Rogers:

> The main security parameters are more likely to be the deep divisions of wealth and poverty across the world, coupled with increasingly dominant global environmental constraints on economic activity and human well-being. Among the end results will be increased migratory pressures, conflict over the control of resources and markets, and violent responses from the dispossessed.
>
> Western military strategists are now steadily reorientating their outlook towards such a world—one polarised more by economic contrasts than by ideology. With this scenario, it will be all too easy to perceive (and justify) the comfortable lifestyles of the global elites as representing civilisation, complete with their own new warrior class (UN peacekeepers, perhaps) protecting them from the barbarians at the gate.

Translated into religious terms, bearing in mind the demographic shift in Christian profession, this would mean that the levers of global economic power would be located in the post-Christian West and East Asia, and will be employed effectively to keep people out. And the Christian faith will be the religion of the relatively and the absolutely poor, centred in the poorest parts of the world, and this would condition the theology and the practice of the Christian church.

Perhaps the proper response comes in the poem, long ago published by the Lovedale Mission Press, that has become the national anthem of the new South Africa:

> Nkosi sikelel' i Afrika : God bless Africa
> Makube njalo. : May it be so for ever.

6

African Christianity in the History
of Religions

In the history of religions, African Christianity appears in two capacities: first, as a new period in the history of African religion, continuing the story begun in the "primal" or "traditional" religions; and second, as a new period in the history of Christianity in which the Christian tradition is being expressed in intellectual, social, and religious milieux that it has not previously entered. If the present chapter is concerned principally with the first aspect, it is with no intention of undervaluing the second, the extent to which African Christianity represents a new chapter in Christian history. Both aspects, the African and the Christian, are essential to its identity. Problems arise only when we use the terms "African religion" and "Christianity" as though they were self-contained, self-explanatory alternative systems, adopted as a whole or abandoned as a whole, like suits of clothes that can be taken off and changed. Actual religious experience, actual lived religion is not like that. There is a case to be made in theory (less easy to demonstrate in practice) for regarding Islam as such a self-contained, self-consistent system; but Christianity, of its incarnational nature, offers no such analysis. It does not make sense to try to separate out from unified experience what is "really" Christian and what is "really" African, as though the identification of one set of aspects somehow invalidates or undermines the other. African Christianity is a new development of African religion, shaped by the parameters of pre-Christian African religion as was the Christianity of the Jerusalem church of the Acts of the Apostles rooted in the religion of old Israel. (I choose that earliest group of Christians advisedly; all subsequent Christian communities have an assured

A Presentation for the African Christianity Project, Centre for the Study of Christianity in the Non-Western World, University of Edinburgh. First published in *Studies in World Christianity* 2 (No. 2, 1996):183–203. Reprinted with permission.

relationship to the Old Testament, but a different one from that of the earliest Christianity.) African Christianity is also a new development of the Christian tradition produced by the interaction of that tradition with the life and lore of Africa, as complex and distinctive in their way as those of the Greco-Roman culture that determined so many of the features of Western Christianity.

Africa and the Demography of Religion

The World Missionary Conference of 1910, held in Edinburgh, was the high-water mark of the missionary movement from the West. It is necessary to recall only two features of that conference to show how huge, and how unpredictable, a degree of religious change has taken place in the ninety years since that conference (*World Missionary Conference* 1910; Hogg 1952: ch. 3).

First, the 1910 conference saw the world as divided between "missionized" and "not yet missionized" areas. The fully missionized areas were, for practical purposes, Europe, North America, Australia, and New Zealand (Latin America was passed over in silence to avoid splitting the conference on the issue of whether Latin America was really Christian). The rest of the world, including the whole of Africa (save for a small section of South Africa), was deemed not yet fully missionized.

Second, as regards the foreseeable future, missionary optimism tended to centre on Asia. It was in Asia that Christianity appeared to have caught the currents of the time, especially in the newly westward-facing China and Japan. It was in Asia that the most striking human products of the missionary process appeared. There was a tier of distinguished Christians from India and China and Japan at the conference itself, and the University of Edinburgh took the opportunity to bestow the appropriate honorary doctorates on some of them; but there was not a single African present. The tendency to look eastward probably also reflected the balance of missionary effort; it had long been the practice to send the missionaries with superior academic or intellectual credentials to India or China, leaving the celestial cannon fodder for Africa. A near contemporary of the World Missionary Conference, with some justification, described medical missions as the heavy artillery of the missionary movement. It is significant that such medical artillery as was used in Africa tended to be rather light and came rather late. Certainly, Western medicine accompanied Christian teaching from the earliest days of Western missions; but Africa saw no equivalent of the medical missionary investment that produced entire medical faculties for the Chinese Empire. The heavy artillery of the missionary movement was deployed in Asia, not in Africa.

Since 1910, not only has the religious situation in Africa changed beyond recognition; there has also been a demographic transformation of the situation of Christianity within the world as a whole. There has been simultaneously a major recession from Christianity and a major accession to it. The recession has been centred in those parts of the world that the World Missionary Conference recognized as fully missionized, so that much of western Europe, for instance, is best described as post-Christian. The accession has been centred in the southern continents and most noticeably in Africa. It is not simply that there has been a massive increase in the number of professing Christians in Africa in the course of the twentieth century; there has been such a degree of change of religious adherence as to alter completely the relative positions of European and African Christianity. In 1910, Europe was part of the Christian heartland, "typically" Christian territory; at the end of the century it was moving towards the Christian margins. The proportion of the world's Christians who are Africans, meanwhile, steadily increases. At the end of the twentieth century Africa was appearing as the Christian heartland (Walls 1976).

The nature of this process was long in coming to notice; generally speaking, not before the years of decolonization. One of the first in the academic world to draw attention to the process of religious change was Roland Oliver in a little paper of 1956 entitled *How Christian Is Africa?* (Oliver 1956). The importance of the topic was signalled a decade later in the conference on Christianity in Tropical Africa, in which Oliver's influence was noticeable, held under the auspices of the International African Institute (Baëta 1968). In the meantime, a series of contributions from David Barrett, notably an article in the *International Review of Mission* for 1970 (Barrett 1970) indicating an expectation of "350 million Christians in Africa by AD 2000," alerted those more directly concerned with the development of world Christianity to its changing centre of gravity. But until recent years specialist studies of the phenomenon of African Christianity did not reflect the importance of the topic. For some time the study of Islam in Africa appeared to have a degree of respectability not accorded to the study of Christianity. Inasfar as African Christianity attracted attention, it tended to be the so-called African independent churches that drew it. (It is interesting to reflect that the fullest account we have of the history and outlook of any body of African Christians is probably still Harold Turner's two-volume study *History of an African Independent Church*, published in 1967.) It was perhaps the thought that these bodies were more "African" than those churches in Africa that acknowledged historic continuity with missionary effort that gave them recognition as a legitimate focus for African studies. If so, this may have obscured an important aspect of the significance of the independent churches: the extent to which they often reflect the concerns, aspirations, and views of large numbers of Christians in the historic churches, and the index that they provide to some of the characteristic features of African Christianity.

A Specifically African Christian History

In other words, the significance of religious change over the past century does not lie solely in the statistical growth of Christianity (or, one may add, of Islam, which has also seen dramatic expansion). It lies also in the nature of the changes and in the developments taking place within African Christianity. There is now a sizable and identifiable African Christian history. This is true not only in the sense of there having been a historic Christian presence in the continent; in that sense Christianity has as long a continuous history in Africa as it has almost anywhere else. But it is also true that there is now a sizable and identifiable *modern* African Christian history, with generations of development, and changing belief systems and organizational structures with different generations displaying different characteristics of those systems and structures.

This gives a double importance to the study of African Christianity. On the one hand, it is an important chapter in the history of Africa, and specifically of African religion. For African Christianity is undoubtedly *African* religion, as developed by Africans and shaped by the concerns and agendas of Africa; it is no pale copy of an institution existing somewhere else. On the other hand, the sorts of development occurring in African Christianity may be important beyond Africa; for instance, as indicating how Christianity itself has been reshaped during the present century. For if the considerations urged here have any validity, and we take the recent accession to Christianity in Africa along with the recent recession from it in the West, African Christianity must be seen as a major component of contemporary *representative* Christianity, the standard Christianity of the present age, a demonstration model of its character. That is, we may need to look at Africa today in order to understand Christianity itself. This is a phenomenon beyond the dreams of the Edinburgh conferees of 1910. Africa can no longer be taken as peripheral to the study of Christianity; it contains too high a proportion of the world's Christians for that. And Africa may be the theatre in which some of the determinative new directions in Christian thought and activity are being taken.

What Has Happened to the Traditional Religions?

Any attempt to survey Christianity in Africa at the turn of this millennium poses the question, What has happened to the traditional religions of Africa in the light of the exponential growth of Christian (and of Islamic) profession in the past century? Clearly, traditional religion has not died out, nor has it been reduced to atavistic or "premodern" enclaves. Nor is it confined to those movements launched every now and again to harness African traditional religion to national consciousness and to the conventions and artefacts of the "modern" world, such as the

Afrikania movement in Ghana.[1] It is my argument that the principal evidence of the ongoing life of traditional African religion lies within
African Christianity. What happens in African Christianity is intelligible
only in the light of what has gone before in the African religious story.
Kwame Bediako picks up the insight of John Mbiti: "Their past is our
present," he says of the ancestors and their religion; and Itumeleng Mos-
ala points out that the roots of so modern a phenomenon as South
African black theology lie in the pre-Christian period. African Christianity is shaped by Africa's past. The continuity of African religious history,
Christian and pre-Christian, with no sharp break in African understandings of relationships with the transcendent world, is cemented in most
parts of Africa by the fact that the Christian God has a vernacular
name—a name in common speech, to indicate the God of Israel and of
the Scriptures. Some of the contemporary academic discussion about the
legitimacy of this process, or its applicability in particular instances,
seems irrelevant; the fact is that the identification has been readily accepted and the consequences are inescapable.

In many instances—over much of West and Southern Africa, for instance—a vernacular name was applied as the indigenous response to
Christian preaching; when missionaries preached the Christian God,
people recognized attributes of Olorun or Ngewo in the missionary
preaching of the Christian God (Sanneh 1989; Bediako 1995). Africans
thus responded to Christian preaching by recognizing God in their
"pre-Christian" past and in their vernacular languages, even where
there was no active cult of the Being named, and where most religious
activity was directed to the ancestors or the local divinities. Among
some East African peoples there was, indeed, no such instant recognition, and the proper choice of term was much more open to doubt. Even
so, a vernacular name was almost invariably chosen. (Among the
Ganda the choice of Katonda seems to have had a remarkable effect,
moving a divinity, certainly associated with creation but marginal to
cult and half-forgotten by most people, into spectacular prominence
[Taylor 1958].) Neither the surprising nature of this feature of African
religious history nor the eventual significance of this identification of
the new with the old in the governance of the universe has perhaps
been fully assessed. There seems to be no historical inevitability about
the process (Walls 1988). The early missionaries had little in their theology to cause them to look for God in African traditional religion. It was

---

[1]The fullest account of Afrikania is probably Samuel Gyanfosu, "The Development of Christian-related Independent Religious Movements in Ghana, with Special Reference to the Afrikania Movement" (Ph.D. diss., University of Leeds, 1995).
Cf. "A Discussion on Afrikania Religion," *Exchange* 13, nos. 37–38 (1984): 98–106.
Cf. H. J. Becken in *Zeitschrift für Mission* 11, no. 4 (1983): 98–106; and Kwame Bediako, *Christianity in Africa: The Renewal of a Non-Western Religion* (Edinburgh, 1995).

certainly possible for them to accommodate any such evidence that turned up; everyone agreed that God "left not himself without witness" (Acts 14:17). But it was not hard to believe that the heathen, "having no hope and without God in the world" (to use a text, Eph. 2:12, equally frequent in occurrence in missionary discourse), might not so much as know the name of God.

Robert Moffat is probably a fair representative of many of his contemporaries—missionary activists of modest theological attainments. Early in his missionary career he concluded that the Tswana had neither God nor religion in the true sense of the words. But as he worked at the translation of the Scriptures into Setswana, the name Modimo forced itself upon his consciousness. God did have a Tswana name; and Moffat found it, not because he was looking for it, but because it was there (Setiloane 1976: esp. ch. 6). Missionary experience in other parts of the world by no means necessarily followed the same pattern. Missionaries in China, for instance, remained grievously divided over the proper names to use for God in Chinese; while in various languages of the Pacific it seems to have been common to use the generic Atua, or some rendering of Jehovah, rather than any vernacular name. One may add that a similar process seems to be generally characteristic of African Islam; African Muslims seem rather reticent of using any vernacular name as equivalent of Allah, and some of the most thoroughly Islamic African peoples no longer recognize any such name. It is Christianity, not Islam, that has struck its roots into the vernacular past. Nor did anything in the Christian experience of the West suggest any easy identification between the God of Christian worship and any entity in the pre-Christian past. In the Mediterranean world, despite the fact that elision of divinities was well established, the Christian God was not identified with Zeus or Jupiter; nor in northern Europe was any identification made with any member of the Celtic or Germanic pantheons. In European Christian history, God came from the outside: God against the gods, the One over against the many. There was little in European experience, therefore, to cause European missionaries to look for the divine name in the pre-Christian past. Yet all over sub-Saharan Africa, by an apparently natural, barely questioned development, the Christian God is known by vernacular names. The relationship between Africa's old religion and its new one is cemented in the conventions of speech. There are implications in this for African theology, for—by contrast with the foundational experiences of Western Christianity—the God of Israel and the Scriptures belongs conceptually to the African past; indeed, as Olorun belongs to the Yoruba, as Ngewo to the Mende past. When Moffat, despite his primary instincts, was forced to recognize that the God he sought to serve was Modimo, the possibility for centuries of interaction between the biblical tradition and Tswana tradition opened up. It is no surprise that so much African theological activity, at both the academic and the practical levels, is devoted to the relationships of the old and the new in African religion.[2]

African Maps of the Universe

The continuity in African religion, pre-Christian and Christian, is due in large measure to continuing worldviews, the application of the material of the Christian tradition to already existing African maps of the universe. It has been the most fruitful single source of misunderstanding of African Christianity that the continuance of such maps somehow makes the resultant practice less Christian. It is true, as we shall see, that the relationships between the components of those maps—God, local divinities, ancestors, objects of power—have changed, and changed radically, as a result of the Christian impact; but as components in understanding the world and society, they remain in one guise or another. In order to have effect in Africa, the Christian tradition has thus had to be applied to these preexisting components; it has been placed on the available maps of the universe, and interpreted within existing categories. Christianity has thus necessarily inherited all the old goals of religion; in particular, the association with protection and with power is undiminished. The operating maps of the universe provide for frequent interventions of the transcendent world in the phenomenal world; for the operation of spiritual forces, whether acting independently or directed by human malice, or indicating neglected familial or social duty. The effectiveness of the Christian faith, or of any particular manifestation of it, is accordingly open to the test of whether it gives access to power and prosperity or protection against natural or spiritual enemies (purposes to which much traditional practice was directed) and satisfactorily enforces familial and social duty.

This has involved a degree of reorientation from the missionary models of Christianity. Missionaries were, generally speaking, children of the European Enlightenment, and their Christianity came adapted to Enlightenment values; indeed, they expected its transplantation to Africa, closely allied as it was to education and modernization, to issue eventually in an Enlightenment universe of discourse in Africa. It has done so, but only partially. The extent to which Africa participates in such discourse certainly reflects the missionary legacy, but the real strength of Christianity in Africa may prove to be its capacity for independence of Enlightenment categories. The independence is seen even in the new forms of charismatic Christianity, which are often skilled in the use of modern communications, and in the background against which they arise.

---

[2]Kwame Bediako, *Theology and Identity: The Impact of Culture upon Christian Thought in the Second Century and in Modern Africa* (Oxford, 1992), draws a parallel between the activity of modern African theologians and the early Christian apologists in this regard.

This background includes a pattern of the recurrence of traditional cult or traditional practice or traditional divination among Christians of the third or even later generations. This is not intended as an act of apostasy from Christianity, but as a fail-safe device for protection against illness or misfortune or spiritual attack. The emergence of new, radical developments within Christianity—seen in different forms in independent or "spiritual" churches, Pentecostal or radical evangelical groups, revival movements and charismatic healers—is part of the same pattern. All oppose traditional practice, but do so in traditional terms, by bringing protection or deliverance into active relationship with the Christian God, and by demonstrating more effective power than that of the traditional practitioner (Hackett 1987, 1990; Ojo 1987; Adubofuor 1994; Smith 1994). The formal parallels to traditional practice, particularly in healing and divination (though given a different rationale and justification), have often enough been remarked, at least in relation to the spiritual churches; but the real continuities between pre-Christian and Christian African religion lie in worldview and perception. It is often said that traditional religion is "this worldly" in orientation, and that African responses to Christianity have been "this worldly" in motivation. Both statements have truth, provided it is not assumed that "this worldly" equates simply to the material-phenomenal universe, as tends to be the case in Western discourse. In an African setting the whole point about "this world" is that it stands at the frontier of human and spiritual activity, and the two are in constant interaction (Okorocha 1987).

To recognize the continuity in African religion in its pre-Christian and its Christian forms is not, however, to say that African religion is substantially unchanged as a result of the Christian impact, that its essential phenomena have simply continued under other names. The Christian period in African religion has brought to it deep-rooted changes. It is convenient to see change in relation to two spheres: the reordering of worldview, and the introduction of new symbols and sources.

The Reordering of African Worldviews

Studies of African traditional religion have conventionally identified four component entities in the understanding of the transcendent: God, divinities (i.e., ruling powers, either of a locality or of a dimension of life), ancestors, and objects of power. Traditional African religious systems vary as to which component is the dominating one; there are God-dominated systems in Africa (especially among the Nilotic peoples), divinity-dominated systems, ancestor-dominated systems. Not all systems have all four components; the Central Luo, for instance, seem to have had no niche at all in their system for God, and the Gikuyu none for divinities or even ancestors (Kirika 1988). Nor were religious systems rigid and immutable. All sorts of forces, from prophetic insight to change of the manner of subsistence or political transformation, could alter the relationships between the components. During Moshoeshoe's long reign, the Sotho moved from an ancestor-dominated to a God-dominated system. This change facilitated the impact of Christianity, but did not originate directly from it; the originating vision was that of the traditional religious reformer Mohlomi (Thompson 1995). With the Zulu, development took another direction; success in building the nation on the basis of a military corps involved a religious reconstruction in which ancestral cult was crucial. Not only might the relationships between the components in the religious system change under the pressure of internal or external forces; they might also look different at different points of community life or ritual, or even differ in different sections of the community. The inadequacy for African religion of the conventional categories of Western philosophy of religion, especially those (like monotheism, polytheism, henotheism, or pantheism) that purport to describe alternative conceptions of the divine, has long been recognized by workers in the field (Parrinder 1970).

God and the Divinities

The widespread adoption of Christianity in Africa, and the equally widespread identification of the God of the Bible with the God component of the traditional universes, have made a substantial difference to African maps of the transcendent world. They are the same maps, marking that busy, constantly crossed frontier of the phenomenal and transcendent worlds (post-Enlightenment Western maps, even when designed by Christian believers, tend to imply a closed frontier, or at most one with defined, regulated crossing points). But the African maps as revised show the relationships of the components to be transformed under the Christian impact. The most regular, and most obvious, feature is the magnification of the God component. In most traditional systems the God component might *in principle* be the dominant concept, but the direction of religious practice towards other components in the system usually prevented this happening in practice; hence the frequent, if inaccurate, application to African religious systems of the term *Deus absconditus*. The identification of the God of Christian preaching with the God component in traditional religion transformed the significance of the God component. It has led in many cases to the virtual extinction of the divinities, the "rulers" behind much pre-Christian practice, as active recognition of the rulers has been seen as incompatible with the worship of God. Western style, post-Enlightenment Christianity would be content to leave it there; the One excluding the many, the true triumphing over the imaginary. But some aspects of African Christianity show that in many cases the old divinities have not simply disappeared; they have become demonized, and are now seen as the embodiment of opposition to the God of church and Bible, now with his vernacular name. Accounts of early conversion movements frequently centre on power encounters between the evangelist (in the stories, almost always African, hardly ever a Western missionary) or some seminal local Christian figure on the one hand, and the local ruling spiritual power) (represented often by a shrine, cult, society or guild) on the other. That victory, however, does not necessarily indicate a final triumph; over the Christian generations, the territorial rulers, the old divinity component, reemerge in various forms. But this reemergence of the divinities does not produce the clear-cut choices of the conversion generation. In later, "Christian," generations, those who resort to the old powers usually intend no apostasy, no abandonment of the Christian framework. They do not have the means, even if they wanted, to reconstitute the pre-Christian religious system in its integrity. Rather, they have run out of resources to face the difficulties of the contemporary world, and are looking for additional resources beyond the Christian framework.

Many of the new forms of African Christianity are responses to this common situation, whereby Christians seek alternative sources of power outside a Christian framework. The answer they bring is emphatic location of power with God, usually in the figure of Christ or the Holy Spirit; all other sources are not so much illusory as illegitimate and dangerous. In terms of the maps of the spiritual universe, they magnify the God component at the expense of the divinity component; but the native significance of the divinity component is reflected in the very vigour of the rejection that demonizes it. Ogbu Kalu's studies of territorial cult in Igboland point in the same direction (Kalu 1996). Igboland saw unusually rapid Christian expansion, but the old rulers retained a circumscribed place over several Christian generations, accommodated, but never really assimilated, into a Christian conceptual framework. Today, as Kalu shows, these rulers are being challenged and confronted by a new "single-source" Christian radicalism. The choice in Igboland is no longer between a "Christian" option and a "traditional" one; it is between different expressions of Christianity, some accommodated, some radical. The explosive effect within hierarchies and kinship networks as people make different responses may be as explosive as in the days when "Things Fell Apart."

But the exaltation of the God component does not always involve the demonization of the divinity component. As the Igbo example indicates, the latter has often been quietly accommodated within the Christian scheme. Long ago, J. V. Taylor pointed out how the Ganda found the empty skies of missionary Christianity hard to cope with. (Missionaries, however attached to the Bible, being mostly children of the Enlightenment, implicitly posited the Western view of a closed frontier between the phenomenal and transcendent worlds.) It was hard for Ganda to recognize in one short visit by the divine Son a long time ago the conceptual equivalent of all the long-recognized activity of an array of spiritual rulers (Taylor 1958: ch. 14). Some forms of African Christianity have filled the gap by recognizing the activity of God through mediating beings, such as angels or other spirit servants of God.

It is perhaps not without significance that some of the interpretations of African traditional religion that stress the contingency of the divinity element, and insist that the divinities are mediators or even "refractions" of God, are themselves the work of scholars who are also Christian theologians (Idowu 1962, 1973). A parallel process may be seen in some of the "spiritual" or "prophet-healing" churches of the Aladura type, which make much use of biblical imagery about the heavenly spirits, and which make angels and angel names prominent in their devotions. If such phenomena reflect the persistence of the divinity component of the old maps, now redrawn with the aid of Christian symbols, it is worth noting that their activity is now firmly and explicitly locked into agency on behalf of God. The divinity component has been drawn inside the activity of the God component, as regards both theory and practice.

One of the features of the Christian situation in Africa in the 1990s was the sharp conflict between the old-type independent churches, the "spirituals," and the new type, the Pentecostal and charismatic radicals (Smith 1994: esp. part 2). Perhaps the core of the conflict, the element that makes relationships so tense, is the issue whether subordinate spiritual beings, who represent the continuity of the religious consciousness demonstrated in the divinity element in the older cosmologies, may be recognized as the obedient agents of God, or must be anathematized as evil entities opposed to God. What both groups take for granted is the existence of this element. In this, the radical evangelicals are as much children of Africa as the older independents, the prophet-healing churches. They use the same maps of the universe, even if they colour them differently.

God and the Ancestors

The impact of Christianity on the relationship between the God component and the ancestor component in African maps of the transcendent has been more ambiguous. Generally speaking, the explicit significance attributed to the ancestors has diminished as the God component expands, especially in religious systems that in the pre-Christian period were ancestor dominated. But the occasions for territorial battle between God and the ancestors have not been of the scale or frequency of those between God and the divinities. Certainly, especially in the early stages of Christian presence, community misfortune might be attributed to ancestral anger at breaches of custom; but, as the Christian presence increased, other explanations come to hand. The converse might be equally true: misfortune might reflect God's anger at resistance, or perhaps indicate that the community's ancestors themselves favoured the Christian message. Signs were recalled from the past—prophetic oracles or diviner's declarations—that indicated that great figures of the past had foreseen and welcomed the coming of Christianity and the Book. (The frequency of stories of such predictions, providing local or ethnic Christian "founding myths" are another indication of how Christianity has been adopted into the African past, emphasizing the continuity of religious consciousness [e.g., Thompson 1995: 36–37].)

As for missionary influence, missionary Christianity was largely disabled from giving clear guidelines on the matter of the ancestors, since there was no precise equivalent in Western experience either of the ancestors or of the family and kinship systems to which the ancestors belonged. The more Protestant strands of missionary teaching tended simply to proscribe any form of ancestral cult as inconsistent with the sole worship of God; the more Catholic ones offered reinterpretations of ancestor veneration in terms of the Latin Christian doctrine of the communion of the saints. But neither of these procedures could abolish, absorb, or fully replace the religious consciousness from which ancestor cult arose.

The relationship between God and the ancestors within African Christianity has been an ill-defined and sometimes uneasy one, with theory and practice sometimes in tension and different inferences drawn from similar premises. In some areas a long tradition of explicit discountenance of ancestral cult on the part of the church has produced a curious outcome. Some of the traditional states of southern Ghana, for instance, now have an honoured royal house and priesthood maintaining traditional custom, with ancestral veneration at its heart, for the good of the nation, and for that reason remaining outside, though by no means hostile to, the churches to which the overwhelming majority of their people are attached. There has been plenty of discussion of whether this dichotomy is necessary (Safo-Kantanka 1993), and at present the new Christian radicals seem to be making the running, with a call for explicit abandonment of ancestor veneration. But on this, as on other matters, the radicals are not simply reinforcing the directives of Western Christianity; their consciousness of the ancestors is inherently African, because it recognizes the potentialities of ancestral action. Thus some of the modern "deliverance ministries," which offer release from oppression by evil spiritual forces, recognize that one source of such oppression may be the religious activities of one's forebears (Larbi 1995). Other Christians have followed other interpretations. Sampson Oppong, the unlettered (and therefore uninhibited) prophet whose preaching brought a mass movement to Christianity in Ashanti during and after the First World War, appealed directly to ancestor consciousness; powerful traditional rulers quailed at his pictures of their ancestors by the lake of blood that they had shed (Haliburton 1965). Some Christians have maintained ancestor veneration (the term "worship" is often a sensitive one) alongside, but separate from, Christian worship. This mode implies a sense of the reality and necessity of both realms of activity, with no clearly understood relationship between them. Others have sought ways of accommodating the two, adopting the ancestors into the Christian framework, using Christian prayer and a theological rationale.

What is clear is that the ancestors have not gone away; they belong at present to the penumbra of African Christianity. Perhaps the most striking witness to their resilience is among the Krio people of Sierra Leone. Torn from the lands of their fathers in the conversion generation, melded from various ethnic groups with Christianity as a badge of their corporate identity, and after some two centuries of Christian history in which Protestant and evangelical strains have been dominant, the community has maintained its characteristic ancestral rituals over the generations, and has developed a set of distinctive funeral and memorial customs (Fyfe 1962; Peterson 1969). Both popular religion and official church policy have varied in their understanding of the relationships of all these practices to Christian worship and teaching. For some they have been parallel and separate, for others complementary and interactive. Krio church reformers such as Bishop T. S. Johnson have sought to redirect them by liturgical innovation; Krio theologians such as Harry Sawyerr sought to reinterpret them in the Christian mainstream.[3] Most of the modern Christian radicals of Freetown's burgeoning Pentecostal congregations set their face against all ancestor-related rituals; but it is worth noticing that some, while maintaining the utter rejection of all other spiritual entities outside the Christian framework, leave ancestor cult as an issue for the future.

Perhaps this reference to the future must serve for wider purposes also. If, as is argued here, a new form of Christianity is emerging, shaped by the configurations of African life, it will be bound to take account in some way—not necessarily always in the same way—of the ancestors.

God and Objects of Power

The fourth component of the traditional worldviews, impersonalized power and objects of power, has been painlessly drawn into the Christian framework. Commentators have often seen resemblance to fetish practice in the activities of Christian congregations, especially in the prophet-healing churches and movements; yet for the members and practitioners themselves, the crucial factor is the source of the power, the God of the Scriptures. The power they claim is not freestanding or inherent; it is identifiable as the power of Christ or of the Holy Spirit. Sampson Oppong

---

[3]M. Markwei, "Harry Sawyerr's Patron (Bishop T. S. Johnson)," in *New Testament Christianity for Africa and the World: Essays in Honour of Harry Sawyerr*, ed. M. E. Glasswell and E. W. Fasholé-Luke (London, 1974), 179–97. Sawyerr wrote extensively of the *awujoh*, or ancestor rituals, and on graveside libations. See John Parratt, ed., *The Practice of Presence: The Shorter Writings of Harry Sawyerr* (Grand Rapids, 1995), 184; and in the same volume, the introductory essay by A. F. Walls, "The Significance of Harry Sawyerr."

often preached holding a white stone; his hearers believed he could read his messages in it, while he himself felt confident before the most powerful chiefs while it lay in his hand. It is easy to call his white stone a fetish; but Oppong himself saw it as the white stone with a new name written on it given in Rev. 2:17 to "those who overcome" (Haliburton 1965:92). In other words, for him the power and the significance of the stone lay not in itself but in its association with Christ. The spiritual churches may offer the divine power mediated through holy water or some other substance, or demonstrate that power in exorcism by a blow on the afflicted head from the Bible; but again it is crucial to their identity that it is *God*'s power that is mediated, *God*'s book that is used in the mediation. All other objects of power are not only inferior ("Jesus Christ power na supa supa power; Mami Wata power na lessa lessa power," runs a chorus popular in Freetown) but also illegitimate; the person who is wearing a protective charm, or who has buried one at home, will receive no healing until he or she has destroyed such things.

If, therefore, the principal feature of cosmological change induced by Christianity in Africa has been the magnification of the God component, that does not mean that the other components have altogether disappeared. They are elements in a process of rethinking and reevaluation in the light of the impact of the biblical tradition. The process may continue for some time and lead Christian theology into new paths.

New Elements in African Religion

It is necessary, even if done cursorily, to point to new elements introduced into African religion under the Christian impact, quite apart from the reordering of the component elements so far discussed.

The central Christian symbol, the person of Christ, is the obvious point at which to begin. The new religious systems of Africa are distinctively Christian in that they not only magnify the God component that has always been present in African religion, but also identify that component with the God of Israel and of the Scriptures, and with the God and Father of the Lord Jesus Christ. That is to say, they bring the elements of African religious consciousness into connexion with Christ. This has led to another crucial development of the God component in African religion: the Christian impact has greatly intensified the sense of the immediacy of the presence of God, particularly in the figure of Christ. God's interventions in the phenomenal world no longer need be attributed to refractions of God's existence (as Idowu claims to be the case with the *oriśa*), or sought through intermediaries—God speaks directly. This is the conviction of innumerable Christian prophets, healers, holiness leaders, and reformers, that they have heard the voice of God. Sometimes it has been as a voice, sometimes as a vision of Christ, sometimes in a dream. Nor are such experiences restricted to the prophet-healing and spiritual churches or even the charismatic groups; hundreds of candidates for the ministry or priest-hood in the so-called mainline churches have been determined in their vo-cation by a voice heard as the voice of God.

No group is so naive as to assume that any dream or vision in itself is self-authenticating; even in the spiritual churches, in which dreams and visions are often institutionalized, there are checks and balances and mechanisms for detecting self-deceit or self-serving. If they have brought the dream into the sphere of revelation and Christian practice, they ac-knowledge the existence of Christian ways of dreaming, and ways of dreaming that are not Christian. But the fact remains that by voices, dreams, and visions, God, usually in the person of Christ, is held to speak directly to people and reveal the divine will. Some years back an Anlo tra-ditionalist elder in Ghana commented to C. R. Gaba on the novelty of this: only the Christians in our country, he said, dream of God (Mawu); just as only the Christians build houses for God. His own explanation for this marks the immensity of the change. Perhaps, he said, the Christian God was not God at all, but a lesser power, a divinity known to the whites and introduced to Anlo Christians by them, and thus capable, like other di-vinities, of appearing in dreams. For Christians, that is, the God compo-nent in the worldview had taken over dreams from the divinity compo-nent and by this means come close to Anlo people—too close for this old man to accept (Gaba 1969).

The same conceptual transformation appears in divination. Under the Christian impact, this becomes the search for the will of God. It is God's word that is sought; no lesser power's word will do. It is God's will that is heard in the revelation of the prophet or the ecstatic utterance in the charismatic assembly. Yet in traditional African divination, it is rarely God's own voice that is heard in ecstatic utterance, but that of the shrine spirit or some other lower spiritual power. Oracular, wisdom-type divina-tion, such as Ifa, which offers no direct voice from the spirit world, is often recognized as a source of knowledge from a higher spiritual source, even if hard and uncertain of interpretation (Bascom 1969).

The mention of wisdom divination leads naturally to the second im-portant new category in African religion: Scripture. The Scriptures, and specifically the vernacular Scriptures, have led to innumerable new effects in African religion.

It is also worth noting that the coming of the Scriptures has led to the Christian reaffirmation of some ancient aspects of African religion that were not part of missionary Christianity at all. The very revelatory phe-nomena already mentioned—dream, vision, trance, ecstatic utterance—now so readily taken for granted, tended to be discouraged or ignored during the missionary period of African Christianity. To Western Chris-tians, whose historic tradition stressed the supreme authority of either Scripture or church, such things were theologically suspect, and they formed no working part of Enlightenment discourse. But these phenomena, or something like them, were clearly visible in the Bible, in the New Testament as well as in the Old. Wider and wider access to the Bible has given a new justification, a new conceptual setting, to various elements in traditional African religious culture, which have been reaffirmed and reinterpreted in Christian terms by rooting them in Christ and the Scriptures. It is hard to overestimate the status of the vernacular Scriptures in some African societies as "owned" traditional property: witness the place of the Twi Scriptures in Ghana, translated in the high style of the royal courts (Bediako 1995: ch. 3); or the Yoruba Scriptures, much revised certainly, but still embodying the first African translation to be largely the work of a mother-tongue speaker, Samuel Ajayi Crowther.

Another effect of the accessibility of the Scriptures has been the development of new models of the church. Many of the spiritual and prophet-healing independent churches are the product of African readings of Scripture. They have completely bypassed the various "classical" polities built up over centuries of Western Christian history by the direct application of their reading of Scripture to local situations. There are signs that some of the new charismatic churches, at first sight so reminiscent of the Pentecostal churches of the West, are doing the same. The new readings of Scripture sometimes involve not strictly a different canon of Scripture, but a different *effective* canon, which brings into use books of the Bible that Western Christians have left on one side—part of the canon, but not part of the *effective* canon, since they no longer have resonance with the conditions of Western life. The Holiness Code of Leviticus is frequently used in the spiritual churches of West Africa. These churches take account of the problems and worries of people with a traditional background for whom issues of ritual purity are important, issues that are left almost without reference in all the codes of church discipline imported from the West. One is reminded that a century and a half ago, Samuel Ajayi Crowther, that first mother-tongue translator, argued that, after obvious candidates such as the Gospels and Psalms, the book of Leviticus (which contemporary Western Christians could hardly use except by forcing allegorical interpretations upon it) should be among the first books of the Bible to be translated.

The effect of the Christian tradition has also been to introduce a new category to African religion: the demonic. We have already noted the frequent demonization of the local divinities and other governing powers in Christian understanding, their designation as antigod; it is a sign of a lively apprehension, especially in the newer forms of African Christianity, of the significance of the powers of evil. These powers are organized under the control of the enemy of God and of human welfare, the devil; the power of Christ signals their ultimate destruction. The dramatic opposition of good and evil forces is one of the distinctive characteristics of African Christianity; and yet such a dualistic model of understanding of the universe seems to have little foundation in traditional Africa. Traditional cosmologies had trickster figures, such as the Yoruba Eṣu; but Eṣu and his like were not originally antigod figures, not embodiments of evil, though they have sometimes become Satan figures nowadays. Among the most remarkable features of the reordering of African religion under the impact of Christianity we may observe not only the magnification of God, but also the emergence of the devil.

In this chapter I have deliberately left aside the association of Christianity with Enlightenment values, and with the matrices of these values—formal education, economic development, modernization. This is done with no desire to deny or downgrade the importance of those associations; a different sort of essay could be written to concentrate upon them and their organic relationship to the Christian faith. But it is important to recognize that Christianity has made itself at home in Africa independently of these things as well as in association with them, and that this is part of its significance. Christianity is at home in African religion; it is African religion. It is thus able to operate in Africa at some of the most important levels of consciousness. It is able, for instance, to operate in the sphere of healing. Western medicine, as commonly administered, is addressed to the disease. Healing in Africa is a more complex business, addressed to the person, and the various influences that are, or may be, concerned in that person's disabilities. Christian missions were crucial to the introduction of scientific medicine, and Christian health services are still important; but amid the ruin of medical and mental health services in so many parts of Africa, Christian healing activity has expanded far beyond the provision of scientific medicine. At first in the spiritual churches, then among the charismatics, and now increasingly in the mainline churches, healing is being addressed to the person as the centre of a complex of influences. It is addressed to the person as target of outside attack, as sufferer from unwanted legacies, as carrier of the sense of failure and unfulfilled duty. It is the long-established African understanding of the nature and purpose of healing that is at work. What distinguishes its Christian phase is that the central Christian symbol of Christ is identified as the source of healing.

The same developments have enabled Christian influences to be deployed actively against witchcraft and sorcery. In the missionary period, such activity was often disabled by Enlightenment principles, which, under the general label of "superstition," sometimes confused the practice of witchcraft and sorcery with belief in their efficacy. In the missionary period, Christianity could protect innocent people from terrorizing accusations of witch activity; but its power to deal with the fear that such activity was taking place was limited. Still less obviously was there any help for the persons who feared that they themselves possessed witch powers, who were conscious of the desire to destroy and longing to be rid of it. Postmissionary Christianity in Africa is able to recognize both conditions, and to deal with the objectified spite and malice that witchcraft and sorcery stand for, the poisoned relations that follow, the frequently accompanying self-loathing. It is able to introduce the possibility of forgiveness, reconciliation, release, and the assurance of safety, again by the use of its central symbol, Christ himself. It has, in fact, only been possible to be more fully Christian by more fully entering into the African inheritance.

The missionary period of African Christianity was, after all, only an episode—an important episode, for it stands for that Christian universality from which the new African Christianity has shown no desire to resile. The features that have marked earlier phases of Christian history are all represented in contemporary African Christianity. African Christians worship the God of Israel; they attribute ultimate significance to Jesus Christ; they acknowledge the activity of God among his people; they recognize their participation in a community that transcends time and space; they read the same Scriptures and are distinguished by the special use of bread and wine and water. But the experiences, traditions, and agendas of Africa are reshaping Christianity. The continent has seen immense theological activity over a long period, and the activity seems likely to intensify. It has hitherto been mainly conducted, not by academics, but by thousands of people who never thought of themselves as theologians, some of them barely literate in English, who have been making Christian choices about kinship obligations, ancestors, shrines, customary rites, healing, possession, divination, reconciliation. Their sources have been the Christian Scriptures (usually in the vernacular), the Christian tradition as they knew it, and their understanding of local patterns of thought, action, and relationship. The result of their work has already meant a substantial enlargement of Christian theology; for, as we have seen, they have had to relate the historic Christian tradition to the preexisting structures of African belief systems and religious consciousness, affirming, denying, suppressing, reshaping, redirecting, and reinterpreting the various elements in the process. It will be one of the tasks of African academic theology to explore and articulate the forms and formulations of Christianity already made in thousands of congregations over several generations. There will be alternative formulations; it is clear that diverse trends are already discernible. Africa is, in fact, a great theological laboratory, dealing with issues—literally—of life and death, of deformation and reformation, of fossilization and revival. It is also in a process of generational religious change, which, as Ogbu Kalu has shown, is critical and may be explosive. And understanding it will give scope for a whole lifetime of African Christianity Projects.

Bibliography

Adubofuor, S. B. 1994. "Evangelical Parachurch Movements in Ghanaian Christianity." Ph.D. diss., University of Edinburgh.

Baëta, C. G. 1968. *Christianity in Tropical Africa: Studies Presented and Discussed at the Seventh International African Seminar, University of Ghana, April 1965*. London: Oxford University Press.

Barrett, David. 1970. "AD 2000: 350 Million Christians in Africa." *International Review of Mission* 59: 39–54.

Bascom, William. 1969. *If a Divination: Communication Between Gods and Men in West Africa*. Bloomington: Indiana University Press.

Bediako, Kwame. 1995. *Christianity in Africa: The Renewal of a Non-Western Religion*. Edinburgh: Edinburgh University Press.

Fyfe, Christopher. 1962. *A History of Sierra Leone*. London: Oxford University Press.

Gaba, C. R. 1969. "The Idea of a Supreme Being among the Anlo People of Ghana." *Journal of Religion in Africa* 2, no. 1: 64–79.

Hackett, Rosalind, ed. 1987. *New Religious Movements in Nigeria*. Lewiston, New York: Edwin Mellen Press.

———. 1990. "Enigma Variations: The New Religious Movements in Nigeria Today." in A. F. Walls and W. R. Shenk, eds. *Exploring New Religious Movements: Essays in Honour of Harold W. Turner*. Elkhart, Ind.: Mission Focus.

Haliburton, G. M. 1965. "The Calling of a Prophet: Sampson Oppong." *Bulletin of the Society for African Church History* 2, no. 1: 84–96.

Hogg, W. Richey. 1952. *Ecumenical Foundations: A History of the International Missionary Council and Its Nineteenth Century Background*. New York: Harper.

Idowu, E. Bolaji. 1962. Olódùmare: *God in Yoruba Belief*. London: Longmans.

———. 1973. *African Traditional Religion: A Definition*. London: SCM.

Kalu, Ogbu. 1996. *The Embattled Gods: Christianization of Igboland*. Lagos: Minaj.

Kirika, Gerishon M. 1988. "Aspects of the Religion of the Gikuyu of Central Kenya before and after the European Contact, with Special Reference to Prayer and Sacrifice." Ph.D. diss., University of Aberdeen.

Larbi, E. K. 1995. "The Development of Ghanaian Pentecostalism, with Special Reference to the Christ Apostolic Church, the Church of Pentecost and the International Central Gospel Church." Ph.D. diss., University of Edinburgh.

Ojo, Matthews A. 1987. "The Growth of Campus Christianity and Charismatic Movements in Western Nigeria." Ph.D. diss., University of London.

Okorocha, Cyril C. 1987. *The Means of Religious Conversion in Africa: The Case of the Igbo of Nigeria*. Aldershot: Gower.

Oliver, Roland. 1956. *How Christian Is Africa?* London: Highway Press.

Parrinder, E. Geoffrey. 1970. "Monotheism and Pantheism in Africa." *Journal of Religion in Africa* 3, no. 2: 81–88.

Peterson, John. 1969. *Province of Freedom: A History of Sierra Leone 1787–1870*. London: Faber and Faber.

Safo-Kantanka, Osei. 1993. *Can a Christian Become a Chief? An Examination of Ghanaian Ancestral Practices in the Light of the Bible*. Accra: Pentecost Press.

Sanneh, Lamin. 1989. *Translating the Message: The Missionary Impact on Culture*. Maryknoll, N.Y.: Orbis.

Setiloane, G. M. 1976. *The Image of God among the Sotho-Tswana*. Rotterdam: Balkema.

Smith, D. Robert M. 1994. "A Survey and Theological Analysis of the Spiritual and Pentecostal Evangelical Churches in Freetown, Sierra Leone." Ph.D. diss., University of Edinburgh.

Taylor, John V. 1958. *The Growth of the Church in Buganda*. London: SCM.

Thompson, Leonard. 1975. *Survival in Two Worlds: Moshoeshoe of Lesotho 1786—1870*. London: Oxford University Press.

Thompson, T. Jack. 1995. *Christianity in Northern Malawi: Donald Fraser's Missionary Message and Ngoni Culture*. Leiden: Brill.

Turner, H. W. 1967. *History of an African Independent Church*. 2 vols. Oxford: Clarendon Press.

Walls, A. F. 1976. "Towards Understanding Africa's Place in Christian History," in J. S. Pobee, ed., *Religion in a Pluralistic Society: Essays Presented to Professor C. G. Baëta*. Leiden: Brill, 180–89.

———. 1988. "On the Origins of Old Northern and New Southern Christianity," in H. Kasdorf and K. W. Müller, eds., *Reflection and Project: Missiology on the Threshold of 2001*. Bad Liebenzell: Verlag der Liebenzeller Mission, 243–55.

World Missionary Conference 1910. Edinburgh: World Missionary Conference.

7

Africa as the Theatre of Christian Engagement with Islam in the Nineteenth Century

The nineteenth-century encounter between Europe and India was notable for the long and close engagement of Christianity in its Western form and the traditional religious culture of India, with momentous consequences for both. The missionary impact, more than any other single factor, led the West into realms beyond all its previous experience. The nineteenth-century encounter with Islam, by contrast, was often shaped, not in the sphere of active engagement between Christian and Muslim, but by factors arising out of the long past histories of Europe and Asia, and in settings where genuine interreligious exchange was well nigh unthinkable. In the meeting with India, Europe was aware of its substantial ignorance, and the missionaries succeeded the early humanists of the East India Company as its sensors. In the meeting with the Islamic world, Europe, while sometimes changing its mind about Islam, believed it already knew all that was necessary, and the missionary was generally marginal in compiling that corpus of knowledge. It is the purpose of this chapter to suggest that Africa was a partial exception, and to explore some of the ways in which West Africa, in particular, was a theatre of Christian Muslim engagement and impinged on the changing debate in Europe.

Some detest the Persians because they believe in Mohamed; and others despise their language because they do not understand it.[1]

Thus, Sir William Jones, the great impresario of Sanskrit studies who handled the Hindu classics as his Western contemporaries handled those

First published in *Journal of Religion in Africa* 29 (No. 2, 1999): 155–74, an issue in honor of Adrian Hastings. Reprinted with permission.
[1]William Jones, "A Grammar of the Persian Language," 2nd ed. (London: J. Richardson, 1775), preface.

of Greece and Rome, explained the neglect in his circles of Persian, the other great language of the Moghul Empire. The emotional charge in his words is evident; as Muslims, the Persians "believe in Mohamed," and to the eighteenth-century English that is detestable. Behind that detestation lie centuries of hostility and terror. The contemporary folk image of Islam is evoked by Robert Burns, who describes the scene as the devil comes into an Ayrshire town and marches off with the hated revenue officer. All the women of the town delight in the deliverance, crying "Auld Mahoun', I wish ye luck o' the prize, man."[2] In eighteenth-century Scotland, that is, the Prophet's name was a demotic periphrasis for the devil.

It was not only old ladies in Scotland who made the equation. The life of Muhammad best known to most educated people of the time was still probably that included in the work of Humphrey Prideaux, the title of which tells its own story: *The true nature of imposture fully displayed in the life of Mahomet; with a discourse attached for the full vindication of Christianity from this charge.*[3] Prideaux's book, first published in 1697, was being reprinted as late as 1808, and someone thought it worthwhile to produce an American edition in 1798. Muhammad was above all the great imposter, or, in Charles Wesley's phrase, "the Arab thief, as Satan bold" whose doctrine should be chased back to hell.[4]

There were not many reasons, even worldly ones, to take up the study of Arabic, the necessary prelude to any deeper engagement. Sir William Jones, enthusiast for languages as he is, urges Arabic only for those of his company's staff who wish to become eminent translators. For all ordinary purposes, Persian would serve; and diligent use of his grammar for a year should enable the student to read and reply to any letter he might happen to receive in that language from an Indian prince.[5] It is noteworthy that when Dr. Johnson and Boswell set up in imagination an ideal university, with chairs held by their learned friends, they thought of appointing a professor of Sanskrit (Jones) but no professor of Arabic.[6]

Nevertheless, Arabic as a field for the learned never quite died out, just as the presence of the emotional charge that could produce detestation of Islam did not inhibit the activities of the Levant Company and other trading ventures in the Muslim East. An Arabic Psalter was produced in 1724

---

[2]Robert Burns, "The Deil's awa' wi' the Exciseman."

[3]The real target of the work is not distant Islam but proximate English deism; its popularity in this sphere of polemics made it one of the more accessible sources of information on Islam.

[4]Hymn, "For the Turks," first published in Bristol, 1758; *Poetical Works of John and Charles Wesley,* ed. George Osborn, vol. 6 (London: Wesleyan Methodist Conference Office, 1870), 137.

[5]Jones, *Grammar,* preface

[6]"Journal of a Tour to the Hebrides with Samuel Johnson," for 25 August 1773, in G. Birbeck Hill and L. F. Powell, eds., *Boswell's Life of Johnson,* vol. 5 (Oxford: Clarendon Press, 1964), 108.

and a New Testament and catechism thereafter by the Society for Promoting Christian Knowledge; but these were intended for use not among Muslims but by Eastern Christians, and the main burden of translation was borne by a Syrian Christian.[7] One of the correctors employed for the New Testament was the lawyer George Sale, who became the earliest major interpreter of Islam to the English-speaking world. Sale's *Koran*,[8] with its massive notes, was the standard English version for a century and a half. How unusual was such activity can be gauged from the fact that many people assumed—and Voltaire apparently actually said—that Sale had spent his life among the Arabs. In fact, he never left England.

By the early nineteenth century it was easier to identify some people who had genuinely lived among the Arabs and had done so not simply as travellers in the East—there had always been such—but as interpreters of the life of Muslims. The most remarkable was probably E. W. Lane, who first went to Egypt for his health and to study the language and stayed on as Mansur Effendi to write *Manners and Customs of the Modern Egyptians*, published in 1836. Though Lane adopted a Muslim identity in Egypt, he never forsook the Christianity of his clerical background, but he was neither a missionary nor even an explorer of Islamic faith.[9]

By Lane's time, however, the new Protestant phase of the modern missionary movement was well under way. Not surprisingly, its American arm early directed itself to the area that had become prominent in American public consciousness as a result of American foreign policy, the Middle East.[10] This brought it to what the West generally saw as the heart of the Islamic world, where the Prophet's deputy, the leader of the faithful, presided over the immense, if ramshackle, Ottoman Empire, which extended over three continents. British missionary interest in the area was much less sustained.[11] But in any case, the official position of the Turkish Empire was never to admit missions to Muslims. Whatever the hopes for the future, missions

---

[7]The background is explored by Daniel L. Brunner, *Halle Pietism in England: Anthony William Boehm and The Society for Promoting Christian Knowledge* (Göttingen: Vandenhoeck und Ruprecht, 1993), especially 154–65. English traders of the Levant Company resident in the East played a part in facilitating the project.

[8]*The Koran: Commonly Called the Alcoran of Mohammed* (London, 1764).

[9]Lane's work is one of the key points of reference for Edward Said, *Orientalism* (London: Routledge and Kegan Paul, 1978). See especially chapter 2, section 5: "Orientalism structures and restructures: Oriental residence and scholarship. The requirements of lexicography and imagination."

[10]See James A. Field, *America and the Mediterranean World 1770–1882* (Princeton: Princeton University Press, 1969); reprinted as *From Gibraltar to the Middle East* (Chicago: Imprint Publications, 1991). Chapter 3 deals with the missionary impulse.

[11]The Church Missionary Society and the British and Foreign Bible Society were early interested in developments that could bring renewal to the ancient Eastern churches. William Jowett, later clerical secretary of the CMS, had been based for fifteen years in Malta with this view; see his *Christian Research as in the Mediterranean, Syria, or the Holy Lands* . . . (London, 2nd ed., 1826).

within the Turkish Empire owed their justification to the old Christian minority communities of the empire. For much of the nineteenth century, writers on missions continued to lament the closed doors of the world's greatest Muslim power. By the century's end, only a fraction of the world's Muslims were living within that empire, but old habits die hard, and Western perceptions of Islam continued to be moulded by its association with the Ottoman Empire in decline, long after the political reality had changed.

The exclusion of missions from what was seen as the heart of the Islamic world, or their presence there on terms that made Christian engagement with Islam at most indirect, meant that, though the expanding missionary movement had by the 1830s reached many parts of the globe, a very small number of its representatives were closely involved with Muslims on any regular basis. First in point of time were some in West Africa, where Sierra Leone, the first Christian settlement, had Muslim neighbours and regular Muslim visitors.

From its inception the "Province of Freedom" in Freetown was intended as a base for missionary operations, and through the 1790s most of the new missionary societies sent representatives there, all intended to reach beyond the colony. Most of the missions were disastrous, but the most durable, first the Edinburgh Missionary Society, and then from 1804 the Church Missionary Society, found a niche among the Susu, who were in process of Islamization.[12] But as early as 1794, representatives of the Sierra Leone Company, the colony's evangelically minded sponsoring body, reached Futa Jallon. They were deeply impressed by the orderly Islamic state they found at Timbo. The king there professed himself interested in further contact with Europeans, while carefully establishing that he was not an independent agent; he was subject to a suzerain beyond. This simply increased the attractiveness of the idea of a mission. Let the gospel be preached in Timbo, and it might soon be preached in Timbuktu. No one supposed it would be easy; it would need to be a special mission, able to recommend itself by the productive methods of agriculture the company wished to see developed in Sierra Leone.[13] It was a task ready made for English Methodists, and Thomas Coke undertook to recruit an agricultural mission staffed by Methodists who could handle both the Bible and the plough.[14] The event had a comic opera outcome, for the

---

[12]Thomas Thompson, who visited the area in 1752, describes the Susu as "a mixt people of Pagans and Mundingos, which are a Sect of Mahometans" (*An Account of the Society for the Propagation of the Gospel* . . . [London, 1758], 30).

[13]*An Account of the Colony of Sierra Leone from Its First Establishment* . . . (London, 1795) contains a full report.

[14]See references in Christopher Fyfe, *A History of Sierra Leone* (London: Oxford University Press, 1962); and John Peterson, *Province of Freedom: A History of Sierra Leone 1787–1870* (London: Faber, 1969); A. F. Walls, "A Christian Experiment: the Early Sierra Leone Colony" in G. J. Cuming, ed., *The Mission of the Church and the Propagation of the Faith* (Cambridge: Cambridge University Press, 1970), 107–29.

party never got beyond Freetown. One of its members immediately created an incident by accosting a Muslim to denounce Muhammad as a false prophet, and the rest were dismayed to realise the implications of the life to which they had committed themselves. The governor of Sierra Leone, fearful for the colony's credit with its neighbours, easily persuaded them to go home. The first modern mission to a Muslim state collapsed before it began.

Despite the shame and embarrassment, the vision of the Muslim hinterland, the lure of Timbuktu, remained in missionary consciousness.[15] In the first two decades of modern West African missions there is little to suggest that either missionaries or their sponsoring societies thought of Muslims as being less likely to respond to the Christian gospel than others. The command was to preach the gospel to every creature; the promise was that Ethiopia would eventually stretch out its hands to God, and Timbo and Timbuktu belonged to Ethiopia as surely as Freetown. The facts of experience were that missions everywhere were difficult, slow, and discouraging in their immediate results. In the case of Muslims, at least they acknowledged one God, so different from the dim mysteries of African traditional belief. And who could say that the Fulani of Futa Jallon (who had at least expressed interest in a mission from Freetown) would *not* be more responsive than the Susu or the Hindus? Experience elsewhere in the world counted for little, since the last significant Christian encounters with the Muslim world were long ago and under very different conditions.

The period of disengagement between Christianity and Islam that followed in West Africa thus arose, not from any avoidance of Muslims as unresponsive, but from the sudden burgeoning of new missionary tasks elsewhere. The most direct in its effect was the urgent need to respond to the crowds of recaptives being brought into the Sierra Leone peninsula from the slaveships, which eventually caused the closure of the Susu mission and the transfer of its missionaries.[16] To this must be added the tantalizing prospects on the Gold Coast,[17] and later the link with the Yoruba states forged by Sierra Leonean recaptives making their way home.[18] These demands on a mission force that never was large, and that was sub-

---

[15]On the relation of Islamic movements in West Africa to Christian progress in this period, see Adrian Hastings, *The Church in Africa 1450–1950* (Oxford: Clarendon Press, 1994), 188–94.

[16]On the shape of the Christian movement in West Africa at this time, see Hastings, *Church in Africa*, 177–87; on Sierra Leone, A. F. Walls, "A Christian Concordat: Two Views of Christianity and Civilisation," in Derek Bake, ed., *Church, Society and Politics* (Oxford: Blackwell, 1975), 293–302.

[17]See F. L. Bartels, *The Roots of Ghana Methodism* (Cambridge: Cambridge University Press, 1965).

[18]See Hastings, *Church in Africa*, 349–58, and J. F. Ade Ajayi, *Christian Missions in Nigeria 1841–1891: The Making of a New Elite* (London: Longmans, 1965).

ject in this period to particularly high mortality, broke the pattern of engagement with Muslim Africa that had earlier been envisaged. By the middle of the century, Christians and Muslims were neither opponents nor competitors in Africa to any marked degree.

The second area of engagement for a brief period was the Russian Empire. The short-lived enthusiasm of Tsar Alexander I to involve Protestants in the conversion of the Tatars caused the Edinburgh Missionary Society, at least, to rate it a higher priority than West Africa. Its remaining missionary with the Susu, Henry Brunton, who had achieved the composition of the first grammar of a West African language, was transferred to the Russian Empire, taking his African assistant, Jellorum Harrison, with him. Harrison provides the spectacle of an African missionary to Russian Muslims in the early years of the nineteenth century.[19]

More substantial was the encounter that took place in India with the appointment to an East India Company chaplaincy of Henry Martyn, who brought a depth of scholarship previously unmatched in the Protestant missionary movement. With Martyn—and Samuel Lee, the Cambridge professor who presented his work to the world—comes the first literary response to arise out of direct encounter with Muslims since the Jesuit missionaries at Akbar's court in the early seventeenth century.[20] Martyn's early death, and the local and occasional nature of his controversy with Mirza Ibrahim, meant that it was not followed up. The nearest Martyn had to a successor in this respect was Karl Gottlieb Pfander,[21] whose own first encounter with Muslims had been in the Russian Empire. The first version of his best-known work, *Mizan-ul-Haqq* (*The Balance of Truth*), was published in Persian in the Caucasus in 1835; five years later, Pfander joined the CMS in India. *Mizan-ul-Haqq*, a treatise in Arabic dialectic style, appeared in many editions and translations directed to every part of the Muslim world; the Religious Tract Society produced a revised English version in 1910, as a basis for further translations.[22] It provided, in fact, the standard Protestant missionary apologetic to Islam for almost a century. Arguing that of all worldviews, only the Christian and Islamic *can* be true, since they alone recognize the one true God who is the source of knowledge, it pits Bible against Qur'an as the source of revelation. The argument is pursued in three stages: first, that the Jewish-Christian Scrip-

---

[19]On Brunton and his work, see P. E. H. Hair, *The Early Study of Nigerian Languages* (Cambridge: Cambridge University Press, 1967); William Brown, *History of Missions; or, of the Propagation of the Gospel among the Heathen* (Edinburgh, 1816). (Brown was secretary of the Scottish, formerly Edinburgh, Missionary Society).

[20]Samuel Lee, ed., *Controversial Tracts on Christianity and Mohammedanism . . . by the Rev. Henry Martyn* (Cambridge, 1824).

[21]Clinton Bennett, "The Legacy of Karl Gottlieb Pfander," *International Bulletin of Missionary Research* 20 (April 1996): 76–81.

[22]W. St. Clair Tisdall, *Mizanul Haqq, or Balance of Truth* (London: RTS, 1910). The argument is substantially that of Pfander's version.

tures have not been corrupted nor abrogated; second, that the teaching of these Scriptures meets the criteria for true revelation; and third, that Qur'an is not miraculous, Muhammad not always estimable, and the methods used in the spread of Islam questionable. The work moves on to establish the evangelical paradigm of sin, law, gospel, forgiveness.

Martyn, Pfander, and their Muslim interlocutors were arguing about the truth of revelation in works published in Asia and in Asian languages. In Europe—a Europe no longer menaced by Saracen or Turkish bogeys, and disposed, indeed, to prop up the Ottoman Empire as a check to Russian ambitions[23]—the depiction of Islam was becoming more benign. A well-known literary landmark of the change is Thomas Carlyle's *Heroes and Hero Worship,* published in 1840. Here Muhammad represents the hero as prophet—a true prophet, a true man, no impostor, his utter sincerity declared by the fact that more people now believe his word than believe any other word. Islam, like Christianity, demands complete surrender to God; indeed, it is definable as a confused form of Christianity, and a better one than that of the miserable Syrian sects squabbling about Christology. And if its morality is not always the highest, it is better than that of penny-counting contemporary utilitarianism.

But the key assumption is revealed when Carlyle says, "As there is no danger of our becoming, any of us, Mahometans, I mean to say all the good of him I justly can."[24] That is, conversion to Islam is culturally impossible for anyone partaking of Western civilization. That assumption was to shape a great deal of subsequent debate about Islam. In the areas of engagement, the debate is about the truth of revelation. By 1840, Europe was suspending that question, and turning to the issue of whether Islam might have been good for *other people.* That issue had more weight in determining attitudes than all the Arabist historical-critical scholarship building up in Germany,[25] or the incipient theology of religion being propounded by F. D. Maurice.[26]

---

[23] A writer in the *Edinburgh Review* in 1853 summed up contemporary attitudes thus: "Three centuries ago, the first vow of Christian statesmen was the expulsion of the Turks from the city of Constantine and the deliverance of the Empire from the scourge and terror of the infidel. In the present age, the absorbing desire of the same cabinets is to maintain the unbelievers in their settlements; and to postpone the hour at which the Crescent must give way to the Cross."

[24] All references are to the lecture "The Hero as Prophet."

[25] The effect of the new scholarship represented by Gustav Weil is reflected in the popular *Life of Mahomet* by Washington Irving, a work that maintains the Western reader's distance from the Prophet by treating him as the hero of an Eastern romance. It appeared more substantially in the new translation of the Qur'an by a London clergyman, J. M. Rodwell, in 1861. And it made its fullest entry into the English-speaking world in the large-scale works of the evangelical Indian civilian Sir William Muir.

[26] *The Religions of the World and Their Relation to Christianity* appeared in 1847. See A. F. Walls, "Islam and the Sword: Some Western Perceptions, 1840–1918," *Scottish Journal of Religious Studies* 5, no. 2 (Autumn 1984): 88–105.

The same middle years of the century that saw these developments in Europe saw the renewal of Christian Muslim engagement elsewhere. The Indian chapter of the story cannot detain us here; but there was also significant encounter in the Upper Niger area. The central figure on the Christian side was the Yoruba clergyman Samuel Adjai Crowther.[27] Already a veteran of the Niger Expeditions of 1841 and 1854, and a seasoned pillar of the CMS Yoruba mission, he was in 1857 appointed to head the mission in the Niger territories, becoming bishop there in 1864. His mission staff was entirely African; most of them had, like himself, been either born or brought up in Sierra Leone.

Sierra Leone, then the most sizable Christian community in West Africa to arise from the missionary movement, was also perhaps the first to demonstrate how resistant to Christianity Muslim communities were; for in this Christian colony Muslim recaptives had maintained their separate identity. As a fervent young evangelist, keeping school in a village where there were numbers of Muslim recaptives, Crowther found a boy wearing a charm. Crowther cut it off, telling the boy to take it home, as such superstitions were not permitted in a Christian school. This brought the father with a wrathful complaint. Crowther offered to answer him in front of the Muslim elders, and duly appeared with his Bible and Sale's *Koran*. At the end of his long life he could still recall the humiliation of that encounter. All his well-marshalled arguments were useless. For Muslims, there was only one argument: God did not have a son.[28]

The interesting feature of this story is the disjunction between cause and outcome. The original point of conflict was not about Islamic belief at all, but about the use of charms, an indigenous African religious practice widely tolerated in Islam. In areas where Muslim and non-Muslim peoples lived on close terms, Muslims often had, paradoxically, a high reputation for the efficacy of their charms. The origin of this reputation may well have lain in the Qur'an itself, in the mystery of writing and its sacred character. Certainly, scraps of the Qur'an were often used as a prophylactic against disease or misfortune, and it may thus have been a qur'anic charm that Crowther had cut from the boy's neck. Later, Christian missionaries came under similar pressures. Crowther himself as a missionary on the Niger found a great demand from Muslim clerics and others for Arabic Bibles. He was cautious about responding to expressions of interest in the Scriptures, fearing the use to which they might be put. He tells of an old cleric who had long begged for a Bible; Crowther declined, since he feared it would be cut up for charms. At last he gave in, but only after

---

[27]Hastings, *Church in Africa*, 338–93, suggestively makes Crowther's life and significance the frame for the mid-century chapter of African Christian history. On Crowther, see Ajayi, *Christian Missions*. A major biographical study by Professor Ajayi is forthcoming.

[28]Samuel Crowther, *Experiences with Heathens and Mahomedans in West Africa* (London: SPCK, 1892).

exacting a promise that the recipient would not use it "for a bad purpose."[29]

Crowther's early experience in Sierra Leone had taught him that confrontation where one party cries "Jesus is the Son of God" and the other "No, he is not" was useless. In his mature years on the Niger, he sought for common ground at the nexus of Qur'an and Bible: the themes of the status of Jesus as a great prophet, his miraculous birth, Gabriel as the messenger of God. Crowther seems to have had courteous and friendly relations with Muslim rulers, and to have nourished a hope of reaching beyond them, through the Christian community, to the as yet barely Islamized peasantry under their control.

He combines stories of his earlier and later attitudes at some length in a small posthumous work, *Experiences with Heathens and Mohammedans in West Africa*. The anecdotal approach adopted by the aged bishop is in fact very revealing; the stories also seem to accord reasonably well with accounts given at the time.[30] He describes, for instance, a meeting in the palace in Ilorin, which he dates as 1872, that offers a striking contrast with his early encounters in Sierra Leone. Crowther opened the debate[31] by asking the court if Jibrila could make a mistake; all agreed he would not. Crowther, showing the Bible both in English and in Yoruba, then read from the first chapter of Luke, the story of Gabriel's visit to Mary, the announcement of the coming birth of Jesus Messiah. The court could assent to this; the qur'anic account has much in common with it.[32] Crowther passed to the reading of two other New Testament passages, John 14 and Matthew 28. The first was intended to indicate

---

[29]A. F. Walls, "Samuel Adjai Crowther," in G. H. Anderson et al., eds., *Mission Legacies* (Maryknoll, N. Y.: Orbis, 1994), 132–39; reprinted as Chapter 8 below.

[30]For instance, the account in *Experiences* of the meeting at the court of the Emir in Ilorin is in line with the more contemporary report in CMS Archives CA3/04 A–B and the printed version, Bishop Crowther's report of the overland journey from Lokoja to Bida, CMS, 1872. See also P. R. McKenzie, *Inter-Religious Encounters in West Africa: Samuel Ajayi Crowther's Attitude to African Traditional Religion and Islam* (Leicester: University of Leicester, 1976), 57f. In a report made to the CMS Parent Committee in 1859, Crowther strongly urged that missionaries should refrain from any suspicion of attacks on Islam: "[Muslims] have great respect for the books of Moses, the Prophets, and the Psalms, and, to some extent the Gospel of Christ also. . . . If they be quietly referred to these books . . . in things concerning Christ Himself, we may have opportunity of bringing before their minds the wholesome substance of those blessed books. Our undue rashness in quarrelling with, and our untimely exposure of, Mohammedanism, can do no good; but may irritate, and prove most injurious to the heathen population." The CMS published this: Samuel Crowther and John Christopher Taylor, *The Gospel on the Banks of the Niger: Journals and Notices of the Native Missionaries Accompanying the Niger Expedition of 1857–1859* (London: CMS, 1859).

[31]This was Sunday afternoon. Crowther had already read the morning service of the Church of England in the compound where he was lodging, with a crowd watching. McKenzie, *Inter-Religious Encounters*, 57.

[32]Sura 3:42–47; cf. Sura 19:16–21.

that the one whom the court agreed had been pointed out by Jibrila had declared himself "the way, the truth and the life." The second was to show that
he also commanded his followers to teach all nations about him, and thus
explain Crowther's own mission. The emir now took a hand, asking if Anabi
(the prophet Jesus) was not to be the judge of the world? Crowther characteristically refused an answer in his own words, but read Matthew 25, the
parable of the sheep and the goats, where "all nations" are assembled before
"the Son of Man." The emir asked when this will take place, and Crowther
read three passages in turn: Acts 1:7 ("It is not for you to know the times and
the seasons"), Luke 12:39 (the Son of Man comes as a thief in the night), and
Rev. 22:10 ("The time is at hand"). The succeeding silence was broken by a
suspicious question from within the court: "What does your litafi say about
Muhammad?" Crowther's reply was that since the Prophet was born 622
years after Christ, the New Testament is naturally silent on the matter. The
next question suggests a Muslim rejoinder: "Which is fuller, your litafi or the
Qur'an?"—in other words, granted your book may be older, is there a continuing need for it in the light of the Qur'an? What do you have that we have
not? Crowther again avoided pitting the Bible directly against the Qur'an,
saying that the Qur'an has selected certain topics from among the range
treated in the Torah and the Injil.

The Muslims now asked Crowther for a prayer. The bishop's choice of
prayer is intriguing. He had, of course, his Church of England Book of
Common Prayer ready at hand, again in both English and Yoruba. From
the second he delivered the "Prayer for the Queen's Majesty" prescribed
for every morning and evening service. It is worth setting out in full the
prayer in the English form that Crowther would have had:

> O Lord, our heavenly Father, high and mighty, King of kings, Lord
> of lords, the only ruler of princes, who dost from thy throne behold
> all the dwellers upon earth; Most heartily we beseech thee with thy
> favour to behold our most gracious Sovereign Lady, Queen Victo-
> ria; and so replenish her with the grace of thy Holy Spirit, that she
> may always incline to thy will, and walk in thy way; Endue her
> plenteously with heavenly gifts; Grant her in health and wealth
> long to live; strengthen her that she may vanquish and overcome
> all her enemies; and finally after this life she may attain everlasting
> joy and felicity; through Jesus Christ our Lord.

Crowther explained that the Christian custom when outside the
queen's dominion was to replace the name of Queen Victoria "by the
name of the sovereign in whose dominions we are living"; that is, he lets
the emir know that Christians in his dominions would pray for him in
these terms. The court agreed that the prayer was very suitable.

"There was no argument," says Crowther, "no dispute, no objection
made, but the questions were answered direct from the Word of God."

This insistence on answering from Scripture, even when another answer might be readily at hand, was essential to Crowther's approach.

> After many years of experience, I have found that the Bible, the sword of the Spirit, must fight its own battle, by the guidance of the Holy Spirit.[33]

Taught by his early years in Sierra Leone, he recoiled from the type of debate that was initiated by setting out the traditional formulations of Christian doctrine that aroused hostility or suspicion. Not that he departed from Trinitarian doctrine, or thought it indefensible; but he recognized the horror that Muslims felt at what they thought Christians to be saying. Often, what Muslims shrank from as blasphemy was not Christian doctrine at all. The way ahead lay in the words of Scripture: establish the joint acknowledgment of the status of Gabriel as messenger, and proceed to the prophecies of Jesus' messiahship, Jesus' own words, and then the testimony of his disciples about him. Crowther was an old and frail man when he wrote *Experiences with Heathens and Mohammedans*, and the latter part of the book dissolves in a shower of texts. But there is enough to show that Crowther, the African leader of an African mission, had developed an African Christian approach to Islam in an African setting. It parted company from the assumptions about Islam that had been current in missionary writing in Crowther's formative years; there was no denunciation, no allegation of imposture or false prophecy. But his approach also differs markedly from the far more influential model being developed in another part of the Islamic world by Pfander, the leading missionary to Muslims in the ranks of Crowther's own mission. The dialectic of *Mizan-ul-Haqq* is meant to force a choice between Bible and Qur'an, to induce the conviction that the latter does not meet the criteria for a final revelation. Crowther steadfastly avoided posing that choice. He began with acceptance of what the Qur'an said of Jesus, and founded the body of debate on that premise. By using the actual words of Scripture, he avoided many of the flashpoints that would immediately arise from the systematic exposition of Christian doctrine in the formulations of the day. His personal theology closely linked the activity of the Holy Spirit with the words of Scripture; and he correctly identified the emerging African Christianity as biblicist in character. For the future he looked to an African Christian community with an effective knowledge of the Bible; already the average African Christian knew the Bible better than the average African Muslim knew the Qur'an. His other ground of confidence lay in the vernacular principle in Christianity: the fact that the rule of faith was typically expressed in the vernacular, not enshrined in a special sacred language. (We have seen his careful recording of the fact that it was the Yoruba Bible, not the English one, that impressed

---

[33]Crowther, *Experiences*, 28.

the court of Ilorin.) This difference reflected different understandings of the application of faith in life. It is a point that has become a focus of the modern debate about Christianity and Islam in Africa.[34]

The significance of the Upper Niger in the mid-nineteenth century as a meeting place of Christian and Islamic proclamation may deserve more attention than it has yet received. And the contribution of Crowther—no Arabist and no formal scholar—and his group of African colleagues may deserve a place in the history of the debate alongside the more formally equipped Christian exponents such as Pfander and Sir William Muir in India. In Persia the *Mizan-ul-Haqq* could be distributed only with discretion, and its arguments whispered. In British India it could be scattered broadcast. Crowther and the black missionaries of the Niger operated in an Islamic context quite different from either, and they developed—with little evident influence, or indeed much notice, from anyone outside—a basis for continuing operations in that context.

The opening they made was not followed up. The troubles that beset the Niger Mission and clouded Crowther's last years are well recorded.[35] The young Englishmen who succeeded the African missionaries, and who sought to expand Christian missions into more Islamized territory than the Royal Niger Company was willing to allow, had a different outlook and approach.[36] But the irony is that in this same period West Africa for the first time became the theatre for a debate about Islam, but once more the fruits of engagement on the field were preempted by an academic debate in Europe that owed nothing to real conversations between Christians and Muslims.

One of the initiators of the debate was Reginald Bosworth Smith, a Harrow schoolmaster who wrote for the papers. In view of the reputation accorded to him at the time as some sort of specialist, it is worth noting that he was in fact one of nature's amateurs. He knew no Arabic, had no cross-cultural experience, and was no theologian. He wrote four books on entirely unrelated subjects.[37] If we except a volume on ornithology, how-

---

[34]Far from being contemptuous of Crowther's not using an Arabic original, the Ilorin court were particularly impressed by the Yoruba Bible, and with how difficult it must be to read Roman script. The question of the different attitudes to the vernacular principle in Christianity and Islam is pursued by Lamin Sanneh, *Translating the Message: The Missionary Impact on Culture* (Maryknoll, N.Y. Orbis, 1989); *Piety and Power: Muslims and Christians in West Africa* (Maryknoll, N.Y.: Orbis, 1996); *The Crown and the Turban: Muslims and West African Pluralism* (Boulder, Colo.: Westview, 1997).

[35]See Ajayi, *Christian Missions*; G. O. M. Tasie, *Christian Missionary Enterprise in the Niger Delta 1864–1918* (Leiden: Brill, 1978).

[36]Andrew Porter, "Cambridge, Keswick and Late Nineteenth Century Attitudes to Africa," *Journal of Imperial and Commonwealth History* 5 (1976):5–34; and "Evangelical Enthusiasm, Missionary Motivation in the Late Nineteenth Century: The Career of G. W. Brooke," *Journal of Imperial and Commonwealth History* 6 (1977).

[37]Apart from the work discussed here, they are: *Carthage and the Carthaginians* (1878), *The Life of Lord Lawrence* (1883), and *Bird Life and Bird Lore* (1905).

ever, nearly all his writing has a single theme: the responsibilities attaching to British imperial and military power.[38] Patriotism allied to moral earnestness sounds through his work. It is in this light that we must view his strangely influential work *Mohammed and Mohammedanism* (1874).

His desire is that British power, beneficent in intent, shall be beneficent in reality. To act in the right way is to act in the Christian way, and Britain is a Christian country. Indeed, he declares that Christianity is the birthright of the English. He has read F. D. Maurice and from him learned to affirm the positives of other faiths rather than to deny their negatives.[39] But to Maurician theology Smith added two new elements. One was the new science of comparative religion. In default of the master, Smith himself undertakes to fit Islam into the systematic history of religion.[40]

The other new element is a cheerful evolutionism. By adding Max Müller to Maurice within an evolutionary framework, Smith arrives at a formulation whereby all religions are moral, rather than theological, in origin. They have come into existence to meet social and national moral needs. They raise humanity gradually towards God.

Since religions arise from a particular need to establish the principle of righteousness at a particular period, one can readily acknowledge that Islam established righteousness at the time of its birth. For instance, while Christians commonly complain of the depressive effect of Islam on women, it can be shown that Muhammad significantly *raised* the status of women in early Arabia. But one can go further. Islam can still establish the principle of righteousness today, whenever it encounters a people at a lower stage of development than itself. Without, therefore, giving up the idea of the superiority of Christianity, and even leaving open the possibility that Muslims will eventually see the need for a higher ethical norm, Islam can be seen, not as the enemy of Christianity but as its ally in the task of raising humanity.

This is not, of course, the vision of missionary Christianity; Smith's vision is that of birthright Christianity, the fortunate inheritance of Britain, which should be Britain's light in dealing with those who have not yet reached the same happy position. As Britain moved towards the high period of its imperial expansion, as that expansion brought British rule to more and more peoples where Islamic influence was already at work or at hand, Smith's book could be read as a tract for the times. The expansion of Islam might actually improve the lot of "native peoples." That was not to say that Islam was true, not to say that Islam was the highest religion, and

---

[38]The theme of *Carthage and the Carthaginians* is the criminal folly of Rome in destroying the province it had conquered; Lawrence is presented as the ideal representative of empire.

[39]*Mohammed and Mohammedanism*, 45ff.

[40]The opening lecture of the series that formed *Mohammed and Mohammedanism* deals with "the Science of Comparative Religion," acknowledging it is still in its infancy.

certainly not to say that it had any relevance to Western society. All questions of truth claims could be bypassed; the administrative convenience was that the general tendency of Islam was, or could be, socially elevating.

Once again Western thought had become engaged, not in a debate *with* Islam, but in an internal one *about* Islam. Its new focus was less on comparative religion than on colonial policy. Smith's views were enthusiastically endorsed by the Afro-West Indian man of letters Edward Wilmot Blyden, who wrote with the authority of one who had himself been a Christian missionary.[41] He could give Bosworth Smith's argument a new dimension, detailing on the one hand the baleful effects in Africa of a Christianity heavily imbued with Western values, and on the other the blessings already brought to Africa by Islam. Islam had brought unity instead of tribal division. It had kept foreign influence at bay; foreign nations had taken over every African state that had any foreign influence, Liberia alone excepted. Islam had provided a basis for economic and cultural progress. It had harmed the African psyche less than Christianity had, for Western colour prejudice and the imposition of Western cultural norms had confused African Christians and inhibited African artistic expression. Islam was less materialistic than Christianity, at least in its outworkings; in colonial society an African had little to gain by becoming a Muslim, everything to gain by connecting with the mission-dominated education system. Africans learned English to profit in this world, Arabic to enter the next:

> I believe that Islam has done for vast tribes of Africa what Christianity in the hands of Europeans has not yet done. It has cast out the demons of fetishism, general ignorance of God, drunkenness, and gambling, and has introduced customs which subserve the highest purposes of growth and preservation. I do not believe that a system which has done such things can be outside God's beneficent plans for the evolution of humanity.[42]

As a rhetorician, Blyden outpaces the gentle periods of Bosworth Smith, but it was Smith who haunted missionary writers and speakers on Islam for a generation to come.[43] And their concern was not usually with

---

[41]See especially the collection of writings in *Christianity, Islam and the Negro Race* (London, 1887; 2nd ed., Edinburgh: Edinburgh University Press, 1967).

[42]J. G. G. Wilkinson, *The African and the True Christian Religion* (New York, 1892); the words are from a letter of Blyden to the author, printed as an appendix.

[43]Blyden noted the progress of Bosworth Smith's views: *Christianity, Islam and the Negro Race*, 189. The introductory paper of the Cairo Conference on missions claims that "many have been led to think of Islam as a mild oriental Unitarianism, well enough adapted to Asiatics and Africans" largely through the "misrepresentations of men like Bosworth Smith." This was thirty years after Smith's book first appeared. S. M. Zwemer, E. M. Wherry, and J. B. Barton, eds., *The Mohammedan World of Today: Being Papers Read at the First Missionary Conference on Behalf of the Mohammedan World . . .* (New York: Revell, 1904), 18.

his facile theology, but with his sociology. It is evident that it was the sociology that was appealing to a great deal of the educated British public opinion forming Smith's audience, opinion that created the climate in which administrative decisions were made.

In West Africa, the growing empires of the Western powers were colliding with the great Islamic grassland empires, the fruit of a complex process of Islamic revival and expansion; in Egypt and the Sudan, French and British interests were confronting each other; in East Africa, the Western powers were absorbing the areas once claimed by the sultanate of Zanzibar.[44] Incremental changes in the rest of the world now meant that the foremost ruler of the world's Muslims was no longer the sultan of Turkey but Queen Victoria. The Royal Republic of the Netherlands also claimed vast numbers of Muslim subjects; and the twentieth century was to bring a time, not far ahead, when, with the caliphate collapsed and Turkey secular, the emir of Afghanistan was almost the only genuinely independent Muslim ruler in the world.

Thus in the age of imperialism that Smith heralded, most of the Muslim world passed under the rule, or at least the dominance, of powers that had always been thought of as Christian. But, despite the optimism of some missionary commentators, such as Robert E. Speer,[45] this did not usher in a great new era of accessibility; the opening to missions of the doors the caliphate kept shut; indeed, the colonial powers were sometimes more efficient at gatekeeping than the sultan had been. Far more importantly, there seemed now good reasons why public policy should control the access of missions, not only to areas that were Islamic, but also to areas in which Islamic influence was, or might soon be, at work.

The era of imperial expansion is, of course, the era of missionary revival. Hundreds of new missionaries from the West pushed the frontiers of mission forward, seeking—in the eloquent title of a popular series of books at the time—the *Conquests of the Cross*.[46] As regards Africa, the idea developed of a race with Islam, a competition for the peoples of the continent. And what appeared to the mission constituency to stand in the way was the colonial administration, so tender of Islamic susceptibilities, it seemed, and so misled by the spirit of Bosworth Smith about the social

---

[44]Hastings, *Church in Africa*, 397–492, under the title "A Variety of Scrambles" relates the political and religious aspects.

[45]E.g., *Students and the Missionary Problem: Addresses Delivered at the International Student Missionary Conference, London, January 2–6, 1900* (London: Student Volunteer Missionary Union, 1900), 423–28. "Dare we say that the Mohammedans are inaccessible until we have tried? . . . When Islam has been won to Christianity we shall be able to give the world missionaries. Who dare say that they will not be even better than the Jews?"

[46]*Conquests of the Cross: A Record of Missionary Work Throughout the World* (London and New York: Cassell, 1890). The series of three volumes was compiled by Edwin Hodder.

effects of Islam, that it encouraged Muslim expansion and hindered Christian conversion. In the race for the soul of Africa, Christianity, it seemed, must contend with handicaps and heavy weights imposed by the administrative policies of Christian countries. The intellectual position of Christianity, the axiomatic character of its benefit to society, could no longer be taken for granted. It is in the heyday of imperialism that an unmistakable note of embattlement comes into missionary discourse.

That note of embattlement is very audible in the proceedings of the special missionary conferences called to consider missions in Muslim lands held in Cairo in 1906 and in Lucknow in 1911. Fifty years earlier the mission constituency had complained that British administration in India was trying to maintain neutrality in India when it should be declaring support for Christianity. At the Cairo conference, W. R. S. Miller, one of the most eloquent missionary figures associated with northern Nigeria, complained not that the British government practised neutrality in religion, but that it did not. Were the government truly neutral, Islam would not be making the progress it was in Nigeria, where the Plateau people had long experience of harsh treatment from Muslims. But while Muslim missionaries were allowed to go anywhere under British administration, Christian missionaries were restricted. "The inevitable results of a slave ridden land, laziness, oppression and dirt have fallen upon West Africa."[47] An American, C. R. Watson, made this general observation about colonialism and missions:

> The displacement of pagan governments by Western governments has generally been to the advantage of the missionary enterprise as a whole. Yet, when we consider only the way in which that change affects the status of Islam . . . the change from a pagan to a Western government has generally been to the advantage of Islam.[48]

The distinguished CMS missionary in Egypt, Temple Gairdner, was more direct. Contemporary British colonial policy was

> cowardly and unchristian. . . . The British official may one day see that all this subservience to the Muslim and neglect of his own faith gains him neither the respect, gratitude nor affection of the people, but the very reverse.[49]

---

[47]"Islam in West Africa," in Zwemer, Wherry, and Barton, eds., *Mohammedan World of Today*, 43–50.

[48]"Statistical and Comparative Survey of Islam in Africa," in ibid., 281–85.

[49]"Islam under Christian Rule" in E. M. Wherry, S. M. Zwemer, and C. G. Mylrea, eds., *Islam and Missions: Being Papers Read at the Second Missionary Conference on Behalf of the Mohammedan World at Lucknow* (New York: Revell, 1911), 195–205. The quotation is from p. 205.

The World Missionary Conference in Edinburgh in 1910 produced a documentation of the discrimination practised by Western governments against Christian missions in Islamic contexts, and made an official protest to what was seen as the chief culprit, the British government.[50]

In a period when the idea was developed of competition with Islam for the soul of Africa, the conclusion was that competition was unfairly skewed towards Islam by colonial policy. The missionary constituency itself became involved in the debate about the social effects of Islam—a theme very apparent in the discussions on Islam in the mission conferences of the last decade of the nineteenth century. The enemy were those, like Bosworth Smith (frequently mentioned by name long after the appearance of his sole book on the subject), who claimed a Christian standpoint yet urged that the effects of Islam on "primitive" peoples were beneficial. What made this so distressing was the opinion, now widely canvassed by European observers and loudly proclaimed by Blyden, that the social effects of Christian missions were, to say the least, ambiguous. It had once been a keystone of Christian thinking about Africa that Christianity and legitimate commerce would spread together, commerce checking the slave trade, which itself was one of the impediments to missions. But at the end of the century, with the Atlantic slave trade ended, commercial relations with Europe well established, and Christian missions in most of the trading centres, the most notable article of trade was distilled spirits. As the pyramids of gin bottles mounted in African villages, the word began to be heard that alcohol was a new slave trade even more devastating than the old one. And the areas in which this was most evident were the coastal territories, the most missionized. And what if the gin traders were Christians—whether from Christian Europe or Sierra Leone? (In the latter case they might well be teaching the people to sing hymns on Sunday.) If an alcoholic haze was truly hanging over West Africa as a result of the confluence of commerce, Christianity and civilization, was it really to be assumed that the social effects of Christianity were better than those where alcohol was renounced? Might not the spread of Islam be to the moral and temporal benefit of Africa?

A little book by C. H. Robinson[51] excellently represents a good deal of missionary writing. Robinson had been a member of the "Soudan Party," an early mission to northern Nigeria; he became lecturer in Hausa at

---

[50]World Missionary Conference 1910, vol. 7 *Missions and Governments* (Edinburgh and New York, 1910), 113.

[51]*Mohammedanism, Has It Any Future?* (London: Gardner Darton, 1897). Many of the same themes are addressed in Robinson's larger book, *Housaland or Fifteen Hundred Miles through the Central Soudan* (London: Sampson Low, 1896). Chapter 13 "Mohammedanism in the Central Soudan" sets out to counter "a considerable number of apologists in England, who, whilst professing Christianity themselves, have maintained that for a large portion of the human race, Mohammedanism is not only as good, but a distinctly better form of religion than that which they themselves profess." He quotes a letter to *The Times* by Sir William Carter, governor of Lagos, arguing for the spread of Islam as an answer to the alcohol problem.

Cambridge; and as editorial secretary for the Society for the Propagation of the Gospel, he was a prolific writer on missionary topics. His specific target in this work is "Christian apologists for Islam," and his purpose is to show that the reality of Islamic lands is not what ought to follow from Bosworth Smith's premises. Interestingly, he does not take the traditional line of denouncing Ottoman corruption: the Mediterranean lands were formerly Christian, and no index to the social effects of Islamic civilization. The theatre for judging that is Hausaland.

And Hausaland proves that Islam does not halt the new slavery of drunkenness: Muslims get as drunk as anyone. Certainly, the further north one goes, the less the incidence of drunkenness; but this simply represents distance from the source of pollution, Western trade—a trade due, not to Christianity, but to the highly secular Royal Niger Company. Nor does the experience of Hausaland suggest that Islam creates an advanced civilization: the celebrated Hausa cloth is pre-Islamic. What Islam has brought to Hausaland is slavery: a third of the Hausa are slaves, one in three hundred of the world's population is a Hausa-speaking slave. To the argument that Christians were for centuries responsible for the slavery of Africans, Robinson replies that slavery is integral to Islam, fundamentally antipathetic to Christianity.

This raises the link between theory and practice, by which the "Christian apologists for Islam" must be tested. Islam, Robinson concludes, may indeed raise "degraded savages" through the idea of the transcendent God and the practice of Arabic literacy. But it has little to offer "civilized heathenism," a category that seems to comprehend the Hausa. The reason is that Islam has a built-in block, a cultural progress *beyond a certain point.*

> Unless we are prepared to contemplate the African civilization . . . of a thousand years hence being on a level with that of the Arab even of today, we cannot look with other than grave mistrust and apprehension at the progress, be it great or small, which Islam is now making in Africa.[52]

In this way a significant element of mission thinking became drawn into the Western debate about the social effects of Islam in a period in which mission strategy became concerned with the idea of competition with Islam. In evangelical circles the German traveller Karl Kümm popularized the idea of competition in the whole "Sudan" (i.e., *Bilad es-Sudan*) region. The object was not to lock horns with Muslims, but to concentrate on non-Muslim peoples before they came under Islamic influence. The Sudan United Mission was one outcome of such thinking.[53] Other mis-

---

[52]Robinson, *Mohammedanism*, 27.
[53]See Hermann Karl Wilhelm Kümm, *The Sudan: A Short Compendium of Facts and Figures about the Lord of Darkness* (London: Marshall, 1906); *Khont-hon-nofer: The Lands of Ethiopia* (London: Marshall, 1910); *From Hausaland to Egypt* (London: Constable, 1910).

sions begged for missionary reenforcements to stem a tide of Islamic advance they expected (an expectation not always justified by the event).[54] In these new crusade days, the immediate challenge was to "occupy," that is, to get there first.

All this activity and controversy about Islam did little to advance direct Christian engagement, encounter, and conversation with Muslims. True, there were new developments in germ. The year 1911 saw the birth both of the journal *The Moslem World*[55] and The Kennedy School of Missions, which together (the latter through its Muslim Lands Department under Duncan Black Macdonald) were to have a deep influence on Protestant missionary thinking about Islam. But to a remarkable extent, and for a variety of reasons, the nineteenth century is a time of disengagement between Christians and Muslims. Every exception is significant, and one of them is Samuel Adjai Crowther and the African missionaries of the Niger.

Adrian Hastings, in the course of a characteristically discerning portrait of Crowther says,

> It might well be claimed that for all-round pastoral maturity he has no peer among nineteenth century Anglican bishops in Africa. . . . A combination of learning, zeal, sound judgment, regular visits to Britain, and the towering status provided by his bishopric set Crowther in a place apart until the end of his life. For his contemporaries, both black and white, he appeared to represent all that they could hope for.[56]

Perhaps he was also one of the nineteenth century's significant Christian conversationalists with Muslims.

---

[54]J. D. Holway, "CMS Contact with Islam in East Africa before 1914," *Journal of Religion in Africa* 4, no. 3 (1972): 200–212.

[55]This journal, the work of Samuel Marinus Zwemer, was designed to be "a quarterly review of current events, literature and thought among Mohammedans, and the progress of Christian missions in Moslem lands."

[56]Hastings, *Church in Africa*, 340.

8

Samuel Ajayi Crowther
(1807–1891)

Patterns of African Christianity in the Nineteenth Century

Samuel Adjai[1] Crowther was probably the most widely known African Christian of the nineteenth century. His life spanned the greater part of it—he was born in its first decade and died in the last. He lived through a transformation of relations between Africa and the rest of the world and a parallel transformation in the Christian situation in Africa. By the time of his death the bright confidence in an African church led by Africans, a reality that he seemed to embody in himself, had dimmed. Today things look very different. It seems a good time to consider the legacy of Crowther.

Slavery and Liberation

The story begins with the birth of a boy called Ajayi in the town of Oṣogun in Yorubaland, in what is now western Nigeria, in or about the year 1807. In later years the story was told that a diviner had indicated that Ajayi was not to enter any of the cults of the *oriṣa*, the divinities of the Yoruba pantheon, because he was to be a servant of Olorun,[2] the God of

---

First published in Gerald H. Anderson, Robert T. Coote, Norman A. Horner, and James M. Phillips, editors, *Mission Legacies: Biographical Studies of Leaders of the Modern Missionary Movement* (Maryknoll, NY: Orbis Books, 1994), pp. 132–39.

[1]Crowther himself spelled his Yoruba name (which he employed as a second name) thus. The modern spelling is Ajayi, and this spelling is commonly used today, especially by Nigerian writers.

[2]On the relation of the *oriṣa* to Olorun, see E. B. Idowu, *Olódùmarè: God in Yoruba Belief* (London: Longmans, 1962). Idowu argues that Olorun is never called an *orisa*, nor classed among them.

heaven.[3] He grew up in dangerous times. Both the breakup of the old Yoruba empire of Oyo, and the effect of the great Islamic jihads, which were establishing a new Fulani empire to the north, meant chaos for the Yoruba states. Warfare and raiding became endemic. Besides all the trauma of divided families and transplantation that African slavery could bring, the raids fed a still worse evil: the European traders at the coast. These maintained a trade in slaves, illegal but still richly profitable, across the Atlantic.

When Crowther was about thirteen, Oṣogun was raided, apparently by a combination of Fulani and Oyo Muslims. Crowther twice recorded his memories of the event, vividly recalling the desolation of burning houses, the horror of capture and roping by the neck, the slaughter of those unfit to travel, the distress of being torn from relatives. Ajayi changed hands six times before being sold to Portuguese traders for the transatlantic market.

The colony of Sierra Leone had been founded by a coalition of anti-slavery interests, mostly evangelical Christian in inspiration and belonging to the circle associated with William Wilberforce and the "Clapham Sect." It was intended from the beginning as a Christian settlement, free from slavery and the slave trade. The first permanent element in the population was a group of former slaves from the New World. Following the abolition of the slave trade by the British Parliament in 1807 and the subsequent treaties with other nations to outlaw the traffic, Sierra Leone achieved a new importance. It was a base for the naval squadron that searched vessels to find if they were carrying slaves. It was also the place where slaves were brought if any were found aboard. The Portuguese ship on which Ajayi was taken as a slave was intercepted by the British naval squadron in April 1822, and he, like thousands of other uprooted, disoriented people from inland Africa, was put ashore in Sierra Leone.

By this time, Sierra Leone was becoming a Christian community. It was one of the few early successes of the missionary movement, though the Christian public at large was probably less conscious of the success than of the appalling mortality of missionaries in what became known as the "White Man's Grave." To all appearances, the whole way of life of Sierra Leone—clothing, buildings, language, education, religion, even names—closely followed Western models. These were people of diverse origins whose cohesion and original identity were now beyond recall. They accepted the combination of Christian faith and Western lifestyle that Sierra Leone offered, a combination already represented in the oldest inhabitants of the colony, the settled slaves from the New World.

Such was the setting in which young Ajayi now found himself. We know little of his early years there. Later he wrote,

---

[3]The story is representative of hundreds that show the God of the Bible active in the African past through such prophecies of the Christian future of Africa.

About the third year of my liberation from the slavery of man, I was convinced of another worse state of slavery, namely, that of sin and Satan. It pleased the Lord to open my heart. . . . I was admitted into the visible Church of Christ here on earth as a soldier to fight manfully under his banner against our spiritual enemies.[4]

He was baptized by the Reverend John Raban, of the (Anglican) Church Missionary Society (CMS), taking the name Samuel Crowther, after a member of that society's home committee. Mr. Crowther was an eminent clergyman; his young namesake was to make the name far more celebrated.

Crowther had spent those early years in Sierra Leone at school, getting an English education, adding carpentry to his traditional weaving and agricultural skills. In 1827 the Church Missionary Society decided, for the sake of Sierra Leone's future Christian leadership, to provide education to a higher level than the colony's modest schools had given. The resultant "Christian Institution" developed as Fourah Bay College, which eventually offered the first university education in tropical Africa. Crowther was one of its first students.

The Loom of Language

This period marked the beginning of the work that was to form one of the most abiding parts of Crowther's legacy. He continued to have contact with Raban, who had baptized him; and Raban was one of the few missionaries in Sierra Leone to take African languages seriously. To many of his colleagues the priority was to teach English, which would render the African languages unnecessary. Raban realized that such policy was a dead end; he also realized that Yoruba, Crowther's mother tongue, was a major language. (Yoruba had not been prominent in the early years of Sierra Leone, but the political circumstances that had led to young Ajayi's captivity were to bring many other Yoruba to the colony.) Crowther became an informant for Raban, who between 1828 and 1830 published three little books about Yoruba; and almost certainly he also assisted another pioneer African linguist, the Quaker educationist Hannah Kilham.

Crowther was appointed a schoolmaster of the mission, serving in the new villages created to receive "liberated Africans" from the slave ships. A schoolmaster was an evangelist; in Sierra Leone church and school were inseparable. We get glimpses of an eager, vigorous young man who, at least at first, was highly confrontational in his encounters with represen-

---

[4]A. F. Walls, "A Second Narrative of Samuel Ajayi Crowther's Early Life," *Bulletin of the Society for African History* 2 (1965): 14.

tatives of Islam and the old religions in Africa. In later life he valued the lessons of this apprenticeship—the futility of abuse, the need to build personal relationships, and the ability to listen patiently.

Crowther began study of the Temne language, which suggests a missionary vision towards the hinterland of Sierra Leone. But he also worked systematically at his own language, as far as the equipment at hand allowed.

Transformation of the Scene

Two developments now opened a new chapter for Crowther and for Sierra Leone Christianity. One was a new link with Yorubaland. Enterprising liberated Africans, banding together and buying confiscated slave ships, began trading far afield from Freetown. Some of Yoruba origin found their way back to their homeland. They settled there, but kept the Sierra Leone connections and the ways of life of Christian Freetown. The second development was the Niger Expedition of 1841, the brief flowering of the humanitarian vision for Africa of Sir Thomas Fowell Buxton. This investigative mission, intended to prepare the way for an alliance of "Christianity, commerce, and civilization" that would destroy the slave trade and bring peace and prosperity to the Niger, relied heavily on Sierra Leone for interpreters and other helpers. The missionary society representatives also came from Sierra Leone. One was J. F. Schön, a German missionary who had striven with languages of the Niger, learning from liberated Africans in Sierra Leone. The other was Crowther.

Crowther's services to the disaster-stricken expedition were invaluable. Schön cited them as evidence of his thesis that the key to the evangelization of inland Africa lay in Sierra Leone. Sierra Leone had Christians such as Crowther to form the task force; it had among the liberated Africans brought there from the slave ships a vast language laboratory for the study of all the languages of West Africa, as well as a source of native speakers as missionaries; and in the institution at Fourah Bay it had a base for study and training.

The Niger Expedition had shown Crowther's qualities, and he was brought to England for study and ordination. The latter was of exceptional significance. Anglican ordination could be received only from a bishop, and there was no bishop nearer than London. Here then, in 1843, began Sierra Leone's indigenous ministry.[5]

---

[5]Crowther was not the first African to receive Anglican ordination. As early as 1765, Philip Quaque, from Cape Coast in what is now Ghana, who had been brought to England as a boy, was appointed chaplain to the British trading settlement at Cape Coast. He died in 1816. Crowther had never heard of him until he went ashore at Cape Coast en route to the Niger in 1841 and saw a memorial tablet. See Jesse Page, *The Black Bishop* (London: Hodder and Stoughton, 1908), 53.

Here, too, began Crowther's literary career, with the publication of *Yoruba Vocabulary*, including an account of grammatical structure, surely the first such work by a native speaker of an African language.

The Yoruba Mission

Meanwhile, the new connection between Sierra Leone and Yoruba-land had convinced the CMS of the timeliness of a mission to the Yoruba. There had been no opportunity to train that African mission force foreseen by Schön and Crowther in their report on the Niger Expedition, but at least in Crowther there was one ordained Yoruba missionary available. Thus, after an initial reconnaissance by Henry Townsend, an English missionary from Sierra Leone, a mission party went to Abeokuta, the state of the Egba section of the Yoruba people. It was headed by Townsend, Crowther, and a German missionary, C. A. Gollmer, with a large group of Sierra Leoneans from the liberated Yoruba community. These included carpenters and builders who were also teachers and catechists. The mission intended to demonstrate a whole new way of life, of which the church and the school and the well-built house were all a part. They were establishing Sierra Leone in Yorubaland. The Sierra Leone trader-immigrants, the people who had first brought Abeokuta to the attention of the mission, became the nucleus of the new Christian community.

The CMS Yoruba mission is a story in itself. How the mission, working on Buxton's principles, introduced the growing and processing of cotton and arranged for its export, thereby keeping Abeokuta out of the slave economy; how the missionaries identified with Abeokuta under invasion and reaped their reward afterward; how the CMS mobilized Christian opinion to influence the British government on behalf of Abeokuta; and the toils into which the mission fell amid inter-Yoruba and colonial conflicts, have been well told elsewhere.[6] Crowther came to London in 1851 to present the cause of Abeokuta. He saw government ministers; he had an interview with the Queen and Prince Albert; he spoke at meetings all over the country, invariably to great effect. This grave, eloquent, well-informed black clergyman was the most impressive tribute to the effect of the missionary movement that most British people had seen; and Henry Venn, the CMS secretary who organized the visit, believed that it was Crowther who finally moved the government to action.

But the missionaries' day-to-day activities lay in commending the gospel and nourishing the infant church. There was a particularly moving incident for Crowther, when he was reunited with the mother and sister

---

[6]Especially by J. F. A. Ajayi, *Christian Missions in Nigeria: 1841–1891* (London: Longmans, 1965). See also S. O. Biobaku, *The Egba and Their Neighbours: 1842–1874* (Oxford: Clarendon Press, 1957).

from whom he had been separated when the raiders took them more than twenty years earlier. They were among the first in Abeokuta to be baptized.

In Sierra Leone the church had used English in its worship. The new mission worked in Yoruba, with the advantage of native speakers in Crowther and his family and in most of the auxiliaries, and with Crowther's book to assist the Europeans. Townsend, an excellent practical linguist, even edited a Yoruba newspaper. But the most demanding activity was Bible translation.

The significance of the Yoruba version has not always been observed. It was not the first translation into an African language; but, insofar as Crowther was the leading influence in its production, it was the first by a native speaker. Early missionary translations naturally relied heavily on native speakers as informants and guides; but in no earlier case was a native speaker able to judge and act on an equal footing with the European.

Crowther insisted that the translation should indicate tone—a new departure. In vocabulary and style he sought to get behind colloquial speech by listening to the elders, by noting significant words that emerged in his discussions with Muslims or specialists in the old religion. Over the years, wherever he was, he noted words, proverbs, forms of speech. One of his hardest blows was the loss of the notes of eleven years of such observations, and some manuscript translations, when his house burned down in 1862.

Written Yoruba was the product of missionary committee work, Crowther interacting with his European colleagues on matters of orthography. Henry Venn engaged the best linguistic expertise available in Europe—not only Schön and the society's regular linguistic adviser, Professor Samuel Lee of Cambridge, but also the great German philologist Lepsius. The outcome may be seen in the durability of the Yoruba version of the Scriptures to which Crowther was the chief contributor and in the vigorous vernacular literature in Yoruba that has grown up.

New Niger Expeditions and a Mission to the Niger

In 1854 the merchant McGregor Laird sponsored a new Niger Expedition, on principles similar to the first, but with a happier outcome. The CMS sent Crowther on this expedition. It revived the vision he had seen in 1841—a chain of missionary operations hundreds of miles along the Niger, into the heart of the continent. He urged a beginning at Onitsha, in Igboland.

The opportunity was not long in coming. In 1857 he and J. C. Taylor, a Sierra Leonean clergyman of liberated Igbo parentage, joined Laird's next expedition to the Niger. Taylor opened the Igbo mission at Onitsha; Crowther went upriver. Shipwrecked, and stranded for months, he began to study the Nupe language and surveyed openings to the Nupe and Hausa peoples. The Niger Mission had begun.

Henry Venn soon made a formal structure for it. But it was a mission on a new principle. Crowther led a mission force consisting entirely of

Africans. Sierra Leone, as he and Schön had foreseen so long ago, was now evangelizing inland Africa.

For nearly half a century that tiny country sent a stream of missionaries, ordained and lay, to the Niger territories. The area was vast and diverse: Muslim emirates in the north, ocean-trading city-states in the delta, the vast Igbo populations in between. It is cruel that the missionary contribution of Sierra Leone has been persistently overlooked, and even denied.[7]

It is possible here to consider only three aspects of a remarkable story. Two have been somewhat neglected.

More Legacy in Language

One of these is the continued contribution to language study and translation. Crowther himself wrote the first book on Igbo.[8] He begged Schön, now serving an English parish, to complete his Hausa dictionary. He sent one of his missionaries to study Hausa with Schön. Most of his Sierra Leone staff, unlike people of his own generation, were not native speakers of the languages of the areas they served. The great Sierra Leone language laboratory was closing down; English and the common language, Krio, took over from the languages of the liberated. Add to this the limited education of many Niger missionaries, and their record of translation and publication is remarkable.

The Engagement with Islam

Crowther's Niger Mission also represents the first sustained missionary engagement with African Islam in modern times. In the Upper Niger areas in Crowther's time, Islam, largely accepted by the chiefs, was working slowly through the population in coexistence with the old religion. From his early experiences in Sierra Leone, Crowther understood how Islamic practice could merge with traditional views of power. He found a demand for Arabic Bibles, but was cautious about supplying them unless he could be sure they would not be used for charms. His insight was justified later, when the young European missionaries who succeeded him wrote out pas-

---

[7]Repeated, for instance, by Stephen Neill, *Christian Missions*, Pelican History of the Church (Harmondsworth: Penguin Books, 1964), 306: "It is only to be regretted that its Christianity has not proved expansive." In fact, few countries can claim so *much* expansion in proportion to the numbers of the Christian population.

[8]See P. E. H. Hair, *The Early Study of Nigerian Languages* (Cambridge: Cambridge University Press, 1967), 82, for an assessment. See Stephen Neill, *Christian Missions* (377f.), for the common impression of the linguistic incompetence of Crowther and the Niger missionaries. Hair's careful catalog of their translations in the languages of the Lower Niger, as well as his descriptions of Crowther's linguistic surveys in the Upper Niger, show how misleading this is.

sages of Scripture on request, pleased at such a means of Scripture distribution. They stirred up the anger of Muslim clerics, not because they were circulating Christian Scriptures, but because they were giving them away free, thus undercutting the trade in qur'anic charms. In discussion with Muslims, Crowther sought common ground and found it at the nexus of Qur'an and Bible: Christ as the great prophet, his miraculous birth, Gabriel as the messenger of God. He enjoyed courteous and friendly relations with Muslim rulers, and his writings trace various discussions with rulers, courts, and clerics, recording the questions raised by Muslims, and his own answers, the latter as far as possible in the words of Scripture: "After many years' experience, I have found that the Bible, the sword of the Spirit, must fight its own battle, by the guidance of the Holy Spirit."[9]

Christians should of course defend Trinitarian doctrine, but let them do so mindful of the horror-stricken cry of the Qur'an, "Is it possible that Thou dost teach that Thou and Thy Mother are two Gods?" In other words, Christians must show that the things that the Muslims fear as blasphemous are no part of Christian doctrine.

Crowther, though no great scholar or Arabist, developed an approach to Islam in its African setting that reflected the patience and the readiness to listen that marked his entire missionary method. Avoiding denunciation and allegations of false prophecy, it worked by acceptance of what the Qur'an says of Christ, and an effective knowledge of the Bible. Crowther looked to the future with hope; the average African Christian knew the Bible much better than the average African Muslim knew the Qur'an. And he pondered the fact that the Muslim rule of faith was expressed in Arabic, the Christian in Hausa, or Nupe or Yoruba. The result was different understandings of how the faith was to be applied in life.

The Indigenization of the Episcopate

The best-known aspect of Crowther's later career is also the most controversial: his representation of the indigenous church principle. We have seen that he was the first ordained minister of his church in his place. It was the policy of Henry Venn, then newly at the helm of the CMS, to strengthen the indigenous ministry. More and more Africans were ordained, some for the Yoruba mission. And Venn wanted well-educated, well-trained African clergy; such people as Crowther's son Dandeson (who became archdeacon) and his son-in-law T. B. Macaulay (who became principal of Lagos Grammar School) were better educated than many of the homespun English missionaries.

Venn sought self-governing, self-supporting, self-propagating churches with a fully indigenous pastorate. In Anglican terms, this meant

---

[9]Crowther, *Experiences with Heathens and Mohammedans in West Africa* (London, 1892), 28.

indigenous bishops. The missionary role was a temporary one; once a church was established, the missionary should move on. The birth of the church brought the euthanasia of the mission. With the growth of the Yoruba church, Venn sought to get these principles applied in Yorubaland. Even the best European missionaries thought this impractical, the hobbyhorse of a doctrinaire home-based administrator.

As we have seen, Venn made a new sphere of leadership for Crowther, the outstanding indigenous minister in West Africa. But he went further, and in 1864 secured the consecration of Crowther as bishop of "the countries of Western Africa beyond the limits of the Queen's dominions," a title reflecting some constraints imposed by Crowther's European colleagues and the peculiarities of the relationship of the Church of England to the crown. Crowther, a genuinely humble man, resisted; Venn would take no refusal.

In one sense, the new diocese represented the triumph of the "three-self principle" and the indigenization of the episcopate. But it reflected a compromise, rather than the full expression of those principles. It was, after all, essentially a *mission*, drawing most of its clergy not from natives of the soil but from Sierra Leone. Its ministry was "native" only in the sense of not being European. Three-self principles required it to be self-supporting; this meant meager resources, missionaries who got no home leave, and the need to present education as a salable product.

The story of the later years of the Niger mission has often been told and variously interpreted. It still raises passions and causes bitterness.[10] There is no need here to recount more than the essentials: that questions arose about the lives of some of the missionaries; that European missionaries were brought into the mission, and then took it over, brushing aside the old bishop (he was over eighty) and suspending or dismissing his staff. In 1891 Crowther, a desolate, broken man, suffered a stroke; on the last day of the year, he died. A European bishop was appointed to succeed him. The self-governing church and the indigenization of the episcopate were abandoned.

Contemporary mission accounts all praise Crowther's personal integrity, graciousness, and godliness. In the Yoruba mission, blessed with many strong, not to say prickly, personalities, his influence had been irenic. In Britain he was recognized as a cooperative and effective platform speaker. (A CMS official remembered Crowther's being called on to give a conference address on "Mission and Women" and holding his audience spellbound.) Yet the same sources not only declared Crowther "a weak bishop" but also drew the moral that "the African race" lacked the capacity to rule.

---

[10]See E. A. Ayandele, *The Missionary Impact on Modern Nigeria: 1842–1914* (London: Longmans, 1966), for a representative modern African view. Neill, *Christian Missions*, 377, reflects the traditional "missionary" view. Ajayi, *Christian Missions in Nigeria*, sets the context, and G. O. M. Tassie notes some neglected factors in his *Christian Missionary Enterprise in the Niger Delta: 1864–1918* (Leiden: Brill, 1978).

European thought about Africa had changed since the time of Buxton; the Western powers were now in Africa to govern. Missionary thought about Africa had changed since the days of Henry Venn; there were plenty of keen, young English workers to extend the mission and order the church; a self-governing church now seemed to matter much less. And evangelical religion had changed since Crowther's conversion; it had become more individualistic and more otherworldly. A young English missionary was distressed that the old bishop who preached so splendidly on the blood of Christ could urge on a chief the advantages of having a school and make no reference to the future life.[11] This story illustrates in brief the two evangelical itineraries: the short route via Keswick, and the long one via the White Man's Grave, the Niger Expedition, and the courts of Muslim rulers of the north.

There were some unexpected legacies even from the last sad days. One section of the Niger Mission, that in the Niger Delta, was financially self-supporting. Declining the European takeover, it long maintained a separate existence under Crowther's son, Archdeacon Dandeson Crowther, within the Anglican Communion but outside the CMS. It grew at a phenomenal rate, becoming so self-propagating that it ceased to be self-supporting.[12]

Other voices called for direct schism; the refusal to appoint an African successor to Crowther, despite the manifest availability of outstanding African clergy, marks an important point in the history of African independent churches.[13] The treatment of Crowther, and still more the question of his successor, gave a focus for the incipient nationalist movement of which E. W. Blyden was the most eloquent spokesman.[14] Crowther thus has his own modern place in the martyrology of African nationalism.

But the majority of Christians, including those natural successors of Crowther who were passed over or, worse, suffered denigration or abuse, took no such course. They simply waited. Crowther was the outstanding representative of a whole body of West African church leaders who came to the fore in the preimperial age and were superseded in the imperial. But the imperial age itself was to be only an episode. The legacy of Samuel Ajayi Crowther, the humble, devout exponent of a Christian faith that was essentially African and essentially missionary, has passed to the whole vast church of Africa and thus to the whole vast church of Christ.

---

[11] Ajayi, *Christian Missions in Nigeria,* 218.

[12] For the story, see Tasie, *Christian Missionary Enterprise.* See also Jehu J. Hanciles, "Dandeson Coates Crowther and the Niger Delta Pastorate: Blazing Torch or Flickering Flame?" *International Bulletin of Missionary Research* 18, no. 4 (1994): 166–72.

[13] See J. B. Webster, *The African Churches among the Yoruba* (Oxford: Clarendon Press, 1964).

[14] See, for instance, H. R. Lynch, *Edward Wilmot Blyden* (London: Oxford University Press).

9

The Significance of Harry Sawyerr

Harry Alphonso Ebun Sawyerr[1] was born in the colony of Sierra Leone, on 16 October 1909. Soon afterwards his father, O'Brien Sawyerr, was sent to the recently opened station of Boma Sakrim, in Mende country in the south of the Sierra Leone protectorate, as an agent of the Sierra Leone church missions, the Sierra Leone church having taken over the Church Missionary Society's missions within the protectorate. Boma Sakrim was his posting until 1916; he afterwards served elsewhere in the protectorate, notably at Bo, the administrative centre, before ordination in 1922 and returning to the Freetown area on the staff of the Sierra Leone Native Pastorate, that first fruit of Henry Venn's missionary policy of self-governing, self-supporting, self-propagating churches.

His son Harry was thus brought up not only in the atmosphere of the church, but also in the midst of missionary work, of the primary encounter between the Christian faith and the old religions of Africa. He also grew into a double heritage. On one side lay the Krio Sierra Leone of the nineteenth century with its long Christian history and remarkable record of missionary enterprise beyond its borders. That tiny country ("the Colony") had appropriated the English language and British institutions; it had also developed a distinctive language and culture of its own, absorbing those Western elements into the soil of Africa. The other side of his heritage was the traditional Africa in which so much of his early life was spent. The British protectorate that effectively fixed the borders of the

---

First published as the introduction to John Parratt, editor, *The Practice of Presence: Shorter Writings of Harry Sawyerr* (Grand Rapids, MI: Eerdmans, 1995). Reprinted with permission.

[1]The distinctively Sierra Leonean spelling of the name originated in a printing error. The brothers Moses and T. J. Sawyer opened a stationers' and booksellers' business in Freetown in 1856, becoming also the local Bible Society agents. They ordered printed invoices from England, which arrived containing the supernumerary *r*. Rather than waste them, they put them to use, and accepted the consequences. See C. Fyfe, *A History of Sierra Leone* (London: Oxford University Press 1962), 304.

modern republic of Sierra Leone was then still new. The Mende heartland, with social and religious structures resilient against change, represented a new Sierra Leone, with power to transform the old one. Harry Sawyerr was one of the people on whom fell the task of assisting the transition to a new nation that would draw from both streams.

Sawyerr was a "one nation" man who united various strands in himself. Much about him was archetypically Krio; the Krio have always moved in the Western intellectual universe as proprietors, not as borrowers or squatters. And he belonged to that Krio tradition which affirmed and gloried in its African origins. He was, for instance, a vigorous champion of the Krio language (and an eloquent exponent of it) at a period when some leaders of the community denigrated it as degenerate English. "It is full of colour and empathy, like all other African languages," he asserted in an early foray into the media, "and sounds African."[2] Yet he was also deeply marked by Mendeland, and his love for and fascination with things Mende never left him. One of his earliest scholarly publications was an article on Mende grammar;[3] one of the most significant is his presentation and expansion of the collected observations of the Methodist missionary W. T. Harris, published in 1968 as *The Springs of Mende Belief and Conduct*.[4] His interest in Mende language never failed,[5] and he could combine his philological and theological concerns, as in his "essay in detection" about the Mende name of God.[6] He also took an interest in the affairs of the Freetown Kru community with its Liberian links.[7] His sense of identity was, in fact, complex, confident, and catholic; and these were qualities much needed in his time and place. Confidence in Africa, confidence in Africanness, were essential, for he grew up in a colonial setting when European paternalism was at its crudest, and in a community that was frequently the butt of European scorn. Not until a late period of his life were many in the West expecting innovative intellectual or cultural

---

[2]*Sierra Leone Weekly News*, 30 October and 6 November 1937. On the controversy, see Akintola Wyse, *The Krio of Sierra Leone: An Interpretive History* (London: Hurst, 1989), 96ff.

[3]"Prepositions and Post-positions in the Mende Language," *Sierra Leone Studies* (1957): 209–20.

[4]Freetown: Sierra Leone University Press, 1968. The Rev. W. T. Harris died in 1959, shortly after preparing articles on Mende marriage and inheritance law, which appeared in the earliest issues of the *Sierra Leone Bulletin of Religion*, published by the faculty of theology at Fourah Bay College. Some years afterwards his widow made available to the faculty the much larger manuscript that he had prepared.

[5]See his article with S. K. Todd, "The Significance of the Numbers Three and Four among the Mende," *Sierra Leone Studies* 26 (1972): 29–33.

[6]"Ngewo and Ngawu: An Essay in Detection of the Origins of the Mende Concept of God," *Sierra Leone Bulletin of Religion* 9, no. 2 (1967): 26–33.

[7]See his article with A. W. Sawyerr, "Dison: A Kroo Rite," *Sierra Leone Bulletin of Religion* 5, no. 2 (1963): 47–54.

contributions from Africa, or anything higher than creditable imitation of Western models, and he and his colleagues had long to put up with a good deal of patronage and condescension. Catholicity, readiness to appropriate the manysidedness of the African heritage, was equally important in the era of emerging nationhood, when ethnic diversity could be so destructively exploited. The Krio tradition has sometimes reflected the parochialism of a small community, but its cosmopolitan origins, international dispersion, and broad knowledge of the world have at other times combined to give a compelling pan-African vision, a vision of Africa's place in the world community. Harry Sawyerr had this vision.

Back in Freetown, young Harry Sawyerr attended the Prince of Wales Secondary School, showing great promise and developing a keen interest in science. At this point he came under one of the crucial influences in his life, the Freetown legend T. S. Johnson, whom in the dedication of one of his books he was to salute posthumously as "Scholar, Teacher, Theologian, Evangelist, a Father in God and my Patron."[8]

The Rev. Thomas Sylvester Johnson, later bishop, was then tutor at Fourah Bay College in the theory and practice of education. He deserves his own footnote in the history of African theological writing. His locally published book *The Fear-Fetish: Its Cause and Cure*[9] is a little-noticed study of the tension felt by many African Christians between the elements of a worldview that emanates essentially from Africa (especially what Johnson calls the "fear-fetish") and a Christian faith that has not been integrated with that worldview. Much of Harry Sawyerr's most creative future work was to be directed to that very issue, and he was to reach dimensions of the question that his mentor never glimpsed.

Johnson's immediate aim at the time of their early encounters was the recruitment of first-rate teachers, and he identified Harry Sawyerr as suitable material, encouraged him in his studies, and eventually brought him to continue those studies with himself at Fourah Bay College. Johnson's vision of education—full, rounded, undiluted—as essential to human development and Christian ministry in Africa was absorbed by his young pupil. Economic development alone would not suffice. "We have also to develop and cultivate our minds so that we can dream dreams and see visions," the good bishop was still telling Fourah Bay students at the end of

---

[8]Dedication of *God: Ancestor or Creator?* (London: Longman, 1970).

[9]Freetown, 1949. Johnson also wrote a history of the (Anglican) Sierra Leone Church: *The Story of a Mission. The Sierra Leone Church: First Daughter of CMS* (London: SPCK, 1953). There is, appropriately enough, a commemoratory essay on him in the festschrift published for Harry Sawyerr: Mateï Markwei, "Harry Sawyerr's Patron (Bishop T. S. Johnson)," in M. E. Glasswell and E. W. Fasholé-Luke, eds., *New Testament Christianity for Africa and the World, Essays in Honour of Harry Sawyerr* (London: SPCK, 1974), 179–97. The same work includes a bibliography of Sawyerr's writings to 1974.

his life; and he enforced it by quoting J. E. K. Aggrey: "Give us Science, yea, more Science, but do not give us less Greek."[10] That is an authentic Sawyerr note too, and it is no surprise to find Sawyerr publishing this sermon of his old teacher long afterwards as a tract for the times.[11] He, too, held with passion that part of Africa's liberation lay in taking hold of the whole corpus of learning and in developing the faculties of scholarship and research. For him, there were no areas or levels of study or learning that could be treated as inappropriate to Africa. He was not particularly afraid of the implicit colonialism that might arise from the form and content of Western learning. His fear was the colonialism that arose from ignorance, underresourcing, or the patronizing judgment that certain expressions of intellectual activity desirable for the West were unnecessary for Africa. This conviction underlay his later attitude to the study of theology. Pioneer of African theology as he became, and one ever anxious to extend its applications, he saw no need to revise the received framework of the theological disciplines, and he vigorously maintained the classical approach to biblical studies, and was wary of attempts to dismiss any particular academic activity as "irrelevant" to Africa.

Fourah Bay, an institution unique in West Africa, claimed Harry Sawyerr's lifelong devotion and unstinting service. He joined it first as a student, took his first arts degree there, and later received the M.A. and the M.Ed. (education was still then his primary field). He became successively tutor, lecturer, head of the theology department, professor of theology (1962), principal (1968), and vice-chancellor of the University of Sierra Leone (1972). This catalog marks not only his own, but also the college's, development over three and a half decades. Founded by the Church Missionary Society in 1827, it had for the succeeding century and more been West Africa's premier educational institution. Since 1876 it had been affiliated with the University of Durham, preparing students for the degrees of that university. It had attracted students from across the length and breadth of English-speaking West Africa. It had produced graduates of distinction (none more so than the first on its roll, Bishop Samuel Ajayi Crowther); it had been a base of serious scholarship (most notably the pioneer work of S. W. Koelle in African linguistics in the mid-nineteenth century); it had been at the centre of successive visionary strategies for Christian expansion, educational development, and academic progress in West Africa. And until after the Second World War, it did this from the re-

---

[10]T. S. Johnson, "New Life for Old: Congregation Sermon Preached in the College Chapel on Mount Aureol on January 20th, 1953," *Sierra Leone Bulletin of Religion* 8, no. 2 (1966): 41.

[11]Harry Sawyerr, at that time editor of the *Bulletin*, adds a note indicating the appropriateness of the sermon to the new situation, the creation of a national university.

sources of a small mission institution.[12] It is little wonder that its history is marked by recurrent failures of nerve, collapsing infrastructure, and threats of closure. There were several such crises during Harry Sawyerr's association with the college, but those years also saw the most remarkable period of development in its long history.

Fourah Bay College was in those days essentially a church institution, even if theological students were a minority of the student body. It was also the apex of Sierra Leone's educational system, a monument in which Sierra Leoneans felt pride; and the link with Durham, and the presence of students from other African territories—who came because there was no such institution at home—gave it a cosmopolitan significance. This early formation lay behind the close relationship of church, education, and national development that conditioned Harry Sawyerr's view of theology. Fourah Bay, even as a national university, never developed the "religious studies" model pioneered by Ibadan and characteristic of African universities generally. Sawyerr's view of the place of theology in the university sometimes surprised secular-minded expatriate educational experts who appeared in Sierra Leone from the 1950s. It was not based on triumphalist claims for supremacy, but on an assumption of the universal relevance of theology to all spheres of human activity, and of the responsibility of the churches to make their contribution in every sphere. It was a Johnsonian view, an expression of the attitude that had kept Fourah Bay College in being so long, and that had frequently to contend with an alternative view, that the church should confine itself to a purely "spiritual" sphere. Harry Sawyerr's own commitment to the church was sealed by his ordination in 1943; his activity in the community, however, was many-sided.

The Second World War brought Fourah Bay College to the brink of extinction. Its buildings were commandeered, and its skeleton staff and drastically reduced student body were moved forty miles out to Mabang; and in this state they were visited by the Elliot Commission on the postwar shape of higher education in West Africa. When the report was considered, the secretary of state decided that Sierra Leone's modest needs for university provision could best be met at the new Nigerian university college in Ibadan.

Freetown was indignant; Sierra Leone had pioneered university education in West Africa. The community rallied to the support of its college, protectorate voices joining with those of the colony, and bringing financial

---

[12]In 1953, Bishop Johnson claimed that throughout the (fifty-nine) years he had been connected with the college, it had never received more than £200 of government aid in a year (Johnson, "New Life for Old," 41, 44 n. 1). From 1918, the Wesleyan Methodist (later the Methodist) Missionary Society participated in the college; subsequently, the third of Sierra Leone's major churches, and the largest in the protectorate, the Evangelical United Brethren (since joined with the American Methodists in the United Methodist Church) also joined.

backing that had been lacking in previous crises at the college.[13] The eventual outcome was the reconstitution of Fourah Bay College, with significant government funding and a broadbased council, on a magnificent new mountain site above Freetown. The place of the churches, and especially that of the Church Missionary Society, in the college history was recognized, and the link with the University of Durham maintained and broadened; but Fourah Bay was now in effect, if not yet in name, a university college, in parallel with its better-known and better-financed siblings in Ghana and Nigeria.

For some of the years of decision, Harry Sawyerr had been absent from Sierra Leone. From 1945 to 1948, accompanied by his vivacious wife, Edith, he was studying theology at the University of Durham. Durham theology at the time was rigorous in the classical mode, emphatic on the importance of the biblical languages and of the theology of the Greek and Latin fathers, and strongly Anglican in flavour. The ecclesiastical traditions of Sierra Leone were those of the evangelical Church Missionary Society; in Durham Harry Sawyerr drank deeply of the Anglican Catholic stream also. It was probably an advantage that his student contemporaries were of the older, war-experienced generation. Outgoing, cheerful, interested, and concerned about everything and everyone, he made abiding friendships, not least among his teachers, including Michael Ramsay, the future archbishop of Canterbury. His attendance at the Pan-African Conference in Manchester in 1945, that landmark in the history of African nationalism, is also significant.

He returned to Sierra Leone to take a responsible place in the new Fourah Bay. His primary assignment was to maintain and develop the place of academic theology in a growing institution no longer under the direction of the church, serving the needs of an emerging nation. Soon after Fourah Bay's new constitution came Sierra Leone's "Stevenson Constitution" of 1951, and elections that brought Dr. Milton Margai, a Mende man from the protectorate, to be head of the government. The pattern was set for the future. Sierra Leone gained independence from Britain in 1961; in the same period, Fourah Bay gained its independence from Durham, as the University College of Sierra Leone. (In 1966 came further legislation by which Fourah Bay College and the University College of Njala became parts of a federal University of Sierra Leone.)

The church to which Harry Sawyerr returned had great traditions, but perhaps a sense of being left behind in the march to nationhood. In several respects it was ill-adjusted to the new age; its ministry was aging, and its centre of gravity lay heavily in the old colony. Sawyerr worked to reinvigorate it and to equip it to play an effective part in national life. In this project the Department of Theology had an important place. An ecumeni-

---

[13]Johnson, *Story of a Mission*, 103ff.

cal ministerial programme and a licence in theology, regular vacation clergy schools, and publication of a series of Aureol pamphlets were all initiatives based in the Department of Theology. In 1962 he became a canon of St. George's Cathedral, Freetown. He was perhaps too controversial a figure to become bishop; but in terms of pastoral care and concern, no one was a more devoted or time-taking shepherd, as countless students, clergy, and other people can testify. The 1960s also saw him making an impact on the wider church as his stature as a theological thinker was recognized in ecumenical circles. From 1962, he was a member of the Commission on Faith and Order of the World Council of Churches, and later of its working committee.

Meanwhile, he was head of a theology department that had to make its way as an academic department among other academic departments. Most of its students did not have the ministry in mind. A high proportion, as in most departments in those days, came from Nigeria, for Fourah Bay long continued to attract students from there. Harry Sawyerr devoted his energies principally to the study and teaching of the New Testament. He developed a novel thesis about the preconversion background of Saul of Tarsus,[14] contributed to the debate about the framework of the Second Gospel,[15] and spent years on a major study of Pauline theology that was not published. He became a conspicuous figure at gatherings of the international (but at that time almost entirely Western) society of New Testament scholars, the Studiorum Novi Testamenti Societas. A glance at the eminent names in the New Testament field that occur in the *tabula gratulantium* of the festschrift published in his honour tells its own story.

But in all this, he never forgot that academic study of theology must interact with its local context; and here he made a truly pioneering contribution. He was not the first modern African constructive theologian; that place belongs perhaps to J. B. Danquah (another figure who touched African life at many points) and that remarkable book, *The Akan Doctrine of God.*[16] But Harry Sawyerr may well be the first *church* theologian of modern Anglophone Africa.[17] Others (Parrinder and Idowu among his contemporaries, E. W. Smith and J. Olumide Lucas among his predecessors) had explored the patterns of the primal religions of Africa, producing both studies in depth and continental surveys; Danquah had attempted to unite such studies with categories adopted from the philosophy of religion. Sawyerr bravely explored the theological implica-

---

[14]"Was St Paul a Jewish Missionary?" *Church Quarterly Review* (1959): 457–63.

[15]"The Markan Framework," *Scottish Journal of Theology,* 14, no. 3 (1961): 279–94.

[16]London: Lutterworth, 1944.

[17]There were stirrings in Francophone Africa among Roman Catholic writers; there is no clear sign of these influences in Sawyerr's work, though he early read Janheinz Jahn's *Muntu* (1961).

tions of their work, the connexions of the old religions with Christian theology, the bridging concepts by which ideas passed in both directions.

He says that he read *The Akan Doctrine of God* at least twenty times in three years,[18] worrying away at the concept of God as ancestor mooted by Danquah. He could not leave the question where Danquah left it, a piece of detached African philosophy of religion. Nor could he ignore it; he knew that the ancestors loom too large in African consciousness to be ignored by theology. *God: Ancestor or Creator?* is an attempt to bring the concept into Christian theological discourse by means of elements already well-rooted in the Christian tradition.

Another aspect of his thought rotated around the theme of sacrifice. Sacrifice is a theme well-worked in classical Christian theology, but in a sense evacuated of much of its significance; few of its Western protagonists have ever actually *seen* a sacrifice performed. The realities of sacrifice in African life, as well as the motives for sacrifice, offer a starting point for reexamining the biblical imagery.

In all this, his pastoral concerns appear. Like Bishop Johnson with the fear-fetish, he was aware of the tensions in the minds of so many Africans between a Christian profession made with complete sincerity and elements of an African worldview not assimilated to that profession. The tension was strikingly represented among his own Krio people: Christian for centuries, Christian at the very heart of their identity, and yet maintaining the ancestral rites of *awujoh* and developing New Year graveside libations. Harry Sawyerr studied such practices and illuminated them;[19] he also sought an integrated Christian approach to them and to the longings and aspirations they reflected. He was completely ready to confess an evangelistic aim in his treatment of the themes of ancestors and sacrifice; they would be the basis of *Creative Evangelism*.[20] It is this concern that gives him a special claim to a pioneering place as a *church* theologian.

He produced excellent students. Among pupils were later colleagues: Prince Thompson, later bishop of Sierra Leone, and his own successors in the headship of the theology department, Edward Fasholé-Luke and Leslie Shyllon. He was a genial, stimulating colleague who produced both affection and respect. *The Sierra Leone Bulletin of Religion* over the years bears witness to the activity of the department in local research; and its expatriate members included scholars of the stature of Harold W. Turner, whose seminal and magisterial studies of African independent churches

---

[18]Sawyerr, *God: Ancestor or Creator?* x.

[19]See, of many, "Graveside Libations in and near Freetown," *Sierra Leone Bulletin of Religion* 7, no. 2 (1965): 48–55; "More Graveside Libations in and around Freetown," *Sierra Leone Bulletin of Religion* 8, no. 2 (1966): 57–59; "A Sunday Graveside Libation in Freetown, after a Bereavement," *Sierra Leone Bulletin of Religion* 9, no. 2 (1967): 41–45.

[20]The title of his first book (London: Lutterworth, 1968).

began within the department, and the New Testament scholar Mark Glasswell.

Harry Sawyerr's labours were never finished. When he retired from Fourah Bay, he continued to serve the church as the principal of the Sierra Leone Theological Hall; and he left Sierra Leone only to teach in Codrington College, Barbados, which shared with Fourah Bay historic associations with the University of Durham.

He died in 1986. He has not yet been accorded his proper place in the developing story of theology in Africa, or of the theology of the southern continents, which now produce most of the world's Christians. It is right that the richly suggestive fragments of his work presented here receive a new lease on life.

Part Three

VIGNETTES OF THE MISSIONARY
MOVEMENT FROM THE WEST

10

Carrying the White Man's Burden

Some British Views of National Vocation in the Imperial Era

Rudyard Kipling the Secular Theologian

Said England unto Pharaoh, "I must make a man of you,
That will stand upon his feet and play the game;
That will Maxim his oppressor as a Christian ought to do,"
And she sent old Pharaoh Sergeant Whatsisname.

Said England to the Sergeant, "You can let my people go"
(England used 'em cheap and nasty from the start)
And they entered 'em in battle on a most astonished foe
But the Sergeant he had hardened Pharaoh's heart.[1]

"Paraoh" is the Egypt of Khedive Ismail; "the Sergeant" represents the British military instructors sent to the Egyptian army for the Sudan campaign. As the story develops, Pharaoh, under the Sergeant's tutelage, produces quite unexpected vigor and resilience; this Pharaoh swarms desert, river, and railway "like Israelites from bondage":

'Tween the clouds o' dust and fire to the land of his desire,
And his Moses, it was Sergeant Whatsisname![2]

First published in William R. Hutchison and Hartmut Lehmann, editors, *Many Are Chosen: Divine Election and Western Nationalism* (Minneapolis: Fortress Press, 1994): 29–50. Reprinted with permission.
[1]Rudyard Kipling, "Pharaoh and the Sergeant," in idem, *The Collected Works of Rudyard Kipling* (28 vols.; New York: AMS Press, 1970), 26:224–26.
[2]Ibid.

The poem is typical Kipling. The rich fund of biblical allusion is detached from any conventional framework of Christian doctrine, with even a touch of cynicism ("that will Maxim his oppressor as a Christian ought to do"). The glory in empire is tempered by *Schadenfreude,* the ultimate betrayal of empire by easygoing metropolitan indifference. Empire is destiny, British destiny; but it is a lonely, burdensome business, with no more tangible rewards than the consciousness of duty done and manhood proven.

It is natural to begin with Kipling, for no one more clearly articulates the British consciousness of chosenness in the high imperial period, and no one perhaps has ever spoken more comprehensively to the British soul. No major writer since Shakespeare has more sharply reflected the reactions of the ordinary soldier. At the same time, Kipling's vision of the world, his sense of history, and his interpretation of East and West gave him something of prophetic status; his wealth of biblical imagery and his capacity to weave it into narrative or sentiment made him a sort of honorary lay theologian. The fact that Kipling's intellectual schema was far from classical Christian theology did not prevent preachers and theologians from drawing on him, nor did it prevent his reaching quasi-canonical status in Christian hymnody. "Almost since the beginning of his career I have read every word he wrote," said John Watson, the popular preacher who wrote still more popular idylls of Christian Scotland under the name of Ian Maclaren; Watson designated Kipling the "real poet laureate" of England.[3] Hugh Price Hughes, Methodist orator and social activist, so antimilitarist that he would shudder on viewing a military parade from the top of an omnibus[4] and devote five whole sermons to a single foolish outburst from a field marshal,[5] was equally anxious to appropriate Kipling. His daughter assures us that he greeted the appearance in *The Times* of the poem "Recessional" "with rapture," and that he attributed the poem to Kipling's partly Methodist background.[6]

---

[3]W. Robertson Nicoll, *Ian Maclaren: Life of the Rev. John Watson, D. D.* (London: Hodder & Stoughton, 1908), 324.

[4]Dorothea Price Hughes, *The Life of Hugh Price Hughes* (London: Hodder & Stoughton, 1907), 562.

[5]Hugh Price Hughes, Sermons, 5–9, in idem, *The Philanthropy of God Described and Illustrated in a Series of Sermons* (London: Hodder & Stoughton, 1890). Lord Wolseley had complained about "people who object to a barrier between nations upon religious grounds," since "I cannot for one moment believe that the strong instinct which has been given to me, and I dare say to most of you, of love of country, and of intense nationality, can be in any way opposed to the teachings of religion" (quoted in ibid., 79–80).

[6]D. P. Hughes, *The Life of Hugh Price Hughes*, 562. Not surprisingly, Charles Gore was more astringent: "One gets weary of [Kipling's] eternal diablerie," he wrote during a visit to India soon after the appearance of *Lux Mundi,* "and his morality seems as lax as his creed. But he is certainly brilliant" (George Leonard Prestige, *The Life of Charles Gore, Great Englishman* [London: Heinemann, 1935], 112).

Clearly, therefore, Kipling offered to many reflective contemporaries (as well to those to whom reflection came less naturally) an interpretation of the British role in the world with which they instinctively identified. This interpretation is famously made explicit in "The White Man's Burden."[7] Although the poem was originally written to encourage the Americans to annex the Philippine Islands, the "burden" was preeminently that of the British white man, going out to bring peace and equity to a new-found empire.

> Send forth the best ye breed—
> Go bind your sons to exile
> To serve your captives' need.[8]

As the poem portrays it, this will be slow, hard, repetitive, wearying work, but essentially vicarious and altruistic.

> To seek another's profit,
> And work another's gain.

Above all, it will be unpopular. The "captives" ("half-devil and half-child") will be sullen; their idleness and folly will endlessly wreck the work of their benefactors. The reward of service will be

> The blame of those ye better,
> The hate of those ye guard.

The "ye" is deliberately reminiscent of biblical injunction, and the point is soon made explicit: the hosts whom the high-souled administrator is slowly humoring toward the light cry:

> Why brought ye us from bondage,
> Our loved Egyptian night?

The White Man's Burden laid upon British shoulders—whether as viceroys of India[9] or as sergeant-instructors in Egypt—involved playing

---

[7]Rudyard Kipling, "The White Man's Burden," in idem, *Collected Works*, 26:221–23.

[8]This quotation and those that follow in sequence are found in ibid.

[9]See Rudyard Kipling, "One Viceroy Resigns," in idem, *Collected Works*, 25:137–43. An imaginary conversation between Dufferin and Lansdowne occurs: "And all the while commend you to Fate's hand (Here at the top one loses sight o' God)" (p. 140). A later parenthesis states, "God help you, if there be a God (There must be one to startle Gladstone's soul)" (p. 141).

Moses to a stiff-necked people, leading them into a land of promise and getting no thanks for it. The people will be watching Moses narrowly:

> The silent, sullen peoples
> Shall weigh your Gods and you.

Kipling's cosmology would allow him neither the use of the singular of the divine name here nor the use of lower case for "Gods." Many of his readers concurred. Aware of Darwin and of the newly opened mysteries of Eastern thought, they could no longer make *ex animo* the old Christian doctrinal affirmations. Their moral code, however, was still shaped by their Christian inheritance. They could recognize the voice of duty and the transcendent sanctions attached to eternal values. They could recognize destiny, and they expected this destiny to involve moral choice. If heaven and hell no longer conditioned their responses, they still expected the path of duty, as of old, to be strenuous and the rewards of this path to be intangible. The gate leading to life was still a strait one, as it was for the earnest evangelical Christian.

Even orthodox Christians, however, could heartily identify with Kipling's "Recessional," written for the Queen's Diamond Jubilee in 1897. Each verse is addressed to the Lord God of Hosts, the Judge of the Nations, who is also "God of our fathers, known of old" and the lord of the far-flung British battle line. God takes ultimate responsibility for the British Empire from Canada to the tropics.

> Beneath whose awful Hand we hold
> Dominion over palm and pine.

> Lo, all our pomp of yesterday
> Is one with Nineveh and Tyre!

"Recessional" recognizes the transitory nature of imperial glory. It also accepts as the national requirement the Psalmist's sacrifice of the humble and contrite heart.[10] It recognizes the danger of becoming drunk with power and the futility of trust in armaments ("reeking tube and iron shard").

Conscientious preachers also insisted on all these things. No wonder Hugh Price Hughes was enraptured; he too called for national humility, national responsibility, and a sense of God's sovereignty and judgment. If all these pieties left the empire intact, so, generally speaking, did the

---

[10]Ps. 51:17.

preachers. Better behavior was to be demanded and expected of Britain than of other imperial nations:

> If, drunk with sight of power, we loose
> Wild tongues that have not thee in awe
> Such boasting as the Gentiles use
> Or lesser breeds without the Law.

It took some knowledge of biblical exegesis to pick up the full implications of "Gentiles," "lesser breeds," and "without the Law" (again the capitalization is important), and it was not necessary to say aloud that these terms really referred to the Germans. All this, however, hammers home the point underlying the whole poem: Britain is God's people, heir to the privileges and the responsibilities of special relationship.

In "The Reformers," the imperial vocation requires a dedicated life that breaks from the easy luxury to which it has been bred. This is the rhetoric of many appeals for missionary recruits and was perhaps influenced by them. Kipling then takes the biblical language where Christian orthodoxy would fear to tread. The imperial devotee becomes a Christ figure and even a propitiatory, atoning sacrifice for his sleek, indolent nation.

> Virtue shall go out of him:
> Example profiting his peers.[11]
>
> Who is his Nation's sacrifice
> To turn the judgment from his race.[12]

In other words, he is the Suffering Servant.[13]

The experiences of the Anglo-Boer War gave the idea of imperial destiny a jolt and gave the preachers a text as well. Kipling's answer was that "it was our fault, and our very great fault and *not* the judgment of Heaven."[14] Not only the military, but politicians, clergy, and clerisy ("Council and Creed and College"), stifled as they were by "obese, unchallenged old things," must take this "imperial lesson" to heart.[15]

---

[11] The reference is to Mark 5:30 (KJV) and its parallels; Jesus is touched by a woman seeking healing and feels that "virtue" has gone out of him.

[12] Rudyard Kipling, "The Reformers," in *Collected Works*, 26:254–55.

[13] The last verse refers to victory being demonstrated in the children and grandchildren. Kipling probably has Isaiah 53 in mind, especially verse 10, where the servant is made a sin offering but afterwards "sees his seed."

[14] Rudyard Kipling, "The Lesson (1899–1902)," in idem, *Collected Works*, 26:248–49.

[15] Ibid.

There were other poets of imperialism. Sir Henry Newbolt in particular produced some influential pieces,[16] as did a whole clutch of novelists of imperialism. It was Kipling, however, who most moved the imagination. Part of the appeal lay in his discreet, but nonetheless pervasive, view of the special chosenness of Britain, the vision of a beneficent, worldwide British Empire of free, consenting partners revealed as part of the emerging purpose of history.

The ambiguity in Kipling's own religious position was helpful here. His discourse was so thoroughly biblical that a knowledge of the English Bible was needed for its elucidation; earnest Christians could identify with so much of it that many were prepared to take their chance with the odd worrying application or pagan reference. It was not necessary, however, to make a Christian affirmation in order to appropriate his biblical allusions; and post-Christian readers influenced by the new comparative religion could identify with his views on God made in man's image, his dislike for judgmental exponents of "the narrow way," his assertion of the need to recognize that "the wildest dreams of Kew are the facts of Khatmandhu,"[17] and his conviction that "there are nine and sixty ways of constructing tribal lays/And every single one of them is right!"[18]

He was thus accessible to all but the most punctilious Christians (and even they could, if necessary, treat him as reflecting an "Old Testament" position). He was also ideally suited to a rising post-Christian generation that retained the memory and influence of its biblical education.

There was no real theology—nor much ideology—attached to Kipling's idea of chosenness. It involved the application to Britain of a series of images of old Israel, but they were still manifestly poetic images, metaphors at most, into which a wide range of theology or ideology could be imported.

> Fair is our lot—goodly is our heritage!
> (Humble ye, my people, and be fearful in your mirth!)
> For the Lord and God Most High
> He hath made the deep as dry
> He hath made for us a pathway to the ends of all the
>   earth![19]

---

[16]One line of "Vitaï Lampada," which links crises on the public school cricket ground and the desert battlefield, long furnished one of the few poetic quotations that "everybody" knew: "Play up! play up! and play the game!" See Henry Newbolt, *Poems: New and Old* (London: John Murray, 1915), 78–79.

[17]See Rudyard Kipling, "Buddha at Kamakura" in idem, *Collected Works*, 26:219–20.

[18]Rudyard Kipling, "In the Neolithic Age," in idem, *Collected Works*, 26:86–87.

[19]Rudyard Kipling, "A Song of the English," in idem, *Collected Works*, 26:3–13.

Imperial Religion

Watts and Wesley—not to mention the apostle Paul—had already used the exodus motif as a figure of Christ's redemption. Kipling used the same figure to describe the preordination of the empire on which the sun never set; from the point of view of classical theology, this represented a secularization, even a degradation. Classical theology, however, was less fashionable in the era of high imperialism than in earlier generations, and some of the pious may have found Kipling's exhortations to humility, self-sacrifice, and moral exertion an acceptable substitute. From the point of view of many earnest post-Christians for whom the old theology held no meaning, such words offered a resacralization of the biblical narrative and gave a transcendent dimension to a code of duty, patriotism, and service to the nation. From muscular Christianity to muscular devotion to duty was not such a great leap.

Elsewhere I have offered a comment on John Hargreaves's contention that "imperialist religion" in the late nineteenth century produced a consensus among exponents of secular rationalism, evangelical piety, and broad Christian humanism, and that outstanding examples of each are to be found among the great proconsuls.[20] I suggested that an examination of the sort of sermons delivered to British missionary bodies in the 1880–1920 period tends to support Hargreaves's observation; many offer some clues to account for this new consensus. The sermons took the empire and its essential beneficence for granted; by contrast with earlier evangelicalism, they represented a spiritualizing of the gospel and its detachment from social context. The secular sphere was thus the concern of someone else, namely, the colonial government. Preoccupied with the responsibility of the West, they were relatively unaware of the existence of indigenous churches in Africa and Asia. In contrast to the midcentury, they saw missions as embattled at home, surrounded by hostile forces of the spirit of the age.

It seems reasonable in considering British concepts of chosenness in this period to look again at preachers who dealt with missionary themes. From the 1880s onward, ideas of British chosenness inevitably have to do with empire. Before that time they had more to do with insularity—with seagirt security, with freedom from invasion and warfare, and with the defense of true religion and the Protestant faith. There is, as we shall see, certainly some continuity with these ideas in the later nineteenth century, but the principal perceptions of Great Britain's distinctiveness centered on its world role. Even

---

[20] Andrew F. Walls, "'Such Boasting as the Gentiles Use . . .' Some Thoughts on Imperialist Religion," in Roy C. Bridges, ed., *An African Miscellany for John Hargreaves* (Aberdeen: Aberdeen University African Studies Group, 1983), 109–16.

the function of the sea changed;[21] it was no longer a bulwark for defense, but a path to worlds beyond. As John Watson put it to a Wesleyan audience,

> Are any man's eyes so blind that he cannot see the mission of England? Have we not been surrounded by the seas and our national character formed for purposes that we can recognize? What nation has ever planted so many colonies, explored so many unknown lands, made such practical contributions to civilization, set such an illustrious example of liberty?[22]

Or, as Kipling phrased it, God has made the sea a path for Britain to the ends of the earth.[23] The empire was believed to be the result of essentially peaceful expansion that brought peace in its train. Hugh Price Hughes decried militaristic and bombastic utterances from politicians and press, but he did so on basically imperialist grounds. The colonial empire, he urged, had been built up not by military operations, but in spite of them. British traders, British explorers, and British missionaries were responsible for the peaceable establishment of empire. All the military had done was to lose America.[24] Even when force was used, it was for peaceful ends, as it had been in Egypt (Kipling's sergeant-instructors, for example). How liberating it was for these timid Egyptian fellows to learn to charge and fight on horseback against dervishes![25]

Naturally, therefore, Britain and the colonies were clasped together in a close family community that foreigners could not understand. For Watson,

> A covenant has been made between England and her Colonies, and the covenant has been sealed with blood, and today England and the colonies are one. They reviled us, those nations of Europe . . . but it does not matter what the outside world says if your own family is true.[26]

Here is Kipling's family of queens; each is daughter in her English mother's house as well as the mistress in her own.[27]

---

[21]Sir John Seeley did most to supply a historical theory for British imperialism. He argued (*The Expansion of England* [London: Macmillan, 1883]) that Britain was, unlike Norway, not a *naturally* maritime country; England had become a maritime country only in the time of Elizabeth.

[22]Nicoll, *Life of the Rev. John Watson*, 266–67.

[23]Kipling, "Song of the English," 3.

[24]H. P. Hughes, *The Philanthropy of God*, 74–75, 96.

[25]D. P. Hughes, *The Life of Hugh Price Hughes*, 555.

[26]Nicoll, *Life of the Rev. John Watson*, 267.

[27]Rudyard Kipling, "Our Lady of the Snows," in idem, *Collected Works*, 26:227–28. Canada is the Queen of the North, who sends word to the Queens of the East and the South—partners in a single imperial destiny, united when "the world's war trumpet blows" (p. 228).

Hughes and Watson, and the preachers generally, took for granted both that Britain had a God-given civilizing mission to its empire, and that, generally speaking, the effect of the empire had been a beneficently civilizing one.[28] In one sense this continued an older tradition of evangelical and missionary apologetic. There were important differences and new emphases, however. Thomas Fowell Buxton, for instance, had thought of Britain's civilizing mission in the 1830s and 1840s in terms of reparation for wrongs done to Africa by Britain; he had no idea of effecting it by British overseas acquisition and rule.[29] By the 1880s an important change in perception had taken place. Buxton had seen "civilization," in Greco-Roman terms, as the answer to "barbarism"; civilization was a self-evidently desirable state that was to be commended to the barbarians, who were nonetheless regarded as responsible beings. A later age, influenced by evolutionary thought, saw these same peoples as languishing at low stages of development ("half-devil and half-child," in Kipling's extreme terms[30]). The term "child races" passed into common currency among those who supported missions.[31] The historic role of Britain thus became transmuted into that of the kind but firm tutor whose guidance was essential for the eventual maturity of the "children" committed to its care.

When this role was linked to a missionary vocation, Kipling's themes were introduced into territory where Kipling himself could not go. Evangelical Christians might agree that civilization was a desirable and regular accompaniment of Christianity, but they did not believe that the two were the same thing. They did believe, however, that Britain's past history and present situation demonstrated its unique role in the worldwide proclamation of the gospel. "We are elect by all signs and proofs to be the great missionary nation," announced the Baptist preacher J. G. Greenhough to the 1896 meeting of the Baptist Missionary Society.[32]

Greenhough's rhetoric, while claiming to abjure the "boastful jingoism of the music hall" in favor of "the humbler patriotism of the sanctuary," often came close to the language of the former. He asked, however, "Have we got all this glory by our own might and power, or is it because He has 'beset us behind and before' and laid His hand upon us?"[33] Green-

---

[28]See Watson (Nicoll, *Life of the Rev. John Watson, 266*): "England, if one can make anything of history, has been God's instrument in spreading civilization and administering justice among savage or oppressed peoples."

[29]See Andrew F. Walls, "The Legacy of Thomas Fowell Buxton," *International Bulletin of Missionary Research* 15 (1991):74–78.

[30]Kipling, "White Man's Burden," 221.

[31]See, for example, Henry Hutchison Montgomery, ed., *Mankind and the Church: Being an Attempt to Estimate the Contribution of Great Races to Fulness of the Church of God* (London: Longmans, Green, 1907); J. N. Ogilvie, *Our Empire's Debt to Missions* (London: Hodder & Stoughton, 1923), chap. 3.

[32]J. G. Greenhough, *Missionary Sermons: A Selection from the Discourses Delivered on Behalf of the Baptist Missionary Society on Various Occasions* (London: Carey, 1924), 265.

[33]Ibid., 265.

hough would have recognized, as many other preachers did, the same sentiment expressed in Kipling's "Recessional," which appeared a year later. Like Kipling, he did not forget "the Gentiles" who, like old Babylon, boast in themselves. (He also made it quite clear that he saw no signs of authentic Christian vitality outside the areas where the English language was used.[34]) The analogy with Israel went further:

> Was [British power and prosperity] not especially with this intent— that we should be more than all others God's messengers of light and truth to the nations that sit in darkness? In all this God's voice has been calling us. God's consecrating hands have been laid on our heads. Thus saith the Lord: "In the shadow of My hand have I hid thee, and made thee a polished shaft, and in the day of salvation have I helped thee, that thou mayest say to the prisoners: 'Go forth.'"[35]

The Uncertain Boundaries of Chosenness

Britain's election as the missionary nation was not evident to all who accepted the necessity of taking up the White Man's Burden. This fact was to cause endless disappointment within the British missionary movement, and it was the source of the embattled note among the preachers as they encountered the post-Christian nature of much British intellectual life. They realized that the British Empire had become the world's largest Islamic power and far more efficient at excluding missionaries than was the Turkish sultan. The potency of the imperial idea of chosenness, which distinguished it from earlier ideas of national election or responsibility, lay in its compatibility with a variety of theologies and ideologies.

For the same reason, there seems to be no agreed body of biblical exegesis behind Christian appropriations of the chosenness motif. The contemporaneous stress on the necessity for historical exegesis as well as the reaction against the older typological methods would have rendered such a thing unlikely in any case. British Israelism, which used exegetical methods to prove that Britain was the legitimate heir of the prophetic promises to Israel and provided etymologies to match, never touched more than a narrow fringe of those who held some belief in national chosenness.[36] At the Baptist Missionary Society meeting of 1897, a Wesleyan minister, W. L. Watkinson, came as close to such a formulation as a mainstream preacher could come. Referring explicitly to the situation in Isa. 19:23–25, he sustained a parallel between this text and the position of Britain:

---

[34]Ibid., 209.

[35]Ibid., 265.

[36]One highly popular writer at the end of the period, the versifier Patience Strong, held British Israelite views; probably only a small minority of those who responded to her homely mass-circulation doggerel, however, realized the nature of these notions.

England stands much in the same position that Israel did. It is the spiritual centre of the world. As Palestine came between Egypt and Assyria, so this island comes in a wonderful manner between the old world and the new. God gave spiritual gifts in a remarkable degree to Israel; the revelation of Himself, the knowledge of His law, the sense of eternity. . . . God in His government has also given to us special powers for the diffusion of the Gospel.[37]

These special powers included the English language and literature, the spirit of adventure, the gift of colonization, and "a capacity of universality."[38] The preachers invariably insisted that these privileges brought responsibility and should call forth humble gratitude and unstinting service.

At certain points, nonetheless, the missionary tradition sat uneasily with the new version of British national chosenness. Most obviously and basically, by the later part of the nineteenth century North America was manifestly becoming quite as important as Britain in missionary effort. Even Greenhough, sure of Britain's election as the great missionary nation, implicitly set America—alone among foreign nations—with Britain among the righteous. ("In nearly all Protestant lands save where our language is spoken religion is feeble or apathetic."[39]) George C. Lorimer, preaching to the Baptist Missionary Society in 1898, announced,

The united energies, faith and wealth of Great Britain and the United States, if intelligently directed, should be able in a few years to conquer heathen darkness. . . . As the flags of the two living nations blend together, let us bathe them in the splendour of the Cross of Christ; and as they move together about the globe let us see to it that between them, and over them gleams the Cross; and then shall follow the sublime resurrection of the nations and then the angels' song of goodwill to men.[40]

A decade earlier, James Johnston, the secretary of the Centenary Missionary Conference, had noted the extent to which the work of evangelization devolved on the Saxon race. He also announced the decline of the Latin race, the great colonizers of ancient times, under Roman Catholic domination. "It is to the race which is sending the blessings of Christianity to the heathen to which God is giving success as the colonisers and conquerors of the world."[41] The latter sentiment, however, does

---

[37]W. L. Watkinson, in *Missionary Sermons*, 209.

[38]Ibid., 209–10.

[39]Greenhough, in *Missionary Sermons*, 264.

[40]George C. Lorimer, in *Missionary Sermons*, 182.

[41]James Johnston, ed., *Report of the Centenary Conference on the Protestant Missions of the World Held in Exeter Hall, June 9–19, London, 1888*, 2 vols. (London: Nisbet, 1889), I.xvi.

not quite agree with the rest of this section of the report, which highlights the importance of the missions of other northern countries, not all of which had the same colonial success. It was hard to talk of vocation to mission without recognizing that other nations shared with Britain in this vocation.

When the focus was turned from the activity of sending missionaries to the life of the mission church, another set of factors came into play. Roland Allen, with his stress on the transitoriness of the missionary function and the primacy of the indigenous church, is a minority voice within the period, but a significant one.[42] The liberal Bernard Lucas saw the British Empire as only a dim, broken pointer toward a far grander empire of Christ in which the hidden glory of India would be revealed.[43] Other missionary thinkers who stressed the catholicity of the church emphasized that each "race" had its own contribution to the fullness of the body; none was complete in itself. This view was another brake on the idea of "chosenness," since in Christ all races were "chosen." In *Mankind and the Church*, a symposium by high-church Anglicans, the secretary of the Society for the Propagation of the Gospel drew a portrait of the English character showing the limitations that could be corrected only by Asia (and, no doubt, in due time, by Africa).[44]

Singing New Songs

So much for the preachers. Preaching, however, is not the only source of religious impressions, and it seems appropriate to give some consideration to a particularly important source for the British religious consciousness: the hymnbook.

Only during the high imperial period did a special section devoted to the nation first appear in British hymnbooks. The 1864 edition of *Hymns Ancient and Modern*,[45] which marked the final acknowledgment by official Anglicanism that the hymn had become an acceptable and regular part of the service, contained no such section; neither did the supplement to Wesley's hymns that was authorized by the Wesleyan Conference of 1876.[46] One hymn in the latter collection was a prayer for the monarch, but this was an old Wesley hymn, clearly written with George III in mind. The Free Church of Scotland hymnbook, com-

---

[42]See Roland Allen, *Missionary Methods, St. Paul's or Ours?* (London: Scott, 1912).

[43]Bernard Lucas, *The Empire of Christ: Being a Study of the Missionary Enterprise in the Light of Modern Religious Thought* (London: Macmillan, 1907).

[44]Montgomery, *Mankind and the Church*, xxxiv–xxxv.

[45]*Hymns Ancient and Modern*, ed. Henry Hutchison (London: Clowes & Sons, 1864).

[46]*A Collection of Hymns for the People Called Methodists by the Rev. John Wesley . . . with a New Supplement* (London: Methodist Book Room, 1876).

missioned in 1878, did not have topical sections at all, but included an index of subjects that identified two hymns as suitable for "National Fast and Thanksgiving."[47] In *Psalms and Hymns*, published for Baptist churches in 1883, the last hymn in the book was headed "Prayer for Our Country."[48] This hymn was W. R. Hickson's Christianized version of the national anthem "God Bless Our Native Land." The first hymnbook to devote a section explicitly to national hymns may have been the Bible Christian hymnbook of 1889.[49] It was the final section, except for benedictions and doxologies, and it contained no fewer than seventeen hymns, beginning with the national anthem. None of the hymnbooks mentioned above included this feature. Among the other hymns were several that rejoiced in Britain's chosenness, including a spectacular rouser by Thomas Hornblower Gill, which began "Lift thy song among the nations/England of the Lord beloved!" and recounted the past discomfitures of invaders, tyrants, and popery. The hymn went on to describe the sword of the Lord gleaming in the hands of British heroes, freedom's fire remaining "where it first did burn and shine." Eventually the congregation recognizes that the Lord still provides for England "boundless realms and tasks divine."[50]

The last hymn in the section was by Isaac Watts. It was one of those updated paraphrases of the psalms in which he endeavored to make David "speak the common sense of a Christian."[51] Late Victorian Bible Christians, humble in station for the most part, invested the late-period Puritan psalm "Shine, Mighty God, on Britain Shine" with a significance Watts could not have contemplated:

> Sing to the Lord, ye distant lands
> Sing loud, with solemn voice,
> While British tongues exalt his praise
> And British hearts rejoice.[52]

The early twentieth century saw a multiplication of new books and supplements, including new books for the Wesleyan, English Presby-

---

[47]*The Free Church Hymn Book* (Edinburgh: Free Church of Scotland, n.d. [1882]). Of the two hymns in question, no. 93 would have been suitable for a national fast, no. 325 equally suitable for a national thanksgiving or a church anniversary.

[48]*Psalms and Hymns with Supplement for Public, Social and Private Worship: Prepared for the Use of the Baptist Denomination* (London: Haddon for the Trustees, 1883).

[49]*Bible Christian Hymns* (London: Bible Christian Book Room, 1889).

[50]Ibid., no. 994 (1924 ed.).

[51]See the preface to Isaac Watts, *The Psalms of David Imitated in New Testament Language Together with Hymns and Spiritual Songs* (London: n.p., 1719); and the discussion in Bernard L. Manning. The Hymns of Wesley and Watts (London, Epworth, 1942), ch. 4.

[52]*Bible Christian Hymns*, no. 996 (1924 ed.).

terian, and Baptist churches; a *Church Hymnary* (1905) for the main Presbyterian churches in and beyond Scotland, the high Anglican *English
Hymnal* (1906), and the quirky Anglican *Songs of Praise* (1925). All of these
had sections of national hymns; all included the national anthem; all except one included Kipling's "Recessional." Hickson's verses appeared in
most, and some had Kipling's lines for children, "Land of our birth we
pledge to thee." The cry of Ebenezer Elliott, the Corn Law rhymer,
"When wilt thou save the people?" was usually present (interestingly, it
was the Wesleyans, not the Anglicans, who modified his language in the
interests of social order). Also a common entry, although not always
placed in this section, was Henry Scott Holland's prayer for national pur-
gation, "Judge Eternal Throned in Splendour," which included the lines,
"Cleanse the body of this empire/Through the glory of the Lord."[53]

In including hymns reflecting the sense of national chosenness, the
Presbyterian *Church Hymnary* was the most restrained; it did not even include Kipling's "Recessional" in its first edition. The *English Hymnal* included a hymn by an Eton schoolmaster, A. C. Ainger, with the significant
opening, "God of our fathers," which gave thanks "for eastern realms, for
western coasts/For islands washed by every sea" and clearly expected
"our fame to wax through coming days."[54]

The Wesleyans included a hymn based on one originally composed
for the official celebrations of the Queen's Golden Jubilee in 1887. It reflected a vision of the British Empire as God's gift to the world:

> Our bounds of empire thou hast set in many a distant isle
> And in the shadow of our throne the desert places smile
> For in our laws and in our faith it's thine own light they
>   see
> The truth that brings to captive souls the wider liberty.[55]

The Baptists were the most rumbustiously patriotic of all, with one of their
own members, Nathaniel Barnaby, designer of battleships for the Royal Navy
and Sunday school superintendent, contributing such strong rhymes as

> God bless our motherland! Cradled in ocean
> Nursed into greatness by storm and by sea

---

[53]Henry Scott Holland, "Judge Eternal Throned in Splendour."

[54]*The English Hymnal* (London: Oxford University Press, n.d. [1906]), no. 559.

[55]*The Methodist Hymn-Book* (London: Wesleyan Conference Office, n.d. [1904]),
no. 995. The author was a Wesleyan minister, Dr. Henry Burton (see John Telford,
The Methodist Hymnbook Illustrated, 2nd ed. [London Culley, 1909], 165). This hymn
was a by-product of Queen Victoria's Golden Jubilee (1887) and was a response to
a request by the composer, Sir John Stainer, for "a patriotic hymn" to a tune of his
own (Telford, *Methodist Hymnbook Illustrated*, 489).

Out on the stormy winds, and in war's commotion
She had no helper, Jehovah, but Thee![56]

All of these pale, however, before the uninhibited flag waving of *Hoyle's Hymns*, popular in the Band of Hope Union and other temperance societies. Band of Hope meetings were, of course, not normal services, but their predominantly working-class companies seem to have been happy to join in such rhapsodies as "Oh proudly stand, my Fatherland, the envy of the world!"[57]

Some of these effusions were pleas on patriotic grounds for the removal of the curse of drink, but there is little sign in this cheerful little collection of national humility, whether in Henry Scott Holland's sense or Kipling's. It is the Band of Hope Union, above all, that celebrates empire without tears.

Two important points are suggested by this sampling of hymnbooks as a whole. First, the most uninhibited assertions of British chosenness were to be found where lay and working-class influence was strongest. Second, the specifically "missionary" sections of all the books are remarkably free from imperial and national allusions. Some deep-rooted instinct kept the idea of God-given empire in a different sphere from the kingdom of God.

Conclusion

National election was not a new theme among English writers. John Milton (who was prepared to believe that Pythagoras and the magi learned their lore from the Druids of Britain) found the evidence for national chosenness in Wycliffe's ministry: "Why else was this nation chosen before any other, that out of her, as out of Sion, should be proclaimed and sounded forth the first tiding and trumpet of reformation to all Europe?"[58] Although episcopal perverseness had in this case inhibited England's primacy and made necessary the ministrations of the foreigners John Hus and Martin Luther, the signs were that "God is decreeing to begin some new and great period in his church," and "what does he then but reveal himself to his servants, and as his manner is, first to Englishmen?"[59]

Conscious participation in a pioneering political and religious revolution ("even to the reforming of reformation itself"[60]) and the sight of a na-

---

[56]The hymn survives in the *Baptist Church Hymnal Revised* (London: Psalms and Hymns Trust, 1933), no. 698. On Sir Nathaniel Barnaby (1829–1915), see *Dictionary of National Biography*, 22 vols. (New York: Macmillan and London: Smith, Elder & Co., 1908).

[57]*Hoyle's Hymns and Songs for Temperance Societies and Bands of Hope: 275 Gems of Song* (London: Partridge and National Temperance Publications Depot, n.d.).

[58]John Milton, "Areopagitica" (1644).

[59]Ibid.

[60]Ibid

tionwide new dawn in learning, science, and education[61] provoked such thoughts in anyone with a strong sense of Providence. The position of imperial Britain in the late nineteenth century was equally suggestive of reflections on national history. The happy gift for peaceable progress struck many observers, and, as we have seen, imperial expansion itself could be viewed as a manifestation of peaceful progress. Providentialist historiography was no longer in vogue; but if historical meditations were now secular in tone, they were by no means materialist. For John Richard Green, "in England, more than elsewhere, constitutional progress has been the result of social development," and he believed the part played by war in English history was smaller than in any of the European nations.[62]

Such views did not demand providentialist convictions, but did not forbid them either. Providentialists continued to find their links with the seventeenth-century revolutions. George Smith, former India journalist addressing the Student Volunteer Missionary Union, could call attention to Oliver Cromwell's new statue in Parliament Square and link him both with Livingstone and (as one of the few English political leaders genuinely interested in overseas missions) with Gladstone—people with "the imperial instinct to recognize missions as the purest handmaid of statesmanship and of geographical expansion."[63]

A new form of the idea of British chosenness based on the empire appeared in the period after 1880. It drew on biblical motifs, but part of its strength lay in the way in which it could receive assent both from committed Christians and from those who were in the process of parting with Christianity and had already abandoned its traditional forms and classical doctrines. For this very reason it was somewhat imprecisely formulated; it represented exactly that combination of sentiment and ethical rigor, "morality tinged with emotion," that Matthew Arnold—John the Baptist to the age—saw as the heart of religion. It needed a climate of theological imprecision in which to develop among Christians. The new idea of chosenness would have had a harder task amid the old certainties and the old formulations about election, judgment, and covenant.

When Charles Haddon Spurgeon, preaching to the Baptist Missionary Society in 1858, said that "the Holy Spirit must be poured on England, and then shall it go to the utmost borders of the habitable earth,"[64] his audience knew well that he meant the *churches* in England, and specifically

---

[61]See R. Hooykaas, *Religion and the Rise of Modern Science* (Edinburgh: Scottish Academic Press, 1972), 141–42.

[62]John Richard Green, *A Short History of the English People* (London: Macmillan, 1876), v–vii.

[63]George Smith, *Students and the Missionary Problem: Addresses Delivered at the International Student Missionary Conference* (London: Student Voluntary Mission Union, 1900), 95. Gladstone and Cromwell are also brought together as ideal figures by John Clifford in *Typical Christian Leaders* (London: Marshall, 1898), 7.

[64]Charles Haddon Spurgeon, in *Missionary Sermons*, 17.

the Baptist churches. Forty years later, however, the words had a different ring, as Greenhough's 1896 sermon to the same constituency shows. In 1858, moreover, a year after the Indian Mutiny, Spurgeon had cheerfully looked forward to the day when Lord Nelson's statue would be hauled from its column to make way for one of George Whitefield and when John Wesley would replace Sir Charles Napier, conqueror in India, in Trafalgar Square: "We shall say about these men, 'They were very respectable men in the days of our forefathers, who did not know better than to kill one another, but we do not care for them now!'"[65] Had they been delivered in the 1890s, such words would have seemed almost profane.

The Scottish dimension is also worth considering. The erosion of the old discourse and the old certainties, along with the arrival of a new imperial consciousness, tended to reduce the traditional difference between English and Scottish perceptions. It is hard to identify any specifically Scottish dimension of chosenness in relation to empire during the period in question. This is especially interesting in view of the importance of the covenant idea in Scottish history. Historically, Scotland was a nation bound by covenant and at times torn apart over covenants. No theological theme was more identifiably Scottish than that of the Crown Rights of the Redeemer as applied to the nation. It underlay the idea of the "godly commonwealth" envisaged by Thomas Chalmers and a broad band of Scottish churchmen in the first half of the century. We hear little of these matters, however, in relation to the imperial age. Covenant rhetoric remained, but it was rhetoric rather than theology and was often transferred to the political sphere.

In 1911, D. S. Cairns, the Scottish theologian most clearly identified with the student movement, addressed Scottish students in a book entitled *The Vocation of Scotland in View of Her Religious Heritage*. He identified the determining elements in this heritage as the kingdom of God ("the central stream of Scottish religious life is theocratic"), the importance of the church (as distinct from "freelances" of the Spirit), and the acceptance of a strong theology.[66] These traditional Scottish emphases were not exactly hospitable to the new version of imperial chosenness, and it is noteworthy that they were not applied to it. Watson was not the only Scot of the period content to call Britain "England," as the Scots, too, clad themselves in the robes of empire.[67]

---

[65]Ibid., 11.

[66]D. S. Cairns, *The Vocation of Scotland in View of Her Religious Heritage* (London: Student Christian Movement, 1911).

[67]The stress here has been on the omissions from contemporary theological discourse. How far contemporary biblical studies actually assisted the notion of chosenness would need further study. It is interesting to note the influence of Sir William Ramsay's stress on the essentially imperial outlook of Paul and how this affected early Gentile Christianity. See especially William M. Ramsay, *St. Paul the Traveller and Roman Citizen* (London: Hodder & Stoughton, 1895). Lucas eagerly seized on this aspect of Paul in an appendix to *The Empire of Christ*, 149–51.

11

The Protestant Missionary Awakening
in Its European Context

Christian history is the story of successive transformations of the Christian faith following its translation into a series of diverse cultural settings. Our topic, the Protestant missionary movement, is intimately related to one of these transformations that helped to change the demographic balance and cultural milieu of Christianity within a couple of centuries or so. When the movement began, the vast majority of those who professed and called themselves Christians—certainly more than nine out of ten—lived in Europe or North America. At the beginning of the twenty-first century something like six out of ten professing Christians live in Africa, Asia, Latin and Caribbean America, or the Pacific, and the proportion who do so rises year by year. The accession to the Christian faith that has taken place in the southern continents has been accompanied by a recession from it in Europe and North America. In the course of the twentieth century, Christianity has become a mainly non-Western religion. The implications of this for the future of Christian theology and liturgy, for Christian intellectual development and Christian impact on society, and for the relations of Christians with those of other faiths have hardly yet come into mature consideration.

This transformation of Christianity clearly arises from the impact of the Western upon the non-Western world. This is not the same as saying that it arises from the rise of the European empires or the establishment of European hegemony. Its relationship to the Western empires is a highly complex question. The Christian impact on the non-Western world sometimes preceded, sometimes followed, the imperial structures, and the accession to Christianity has become most noticeable since their collapse.

Presentation for the Conference Missions and the Enlightenment, organized by the North Atlantic Missiology Project, Cambridge University, 1977. Also published in Brian Stanley, editor, *The Missionary Movement and the Enlightenment* (Grand Rapids, MI: Eerdmans, 2001).

And we can now see that in the very period in which Christianity was taking hold in Africa and Asia, it was also being quietly but surely eroded in Europe. It is also possible to argue that the Western contact with the non-Western world, and the attempt to establish hegemony over it, contributed significantly to dissolving the special form of relationship between church and society that we call Christendom, a phenomenon that grew out of the early encounters with Christianity of the European peoples before the Roman Empire and that persisted long enough to be thought of as characteristic alike of Europe and of Christianity.[1] Experience taught that the religious settlements, achieved with such pain in so many European countries, could rarely be reproduced overseas, and that realization may well have hastened the decay of Christendom. But Christendom—the concept of Christianity as territorial—which lay at the heart of the European Christian experience, was not essential to the future of Christianity, and new expressions of the Christian faith have developed, and continue to develop, beyond Christendom in African and Asian societies. Africans and Asians and Australasians became Christians for African and Asian and Australasian reasons. The most vigorously growing sector of contemporary Christian studies, the area of most potent discovery, is that which uncovers those processes and their subsequent manifestations within African, Asian, and Australasian Christianity.

All this indicates that African and Asian and Latin American church history is not the same as missionary history; in itself, the missionary movement is a product of Western church history. Nevertheless, the missionary movement is the terminal by which Western Christianity was connected to the non-Western world, and as such it has special importance as an object of study. It was both the principal medium in which Western Christianity made its impact on the non-Western world, and the principal sense organ by which Western Christianity itself felt the impact of the non-Western world. There is therefore a good case for regarding it as one of the most permanently significant topics of Western Christian history. To understand it would be to understand better the present and perhaps the emerging state of the Christian faith. And yet, considered as an object of study, the missionary movement is by no means a well-worked field. Excellent standard treatments of the history of the church in the modern West hardly mention it, and in this they accurately reflect the principal concerns of Western Christianity. The truth is that for most of the period of its existence, the missionary movement was not a major preoccupation of the Western church. Those were periods, certainly, when the work of missions was celebrated and acclaimed in the West, but even then it was a marginal activity for all but a minority of Western Christians. There were other times

---

[1]See Andrew Walls, "Christianity in the Non-Western World: A Study in the Serial Nature of Christian Expansion," *Studies in World Christianity* 1, no. 1 (1995): 1–25.

when suspicion or contempt, or lukewarm recognition, or simple indifference was the prevailing sentiment within the Western church towards the missionary movement. But for most of the time that church was simply too busy about its own local concerns to take much notice of what was known as "the mission field." Throughout their history, whether we are thinking of the leadership of the Western churches or of their membership, missions were the province of the enthusiasts rather than of the mainstream.

In the conventional historiography of the Western missionary movement, Roman Catholic writers, after due acknowledgment of such early figures as Ramon Llull and St. Francis, highlight the Iberian voyages of the late fifteenth century. They see the flowering of the movement in the early seventeenth century, followed by a loss of impetus and partial stagnation by the middle of the eighteenth century, then new life and vigour bursting out in the nineteenth to produce an unprecedented *plantatio ecclesiae*. Protestant writers ponder the question why the sixteenth-century Reformers say so little about the evangelization of the world, point to a dawning missionary consciousness among the Puritans (especially in their American manifestation) hail new signs of activity in the Moravian missions and in eighteenth-century India, and then describe the "real" Protestant awakening in the last years of the eighteenth century. This is symbolized (and many see as initiated) by William Carey's *Enquiry into the Obligations of Christians to Use Means for the Conversion of the Heathens*, and issues in the emergence of the early British missionary societies, following broadly denominational lines. This development in Britain, on this interpretation, is followed by an analogous movement in America and by another crop of societies in continental Europe. Bringing the basic elements of these stories together, one arrives at a picture of the missionary movement (and the author must confess to having written in such terms)[2] with two cycles, rather like the two cycles of imperialism, centered respectively on the Americas and on Asia, identified by D. K. Fieldhouse.[3] Of the equivalent cycles of missionary enterprise, the first is seen as originating in the last years of the fifteenth century and fading in the course of the eighteenth. This cycle is essentially one of Roman Catholic activity, though with a burst of Protestant growth in the later part of the period. The second cycle is identified in the second half of the eighteenth century, and gathers momentum in the nineteenth. This cycle, beginning in a period of decline for Catholic missions (symbolized by the suppression, through the influence of Catholic powers, of one of the most effective Catholic mission agencies, the Society of Jesus), is predominantly a Protestant movement in its origins, and its motor is the Evangelical Re-

---

[2]*Theologische Realenzyklopädie*, 4th ed., s.v. "Mission VI."
[3]D. K. Fieldhouse, *The Colonial Empires: A Comparative Study from the Eighteenth Century*, 2nd ed. (London: Macmillan, 1982).

vival. New movements within the Catholic church, however, produce a missionary revival during the nineteenth century, and the age of imperialism heightens the competition between traditionally Protestant and traditionally Catholic powers. Refinements of this model indicate how by the mid-nineteenth century, all shades of Protestant ecclesiasticism had endorsed the missionary movement, so that it was no longer an Evangelical monopoly, and that from a point early in the twentieth century, North America progressively replaced Europe as the base of the missionary movement from the West. We need follow the second cycle no further into the period of decolonization and ecumenism, which also reflects decline and confusion in Western Christianity. Some would now see a new cycle of missionary movements emerging outside the West; no country now has a more focused missionary consciousness than Korea, nor has any other country mobilized a greater proportion of its population as missionaries, and this despite the fact that Korea's modern Christian history commenced only late in the nineteenth century.

The topic of this chapter involves an attempt to read the history of the missionary movement in a European context; and this exercise raises questions about the two-cycle model, and in particular its stress on the initiatives of the late-eighteenth century. In the first place, a European context causes the Catholic and Protestant movements to be taken together, as representing the interaction of the peoples of Europe (including their descendants settled in North America) with those of the non-Western world. From a Western viewpoint, the issue of Catholic or Protestant missionary proclamation might be one about whether the authentic faith of Christ was transmitted to the non-Western world, or a perverted and destructive misrepresentation of it. For those who heard these proclamations, however, the differences, with roots deep in the intellectual and religious life of Europe, were—both in their attractive and their repellent aspects—often less significant than what the proclamations had in common. In the modern debates about gospel and culture that have arisen out of the manifestations of Christianity in the southern continents, Catholic and Protestant theologians work on similar agendas. A recent study has shown that the conceptual problems in Andean languages faced by modern Protestant evangelists are precisely those that faced the Spanish friars who constructed the first Quechua catechisms in the sixteenth century.[4] The crucial questions for the communication of the Christian message were the same. We have become used to the idea that Christianity exists in three modes: Catholic, Protestant, and Orthodox. That distinction is rooted in European cultural history. In the non-Western world these

---

[4]William Mitchell, "The Appropriation of the Quechua Language by the Church and the Christianization of Peru in the Sixteenth and Early Seventeenth Centuries," Ph.D. diss., University of Edinburgh, 1991.

modes still have significance as indicators of affiliation and organization, but they are becoming less and less helpful as descriptors; and huge areas of non-Western Christianity cannot be meaningfully comprehended under any of the three modes. One wholly unexpected effect of this missionary movement has been the diversification of Christianity, with the prospect of whole new traditions of Christianity, as clearly reflecting historical and cultural developments in the southern continents as the Catholic, Protestant, and Orthodox modes reflect those of Europe.

We return now to the European experience of encounter with the non-Western world. The demographic basis of European Christianity, for all its inheritance from the Christian Roman Empire, lay in the conversion of the tribal and semisettled peoples beyond that empire's frontiers. Here it was that the concept of Christendom developed, as the gospel was gradually adopted as basis and undergirding of customary law. Christendom, the total body of Christian princes and their subjects, all (whatever their actual, often highly dysfunctional, relations with one another) owing allegiance to the King of kings, notionally represented unbroken Christian territory, subject to the law of Christ, from the Atlantic across the European land mass. All born within that territory were born under the law of the King of kings; within that territory idolatry, blasphemy, or heresy should have no recognized place. East and south of Christendom lay another realm, and the only other one of which Western Christians had much close knowledge before 1500. The lands ruled by the Turks included lands once Christian, and the lands where the Saviour had walked, which *ought* therefore to be Christian, but which were beyond immediate reclamation. By 1500, the period when European maritime expansion began to open contact with worlds hitherto outside European consciousness, Europe had become Christian territory in a way it had never been before. The last pagan peoples (apart from some in the extreme north), the populations of the Baltic region, had been dragged within the orbit of Latin Christendom. Still more significantly, the most successful of all the crusades had recently removed the open Muslim presence from southern Spain. At roughly the same period, Christianity became more European than it had ever previously been. Other Christian centres faded. The long-lingering Second Rome on the Bosphorus collapsed, the once vigorous Christianity of central Asia was eclipsed, the Christian presence in China disappeared from view, the Nubian Christian state folded, the Ethiopians stood in mortal danger, and the old Christian populations living under Muslim rule saw steady erosion. The remaining Christian populations in Asia and Africa impinged little on European Christian consciousness, unless in confused impressions such as fueled the stories of Prester John. For all practical purposes there was Christian territory, which was subject to the rule of Christ, and pagan territory, which was not. And this representation was, if anything, strengthened by observation of the other realm, which recognized the lands of Islam and the lands of warfare. The only model of Christianity that Western Europe knew was the Christendom model, the model of Christian territory. Faced with accessible territories where Christ was not known, the manifest duty of Christians was to bring their peoples into the sphere of Christendom, to make those lands Christian territory. The fact that God had so significantly and recently blessed the use of the sword in reclaiming Granada could only reinforce the conviction. Conquest and conversion belonged naturally together.

There is no need here to pursue the Spanish story through Peru, Mexico, and the Philippines. This is a story of the expansion of Christendom, but it is not the story of the origins of the missionary movement. The modern missionary movement began not in the Spanish territories but in the Portuguese, and in those great Asian empires to which the Portuguese trading settlements were neighbours or customers. The Portuguese, with exactly the same theology as the Spanish, and the same inherited experience, found the task of expanding Christendom by the sword all but impossible. They tried, but only in the small enclaves under their direct control; and then often imperfectly could they enforce it. Hindu and Buddhist and Islamic traditions refused passive surrender. New Christian populations did emerge in Asia, but there was no parallel to the events of Mexico and Peru. And there was not the remotest hope of bringing about the conversion of the Moghul or the Chinese Empires by the means adopted in the Americas; and the strange story of Japan's "Christian century" simply served to underline the point.[5] It was necessary to accommodate the Christendom idea to political and military reality.

That reality laid a new requirement upon those for whom the universal claims of Christ's kingship overrode all other considerations. It was necessary to develop a new category of Christian personnel whose function was to commend, explain, and illustrate the Christian message without the power to coerce acceptance of it. Further, in order to attain this uncertain end, those involved must adapt themselves to the modes of life of another people, acquire another language at a fundamental level, and find a niche in another society that enabled them to function within it. This is the style of life exemplified in the Jesuit missions at the Moghul and Chinese courts and in far humbler situations in many other places. It is a new development, one born out of frustrated colonialism. It was far from new in the total Christian history, nor without precedent in Western Christian experience, but counter to the natural first instincts of Western Christianity and to its domestically developed patterns. The idea of living on terms set by other people, which lies at its heart, remained the expression of the essential missionary experience, the missionary ideal for both Catholics and Protestants for centuries to come. It was perhaps the first learning experience that European Christianity received from its contact with the non-Western world.

---

[5]C. R. Boxer, *The Christian Century in Japan, 1549–1650* (Berkeley: University of California Press, 1976).

For its accomplishment this missionary ideal required a combination of three factors. First, it needed a substantial corps of persons with the degree of commitment capable of sustaining such a life and the intellectual equipment to further it. Second, it needed a form of organization that could mobilize and maintain such a force. Third, it needed sustained Western access to specific locations, with reasonable expectation of continued communication. Throughout its history, Western missionary enterprise depended on these three factors, and the presence or absence of one or more of them has brought about its upswings and its downswings. These factors account, among other things, for the periods when Western Christians talked of missions but did not establish them, as well as for the periods when they did not even talk of them.

The first factor, the corps of competent personnel, implies powerful religious influences, informed by a tradition of mental training. The second, organizational viability, implies political and ecclesiastical conditions that allow for innovation and flexibility. The third, the logistical factor, implies maritime capability, with access to transoceanic bases and communications, and a certain level of public consciousness about such things. The logistical factor in the Western missionary movement requires more attention than it has so far received. The earliest missionary concern arose from the new Iberian maritime consciousness; the Jesuit missions in India, China, and Japan depended on the Portuguese enclaves in Asia for their communications and supplies. When control of maritime access passed from the Portuguese to the Dutch, the Netherlands assumed, though without great enthusiasm, the Portuguese role of the extenders of Christendom. It was the only Protestant power to make the attempt. With the accession of the British to maritime leadership, all pretence of responsibility for the extension of Christendom as the aim of public policy (if we except a brief period under the English Commonwealth) came to an end. But the logistics of the missionary movement, the business of getting its personnel to viable overseas stations, still depended very much on the use of British facilities. In what follows, an attempt will be made to show that the significance of the institution of missionary societies in Britain lies not in their initiating the Protestant missionary movement (an impression created by much earlier writing), nor solely in their initiating a British missionary movement, but in the logistical support and expanded outlets they provided for a preexisting continental missionary movement. We may note that among smaller European nations none maintained a higher level of missionary consciousness than Norway, an incorrigibly maritime nation; while the Protestant population of landlocked Hungary produced only a couple of missionaries—and those from the German minority—in the whole of the nineteenth century, and no mission agency before the twentieth.[6]

---

[6]See A. M. Kool, *God Moves in a Mysterious Way: The Hungarian Protestant Foreign Mission Movement 1756–1951* (Zoetermeer: Boekencentrum, 1993).

Maritime access in itself, however, was not enough to promote missionary consciousness. This question is worth considering in relation to the sources of personnel for the early missionary movement, and the organizational means used to recruit missionaries and maintain missions. For the early Catholic missions the organizational models were already at hand in the orders, and the religious and political conditions of the Catholic Reformation favoured their adaptation and development for missionary purposes, enabled the emergence of new custom-built orders and societies, and provided the motivated personnel for both the older and the newer. Protestants had no ready equivalent of the orders to provide the backbone of a mission force or sustain one if provided. It is frequently said that it was the Evangelical Revival that provided the committed corps of personnel for the missionary movement; and it can be further argued that the eighteenth-century development of the voluntary society provided Protestants for the first time with a focused and flexible form of organization as the order had provided for Catholics.[7] The evangelicalism that emerged from the revival in Britain and North America provided a highly successful form of Christian adaptation to the European Enlightenment. It reconciled the developed consciousness of individual responsibility, so characteristic of Enlightenment thought, with Christian faith, while the development of close fellowship that it fostered among the likeminded provided an antidote to the societal and ecclesial atomization that individualism could produce. At the same time, its distinction between "nominal" or "formal" and "real" Christianity made it possible to retain the concept of an overarching Christendom that had been fundamental to European identity for centuries.[8] Such a combination of levels of consciousness—the personal relationship with God, the fellowship of "real" Christians and the larger territorial entity Christian in principle—when equipped with the new instrument of the voluntary society as a "use of means" (as William Carey called it), made possible the mobilization and deployment of a Protestant missionary force.

At first sight, such a view would seem to coincide with the view that the Protestant missionary awakening begins in the late-eighteenth century, with such representative figures as Thomas Coke and William Carey. If, however, we view the origins of the Protestant missionary movement in a European context, the picture looks rather different, and the late-eighteenth century looks much less like a new beginning. For one thing, the achievement of the Evangelical Revival in combining a renewal of Christian faith and zeal with the Enlightenment values of the individual, and in reconciling the type of ecclesial commitment formerly characteristic of the

---

[7]See Andrew F. Walls, *The Missionary Movement in Christian History* (Maryknoll, N.Y.: Orbis, 1996), 79–85.
[8]Ibid., 241–54.

Anabaptist congregation with the recognition of Christendom and its territorial expressions, had been foreshadowed in Germanic and central European Pietism. Pietism had already provided a Protestant religious dynamic that produced the sort of people who could accept martyrdom, "red" or "green";[9] and that dynamic was backed by a tradition of learning and by commitment to active philanthropy. Halle and Herrenhut are the twin poles of Pietism. The former and its key figure, A. H. Francke, were inevitably associated with the famous university and the equally famous orphan house, the latter for the sort of Protestant-Franciscan spirituality that made people ready to become slaves in order to preach to slaves.

Continental Pietism had a missionary consciousness long before British evangelical consciousness was fully developed. When in 1699 the king of Denmark decided to institute a mission (using, of course, the ready-made base of a Danish colony, Tranquebar), he could find none of his own subjects suitable and willing to act as missionaries. The needed missionaries were found among Francke's former students in Halle. Bartolomäus Ziegenbalg and Heinrich Plutschau opened a mission that was to operate and expand throughout the eighteenth century and into the nineteenth, establish a significant Christian community, achieve major feats of translation, and survive the vicissitudes of a highly volatile political situation in India. Its membership included such figures as Christian Friedrich Schwarz, who built up a remarkable relationship of trust with the rulers of Thanjavur.[10] Daniel Brunner[11] has explored the labyrinthine procedures by which the king of Denmark's mission came, for logistical reasons arising from the changing political situation, to be linked with London and the Anglican Society for Promoting Christian Knowledge (SPCK). One of the two key figures in establishing the connexion was Heinrich Wilhelm Ludolf, formerly secretary to Prince George of Denmark. The prince, himself deeply influenced by Pietism, became the husband of Princess Anne of England, the future queen, in 1683. Ludolf was a peripatetic promoter of "inner" Christianity, and found his ideal in Halle. An even more significant figure was Anton Boehm, a Pietist preacher who became London chaplain to the prince. Of the whole succession of SPCK missionaries in India, all were German, and all were Pietists endorsed by Francke or his successors in Halle. They held Lutheran, not Anglican, or-

---

[9]Adopting the early Celtic identification of the self-offering of the ascetic in a "green" setting with the "red" shedding of blood for Christ's sake, the latter being characteristic of the age of persecution.

[10]See Daniel Jeyaraj, *Inkulturation in Tranquebar: Der Beitrag der frühen dänisch-halleschen Mission zum Werden einer indisch-einheimischen Kirche (1706–1730)* (Erlangen: Verlag der Ev.-Luth. Mission, 1996).

[11]Daniel L. Brunner, *Halle Pietists in England: Antony William Boehm and the Society for Promoting Christian Knowledge* (Göttingen: Vandenhoeck und Ruprecht, 1993).

dination, and conveyed that ordination to Indian successors. The SPCK seem to have consulted Halle in relation to every missionary appointment. At various times the question of Anglican ordination was broached in SPCK circles, but never forced to an issue. At other times the question arose of the appointment of English persons to what was technically a mission related to the Church of England; none were ever identified. It was only in 1825 that this remarkable arrangement came to an end.[12]

But Halle was not the sole expression of the growth of a European Protestant missionary consciousness. Equally important, and probably making a heavier impact on a wider public, was the Moravian enterprise associated with Zinzendorf and Herrenhut. The radical nature of the Moravian version of Christian discipleship, the choice of such harsh environments as Greenland and Labrador for mission work, and the eminently practical aspects of their mission activity (exemplified in the new Eden they were held to have planted at the Cape of Good Hope),[13] all made an impression on a range of Christian readers. Recent scholarship has illuminated the variety of groupings within Pietism, W. R. Ward distinguishes Spener-Halle, Moravian-Zinzendorf, Württemberg, Reformed, and Radical, and he has highlighted the conflicts between them, notably between Halle and Herrenhut.[14] To a growing British audience with interest and concern for missions, such conflicts mattered little. What they could see was that pious continental brethren were preaching the gospel among the heathen, and they wanted to emulate them.

If we read William Carey's famous *Enquiry*,[15] so often seen as heralding the new era of missions, against the setting of Baptist thought of the time (as laid out for us by G. F. Nuttall[16] and others), there is little sense of a new beginning. Carey is clearly conscious that missionary work is al-

---

[12]See W. K. Lowther Clarke, *A History of the SPCK* (London: SPCK, 1959), 59–76.

[13]See Bernhard Krüger, *The Pear Tree Blossoms: A History of Moravian Mission Stations in South Africa, 1737–1869* (Genadendal: Moravian Church, 1967). The title alludes to the horticultural emphasis of the early Moravian mission to the Cape, seen at the time as reinforcing the association of Christianity with civilization, and in fact affording the few Khoi ("Hottentot") converts a means of subsistence and source of dignity in a white-dominated society. The pear tree outlasted the early mission.

[14]W. R. Ward, *The Protestant Evangelical Awakening* (Cambridge: Cambridge University Press, 1992).

[15]William Carey, *An Enquiry into the Obligations of Christians to Use Means for the Conversion of the Heathens* (Leicester, 1792). There are several facsimile reprints of this tract; that of 1961 (London: Carey Kingsgate Press) has an introductory essay by Ernest A. Payne. Payne also wrote a book with the eloquent title *The Church Awakes: The Story of the Modern Missionary Movement* (London: Livingstone Press, 1942), which begins with the Napoleonic Wars and the early British societies.

[16]Geoffrey F. Nuttall, "Northamptonshire and the Modern Question: A Turning Point in Eighteenth-Century Dissent," *Journal of Theological Studies*, n.s. 16 (1965): 101–23.

ready and has long been in progress, and he wants his own constituency to become involved in it. The objections to missions that he demolishes are merely such as he met within his own circle, and he deals with them *ad hominem*. (In response to the demand for a specific scriptural warrant for preaching the gospel to heathens in any period following the apostolic age, he points out to his Baptist audience that postapostolic baptism is subject to the same deficiency.) His review (section 2 of the *Enquiry*) of "former undertakings for the conversion of the heathen" is presented as a continuing story from New Testament times to the present day. The story reaches a high point in the establishment and growth of gospel churches in America, evidence that "the Redeemer has fixed his throne in that country, where but a little time ago, Satan had a universal dominion."[17] His last words on America are to record that Mr. Kirkland and Mr. Sergeant are employed in the same good work (i.e., with regard to the Native Americans, taking up Brainerd's mantle).

For the rest of the world he had only the resources of the Leicester Philosophical Institute and a small circle of modest Dissenter ministerial libraries to draw on, so he knows little about the Halle missionaries in India. He has heard, however, of the king of Denmark's mission in Tranquebar, and of conversions there, though his information comes down no later than Ziegenbalg's time. On the Dutch missions in Southeast Asia he is still more out of date, and unduly optimistic, since he seems to assume that "though the work has decayed in some places," the general conditions applying in the late-seventeenth century were still in force. Then comes a salute to the Moravians.

> But none of the moderns have equaled the Moravian Brethren in this good work; they have sent missions to Greenland, Labrador, and several of the West-Indian Islands, which have been blessed for good. They have likewise sent to Abyssinia, in Africa, but what success they have had I cannot tell.[18]

The last words in the review are for the efforts of "the late Mr. Wesley's efforts in the West Indies" (Wesley had died only the year before) and to pleasing accounts of Methodist successes there.

It is clear, then, that Carey saw himself and those whom he was stirring to action as entering into a process already in motion, not as initiating that process. And the leading elements in that process in his own time, and for some time past, have their roots in continental Europe.

A similar outlook is reflected in the early volumes of the *Missionary Register*, which appeared during the Napoleonic Wars. The *Missionary*

---

[17]Carey, *Enquiry* 36.
[18]Ibid., 37.

Register was published by the Church Missionary Society as an ecumenical adjunct to its more "in-house" publications. Its first issue begins the serialization of a *History of the Propagation of Christianity* by Hugh Pearson, an essay awarded the prize endowed by Claudius Buchanan for publication on missions. The earlier part of the essay is heavily dependent on the pioneer work by Robert Millar, minister of Paisley Abbey, which had appeared as long before as 1723.[19]

Of the modern chapter of the story of the propagation of the faith, Pearson identifies the foundation of the Danish Missionary College as a landmark. He describes the Tranquebar mission from much better sources than Carey's and enthuses over the work and devotion of the Moravians. They are entitled to hold very high rank in the roll of missionary enterprise, never surpassed by any denomination, with a "strong and peculiar claim" on the assistance of the Christian world at large. Later that year the *Missionary Register* published a lengthy life of "the eminent missionary Schwarz," the outstanding name among the Halle missionaries in India. Schwarz had died in 1798, but his career as an Indian missionary had begun back in 1750.

There are even examples of missionaries who personally link the British movement that began in the late-eighteenth century with the continental precursor. The notable, if eccentric, Wilhelm Ringeltaube, who was involved in one of the first mass movements to the Christian faith in India in the Protestant period, studied in Halle, was converted there, came under Moravian influence, and worked in India in connexion with the SPCK. He left it in 1799, and in 1804 was appointed elsewhere in India by the London Missionary Society. He served with that society until 1816, shortly before his mysterious disappearance. Another SPCK missionary was Josef Jänicke,[20] who was the younger brother of Johannes Jänicke, founder of the Berlin Missionary Seminary, which provided the Church Missionary Society with most of its first candidates.[21]

In short, the Protestant missionary awakening did not begin in 1792 or anywhere near that date. What happened in that period was British entry into a well-established continental tradition. This was, indeed, no insignificant event. The Evangelical movement as it had developed in Britain made possible a larger supply of committed mission personnel than had been available previously; though, as we shall see, the supply took some time to build up. The organizational capacity for mission was given new scope by the voluntary society, for development of which, es-

---

[19]Robert Millar, *The History of the Propagation of Christianity and the Overthrow of Paganism*, 3rd ed. (London, 1731).

[20]On J. D. Jänicke, see the article by E. M. Jackson, in D. M. Lewis, ed., *Blackwell Dictionary of Evangelical Biography*, vol. 1 (Oxford: Blackwell, 1995), 604.

[21]On Johannes Jänicke, see the article by David Bundy, in ibid., 603f., and references there.

pecially given the conditions of a major continental war, Britain offered the fullest possibilities. And, on the logistical side, British maritime access allowed for a considerable extension of the geographical scope of missions. All these are substantial matters, involving a major enlargement of the missionary movement; but it is an enlargement, a new phase rather than a new beginning.

The entry into the missionary movement of British societal organization and British logistical capability was important not only because it established the missionary contributions of English and Scottish personnel, significant as that was, but also because it provided a new framework in which the continental missionary consciousness could operate. It is commonly pointed out that the emergence of the new British missionary societies (the Particular Baptist Society in 1792, the Missionary Society soon known as the London Missionary Society in 1795, with the Edinburgh and Glasgow societies soon after, the Church Missionary Society in 1799, and the British and Foreign Bible Society and other agencies in the new century) was followed by the establishment of a succession of missionary societies and agencies on the continent—Berlin, Basel, St. Chrischona, Leipzig, and the others. This picture furthers the idea of British primogeniture in the movement. It also obscures much of the importance of continental Europe to the British missionary movement, and the extent to which the new British societies depended, especially in their early years, on continental missionary candidates. In fact, the British societies provided a new outlet for a continental missionary already in being, and to a remarkable extent continued to do so after the new continental agencies had been formed. We may approach the matter with crude statistics. Over the period from its inception in 1799 up to 1850, more than one in five of the missionaries sent out by the Church Missionary Society, a society that had come into being for the very reason that the special concerns and ethos of evangelical ecclesiastics of the Church of England could not be safeguarded by the mission agencies then available, came from continental Europe. If we take the period up to 1830, the tally is higher still—well over a quarter, and not far short of a third. And if we close the count with the Napoleonic Wars in 1815, the proportion is seventeen out of twenty-four, more than two-thirds. Nor does the connexion close even in 1850; throughout the nineteenth century, and long afterwards, continental recruits came to the CMS,[22] even after the special arrangements with the Berlin and Basel seminaries, so important in the early years, came to an end.

Of those serving with the CMS before 1850, the great majority were German, but there were a good number of Swiss, a few Dutch and Danes,

---

[22]The principal source is the Church Missionary Society *Register of Missionaries (Clerical, Lay and Female) and Native Clergy from 1804 to 1904*, first printed for private circulation in 1896 with a supplement ca. 1905.

and at least one Swede. Among the Germans, the largest single constituency is Württemberg, but many of the earliest were from Prussia, and there are others from all over—from Alsace to Saxony, and from Hamburg to Bavaria. There is even one name from Livonia.

If we turn to the London Missionary Society (LMS), the principal missionary vehicle for evangelical Dissenters in the first half of the nineteenth century, the picture, while not as impressive as for the CMS, is striking enough. One remarkable aspect for a London-based society is the size of its Scottish component, and this although the foundation of the society immediately produced emulation north of the border.[23] The LMS received a disproportionately large number of Scottish candidates, and its secretariat in its early days was sometimes dominated by expatriate Scottish ministers living in London. But leaving the question of the Scots presence aside, there appears to be not less than fifty-seven, and perhaps as many as sixty-three, missionaries of the LMS before 1850 whose origins are in the European continent, out of a total of 506.[24] If we add a further five missionaries born in South Africa but of Dutch origin, then something like 13.5 percent of the missionaries of the main agency of the English Dissenters before 1850 had their roots in continental Europe. While not so crucial to the society's existence as to the CMS, the continental mission personnel were none the less significant, especially in the period of the Napoleonic Wars. In 1811, five of the society's thirteen new missionaries were German; in 1814, the new missionaries consisted of two German, one Dutch, one Swiss, and one English. The Netherlands was the main continental source of supply for the broadly Calvinistic LMS; but their register indicates recruits from several parts of Germany, and from Switzerland, Sweden, Denmark, Bohemia, and other parts of the Austrian Empire, with an important group of French Reformed missionaries.

It is clear, then, that the two principal English missionary societies continued to draw heavily on continental sources for their mission personnel well into the period when continental societies were active on their own account. Such arrangements, sometimes formal, sometimes informal, suited both sides. The British societies gained much needed candidates to fill vacancies in the field; the continental agencies received effective outlets for missionary energies. The relationship continued even when the

---

[23]See A. F. Walls, "Missions," in N. M. de S. Cameron et al., eds., *Dictionary of Scottish Church History and Theology* (Edinburgh: Clark, 1993), esp. 568–70. See also William Brown, *The History of the Propagation of Christianity among the Heathen, since the Reformation* (Edinburgh, 1854). Brown was secretary of the Scottish Missionary Society.

[24]The calculation is based on the information given in James Sibree, *London Missionary Society: A Register of Missionaries, Deputations, etc. from 1796 to 1923*, 4th ed. (London: London Missionary Society, 1923) The information provided in the *Register* varies in extent from entry to entry; many of the early entries in particular do not record place of birth or origin.

price for continentals was high: not only Anglican ordination (which had not been required in the eighteenth century for the Halle missionaries of the SPCK in India), but also reordination for those already in Lutheran or Reformed orders.[25]

For the CMS, the continental supply was not just advantageous, but vital. As is well known, for several years after its foundation (which itself had been the focus of a good deal of theological and ecclesiastical angst), the CMS had no missionaries at all. Its successive reports had little to report except hopes. The CMS was rescued from this absurd situation by a continental contact. This was the seminary for the training of missionaries, organized in Berlin by Johannes Jänicke, a missionary enthusiast already linked with Halle and the India mission. The connexion was forged by a man whose name constantly appears in Evangelical and philanthropic circles in England: Carl F. Steinkopf, the German minister of the Savoy Chapel.[26]

The first seven names covering 1804 to 1809 in the register of CMS missionaries are all of Germans. Then follow two English artisans whom the CMS would like to have called catechists, but had to designate as "lay settlers" for New Zealand.

Between 1811 and 1814 there follow seven more Germans, with only one further English missionary, the lay schoolteacher Thomas Kendall. Not until 1815 was this society, set up sixteen years earlier to channel the missionary concern of English Evangelicals anxious to preserve Anglican church order,[27] able to send any English clergy to the mission field. Long after 1815 it continued to rely on German mission staff for its oldest and, in terms of mortality, most dangerous field, West Africa; so that even in the middle of the century it was possible for the supercilious to describe the lingua franca growing up in Sierra Leone as "German English."[28]

If the continental missionaries stood in the breach where the dead fell into the trench,[29] they also supplied materials often lacking in the British

---

[25]See J. Pinnington, "Church Principles in the Early Years of the Church Missionary Society: The Problem of the 'German' Missionaries," *Journal of Theological Studies*, n.s., 20 no. 2 (1969): 523–32.

[26]Eugene Stock, *The History of the Church Missionary Society, Its Environment, Its Men and Its work*, vol. 1 (London: Church Missionary Society, 1899), 82f.

[27]The issue is dealt with at length in M. M. Hennell, *John Venn and the Clapham Sect* (London: Lutterworth Press, 1958), ch. 5.

[28]See Walls, *Missionary Movement*, 103; and contemporary descriptions such as R. Clarke, *Sketches of the Colony of Sierra Leone and Its Inhabitants* (London, 1863).

[29]David Hinderer, the distinguished German CMS missionary in Yorubaland, is said to have used this metaphor in response to his English bride's dismay at the short periods of service and high mortality reflected in the CMS roll of missionaries. The Christian siege of Africa would triumph when missionaries were able to step over the bodies of their fallen comrades into the trench that had so far prevented access to its citadel. See Stock, *History*, vol. 2, 116.

missionary commissiariat. One of these was scholarship. English missionary recruits were often of modest educational attainments, and the Church Missionary College at Islington was set up to give such people basic education. Many of the Germans, too, came from a humble background, but their academic potential was often evident. This was especially important in West Africa, since the practice of the CMS was long to send its better-educated English and Irish personnel to India. Germans soon took the leadership in African linguistics. The first major figure in this area was J. F. Schön, who came to the CMS from Baden via the Basel Missionary Seminary. He served the society for twenty years, but continued long afterwards as linguistic adviser, publishing works on Hausa, Igbo, and Mende, and receiving scholarly recognition.[30] Still more significant was the Württemberger Sigismund Wilhelm Koelle. He, too, came from the Basel seminary, was brought, as the Germans often were, to Islington for orientation and English, and then studied Arabic at Tübingen under Ewald. For most of his career he worked in Muslim contexts in the Middle East; but for a brief, fruitful period he worked in Sierra Leone, producing *Polyglotta Africana*, the pioneer work in the science of comparative African linguistics, based on specimens of a hundred African languages. The CMS often looked to Germany for its linguists, of whom Koelle was perhaps the most distinguished of many.[31] Henry Venn, its ever busy secretary, got his commercial advice from Manchester, but his linguistic counsel from Germany.[32]

The London Missionary Society also received continental recruits of considerable stature. It was indebted to continental Europe for at least one candidate whose coming marked for the society a turning point in its affairs. Johannes Theodorus Van der Kemp entered LMS service in 1798, when he was already fifty years of age. Even apart from his age, he was a new type of missionary. For one thing, while most LMS candidates lamented their early sins and misimproved talents and opportunities, this ex-dragoon officer really had been a sinner on a fairly spectacular scale. He had also been a deist and a rationalist author. At that time the LMS

---

[30]Schön (CMS, *Register*, no. 181) received the Volney prize from Paris and an honorary D.D. from Oxford for his linguistic work.

[31]On S. W. Koelle, see CMS *Register*, no. 379. Koelle, *Polyglotta Africana: or a Comparative Vocabulary of Three Hundred Words and Phrases in More Than One Hundred Distinct African Languages* (London, 1854). On the background of all these translations see P.E.H. Hair, *The Early Study of Nigerian Languages: Essays and Bibliographies* (Cambridge: Cambridge University Press, 1967).

[32]Venn called in the assistance of Lepsius, as well as of scholars—including Max Müller—resident in Britain, for questions related to the Yoruba Bible, one of the landmark mission translations, and this orthography was used in later translations. See J. F. Ade Ajayi, *Christian Missions in Nigeria 1841–1891: The Making of a New Elite* (London: Longmans, 1965), 127.

were not expecting well-endowed candidates and had been conditioned to recruiting missionaries of artisan background. Moravian advice even indicated that these made the best and toughest missionaries. The appointment of Van der Kemp to open the new field at the Cape of Good Hope revolutionized the concept of a missionary as it stood in 1798. It is safe to say that no English equivalent of Van der Kemp, whether from Anglican or Dissenter circles, would have been a potential missionary candidate at that date.[33]

The appointment of people of such stature did not always make for easy relationships. Van der Kemp had been brought to South Africa as a Dutchperson to talk to Dutchpeople, at a time when Britain had newly acquired the colony only through the fortunes of war, and was not committed to staying there. His uncompromising behaviour brought the question of race relations onto the missionary agenda, and kept it there. Notwithstanding the importance of the later activity of John Philip,[34] it is doubtful whether the mission would or could have maintained so firm a stand in a hostile environment without the initial confrontations with Van der Kemp, a man who could not be ignored. Missionaries of stature could also prove uncomfortable for the committee, as the CMS early found out in the matter of C. T. E. Rhenius. This young Prussian was in 1814 one of the first two missionaries appointed by the society to India. Besides being a major Tamil linguist, he proved remarkably effective in building up the church. He can now be seen as far ahead of his time in his vision of what an indigenous church should and could be. At that time, however, the society could only see that its carefully preserved ecclesiastical principles were being jeopardized by Rhenius's proposals for ordination of local ministers. Rhenius was disconnected; the test of his work is the extent to which the Indian congregations continued with him.[35]

This chapter has considered the European dimension of the missionary movement very much in terms of the British missionary movement in the context of the continental. The justification for this is the common assumption that the Protestant missionary movement was essentially a British product that received eventual reinforcement from the continent. It is argued here that its origins are continental and that continental Protestantism helped to sustain the British movement through its fledgling period, while the organizational and logistical features of the British move-

---

[33]On Van der Kemp (Sibree, *Register,* no. 34), see Ido Hendricus Enklaar, *Life and Work of Dr. J. Th. Van der Kemp, 1749–1811: Missionary, Pioneer and Protagonist of Racial Equality in South Africa* (Cape Town: Balkema, 1988).

[34]See Andrew Ross, *John Philip (1775–1851): Missions, Race and Politics in South Africa* (Aberdeen: Aberdeen University Press, 1956).

[35]On Rhenius (1790–1838), see C. J. Rhenius, *Memoir of the Rev. C. T. E. Rhenius* (London, 1841); and the article by R. E. Frykenberg and R. V. Pierard in Lewis, *Evangelical Biography,* vol. 2, 926–28.

ment, products of peculiarly British conditions, gave impetus and new outlets to the continental movement. Other important aspects of the context have been neglected; some of these are highlighted by the relationship between the British and continental movements.

One issue is the extent to which Pietist and Evangelical religion created a sense of common understanding and purpose between groups separated by geography, nationality, and confession. The expressions of Pietist and Evangelical faith could be very diverse; Halle, Herrnhut, and Würrtemberg produced manifestations that were not just divergent from one another but conflicting; the Evangelical Revival as it operated in the British Isles and North America, and the *Réveil* in Switzerland and France produced an equally diverse array. It is a perplexing feature of Pietist and Evangelical religion that it could be grafted on to practically any of the existing theological, confessional, or ecclesiastical traditions, sincerely affirm loyalty to the "true" nature of any historic church, and adapt itself to any national or local cultural ethos. But all forms acknowledged the primacy of personal religion, all sought to express "real" Christianity within a society whose symbols, confessions, and sense of historic identity were already Christian. The distinction between "real" or "inward" and "nominal" or "formal" Christianity in Pietist and Evangelical religion posed an implicit challenge to the idea of Christendom, that territorial expression of Christianity, the idea of the comprehensive Christian realm, which had been a constituent of the European experience since the conversion period that accompanied the collapse of the Western Roman Empire. The challenge was implicit, not explicit; far from desiring to overthrow the Christendom model, with its communal acknowledgment of the Lordship of Christ in the national sphere, Pietists and Evangelicals frequently sought to bolster it and deepen communal Christian allegiance by the infusion of "real" Christianity. This could produce alliances that at first sight seem unlikely, such as that which we have already noticed between Halle Pietists, whose theology could react sympathetically to English Puritanism, and the High Church Anglicans of the SPCK, eager to encourage the practice of a devout and holy life but reacting to the Puritan tradition with revulsion. Perhaps neither Pietism nor Evangelicalism ever fully resolved the tension between the desire to retain a Christian society and the recognition of personal responsibility in response to God's initiative for human salvation. Perhaps too, the missionary movement was to reveal this tension in a particularly significant way, especially as it entered the colonial era.

And this brought the Pietist and Evangelical movements into currents of their times that had quite different origins. The underlying principle of Christendom was initially breached by the Protestant Reformation itself, which replaced the thought of a universal territorial church by mutual recognition of national churches; and Pietists and Evangelicals of all descriptions found their identity in the Reformation. A further breach was opened in the original idea of Christendom whenever political realities forced some degree of religious toleration in place of national religious uniformity. Such developments, even though they left the national symbolic apparatus intact, had the effect of moving religion from the sphere of the public and communal to the sphere of the private and personal, and thus to the sphere of group and family, and ultimately to individual responsibility and choice. Such developments in turn were fertile soil for the intellectual movements arising in the various expressions of the Enlightenment in different parts of Europe. These emphasised the responsibility and even the autonomy of the individual, and developed the principles of contract and association as the modes by which this responsibility could be collectively expressed. These emphases and processes posed a direct threat to the idea of the territorial Christian realm that lay at the heart of European Christianity. Such a further impetus to the movement of religion from the sphere of public requirement to that of private choice could easily be seen as an attack on Christianity as it had hitherto been understood in European history. Paradoxically, such thoroughly Christian developments as Pietism and Evangelicalism, by radically adopting the principle of personal responsibility in religion, and developing with marked success the principles of contract and association to give that religion communal form, helped Protestantism to adapt to the Enlightenment, perhaps even enabled it to survive. Whether this constituted a rescue or a temporary reprieve lies outside the scope of this enquiry; but it is clear that the missionary movement played its part in developing the sense of personal responsibility in religion, and the use of contract and association to give it communal expression.

We have seen how a sense of common purpose could link groups in different countries who stood for "real" Christianity, the Pietist and Evangelical islands, some large, some tiny, in the sea of Christendom. There have been illuminating studies of the networks developed among Evangelicals in Britain,[36] and how those networks crossed the Atlantic; it is also clear that the networks crossed Europe. The significance for the missionary movement of two German ministers living in London, Anton Boehm and Carl Steinkopf, has already been mentioned. Boehm has been well served by Brunner, but Steinkopf, who forged the link between the CMS and the institution that blossomed into the Berliner Missionsgesellschaft, and whose name appears in connexion with so many evangelical agencies and activities, deserves more attention. Evangelicals all over Europe visited the American businessman Wilder, who later became American min-

---

[36]See Susan O'Brien, "Eighteenth-Century Publishing Networks in the First Years of Transatlantic Evangelicalism," in M. A. Noll, D. W. Bebbington, and G. A. Rawlyk, eds., *Evangelicalism: Comparative Studies of Popular Protestantism in North America, the British Isles, and Beyond, 1700–1990* (New York: Oxford University Press, 1994).

ister in Paris. (He had other visitors too; he was party to a plot to spring Napoleon from St. Helena.) He provided the safe house in which the Paris Evangelical Missionary Society could be born in the heart of Bourbon France.[37] The radical Evangelicals—Scottish, English, French, and Swiss—who gathered in Geneva, had their visitors too, and were the source of some important minority movements in mission theory and practice.[38]

With varying degrees of formality, links were established between missionary societies in different countries. The association between the Netherlands Missionary Society and the LMS was first realized in Van der Kemp and his colleague Kicherer; and Van der Kemp was screened for the LMS by an elder of the Scots Kirk at Rotterdam. Peter Fjellstedt, who worked with the CMS in India and Syria between 1831 and 1840, left to become the pioneer architect of Swedish missions, and the founder of the Lund Missionary Society. He did not forget the CMS; he was responsible for recruiting to its ranks Johann Ludwig Krapf, the pioneer and prophet of East African missions.[39] One of the most unusual developments of the missionary movement was the emergence of a Roman Catholic priest, Johann Evangelista Gossner (1773–1858), first as revivalist preacher, then as Lutheran pastor, and eventually as founder of a major missionary society. At one point Gossner tried to hand his mission, which had some rather radical features, to the CMS.[40] The transfer failed, but Gossner's successor was Johann Detloff Prochnow,[41] a Prussian in the service of the CMS in India.

All the springs for the Protestant missionary movement lay in the movement for "real Christianity" within Christendom. Overseas missions were not a separate growth from home missions or European missions; they arose in the same soil, and were rarely rivals. Enthusiasts for one were frequently enthusiastic for the other, and their histories overlapped. In 1801, at a period when the six-year-old LMS was engaged in strengthening its missions in the Pacific and in South Africa, it appointed a French prisoner of war, Louis Cadoret, as a missionary to other prisoners of war. During the Peace of Amiens, the society assisted his removal to France where he worked as a minister.[42] Gossner, before founding the mission

---

[37]On Wilder, see *Records from the Life of S.V.S. Wilder* (New York: American Tract Society, 1865). On the foundation of the Paris Evangelical Missionary Society, see J. Bianquis, *Les origines de la Société des missions Évangéliques de Paris, 1822–1829* (Paris, 1930).

[38]See T. C. F. Stunt, *From Awakening to Secession* (Edinburgh: Clark).

[39]On Fjellstedt (CMS, *Register*, no. 169), see Olaus Bränström, *Peter Fjellstedt; Mångsidig men entydig kyrkoman* (Uppsala: Instituet för Missonsforskuing, 1994).

[40]On Gossner, see Johannes Aagaard, *Mission, Konfession, Kirche: Die Problematik ihrer Integration*, vol. 2 (Lund: Gleerup, 1967); and W. Holsten, *Johann Evangelista Gossner* (Göttingen: Mohr, 1949).

[41]See CMS, *Register*, no. 333.

[42]See Sibree, *Register*, no. 84.

that was to bear his name, travelled widely, including to Finland and Russia, with his revival message. Ebenezer Henderson and John Paterson were originally designated by Robert Haldane as missionaries to India. Finding themselves in Copenhagen in transit to their appointment there, they became impressed with the spiritual needs of northern Protestantism. Henderson's remarkable career as preacher, translator, and Bible distributor led him from Denmark to Sweden, thence to Iceland and, above all, to Russia.[43] In the Russian Empire the mission to Christendom and the mission to the non-Christian world met. Tsar Alexander I had for a time such a zeal for the Bible, and such favour for the Bible society, as to give rise to a belief that he had undergone evangelical conversion. He was also ready to allow Evangelical missionaries to the Tatars and other non-Christian peoples of his empire. No chapter of Protestant missionary activity raised higher hopes, or induced bleaker despair, than that associated with the Russian Empire. Within that story are different layers of the movement's early vision: the evangelization of unknown peoples, the renewal through the Scripture of ancient churches, and the spiritual revival of Protestantism and its return to the Reformation roots.

The missionary movement in its European context had the whole world in its sights. Those sights had as their prism the Pietist-Evangelical understanding of "real" Christianity. But there were to be strange events in the movement's itinerary. The very success of the Pietist-Evangelical project brought almost every section of the Western church into the missionary movement. The advance of Western hegemony and the colonial era raised the issue of territorial Christendom in a new form. New Christian communities came into being as a result of missionary activity without the clear distinction between "nominal" and "real" Christianity so formative in Europe. Christianity independent of Christendom appeared. And some of those communities, though emerging from the work of missions that were in so many ways products of the Christian encounter with Enlightenment, produced in due time versions of Christianity that were independent of the Enlightenment. These are not topics that can be pursued at the end of a chapter, but they suggest something of the range that the study of the Protestant missionary movement opens up, not least when viewed in its European context.

---

[43]On Henderson, see Thulia Susannah Henderson, *Memoir of the Rev. Eberezer Henderson, Including His Labours in Denmark, Iceland, Russia* (London, 1859).

12

The Missionary Movement

A Lay Fiefdom?

In *Mansfield Park,* Jane Austen describes the final interview between Mary, a young lady of the smart London set, and the earnest young clergyman to whom she has become attracted. The occasion is the news of a scandalous affair involving her own brother and the clergyman's sister. The young clergyman expresses his disapprobation of their moral conduct. Mary's reaction is:

> A pretty good lecture, upon my word! At this rate, you will soon reform everybody at Mansfield and Thornton Lacey, and when I hear of you next it may be as a celebrated preacher in some great society of Methodists, or as a missionary into foreign parts.[1]

For the London smart set in Jane Austen's day, there was only one step on the ladder of enthusiasm higher than that of Methodist preacher, and that was foreign missionary. Edmund, to whom the words quoted were addressed, was a beneficed clergyman of the Church of England. In 1811, when *Mansfield Park* was being written, not a single beneficed clergyman had become, in Mary's meaning of the words, "a missionary into foreign parts."

Forty years later, another country parson's daughter was writing about the style of life she knew. In Charlotte Brontë's *Shirley,* the heroine is struggling with her responsibilities towards the institution known variously as "the Jew basket" or "the missionary basket." The author explains:

> The "Jew basket" and "Missionary basket" . . . are willow repositories, of the capacity of a good-sized family clothes basket, dedicated to the purpose of conveying from house to house a monster

---

Presentation for the Conference on Evangelicalism and the Laity, University of Saint Andrews, 1999.
[1]Jane Austen, *Mansfield Park,* vol. 3, ch. 16, of the original edition.

collection of pin-cushions, needle-books, card racks, workbags, articles of infant wear, etc., etc., etc. made by the willing or reluctant hands of the Christian ladies of a parish, and sold per force to the heathenish gentlemen thereof, at prices unblushingly exorbitant. The proceeds of such compulsory sales are applied to the conversion of the Jews, the seeking up of the ten missing tribes, and to the regeneration of the interesting coloured population of the globe. Each lady-contributor takes it in her turn to keep the basket a month, to sew for it, and to foist off its contents on a shrinking male public. An exciting time it is when that turn comes round; some active-minded women, with a good trading spirit, like it, and enjoy exceedingly the fun of making hard-handed worsted spinners cash up, to the tune of four or five hundred per cent above cost price, for articles quite useless to them; other feebler souls object to it, and would rather see the prince of darkness himself at their door, than that phantom-basket, brought with "Mrs. Rouse's compliments, and please, ma'am, she says it's your turn now."[2]

These sound like words from the heart. One suspects that the missionary basket was a bane of Charlotte's life at Haworth Parsonage. But its inescapable presence shows the middle classes of small-town and rural England in the 1840s mobilized in support of overseas missions, with the women at their head. The menfolk, even if far from devout themselves, are systematically laid under tribute. The missionary basket releases entrepreneurial gifts among people who could have few other outlets for the skills that realize a profit of 500 percent. And even those who tremble at the basket's arrival cannot avoid taking their turn. That they cannot do so has nothing to do with the church or the clergy. It is lay peer pressure—and female lay peer pressure at that—that drives the missionary basket on its way.

The two passages well illustrate the change in social attitudes over the forty-year period that separates Jane Austen from Charlotte Brontë. The difference was noted by contemporary observers. Edward Steane, preaching the fiftieth anniversary sermon of the Particular Baptist Missionary Society in 1842, comments on the remarkable change in public opinion about missions since William Carey began his work:

Where at the present day are the statesmen who would prohibit the missionary from setting his foot on any shore that owes allegiance to the British crown? Where are the writers who affect to treat his self-denying labours with contempt? Where are the wits and reviewers who turn them into ridicule . . .? And where is that large portion of the public who gratified their impious merriment at the expense of methodism and missions?. . . Men enriched with the noblest intellec-

---

[2]Charlotte Brontë, *Shirley* (first published 1849), ch. 7.

tual endowments are found among [the missionary cause's] advocates; senators extol it in parliament . . . it moulds much of the current literature of the day, and tinctures more. It has even created a literature of its own. The popular feeling has turned almost entirely in its favour, so that you shall hear it spoken of in terms of commendation in almost all circumstances into which you can go.[3]

Allowing the usual discount for the eloquence of the pulpit, Steane is pointing to a genuine transformation in the attitudes expressed in society at large. Within half a century, missions passed from being one of the enthusiasms of the evangelical to a cause supported by earnest ecclesiastics of every strand of opinion. Whereas at one time a concern for missions might give rise to a suspicion of religious fanaticism or even political disaffection, the time came when the secretary of the Church Missionary Society, if burdened by government action or inaction in Africa, could be sure of a sympathetic hearing from his brother-in-law, the under secretary for the Colonies.

Part of the change, of course, is due simply to the general rise in the public significance and general respectability of evangelicalism in British life; by the beginning of the Victorian period, evangelical norms were adopted by all sorts of people who were not evangelicals. But it is necessary to make certain qualifications. For one thing, general approbation of the missionary project did not translate into general participation in that project. The missionary basket might pass around middle-class households, but throughout the nineteenth century the active promotion of missions remained the concern of a minority. Financial embarrassment dogged mission agencies throughout the century. In the very period of general approbation we have mentioned, the Wesleyans dismissed their most high-profile missionary, a man who had opened up untold new possibilities for missions, essentially because he was spending too much money.[4] The entire income of all the Bible and missionary societies, says Thomas Chalmers in 1819, would not maintain one ship of the line for a year.[5] By the end of the century, the insignificance of missionary contri-

---

[3]The sermon is reprinted in the collection *Missionary Sermons* (London: Carey, 1924).

[4]Thomas Birch Freeman superintended the Wesleyan mission in the Gold Coast from 1838 to 1857, and his journeys to Ashanti, Yorubaland, and Dahomey, and his negotiations with African rulers there, attracted much attention. But he was in constant disputes with his home committee, from at least 1844, about escalating expenses; in 1848 the committee declined to honour some of his bills; by 1856 his resignation was inevitable. See Thomas Birch Freeman, *Journal of Various Visits to the Kingdoms of Ashanti, Aku, and Dahomi, in Western Africa*, 3rd ed., with an introduction by Harrison M. Wright (London: Cass, 1968); Allen Birtwhistle, *Thomas Birch Freeman* (London: Epworth, 1950); Paul Ellingworth, *Thomas Birch Freeman* (Peterborough: Foundery Press, 1995).

[5]Thomas Chalmers, *The Influence of Bible Societies on the Temporal Necessities of the Poor* (Edinburgh, 1819):39.

butions in comparison with expenditure on luxury goods and positively harmful products became a preacher's commonplace.[6] Until the 1880s, missions were also generally short of missionaries. Sometimes the shortage was chronic: the Church Missionary Society spent its first five years without a single missionary on the field. A prime reason for the widespread recognition given in midcentury to the policy of self-governing, self-supporting, self-propagating churches was that there were simply not enough missionaries for the dual task of maintaining existing churches and founding new ones; nor could the agencies envisage that there ever would be, nor that they would be able to support them if there were.

The Victorian churches appropriated the missionary movement, but never saw it as more than marginal to their principal concerns. However fervently they sang "From Greenland's Icy Mountains," domestic concerns concentrated the minds of English and Scottish ecclesiastics far more than how to deliver other lands from error's chain. And those domestic concerns that so absorbed them could wreak havoc on the mission field. The Scottish Disruption, for instance, occurred just at the point where the church's India mission (its first and then only mission) might be regarded as soundly established. All the missionaries declared for the Free Church; all their buildings and facilities remained the property of the Church of Scotland. The work was relocated; but it was also duplicated, because, with the whole of the subcontinent before them, both Auld Kirk and Free Kirk found it necessary to continue what they saw as *their* mission. Unions could be still more destructive than schisms. The union of the Free Church of Scotland with the United Presbyterian Church in 1900 produced such a vast array of overseas commitments that the emergent United Free Church reduced the range, and the Japan field was given up. Union produced retrenchment rather than the expansion to be expected from combining resources. Worse was to follow when the House of Lords settled the resultant property dispute in favour of the remnant of the Free Church that did not join the union. The mission budget of the United Free Church went into crisis, just at the time when there was an increased demand for missionaries, for instance in West Africa, where the Calabar mission was no longer confined to its creeks.[7]

---

[6]See the Student Volunteer Missionary Union conference reports *Make Jesus King!* (London: SVMU, 1896); and *Students and the Missionary Problem* (London: SVMU, 1900).

[7]For the background of the examples quoted, see A. F. Walls, "Missions," in N. M. de S. Cameron et al., *Dictionary of Scottish Church History and Theology* (Edinburgh: Clark, 1993); on the specific Calabar question, see Geoffrey Johnston, *Of God and Maxim Guns: Presbyterianism in Nigeria 1846–1966* (Waterloo: Wilfred Laurier University Press, 1988).

Further, general approbation of the missionary project was not to be permanent. Paradoxically, at the end of the century, when missionary enthusiasm reached its peak, when the numbers of British missionaries achieved unprecedented levels, when the upper levels of society, and the privileged educational institutions linked with them, began to produce missionary candidates in significant numbers, the signs of change appeared in the intellectual climate. Even good ecclesiastics were now beginning to argue that, for lower races, Christianity might be too difficult; perhaps Islam was better fitted to raise Africans in the scale of civilization.[8] In 1842, Steane could believe that no official of a British government would dare to exclude missionaries from British territory. By the end of the nineteenth century, however, Queen Victoria had become the world's leading Islamic ruler, and in her name missions were excluded from more than one territory; and Queen Victoria kept missionaries out more effectively than the sultan of Turkey had ever done. For all the militant enthusiasm of missionary literature in the late-nineteenth century, the note of embattlement is evident. The heyday of the empire, which ought to have given missions their greatest opportunity, was bringing disappointment, frustration, and inhibition. And the intellectual and literary worlds, apparently so favourable in the 1840s, had become even less friendly to missions than the political.[9]

If, therefore, we take the concept of the laity to comprehend the whole professing Christian body of the nation ("Remember," says another of Jane Austen's characters, "that we are English, that we are Christians"[10]), and its opinion-forming and decision-making classes in particular, there was a relatively short period when overseas missions were, in this special sense, a lay fiefdom. But full commitment to the cause of missions was in practice always an elite movement, and there were good reasons why it should be. The reasons require a digression on the origins of the missionary movement and the nature of Western Christianity.

The peoples of northern and western Europe accepted Christianity, in the course of a long, painful process, by adopting it into their customary

---

[8]On the debate sparked by Reginald Bosworth Smith's lectures on *Mohammed and Mohammedanism: Lectures Delivered at the Royal Institution of Great Britain* (London: Murray, 1874), see Andrew Walls, "Africa as the Theatre of Christian Engagement with Islam in the Nineteenth Century," *Journal of Religion in Africa* 29, no. 2 (1999): 155–74, reprinted as Chapter 7, above.

[9]See Eugene Stock, *History of the Church Missionary Society*, vol. 3 (London: Church Missionary Society, 1899), ch. 77, "Controversies from Within and Attacks from Without." See also W. H. Temple Gairdner's paper in E. M. Wherry, S. M. Zwemer, and C. G. Mylrea, *Islam and Missions* (New York: Revell, 1911), vol. 2, 195–203.

[10]Jane Austen, *Northanger Abbey*, vol. 2, ch. 9, of the original edition. Henry Tilney is making clear to the young heroine the folly of believing that English landowners can routinely murder their wives.

law, and making it the basis of that law. In its essence, Western Christianity is tribal religion; and tribal religion is fundamentally more about acknowledged symbols, and custom and recognized practice, than about faith. At the same time, it can be a powerful constituent of identity ("Remember that we are English, that we are Christians"). The circumstances of the conversion of Europe created Christian communities that were notionally subject to the law of Christ. The political development of Europe ensured that the Western experience of Christianity would be in territorial terms. On one side lay Christendom, Christian territory, the assembly of Christian princes and their peoples, subject to the law of Christ, territory in which idolatry, blasphemy, and heresy could have no place; on the other side lay heathendom, the world outside. The fact that the only substantial non-Christian entity known to Christendom directly made an analogous distinction between Dar al-Islam and Dar al-Harb could only strengthen the habit of mind. The long and troubled story of relations with the Islamic world also suggested crusade as the natural model for encounter with the non-Western, which was also the non-Christian, world. Crusade was the attempt to extend the territory within which the law of Christ was observed. It was the model adopted in the Middle East and North Africa, where it generally failed; it was adopted in Granada, where it succeeded. It was extended by the Spanish into the Americas, where at first (if deceptively) it appeared to succeed. But it had not the slightest chance of succeeding in the vast territories of Asia and Africa in which the Portuguese were granted the papal monopoly. It was a situation in which the crusade model was not only inappropriate but impossible to apply that forced the creation of a new model for the spread of Christian allegiance. In this model the representatives of Christendom were to commend, demonstrate, and illustrate the gospel; to persuade without the instruments to coerce. To undertake this task implied a readiness to enter someone else's world instead of imposing the standards of one's own. It meant learning another's language, seeking a niche within another's society, perhaps accepting a situation of dependence.

This is the origin of the missionary movement. It was a model of Christian activity entirely foreign to the mainstream of European experience. In consequence, it needed new structures to express it. In Catholic Christianity, where the movement began, there were already institutions that could be adapted to serve the new purpose, and the religious orders developed new forms and functions. A Protestant missionary movement emerged in due course. Protestant concepts of Christendom were not basically different from Catholic, and the sixteenth-century Reformation left the foundational assumptions of European Christianity essentially untouched. But the structures to give effect to the missionary movement took much longer to develop. The Catholic movement had been able to develop on the basis of the religious orders, but the Reformation had slain the goose that laid that particular golden egg.

Missionary activity needed three preconditions, and the absence of one or more of these factors accounts for the long periods in which Protestants did not establish missions, even though they sometimes desired to do so. The first necessity was a body of people with the degree of commitment needed to live on someone else's terms, together with the mental equipment for coping with the implications. Such commitment was in turn most likely to arise in the wake of powerful religious influences. Times of religious renewal were necessary for the recruitment of a sizable company of such people, and the maintenance of a succession of them. A tradition of mental training, however, was also needed; charismatic inspiration alone would not suffice, and indeed, the plodder might succeed better with a new language and a new society than the inspired preacher. The second need was for a form of organization that could mobilize committed people, maintain and supply them, and forge a link between them and their work and the wider church. Since in the nature of things both their work and the conditions in which they carried it out were exceptional, the necessary structures could not readily emerge in very rigid regimes, whether political or ecclesiastical. They needed tolerance of the exceptional, and flexibility. The third factor necessary to overseas missions was sustained access to overseas locations, with the capacity to maintain communication over long periods. This implies what might be called maritime consciousness, with maritime capability and logistical support.

All three factors were present in the first, Catholic, phase of the missionary movement. The Catholic Reformation released the spiritual forces to produce the committed worker, the religious orders offered possibilities of extention and adaptation that produced the structures for deploying them, and the Portuguese enclaves and trading depots provided the communication networks and transoceanic bases. When in the course of the eighteenth century the Catholic phase of missions began to stutter, it was partly because the three factors were no longer fully in place.

The Protestant movement developed as the Catholic movement weakened. It began not at the end of the eighteenth century (that is a purely British perspective), but at the end of the seventeenth and not in England, but in Germany and central Europe. Its main motors were in Halle and Herrnhut, though, just as German Pietism drew on the English Puritan tradition, it had a Puritan prologue. William Carey's *Enquiry*[11] does not initiate it; the object of that famous tract was rather to urge English Baptists to become involved in a work already well established by the hands of others.[12] But the awakening of missionary interest

---

[11]William Carey, *An Enquiry into the Obligations of Christians to Use Means for the Conversion of the Heathens.* (Leicester, 1792).

[12]See Andrew Walls, "The Protestant Missionary Awakening in Its European Context," in Brian Stanley, ed., *The Missionary Movement and the Enlightenment* (Grand Rapids, MI: Eerdmans, 2001), reprinted as Chapter 11, above.

in Britain that the *Enquiry* represents did have a profound effect on the Protestant movement. It greatly enhanced the second and third of the prerequisites we have noted, the organizational and the logistical. The political and economic situation in Britain (and, as soon became plain, still more in the United States) favoured the development of what was to become the most potent instrument of the Protestant missionary movement: the voluntary society. British maritime consciousness and capability opened vastly expanded possibilities to a missionary movement that had hitherto been based in the continental landmass.[13] Pietism in its various branches had already helped to fulfil the first prerequisite by providing the spiritual dynamic and the intellectual fibre capable of producing a corps of qualified mission workers. The Evangelical movement in Britain and North America increased the flow, slowly at first, eventually in a flood.

The logistical prerequisite does not particularly concern us here; but the other two have some relevance to the theme of the emancipation of the laity.

The first prerequisite, the recruitment of a corps of competent personnel, leads us to the Western understanding of the proclamation of the gospel. Western Christianity, being essentially territorial in conception, had always operated on a territorial understanding of Christian ministry. That understanding was also monarchical: the ordained pastor in his parish. Inheriting this understanding, the Protestant missionary movement took for granted that the missionary, as a preacher of the gospel, would be an ordained minister. The early promoters of mission therefore considered recruitment of missionaries in terms of the sources from which the home ministry was recruited.[14]

Evangelical Anglicans of the "regular," Simeonite type, committed to Anglican liturgy and discipline, were accordingly in particular difficulty. They were pledged to honour the monarchical ordained parish ministry,

---

[13]Even before the British movement developed, the Halle-inspired branch of the continental movement was relying on British logistical support. The inspiration, and all the missionaries, for the Danish-Halle mission throughout the eighteenth century came from Halle Pietism, but for a variety of reasons it was convenient to organize the mission under the Society for Promoting Christian Knowledge. The solid High Church ecclesiastics who formed the basis of the London Society endeavoured from time to time during the century to place English church missionaries in what was theoretically an English mission. They never found any. See W. K. Lowther Clarke, *A History of the SPCK* (London: SPCK, 1959); and Daniel L. Brunner, *Halle Pietists in England: Anthony William Boehm and the Society for Promoting Christian Knowledge* (Göttingen: Vandenhoeck and Ruprecht, 1993).

[14]So even Carey: "And this [living in native style] would only be passing through what we have virtually engaged in by entering the ministerial office. A Christian minister is a person who in a peculiar sense is *not his own*" (*Enquiry*, 71f.).

and were sensitive to accusations of Methodist freewheeling. The official mechanism for the maintenance of the Church of England overseas, the Society for the Propagation of the Gospel, did not reflect an Evangelical understanding of mission; the London Missionary Society, with its boldly ecumenical pretensions, did not reflect an Anglican understanding of the church. These difficulties were circumvented by the creation of a new organization, the Church Missionary Society (CMS), with the structure of a voluntary society but a commitment to Anglican principles and formularies.[15] The implication was that its missionaries would be episcopally ordained clergy. But for a long time, episcopally ordained clergy simply did not offer for missionary service. Charles Simeon's circle of pious young students, the nursery of so many Evangelical clergy, did not produce a single volunteer.[16] Soon, the leaders of the CMS ceased to expect such recruits. "It is hopeless to wait for missionaries," growled Simeon, "send out catechists."[17] And John Venn did draft for the CMS a memorandum on the advantages of recruiting lay catechists for service overseas. The memorandum was full of references to the practice of the early church, and pointed out that in the early church, catechists, whose duties included teaching Christian truth and instructing new converts, were sometimes ordained if they proved themselves worthy. Here was excellent precedent for the CMS to appoint for missionary service pious laity whose social and educational background were obstacles to their ordination.[18]

The proposal provoked a notably hostile reaction from the circle of regular Evangelical clergy who formed the society's backbone. How could people whose identity lay in uniting Evangelical doctrine and Anglican discipline institute a process so flagrantly at variance with that discipline? The catechist proposal was quickly dropped; missionaries must be ordained clergy. Venn had previously toyed with the idea of a special ordination for overseas service, which would be justified on the ground that preaching to people at a "low stage" of civilization did not demand the social and educational attributes necessary to the place that clergy held in English society. But the counter was obvious: a person ordained for overseas service could not be prevented from returning to an English benefice. The mission field would then become an open invitation to social climbers.

---

[15] Eugene Stock, *History of the Church Missionary Society: Its Environment, Its Men and Its Work*, vol. 1 (London: Church Missionary Society, 1899); Charles Hole, *The Early History of the Church Missionary Society for Africa and the East to the End of AD 1814* (London: Church Missionary Society, 1896).

[16] Stock, *History*, 74.

[17] Ibid., 64.

[18] See Michael Hennell, *John Venn and the Clapham Sect* (London: Lutterworth, 1958), ch. 4.

It was for this reason that the CMS took five years to get its first missionaries to the mission field.[19] The office of missionary was a clerical one, not to be filled by a layperson. But neither the clergy, nor the sources from which the clergy came, were able to supply the mission field. There was, everyone recognized, a lay constituency able and willing to do so; but there was no way of utilizing this supply without ordination, and little prospect of that ordination from a largely hostile episcopate.

The CMS was able to square this circle only with the help of German Pietism. Rescue came through a link forged by C. F. Steinkopf, German pastor in London, with Johannes Jänicke of the Berlin Seminary. From its foundation in 1799 to the end of the Napoleonic Wars, the society sent out twenty-four missionaries. Seventeen of the twenty-four were Germans. Most of these were already in Lutheran orders.[20] This took care of the ordination question, and, it was quietly observed, provided for future ordinations on the field without involving the English bishops, while the nationality of the missionaries removed the fear of the mission field becoming a shortcut to an English benefice. Of the seven English missionaries in the list, only three were ordained, and all of these were sent out during the last year of the period, 1815. Only one of them was a university graduate. Of the four English laypersons, one was sent briefly to Sierra Leone as a schoolmaster, under an arrangement with the colonial government to provide schoolmasters as well as clergy for every village. Two were artisans sent to New Zealand as "lay settlers." This was really another version of the catechist idea, but defended on the theory then being advanced by Samuel Marsden that the Maori could be prepared for Christianity by the introduction of "civilization," that is, Western arts and technology. They later were joined by a more educated man, Thomas Kendall, a schoolmaster who was intended to supply the arts.[21] The situation improved for the CMS after 1815, partly through a greater degree of sympathy among the bishops, and partly, as I shall argue later, because the development of a mass-membership system increased the pool of potential

---

[19]The Society for Missions to Africa and the East was founded in 1799. Its first missionaries, Melchior Renner and Peter Hartwig, recruited from Germany as indicated below, were accepted in 1802, and began fifteen months of study at Clapham. They left for Sierra Leone in 1804; for the first two years Renner served as colonial chaplain, so that until 1806, Hartwig, whose career was brief and colourful, was, strictly speaking, the society's only missionary. See *Register of Missionaries (Clerical, Lay and Female) and Native Clergy from 1804 to 1904* (London: Church Missionary Society, n.d.).

[20]On the question of Lutheran orders of Anglican missionaries, and changing attitudes in England, see J. Pinnington, "Church Principles in the Early Years of the Church Missionary Society: The Problem of the 'German' missionaries," *Journal of Theological Studies*, n.s., 20, no. 2 (1969): 523–32.

[21]On Kendall, see Judith Binney, *Legacy of Guilt: A Life of Thomas Kendall* (London: Oxford University Press, 1968).

candidates. But it was long before the CMS dependence on Germany (and some other parts of continental Europe) faded completely. In the period up to 1830, the missionary roll rose to 166, and of these, forty-nine, something approaching one-third, came from continental Europe. In the whole period up to 1850, more than one-fifth of the missionaries sent out by a society that had come into being to represent the missionary concerns of the regular Evangelicals of the Church of England, came from outside England or Ireland.[22]

In Scotland, missionary activity before 1829, when the Church of Scotland began its own mission, was mainly conducted through voluntary societies based in Edinburgh and Glasgow on the ecumenical model of the London Missionary Society.[23] In Scotland this involved less the bridging of denominational divides than uniting Presbyterians of diverse affiliation, holding together members of the established church with those of the various voluntarist seceding bodies. (The strain eventually became too much for the Glasgow Missionary Society, which split into establishment and voluntarist sections.) Both societies adopted a rule that their missionaries should have completed the procedures for ordination in their respective churches before being sent out. The rule proved impossible to implement; most of the early offers of service were from artisans, and few of the early missionaries completed the course of study for the ministry. The results of the early commissions were not uniformly encouraging; one missionary turned slave trader, another returned to promote atheism in Scotland. The Glasgow society decided to send no more artisans; the Edinburgh society decided to establish its own hall for training missionaries. The society had been in existence twenty-five years before the hall was set up.[24]

William Carey's Particular Baptists started on a modest scale; the basis was a minister's fraternal and the initial finances a little over £13. They had some marked advantages, however; they began with two offers of service, one of them from Carey, the principal architect of the project. He was himself of artisan background, but this was not uncommon among ministers of his denomination. A formidable autodidact, he had combined in varying proportions the roles of shoemaker, schoolteacher, and pastor. The tract that he wrote clearly envisages that missionaries would be self-

---

[22]Data and calculations in this paragraph are based on *Register of Missionaries* between 1804 and 1850.

[23]See Walls, "Missions," n. 7. It should be noted that the society founded as the Edinburgh Missionary Society became generally known as the Scottish Missionary Society.

[24] An account of the Scottish societies occurs in William Brown, *History of the Propagation of Christianity among the Heathen*, vol. 2 (Edinburgh, 1854). Brown was long the secretary of the Scottish Missionary Society. See also John Kilpatrick, "The Records of the Scottish Missionary Society (1796–1848)," *Records of the Scottish Church History Society* 10, no. 3 (1950): 196–210.

supporting; he even lists the equipment they would need to take for shooting and for growing their own food. In view of the subsequent history, in which his society disconnected him, this self-reliance was just as well. And for most of his long career, Carey was self-supporting—in his early days as an indigo plantation overseer, later as a teacher in government service at the College of Fort William. Partly from the special vision and position of their leading missionary, partly through their own basis in the lower ranks of English society, the Particular Baptists managed the matter of missionary recruitment better than most.[25]

By contrast, the all-embracing Missionary Society, established in 1795 and soon identified as the London Missionary Society (LMS), started with a flourish. It had the support of many prominent Dissenter ministers, of the expatriate Scottish community in London, and of such notable, if irregular, Anglicans as Thomas Haweis and Rowland Hill. In an inaugurating sermon, Haweis made it clear that the missionaries they should expect would come from the shop or the forge rather than the normal sources of the ministry. Their deficiencies in formal education would not be inhibiting, since a knowledge of the dead languages was not necessary to the communication of the truth in living ones, and their practical skills would be a positive advantage. And find them they did; not less than thirty missionaries, with some wives and children, went off to the Pacific together in 1796. Four were ordained as ministers, one was a surgeon, and most of the rest were artisans or labourers. One was so anxious to go that he worked his passage on the ship and was accepted as a missionary on arrival. The voyage took eight months, so the group naturally formed a gathered congregation on-board ship (and had the sadness of having to excommunicate some of their number on doctrinal grounds). A short period in the islands produced a drastic thinning of the ranks by death and desertion, though one of the labourers went on to devote forty-eight years to the service of the mission, and one of the artisans to give forty-five. Another group of twenty-three missionaries was sent to the Pacific in 1798, but never got there, being intercepted by a French warship.[26] By 1799, the year that saw the founding of the CMS, the LMS had already sent out sixty-seven missionaries.[27]

---

[25]Carey's early views on missionary supplies ("a few knives, powder and shot, fishing tackle and the articles of husbandry") are indicated in *Enquiry*, 73–75. On the subsequent history see, E. Daniel Potts, *British Baptist Missionaries in India, 1793–1837* (Cambridge: Cambridge University Press, 1967).

[26]On the early events, see Richard Lovett, *History of the London Missionary Society 1795–1895* (London: Oxford University Press, 1899), vol. 1. See also Andrew F. Walls, *The Missionary Movement in Christian History* (Maryknoll, N.Y.: Orbis; Edinburgh: Clark, 1996), ch. 12.

[27]Data in James Sibree, *London Missionary Society: A Register of Missionaries, Deputations, etc. from 1796 to 1923*, 4th ed. (London: London Missionary Society, 1923).

This total had included one person who represented a new class of missionary. Johannes Theodorus van der Kemp was a doctor of medicine, a former dragoon officer, a former rationalist philosopher, an established author, and already fifty years old. Furthermore, while missionary candidates routinely bewailed the misspent periods of their youth, van der Kemp's sins truly had been as scarlet.[28] He and his colleague Kicherer were the first LMS recruits from the Netherlands. The Dutch missionaries with the LMS, while not occupying the place that the Germans did with the CMS, were to be a significant factor for many years.

But van der Kemp and Kicherer were exceptions. Typically, early LMS missionaries had been pious artisans; and while some proved splendid successes, there was a disproportionate number of casualties—physical, mental, moral, spiritual. The experience of the Scottish societies had been similar; only Anglican principle and prejudice, and the resources of German Pietism, had kept the CMS from the same outcome.

The early missionary societies had proved that the missionary vocation could attract numbers of lay volunteers. But the societies were not interested in lay volunteers as such; they were trying to tap nontraditional sources for the ministry. The disappointments led them to attempt to bring the average missionary candidate closer to the general standards expected of the ministry. The LMS appointed David Bogue, a substantial Scots theologian, to superintend the training of their candidates. The CMS set up a college in Islington to bring candidates without the education and social graces for immediate presentation to a bishop to at least the level tolerated of ordinands in the province of York.[29] Islington had an impressive record, and produced missionaries of scholarly attainment; yet even in the 1860s, Henry Venn, the CMS secretary, was saying that the college would not be necessary if the Society could get enough candidates from the universities. Even at that late point the missionary vocation was seen as essentially belonging to the sphere of the ordained ministry, even though it was manifest that the ordinary sources for supplying that ministry could not fulfil it.

Ministerial status remained the missionary norm until the last third of the nineteenth century. In some missions it was hard to envisage any other pattern. The Scottish church missions in India concentrated on higher education as the main missionary tool and took for granted the full Scottish university course in arts and divinity as the teacher's rudimentary equipment. The Wesleyans, subject to a connexional committee

---

[28]On van der Kemp's career, see Ido H. Enklaar, *Life and Work of Dr. J. Th. Van der Kemp, 1747–1811* (Rotterdam: Balkema, 1988).

[29]See Alison Hodge, "The Training of Missionaries for Africa: The Church Missionary Society's Training College at Islington, 1900–1915," *Journal of Religion in Africa* 4, no. 2 (1971–72):81–96.

rather than a lay-dominated society, were perhaps the most resolutely clerical of all. This is not to say that there was no place at all for lay participation in the mission field; the CMS, the LMS, and, in their early African undertakings, the Scottish church missions all continued to send laity, particularly artisans; but these were seen essentially as auxiliaries, working under the direction of clerical missionaries. Sometimes, as in the Scottish missions in Africa, laity were appointed specifically for industrial or agricultural functions. (In the Scottish missions, not only salary but also rations for artisan missionaries were calculated according to their rank in Scottish society, while those of clerical missionaries reflected their ministerial status.[30]) Sometimes, especially in areas of acute personnel shortage such as faced the CMS in West Africa, good service as a layperson could be recognized by subsequent ordination,[31] just as John Venn had intended with the abortive scheme for catechists.

Three discrete factors gradually eroded the clerical norm of the missionary. All three had begun before the middle of the nineteenth century; their cumulative effect was not fully felt until towards the century's end.

The first of these was the rise of medical missions. Medical training was from the beginning a frequent part of missionary preparation. A surgeon was, as we have seen, among the large LMS party for the Pacific in 1796; many early missionaries routinely gave medical attendance and some held formal medical qualifications.[32] But their medical function was long seen as purely ancillary to their regular, that is, their ministerial, duty. Medical missions in the strict sense, that is, missions directed primarily at medical practice by missionaries whose primary ministry was medical, first arose in China. They were the fruit of a situation in which antiforeign feeling was so intense that missions on the traditional pattern were severely limited in what they could accomplish. The first medical missionary is usually identified as the American Peter Parker.[33] The first British medical missionary was probably

---

[30]The question needs fuller study. In the meantime, T. Jack Thompson, *Christianity in Northern Malawi: Duncan Fraser's Missionary Methods and Ngoni Culture* (Leiden: Brill, 1995), offers a view of a Scottish mission at work.

[31]For example, Henry Townsend (CMS, *Register*, no. 231), who became the patriarch of the Yoruba Mission, was appointed to Sierra Leone in 1836, at only twenty-one years of age, and after a brief spell at the Islington College. In 1844 he was ordained successively deacon and priest, and appointed to Yorubaland, where he had already carried out distinguished reconnaissance work.

[32]Among well-known missionaries of the London Missionary Society, Robert Morrison, who took medical studies along with other forms of missionary preparation, is an example of the first category, David Livingstone, who was a licentiate of the Faculty of Physicians and Surgeons, of the second.

[33]On Parker, see *The Life, Letters and Journals of the Rev. and Hon. Peter Parker, M.D., Missionary, Physician and Diplomatist* (Boston: Congregational Publication Society, 1896).

William Lockhart of the LMS, appointed to China in 1838, who established his hospital in Shanghai in 1843. Thereafter, medical missions burgeoned, especially in China and India. They were not universally adopted; Henry Venn, for instance, was distinctly cool on the subject, and the CMS was slow to develop them. But where they were established, they sometimes proved a Trojan horse for mission-field organization. The missionary doctor was often, though not always, a layperson, but could neither be treated as an ancillary worker nor fitted into the clerical command structure.

This was ensured by the professionalization of medicine in the middle of the nineteenth century; indeed, before that time Western medicine probably had little, at least outside of the field of surgery, to offer the rest of the world. (Many of the missionaries who died in the "White Man's Grave" of West Africa must have been offered on the grisly altar of medical science.[34]) Early mission hospitals were simple affairs, often in the missionary's house, but they rapidly developed into large and ambitious institutions. Their equipment was equally ambitious; medical missionaries were frequently young, recently trained with the latest and best facilities, and they coveted the latest and best facilities for their own hospitals.[35] Hospital staffs increased the number of personnel in the service of the missions exponentially, and became increasingly specialized: nurses, dressers, dispensers, cleaners, watchmen—and evangelists and catechists, for the mission hospital was an evangelistic and pastoral institution as well as a medical one. There were services on its premises, and there was interaction with patients and ex-patients at various stages of sickness and recovery. The medical, evangelistic, and pastoral functions must be harmoniously integrated; and the only person who could do this, the only person who could hold together the spider's web of hospital staff and make decisions in what could be life-threatening situations, was the medical superintendent. No ministerial senior could meaningfully overrule him or question his judgment in his own field; and the ordained chaplain, if there was one, must work under his direction.[36] I have hitherto spoken of the medical missionary as "he"; when, as in

---

[34]See Philip D. Curtin, *The Image of Africa* (Madison: University of Wisconsin Press, 1964), chs. 3 and 5.

[35]See Walls, *Missionary Movement*, ch. 16.

[36]This is clear, for instance, in an address by Dr. Herbert Lankester, Secretary of the CMS Medical Committee to the Student Volunteer Conference of 1900. He recommends the appointment of evangelistic missionaries to busy hospitals, but clearly takes for granted the responsibility of the medical superintendent for the oversight of the whole work, medical and spiritual. See *Students and the Missionary Problem: Addresses Delivered at the International Student Missionary Conference, London, January 2–6, 1900* (London: SVMU, 1900), 497–99.

due course occurred, the medical missionary was a woman, the capacity of the Trojan horse was enlarged.[37]

There were those who were not content with an arrangement made on pragmatic grounds. The China Missions Conference held at Shanghai in 1907 produced a particularly interesting statement on medical missions, for which the lead paper was prepared by Dr. Dugald Christie of the United Free Church of Scotland mission in Manchuria (the founder of the Mukden Medical College). Christie had come to China specially as a medical missionary, insisting on his own hospital. He had later received ministerial ordination from the Presbytery of Manchuria. Far from holding up his own experience as a model, Christie argues in his paper that the office of medical missionary is a ministry of the church that continues the healing ministry of Christ. It should therefore be marked by a special sort of ordination and commissioning parallel to that which marked the ministerial office.[38]

Through the door opened by the doctors the other nonministerial professions were able to enter. The lay schoolteacher had been in the mission field since early days but had so long been the lowly auxiliary of the ministerial missionary that it was hard even for the new breed of trained educationists to break free. At the World Missionary Conference of 1910 there were still complaints that in some locations the headship of any educational institution must be held by a minister, however pedagogically unqualified, even when there were abundantly qualified teachers on the staff. But the process set on foot by the doctors was inexorable. A range of missionary specialists, their specializations professionalized by developments mirroring those in medicine and education, came to the mission field in the wake of the Student Volunteer movement.[39] The clerical conception of the missionary office, which had been a feature of the Protestant missionary movement from its early stages, was radically altered. And one of the principal contributing factors was the social transformation of the mission field brought about by the student volunteers and other young people of the middle and higher echelons of British society, so different from the homespun missionary material characteristic of the earlier days of the movement.[40]

---

[37]The LMS appointed its first female medical missionary in 1889. It appointed another fifteen up to 1921. Marriage sometimes complicated the structures of responsibility. The Rev. George Kerr and his wife, Dr. Isobel Kerr, jointly superintended the work of the Dichpalli leprosy settlement maintained in Hyderabad by the Wesleyan Methodist Missionary Society. See Dermott Monahan, *The Story of Dichpalli: Towards the Conquest of Leprosy* (London: Cargate, 1949).

[38]See *Records of the China Centenary Missionary Conference, Shanghai 1907* (Shanghai, 1907); and Dugald Christie, *Thirty Years in Mukden* (London, 1914).

[39]The LMS list includes agriculturalist, architect, building superintendent, chemistry professor, engineer, marine, pharmacist, and kindergarten teacher besides categories such as "educational superintendent" and "lady superintendent" of a hospital, and various grades of nursing. Artisans, teachers, and printers had been on the mission staff much earlier.

[40] See Walls, *Missionary Movement*, 106ff.

The second, and still more transformative influence, was the steadily increasing indispensability of the woman missionary. As with so many aspects of the Protestant missionary movement, the woman missionary happened by accident; no one planned her or developed her concept as a strategic instrument. Even leaving out of consideration such wholly exceptional figures as the extraordinary Hannah Kilham, exercising her Quakerly concerns in West African education, linguistics, and agriculture in the early nineteenth century (and one might add equally extraordinary Roman Catholic women such as La Mère Anne-Marie Javouhey), it is hard to identify the first female missionary. From the earliest times wives of missionaries, regarded by the missionary societies as present essentially for their family role, regularly undertook missionary duties. Many early missionaries commenced schools; their wives frequently commenced schools or classes for girls, and extended their responsibilities into other aspects of the women's world, still envisaged as an extension of their husbands' activity. Every so often, wifely enterprise would blossom into a significant institutional commitment; and in such cases a crisis might arise on the death or departure of the lady or her husband, which could be resolved only by appointing a female replacement. This was happening at least from 1820.[41] No one was intending to create a category of women missionaries, nor questioning the assumption that a "real" missionary was an ordained minister of the gospel; they were simply seeking a means of maintaining the valuable work begun by the late excellent Mrs. Jones. Then it became clear that India in particular had whole areas of life shut off from male view; only women could ever have any hope of entering those areas. So in India, and then in England and Scotland, societies for female education emerged to recruit Christian teachers to reach women and girls. It was some time before these societies, often the result of the concern of devout residents of India, came formally within the orbit of the missions; but they usually worked in relation to missions, and (sometimes to the dismay of their organizers) their teachers often married serving missionaries. It took some time for the missions to realize how important, and how nearly autonomous, women's work had become, in both its home and its overseas organization.[42]

In the 1860s, the newly formed China Inland Mission, which challenged many of the orthodoxies of mission practice, took actions that clarified the position. It not only accepted women as missionaries in their own right, but also assigned them, usually in pairs, to work as field missionaries independently of resident male oversight. By the end of the nineteenth century, women had changed the entire face of the Protestant

---

[41]See Church Missionary Society, *Register,* List II, p. 260, nos. 1 and 2.

[42]A British equivalent is urgently needed to the comprehensive investigation by Dana Robert, *American Women in Mission: A Social History of Their Thought and Practice* (Macon, Ga.: Mercer University Press, 1996).

missionary movement by sheer force of numbers. The proportion of women in the medical profession in Britain remained small; the proportion of women among medical missionaries was much larger. By the First World War, Britain was giving place to North America as the main source of missionaries; and both during and after the war the number of women in the British missionary force came first to equal and then to outstrip that of men.[43] It became a commonplace among those who appealed to university audiences for recruits for the mission field that, by contrast with its great days of the student volunteers, the response of the young men of the day to the missionary call had become, "Lord, here am I; send my sister." If we are thinking of its personnel, the missionary fiefdom had become not only lay but female.

But there is another way of considering the missionary fiefdom, which takes us to the third of the transformative factors of the nineteenth-century missionary movement. It also takes us to the second of the prerequisites identified early in this essay, the development of effective organizational structures capable of recruiting, maintaining, and supplying missionaries and linking their work with that of the wider church. This is not the place to speak at large about the voluntary society, the main organizational engine of the Protestant movement, nor of the way in which, when applied to the missionary movement, it subverted all the traditional European forms of church government.[44] All these forms of government had arisen in the setting of territorial Christianity; they had mostly proved impotent for the presentation of the gospel outside the territorial context. But while the voluntary society subverted church structures, it did not always or necessarily declericalize or laicize them. The voluntary society certainly gave the potential for lay involvement. By its means, Miss Pym of the Mission to Lepers could exercise quasi-episcopal functions; and within it, the services of many a captain of industry were called on to assist in computing the cost of many a projected tower. Nevertheless, some missionary societies managed to keep their inner counsels resolutely clerical, assisted in so doing by the clerical assumptions about the missionary's office. The CMS, however, eager to maintain loyalty to Anglican formularies and polity, could defend itself from predatory bishops only by the assertion that it was a lay society, even on occasion unconvincingly claiming a status analogous with that

---

[43]For the Church Missionary Society, the trend is visible early: in the ten-year period 1895–1904, the Society sent out 391 male and 425 female missionaries. For the London Missionary Society, parity is achieved in 1908, with eleven men and eleven women, but it is not until the First World War that the women come into their own. In the years 1915 to 1918, the LMS sent fourteen men and thirty-eight women. Even with the peace and the release of the male backlog, the women remained significant: seventeen men to eight women in 1920, four to seven in 1921, ten to eleven in 1922, and, wartime distortion over, fourteen to nine in 1923.

[44]On this question, see Walls, *Missionary Movement*, ch. 18.

of a lay patron.[45] After 1829 the Church of Scotland might claim to have integrated church and mission; but a glance at the origins of the various missionary operations of the Scottish churches reveals a patchwork of private initiatives.[46] The most substantial laicization of the inner counsels of the missionary movement took place with the second wave of voluntary societies that followed in the wake of the China Inland Mission and took a great part of missionary activity outside the denominational churches altogether. That is a story needing separate treatment.

But a form of laicization, while not necessarily taking control of the inner counsels, nevertheless brought new life to the missionary societies of the first wave. To see its significance we must return to Charlotte Brontë's missionary basket and the ladies who sewed and sold for it.

The origin of such activity probably lies in a development initiated by the British and Foreign Bible Society and copied by missionary societies, including the CMS, of establishing local auxiliaries. The local Bible societies had a dual function: they distributed the Bible in their own localities by arranging easy-payment subscriptions, and enrolled those who already possessed a Bible to contribute to making it available elsewhere in the world, both at home and overseas. In Scotland, where a higher proportion of households than in England already had Bibles, there was little scope for the first function, but plenty for the second; and in both England and Scotland the second function was readily applied to overseas missions. It was a new sort of society; for while its leadership was inevitably dominated by clergy and local bigwigs, its membership straddled a vast range of income and social standing, since the subscription could be as little as a penny a week. Subscription was encouraged and sustained by a flow of information, information from and about lands with which the subscribers had had hitherto nothing to do, but in which by their subscriptions they were now personally involved. Thomas Chalmers, in 1819, reflects on the educational function of such societies, their capacity for enlarging minds by up-to-date reporting from every continent. Characteristically, he also assesses their socioeconomic effect. He had been deeply impressed to come upon an Aberdeen Female Servants' Society for Distributing Scriptures among the Poor, where the subscription was only a halfpenny a week. This meant that female domestic servants, who were

---

[45]See the detailed discussions in Hans Cnattingius, *Bishops and Societies: A Study of Anglican Colonial and Missionary Expansion 1698–1850* (London: SPCK, 1952); and T. E. Yates, *Venn and Victorian Bishops Abroad; The Missionary Policies of Henry Venn and Their Repercussions upon the Anglican Episcopate of the Colonial Period 1841–1872* (Uppsala: Swedish Institute of Missionary Research, 1972).

[46]A survey of the origins of the different fields of the missions of the Scottish churches reveals a variety of initiatives—by concerned nationals and expatriates in India, and individuals and groups in various parts of Scotland. See Walls, "Missions."

at the very bottom of the earned-income scale, could contribute to the improvement of the lot of people who were poorer still. It led Chalmers to consider *The Influence of Bible Societies on the Temporal Necessities of the Poor.*[47] Bible and missionary associations, he argued (and much to the dismay of some Bible society committee members, he wanted to amalgamate the two),[48] were a bulwark against pauperism. There could be no surer form of social and economic insurance than to raise the dignity of poor people to the level of their social superiors by recognizing them as donors in their own right.

The missionary societies followed the Bible society example. We have already seen how long the CMS waited in vain for English missionary candidates. From its beginning it was a voluntary society, but in its early years it was essentially a clerical society, a network of Evangelical clergy who kept up a correspondence based on their knowledge of their own parishes and congregations. Around 1812, the CMS began to develop local auxiliaries, with a penny a week subscription. Not only was there an increase in finances, but also the Society began to receive applications from viable candidates of whom the members of the clerical circle had never heard—and this at a point when missionary work was being identified with the White Man's Grave and heavy mortality.

The broadened base of support, the approach to something like mass membership, necessitated a broader literary appeal. A whole new literature appeared along the trail first blazed by the Baptist *Periodical Accounts.*[49] Missionary literature got beyond the formal reports intended for clergy and the middle-class subscribers of guineas; it produced "missionary intelligence" from all over the world that could be read aloud in church meetings or in groups, as well as quietly at home. A new, middle-brow readership was created, and the *Missionary Register* and its Scottish counterpart reached a broader spectrum of homes than the *Edinburgh Review* or the *Quarterly Review* ever did.

On one occasion Henry Venn noted with satisfaction the news from West Africa that the attack by the king of Dahomey upon the city of Abeokuta, the centre of CMS activity in Yorubaland, had been repulsed. The news, he says, caused many to rejoice, from Her Majesty's ministers to the humble collectors of a penny a week. To a high proportion of even the educated British public (and perhaps even to some few of Her Majesty's ministers), the king of Dahomey must have been a shadowy fig-

---

[47]Edinburgh, 1814. An enlarged edition appeared in 1819.

[48]"An old member" of the Bible Society Committee wrote a refutation, Remarks on a Late Publication of the Rev. D. Chalmers (London, 1819).

[49]*Periodical Accounts Relative to the Baptist Missionary Society,* which appeared between 1800–1817, circulated widely outside Baptist circles, and the Scrampore mission, especially its translation work, received support from many outside the denomination.

ure, hardly to be distinguished from the Queen of Sheba. But to the collector of a penny a week, who had been following the missionary intelligence and sharing with other subscribers the news of the perilous attack, with all its dread potential, the slave-raiding king of Dahomey was a clearly defined personage. Chalmers's vision of a nation transformed and made prosperous by the universal presence of Bible societies may not have materialized; but at least he was right about the cultural impact of the missionary movement on a section of the public that hitherto had had little reason to think of the world outside.

Enthusiasm for missions remained for the most part the concern of an elite group in churches that were busy mainly about other things. Few in ecclesiastical leadership had the remotest idea that the so often struggling movement was to be instrumental in the transformation of the demographic and cultural composition of the Christian church. A movement that arose in the heart of Christendom helped Christianity to survive the death of Christendom. A project that was soaked in the Enlightenment helped to produce a Christianity whose strength now lies in its independence of the Enlightenment. An expression of Christianity that arose from interaction with deep currents in European culture has helped to foster a Christianity that will depend for its future on its critical interaction with the ancient cultures of Africa and Asia.

The elite group kept alive the movement that had such epoch-making significance. It was not entirely a socially elite group, but rather, mixed, fairly representative of active Protestant Christianity. It held seigneurial rights to a lay fiefdom; and its symbolic figure is a penny-a-week collector, reading a missionary magazine.

13

The Multiple Conversions of Timothy Richard

A Paradigm of Missionary Experience

Timothy Richard's active career, beginning in 1869, covered almost fifty years, over which he published hundreds of separate items, some in English, some in Chinese; and, as secretary of the Society for the Diffusion of Christian and General Knowledge among the Chinese, he was responsible for the appearance of hundreds more. The archives of the Baptist Missionary Society at Regent's Park College, not to mention other repositories elsewhere, contain a multitude of his letters and memoranda and other unpublished materials. Richard was an inveterate word processor. At a period when most mission societies, let alone individual missionaries, were still operating by the copy letter book, we find him appealing through the pages of the missionary magazine for a specific make of typewriter (an indulgence excused by convalescence after illness and justified by the plea of freeing his wife to undertake more directly missionary duties).[1] Had he lived in a later era, he could be safely predicted to have been the first missionary to have his own web site; with the Internet at his disposal, he might never have gone to bed at all.

What follows here must be preliminary study, resting on only a fragment of Richard's vast output; nor can I claim to have fathomed even that fragment. Richard was a complex person—deceptively complex. One who admired him called his an intuitive rather than a strictly philosophical mind.[2] A less sympathetic reviewer might have called him slapdash. He was ready to sally forth confidently into such arcane fields as comparative prehistory,

A Presentation for the First International Conference on Baptist Studies, Regents Park College, Oxford, 1998.

[1]*Missionary Herald* (1890): 140. (The *Herald* was published in London.)

[2]Donald MacGillivray, *Timothy Richard of China: A Prince in Israel: An Appreciation* (Shanghai: Christian Literature Society, 1920), 18: "His mind was of the intu-

undaunted by difficulties and untrammeled by evidence. The difficulty of fathoming him is increased by the fact that most of his writing is occasional, often ad hominem, rather than systematic. Even his two volumes entitled *Conversion by the Million,*[3] which came as near as he ever got to a statement of his mature position, make up a ragbag of a collection of items of different date and on diverse topics. They come to a climax in a single-page statement, printed in bold type, about the "Ancient and Modern Bible." The Ancient Bible, the statement says, was inspired by God's Holy Spirit over a period of 1,600 years from Moses to John and, following its wider circulation brought about by the invention of printing, led to the regeneration of Christendom in one generation. The Modern Bible has been inspired over a similar period since the apostolic age by the same Holy Spirit.

> When the Modern Bible as well as the Ancient shall be fully and widely circulated the regeneration not only of Christendom but of the whole world will be possible within one generation.
>
> God's Holy Spirit was promised by our Saviour to guide us unto *all truth*. He is life, light and love. When we accept all His teaching, then conversions will take place by the million![4]

This gnomic utterance, with its sidelong glance at the missionary watchword of the Student Volunteers, is not illuminated by its immediate context; it is presumably to be read as the culmination of the drift of all the fugitive pieces that precede it. Taken by themselves, the words could amount simply to a bold restatement of the traditional Baptist affirmation that God has yet more light and truth to break forth from the Word. Or they could stand for something much less conventionally Christian. This open-endedness and this dicing with danger are characteristic of Richard, and give him special significance in Baptist history. They also make him an interesting figure in the wider story of the Western missionary movement.

---

itive rather than the logical type, but it was very fertile in ideas. . . . A certain mistiness in his writings sometimes tantalized the readers, but such is ever the concomitant of prophetic speech. The ideas were too big for the vehicle." W. E. Soothill, a fellow missionary who became professor of Chinese at Oxford, describes Richard's work on Buddhist texts as "more valuable for its suggestiveness that for its literal accuracy. . . . At times his imaginative sense carried him into regions beyond the reach of other eyes." (*Timothy Richard of China: Seer, Statesman, Missionary and the Most Disinterested Adviser the Chinese Ever Had* [London: Seeley, Service, 1924], 319). Elsewhere he says, "For a man who could work so hard, so long and persistently, his reasoning at times had perplexing gaps. He was not built, for instance, for the patient, meticulous work of translation. Had Mrs. Richard lived, much of his later work . . . would have been better done because of her revision" (*ibid.*, 280).
    [3]Shanghai: Christian Literature Society, 1907.
    [4]*Conversion by the Million*, vol. 2, inside end page.

The missionary movement was the great learning experience of Western Christianity. By its very nature it brought the Christian faith, when it had become thoroughly accommodated to the life and thought of the West and the conceptual categories of western Europe, into massive interaction with totally different styles of life and thought. Some missionaries—some at all times, and perhaps most at first—assumed that the interaction merely reflected the conflict of light with darkness, and maintained their Christian thinking and proclamation in the terms they had always used. But, taking the movement as a whole, the Christian encounter with new cultural situations and the unprecedented questions that that encounter raised, had a profound effect on missionaries. If they were to do what they had come to do—to talk about Christ—they had to engage, at a more fundamental level than most other Westerners were ever called on to do, with the traditions and the cumulative effect of the languages, histories, and literatures, written and oral, of Africa and Asia. The fact that so many people within these cultures showed no inclination to respond to the gospel forced open new areas of Christian thinking. (Perhaps even more drastic revisions of Christian thought arose in those situations where people *did* respond to the Christian proclamation.)

Timothy Richard offers a convenient paradigm of the experience of the missionary movement as a whole. The length of his career facilitates such a study. He did not take a furlough until he had been fifteen years in China; it was another ten before the second, and eight more before his third, and final, period of leave. When he retired, reaching Britain in 1916, he was a sick and broken man with less than three years to live. While, therefore, he was aware of and responsive to the changing currents of thought in the Western world, they invariably came to him coloured by the Chinese situation and by Chinese priorities. It is as a paradigm of the missionary movement, therefore, that primarily we shall consider him here. It is as a missionary that his status in legend has been accorded, and that is how he saw himself.

Creative missionaries have often had troubled relationships with their mission boards, and open rupture is a recurrent feature of the missionary story. Richard's relationships with the society that sent him to China were often tense, sometimes at breaking point, but never quite broken. It was perhaps fortunate, though unplanned, that, after four acclimatising months he found himself alone even in his first appointment. Alone, or with a single sympathetic colleague, such as A. G. Jones, he worked best. He would sometimes issue appeals for more missionary colleagues; but when they came (as when the work in Shanxi opened up), he could not work with them. His best working relationships were sometimes with colleagues who were not Baptists—the Wesleyan David Hill,[5] the American

---

[5]Hill needs a modern study. The fullest biography is still W. T. A. Barber, *David Hill, Missionary and Saint* (London: Kelly, 1898; 5th ed., 1909); the most recent is H. B. Rattenbury, *David Hill, Friend of China* (London: Epworth, 1949).

Methodist Young J. Allen,[6] and his colleagues in the Society for the Diffu-sion of Christian and General Knowledge—where the question of author-ity did not arise.

At one time Richard reached the point where he believed he could no longer work with the Baptist Missionary Society (BMS). He could not as-sent, he said, to the proposition that ministers at home knew the needs of China better than the missionaries themselves. He therefore told the com-mittee that though, with the knowledge of China that they had, they might be doing the best they could, with the knowledge of China he pos-sessed, he would be doing wrong in consenting to do as they wished.[7] In this explosive situation he did what sensible students often do in similar circumstances, and took a year out. The highly influential Li Hung Chang offered him the editorship of his progressive daily newspaper, *Shih Pao*, published in Tianjin (Tientsin). By the time this temporary assignment was finished, Richard was able to move to the secretaryship of the Society for the Diffusion of Christian and General Knowledge among the Chi-nese, better known by the title of its fundraising auxiliary organisation, the Christian Literature Society for China. This was in 1891. The rest of his missionary service, twenty-five years in all, was spent in that Society's service, with the BMS paying his salary but not directing his work—an arrangement that suited Richard to perfection. He and the BMS officers clearly reached the point of exasperation with each other at times; but if one turns to the pages of the *Missionary Herald*, the BMS magazine, no missionary's name appears more frequently, nor with more honourable mention. In the years when he was an agent of the Society, his letters were not only quoted in the magazine, but also often introduced with some laudatory comment. His leaving the Society to edit a Chinese daily news-paper is announced in the *Missionary Herald* as if such a step were a natu-ral development of a missionary's work, with note taken of the additional advantage that it would relieve the Society of the burden of his salary.[8] After his departure to the SDK (as I will hereafter denominate the Society

---

[6]On Allen, see Adrian A. Bennett, *Missionary Journalist in China: Young J. Allen and His Magazines, 1860–1883* (Athens, Ga.: University of Georgia Press, 1983). Allen foreshadows some aspects of Richard's work. Richard speaks of Allen's work on the production of Chinese magazines as "first class" (*Missionary Herald* [1889]: 170).

[7]This account follows the language Richard used later to describe the incident in the brief autobiography reprinted in *Conversion by the Million*, vol. 1, ch. 6, 79–109.

[8]*Missionary Herald* (1891): 196. Richard has previously told readers of the reply he had composed to Li Hung Chang's public question "What is the good of Chris-tianity?" with an essay showing the material, intellectual, political, social, moral, and spiritual usefulness of the gospel as illustrated in history (*Missionary Herald* [1890]: 177).

for the Diffusion of Knowledge), he was still treated very much as one of the BMS family; indeed, in some respects, more so than ever, since he had his own dedicated section in the BMS annual report. There is no obvious sign of censorship of even his most provocative statements, even if more traditional fare from old lights such as Alexander MacLaren is inserted to show that the old ways have not been deserted.[9] In retirement, Richard was honoured as a denominational patriarch; and when he died, his funeral was conducted by denominational luminaries, ancient (W. Y. Fullerton) and modern (T. R. Glover).[10]

For people of my age who went through Baptist Sunday schools, Timothy Richard was the name to associate with China in the way that Carey stood for India or Grenfell for Congo. One of the imperial Chinese decorations that Richard received conferred nobility on his ancestors for three generations back,[11] a dignity that must have astonished those worthy Welsh farmers if notification of it reached them in the celestial fields. But the honoured place that Richard has received in Baptist legend is quite as remarkable. It shows how a rather conventional missionary's ideas and activities developed in unconventional ways; and in this, Richard represents what happened to the missionary movement as a whole.

Richard's story has paradigmatic value of another kind. It is not just that his theological position changed over the years; that is common enough. It is a distortion, I think, to treat his career as that of a simple evangelical who moved progressively in a liberal direction; still more distorting to see him as a missionary who departed from the original missionary vocation by transforming it into something else. Richard had

---

[9]So, e.g., *Missionary Herald* (1897): 568, where MacLaren is quoted as saying at a missionary meeting, "I believe that ninety percent of theological error comes, and always has come, from underrating the significance of sin." Occasionally, the *Herald*'s editor undertakes to clarify or point up a statement. Thus *Missionary Herald* (1893): 210, describes and applauds Richard's appointment to the secretaryship of the SDK. Richard's explanation of the Society's work is quoted at length: "By enlightening these students gathered at the chief centres of the empire, we shall touch the spring of untold happiness for our fellow men. One provincial examination centre will reach the leaders of a hundred centres. . . . *But light must precede reform.* We possess the much needed light, shall we not give it to them?" At this point the editor adds, "They need above all else the Gospel, are we not prepared to give it to them?" After paying tribute to the work of John Murdoch and the Christian Literature Society in India, the editorial comment then reaffirms Richard's argument about the value and importance of literature in guiding intellectual change.

[10]Though Soothill remarks on the "quiet" nature of the service: "One could not help thinking of the contrast between the present small congregation and the public funeral that would have been his in the land where he was known and revered. Among his own people he was almost a stranger" (*Richard of China*, 326).

[11]*Ibid.*, 324.

several opportunities to leave mission service in order to implement the modernising programmes he came to recommend for China, and he turned them all down. He never saw himself as anything other than a missionary, and never wanted to be anything else. For Richard ordinarily does not abandon a position and move to another; he retains the original position but steadily clears more and more space around it and occupies that. He never rejects his past; he finds new affirmations of it somewhere else. He dated his personal awakening of faith to the revival of 1859;[12] back in Wales in 1905, and preparing to batter down the doors of the Foreign Office and, if necessary, Lambeth Palace too, he noted the effects of the recent Welsh Revival, and was particularly moved by the singing.[13] Occupied around the same period with ambitious schemes of ecumenical cooperation, he looked back to "the grand work of Moody and Sankey" as an example of ecumenism in practice.[14] Richard was not really a liberal in the conventional sense at all. I cannot see, for instance, that he was at all interested in biblical criticism. He was passionately interested in science, but had no sense of any warfare between science and religion. It is easy to point to expressions and statements of his that no traditionally minded Christian of that day would dream of using; but it is less easy to point to explicit denials or rejections of traditional Christian doctrine.[15]

Throughout his career Richard quoted one scriptural injunction as the foundation of his missionary work. It was Matt. 10:11, within the instructions given by Christ to his disciples when he sent them out to preach: "When you come to a town, enquire who there is worthy, and stay with them until you leave that place." The priority of the quest for the open-minded "worthy" over indiscriminate missionary preaching was a theme to which Richard constantly returned.

One of his early biographers attributes this principle to the valedictory charge given by Edward Tretrail on behalf of the BMS when Richard

---

[12]Timothy Richard, *Forty-five Years in China* (New York: Stokes, 1910), 22.

[13]Soothill, *Richard of China*, 286; cf. Richard, *Forty-five Years*, 326, where Richard describes speaking at an open-air meeting during the Welsh Revival and the impact of the testimony and song of a miner.

[14]Richard, *Conversion by the Million*, vol. 1, ch. 6.

[15]Richard was clearly wounded by Hudson Taylor's insistence on China Inland Mission (CIM) members breaking off relations and establishing a separate church in 1881 because he was not "orthodox" (Richard, *Forty-five Years*, 152f.). The decision came back to haunt him in his rejection by his younger Baptist colleagues in Shansi (ibid., 204f.), who, he claimed, "misrepresented" his views. Soothill (*Richard of China*, 156) sees CIM influence behind his colleagues' action. But there and elsewhere Richard continued to have the most cordial relations with CIM missionaries. Cf. MacGillivray: "He was not wedded to formal statements of dogma, for his mind was constantly open to new ideas. . . . He disliked controversy, and delighted in the constructive" (*Richard of China*, 18).

began as a missionary in 1869.[16] Richard himself, who in his autobiography dates his actual embrace of the principle some years later, always insisted that his departures from conventional mission practice arose from the study of Scripture. At some point he came upon a copy of the published form of the highly charged address that Edward Irving delivered to the London Missionary Society on "Missionaries after the Apostolical School."[17] This tract advocated a new mode of missions. The prudence that Irving believed to be the watchword of the mission agencies of his day should be abandoned in favour of the literal fulfilment of the Lord's mission charges to the Twelve and the Seventy, which should be seen as permanent charters for missions. In 1887, more than sixty years after its first issue, Richard had Irving's manifesto reprinted in Tianjin ("I know of none dealing with the MOST FUNDAMENTAL principles of Christian missions that will for a moment compare with this"), and sent it to missionaries all over the world.[18] He retained his admiration for Irving's radical biblicism all his life, and regarded it as a basically sound critique of ordinary mission policy. By 1906 he was declaring it to be the source of the principle of seeking out "the worthy."[19]

In fact, when due allowance is made for his loose and unsystematic modes of expression, it is truer to say that Richard expanded his vision than that he altered his theology. The expansion of vision came through the inexorable pressure of Chinese conditions. The original missionary aim was never abandoned; but in the process of fulfilling that aim new dimensions of the task were recognised, dimensions not visible at the beginning. This is very much the story of the missionary movement as a whole; in Richard we can see it within a single long career. What Richard lacked was the theological equipment to interpret effectively what had happened to him and to much of the missionary movement to which he belonged. But the missionary movement as a whole suffered from a similar lack. It was long in recognising that a huge new theological agenda was developing as a result of its own work. Over most of the nineteenth and even the

---

[16]E. W. Price Evans, *Timothy Richard: A Narrative of Christian Enterprise and Statesmenship in China* (London: Carey, 1945), 25. I cannot find any explicit statement by Richard himself to this effect. However, Donald MacGillivray, who knew Richard well through the SDK, says that Trestrail urged Richard to study the Lord's instructions to the Twelve on the occasion of their mission (*Richard of China*, 5).

[17]Edward Irving, *For Missionaries after the Apostolic School: A Series of Orations* (London: Hamilton Adams, 1825). This work appeared substantially after the sermon on which it was based, and in a form larger than the sermon. See Gavin White, "'Highly Preposterous': Origins of Scottish Missions," *Records of the Scottish Church History* 19 (1977): 111–24.

[18]Edward Irving, *Missionaries after the Apostolic School: Three Addresses* (Tientsin: Tientsin Printing Co., n.d.). The preface, from which the quotation comes, is dated "Peking Dec. 1887."

[19]In the autobiography reprinted next year in *Conversion by the Million*.

twentieth centuries, centuries that have entirely changed the face of the Christian world, most missionaries saw theology as a given, something already formed and ready for transfer to China or India or Africa. They made accordingly immense contributions to many branches of learning—linguistics, anthropology, Asian history and literature, tropical medicine, even comparative religion—to every branch of learning, one might say, except theology.[20] Yet theology was the branch of learning that more than any other was being opened up as a result of missionary activity. Richard's later writing, such as *The New Testament of Higher Buddhism*, an exasperating book with wild, even irresponsible, flourishes, represents the uneasy theological conscience of the missionary movement. It recognises the presence of theological issues that it cannot properly articulate. Richard was not a very proficient theologian; but he appreciated more fully than many of his contemporaries that the churches coming to birth in China, as in other parts of the world, might be new in terms of missionary effort but were centuries old in terms of the preparatory work of the Spirit of God. He realised also, again better than some whose doctrinal affirmations were more circumspect, that East Asia under the gospel had the potential to transform the life, thinking, and theology of the Christian church.

It is time to look at Richard's evolution as a missionary, and the events and processes that created turning points—occasions of conversion—in his life.[21] His personal background was quite in keeping with the norms for the missionary movement during the first two-thirds of the nineteenth century. He was born on 10 October 1845 in rural Wales, in West Carmarthenshire, where his father was a working farmer who also served as the community blacksmith. It was a Welsh-speaking area, so English, though he came to it early, was Richard's second language. Like the apostle Paul, he seems to have been sometimes more impressive on paper than before an audience; in the days of his celebrity status, audiences were sometimes disappointed. (It was not only that his English did not always flow readily; he spoke Chinese with the local dialect he had learned in his early days.) The religious influences of his home and neighbourhood were thoroughly evangelical, and his district was deeply affected by the revival movement of 1859–60. Richard's response was baptism on profes-

---

[20]See Andrew F. Walls, *The Missionary Movement in Christian History* (Maryknoll, N.Y.: Orbis, 1996), chs. 14, "The Nineteenth-Century Missionary as Scholar," and 15, "Humane Learning and the Missionary Movement."

[21]Richard was his own biographer, reprinting a memoir that had first appeared in a periodical in *Conversion by the Million*. A fuller form followed in *Forty-five Years in China*. Soothill, *Richard of China*, the fullest biography, uses this, quoting from it substantially; and Price Evans, *Timothy Richard*, largely follows Soothill. Bohr's study of the famine, cited below, indicates how the different aspects of Richard's work would repay study.

sion of faith, the youngest of scores of people baptised in the river on a single day. He grew up on the farm and did farm work. His schooling was somewhat episodic; he was twenty when it reached its climax with his admission to the Baptist College at Haverfordwest to prepare for the ministry.

So far, Richard is a fairly standard representative of the constituency from which Dissenter missionaries came, alike in social background, religious influences, and educational equipment. His career at Haverfordwest was notable for two developments. One was a student revolt. Haverfordwest College offered a traditional curriculum of liberal and theological education. The students of the 1860s demanded less of the dead languages and more of living ones, a wider history syllabus that included India and China as well as Greece and Rome, and an infusion of natural science. Such a revolt is a reminder that nineteenth-century missions were part of an Enlightenment project, stamped by Enlightenment ideals; the evangelical Christianity that underlay them had made its peace with the European Enlightenment and operated in its categories. In later years, Richard was to lament that his theological training had not prepared him for the mission field. He attributed his real theological education to enlightened missionary colleagues, such as Alexander Williamson of the National Bible Society of Scotland, and the American J. L. Nevius. These took Chinese religions seriously and shared their knowledge in weekly Bible studies that opened new vistas for the recruit. In his early years of service he could urge that the need for missionaries was so pressing that it was not necessary to wait for the college course to be completed. Later, complaining that most missionaries arrived miserably undertrained, Richard argued that mission societies should invest in thorough preparation for their candidates, especially in the fields of comparative religion and the science of missions—disciplines that he had acquired, not at Haverfordwest, but from the example of Williamson and Nevius.[22]

The second notable development of his college career was a visit there by Mrs. Grattan Guinness, which directed him to missionary service. The influence of this impressive lady on the British missionary movement in the later-nineteenth century deserves much more study than it has received; her influence on Richard is an early example of it. It is interesting that Richard's initial offer for missionary service was to the harbinger of a new type of missionary society, the infant China Inland Mission. This offered a radical rethinking of mission finance and governance, a stress on faith and on the primacy of the evangelistic task. The CIM did not accept him; perhaps, since they suggested he apply to his denominational society, they thought him too committed a Baptist. In later years, they must

---

[22]Thus the account in the autobiography, *Conversion by the Million*, vol. 1, 79ff.

have rejoiced in their escape. Timothy Richard took the advice, applied to the BMS, and was accepted. But in many ways he continued to bear marks characteristic of the CIM: the concern with the interior, the sense of the sheer magnitude of China, the burden—so typical of Mrs. Guinness—of the "regions beyond." Friendship with CIM missionaries was an important feature of his missionary career; and, in line with CIM practice, he adopted Chinese dress.

In origin, then, Richard was a typical missionary of his generation, a generation that saw the missionary task essentially in terms of the verbal communication of the gospel to as many people as possible as quickly as possible. His early field experience suggested, however, not only that his efforts to this end were not noticeably successful, but also that most of his colleagues were not having much effect either. There were two evangelistic methods in common use. One was daily preaching, either by missionaries or by Chinese taught by missionaries, in small street chapels. The preaching followed the paradigm of sin, atonement, and salvation typical of evangelical preaching in Britain, reinforced by scriptural proof texts. The other method was the distribution of the Scriptures—the handing out of portions of the Chinese Bible to any who would receive them. Richard became oppressed by how alien all this was to the people of the street. It was simply the ranting of ignorant foreign barbarians. The very name of Jesus was just another foreign word; and as long as it remained simply the title of a foreign deity, it could have no more than curiosity value. Much effort produced few converts; still more disturbing, most of those remained dependent on missionaries for their continuance as Christians. In his valedictory charge, Trestrail had urged Richard to lay hold of the teachers of China, but no one had told him how. The teachers of China—the literati, schooled in the Confucian classics, who provided the magistracy and administration at every level—were usually among the most implacable foes of the missions. From their point of view, missions belonged to the battery of foreign barbarian influences, imposed by force, that were introducing corrupt practices and undermining stable government. The very presence of foreigners was an insulting sign of China's weakness, of its inability to keep out undesired influences. The neutralisation of foreign influences as far as possible was therefore a natural policy for "the teachers of China" to follow.

Any response to this must take China seriously, and take Chinese history, literature, and traditions seriously. This was the path that Williamson and Nevius were already following. Richard decided to pursue the theme of "enquiring who is worthy," interpreting "the worthy" of Matt. 10:11 as "the open-minded." Instead of indiscriminate preaching, and indiscriminate Bible and tract distribution, would it not be better to follow the Lord's own counsel to those he sent as missionaries, and seek out those "worthy" who were prepared to listen? Richard believed that these would be found especially among members of the Buddhist sects, "the religious cream of the land." He may have come to this conclusion less by empirical study of the sects than by noticing that a high proportion of Christian converts came from this very background; Pastor Hsi, the best-known Chinese figure associated with the CIM, had been a member of the Golden Pill sect.[23] Richard concluded that the sects were the natural home of seekers after truth, those who were not content with conventional religious practice. He may also have noticed that they were also the group with least interest in the maintenance of Manchu domination in China.

But there was another clue in the New Testament about how "the worthy" were to be found. It lay in the use of parables. These were not simple, self-explanatory stories; as the Lord's own commentary indicated, they required a key, and only "the worthy" sought and found it.[24] Richard sought to emulate this method in a Chinese setting, using the established Chinese medium of the wall poster. Instead of handing out densely written tracts, he set up posters bearing short gnomic utterances: "A hundred years old and persecutions, and endless life in the world to come." That, he found, brought in "the worthy" to enquire further. The church in Shandong grew, and it worshipped Christ under a translated Chinese name, Saviour.

But—Irving again—the missionary's function was apostolic, not pastoral. The missionary must sow the seed of the church, but not become its pastor, or a deacon, above all not its secretary or treasurer. Chinese Christians could carry out all these functions far better than any missionary; and any action that caused them to become dependent on missionaries should be resisted. Richard was already working out a principle that he was to declare a cardinal one, the principle of economy in missions. The evangelisation of China would ultimately depend not on multiplying foreign missionaries but on stimulating Chinese. This is the point he seems to have reached by the end of his first six years in China, which had taken him from the treaty port of Zhifu (Cheefoo) to the interior of Shandong (Shantung) province. He had made some radical departures from standard mission methods, but these had hardly affected substance. Mission was still in essence the communication of the gospel by word, even if the style of communication had been transposed into a new key. And the religious ethos of Richard's work was still the evangelical religion in which he was nurtured, with the biblical, crucicentric, conversionist, and activist

---

[23]Hsi was the subject of a once popular biography: Mrs. Howard [Mary] Taylor, *Pastor Hsi (of North China): One of China's Christians* (London: Morgan and Scott, 1903). There were various versions, titles, and abridgements. A new version, *Pastor Hsi*, was published in 1997 (Singapore: Overseas Missionary Fellowship). Richard refers to Hsi's conversion through friendship with David Hill (*Forty-five Years*, 150). Characteristically, he says that the sect (Kin Tan Chiao) "greatly resembles Nestorianism."

[24]Cf. Mark 4:10–12.

marks that David Bebbington has identified as its essential features.[25] Furthermore, it was christocentric, and the christocentric pattern is especially clear; the function of the missionary is, by whatever means, to proclaim Christ.

Richard's view of the missionary task was diversified in an unexpected way. Famine broke out in the province. Famine led to riots, riots to military repression. Disease followed famine. What was a missionary to do? The reason for his being in China was to preach the gospel, and Richard's first response was in evangelistic terms. He set up his wall posters again, but now to urge people to repent and turn to God. A surprising number did; it was not difficult to see famine and pestilence as the outcome of evil deeds. The magistrate in charge of Richard's district had even had himself put in chains, in recognition that his own faults had played a part in bringing about the calamity. People came to Richard in numbers, acknowledging their sins, and asking him to pray to his God for their deliverance. The *Missionary Herald* noted how the famine was leading to the founding of new churches.[26] But the famine went on, until local resources of every sort were exhausted. There was no imperial transport system that could move grain from one province to another. Confucian social ethics urged benevolence, but left its exercise to the educated elite, the family, and voluntary philanthropy. Indigenous structures thus appeared powerless in the face of disaster. Was it, then, an adequate Christian response to exhort sinners to return to God? Richard became a prime mover in developing a Christian policy towards famine. This was by no means something that could be taken for granted in the 1870s. Missions had certainly engaged in famine relief in India, and famine had been the background of some mass movements to Christianity there, but conditions obtaining in China were entirely different. The limited attempts at missionary philanthropy hitherto set on foot in China had not been encouraging in their outcome. An attempt to distribute food had caused a stampede and further breakdown of order. Magistrates had made it clear that they would not tolerate foreigners using the famine to alienate the people further from the government.

Richard identified the first issue as the release of all remaining local supplies, as the state of China's transport and communications prevented rapid movement of commodities. This required money; and the missions had no great financial resources available in the field. The first approach must be to the commercial interests in Shanghai and the treaty ports, raising money from the foreign communities in China. The second was to reach the Christian public in the West, the churches that pro-

---

[25]D. W. Bebbington, *Evangelicalism in Modern Britain: A History from the 1730s to the 1980s* (London: Unwin, 1989).

[26]*Missionary Herald* (1878): 14.

duced the mission-supporting community, and move them urgently to practical Christian compassion. Month after month the *Missionary Herald* featured the famine, placed the appeal in large print, and gave it priority in its pages. Other mission sources did the same, and Nevius moved American missions in a similar direction. The famine in China entered the Western Christian consciousness and became a theatre of concern for its churches.

The Great Famine of 1876–79—the largest famine known to history, Richard was fond of saying—was a watershed in Western awareness of hunger and natural disaster as a field of Christian activity, and in missionary involvement in relief work. Never before, at least since the days of slave emancipation, had such consciousness raising about basic human need operated on such a scale. Thereafter it became common; the *Missionary Herald*, for instance, regularly recorded famines in India, with calls for special funding and urgent remittances. Such activities, in fact, became part of the general conception of what missions were about, a normal expression of Christian concern. But such things were far from the minds of those who established the missionary movement, and by no means part of normal conception of missionary duty at the time when Timothy Richard first volunteered for service overseas.

It was not simply that the Western mission-minded public, and through them their less enthusiastically mission-minded associates, gave abundantly for famine relief at the urging of those missionaries they had sent to preach the gospel in China. Those missionaries undertook the administration of famine relief as their principal missionary concern for a significant period of time. In this, Richard, with the English Wesleyan David Hill, took a leading part. Interestingly, it was once more to the Gospels that Richard attributed his inspiration. He pointed to the story of the feeding of the five thousand, in which Jesus fed a multitude with apparently neglible resources at hand. The key lay in the Lord's words "Make the people sit down";[27] it was this that secured orderly distribution.

In China orderly distribution was equally the key to meeting the need of multitudes; careful planning and calculation marked the methods developed by Richard and Hill. But it was equally important that they took care to operate within, and not independently of, the official Chinese administration. One by one the harassed local officials were won over; the missionaries worked through the government's own distribution centres, setting up no separate agencies. There was no attempt to "own" the foreign relief supplies, or identify them as "Christian." The missionaries, however, maintained a personal involvement in the administration of relief, rather than simply handing over the foreign contribution.

---

[27]Luke 9:14.

The result was encouraging. It produced a noticeable mitigation of the degree of suffering, at least in urban areas (there was as yet no way of reaching deep into the countryside). Relieved local officials were in general grateful for the supplies and assistance from foreign sources; and they recognised that these foreigners had not abused their position, had respected established authority, and appeared to act with the genuine benevolence that classical Confucian teaching recommended. That is, they were evidently good people in Chinese terms. Nothing could have been better calculated to ease the way for spreading Christian teaching. Tablets recording gratitude to the foreigners for their benevolence were set up, and Richard and Hill had some difficulty in preventing the use of their photographs for veneration in temples.[28] Then famine struck in interior China with increased virulence. Richard followed it into Shansi, where feeling was militantly antiforeign, and where Protestant missions had never taken root at all. The famine was ghastly. In Shandong, it had been said that people sold their children; in Shansi, it was said that they ate them. Richard and a small group of colleagues applied there the methods that had worked in Shandong. Again they succeeded, inasfar as one can ever properly speak of success in such a situation. From a missionary point of view, Shansi presented two new features. In Shandong, the missionaries had been working long before the famine came, and there was a church, even if a tiny one, already in existence to act as the base for Christian involvement. In Shansi, there was no church, and the Protestant missionaries came only with the famine. In other words, the first mark of the mission's presence in Shansi was not preaching, but famine relief. The traditional mission paradigm was altering in more than one respect. The other new feature in Shansi was the presence of a Catholic mission and a Catholic church as the sole prior representatives of the Christian faith. It was necessary for Richard to open relations with the French Catholic bishop for effective prosecution of the famine relief scheme.

Without wishing to exaggerate the schematic importance of the Great Famine, one must accord it special significance in Western missionary history. It had a permanent impact on mission thinking in that it made emergency relief an ongoing feature of mission concern, and developed the capacity for responding to it. More fundamentally, it marked a development in missionary consciousness. Missionaries went out to preach the gospel; they found themselves feeding the hungry. They fed the hungry because it was the only authentically Christian way to respond to the situation in which they had gone to preach the gospel. It was not done in order to help the preaching of the gospel, even if that followed. If justification were

---

[28]The whole area of famine relief is throughly discussed by Paul Richard Bohr, *Famine in China and the Missionary: Timothy Richard as Relief Administrator and Advocate of National Reform, 1876–1884* (Cambridge: Harvard University Press, 1972).

needed, such justification lay in the example of Christ. Mission was still, in the way of evangelical religion, christocentric, but it was no longer solely a matter of the word of the gospel. Mission was not only about speaking, but about being and doing. The famine question clarified issues that the more complex debate about medical missions left obscure.[29]

Timothy Richard had begun his career as an evangelist, in which capacity he had developed an early sort of church-growth theory. It had continued with famine relief, for which he had developed guiding principles of disciplined organisation and respect for indigenous institutions and structures. Richard never repudiated either of these forms of missionary activity; he continued to see them as essential in the missionary enterprise and to glory in his own participation in both. Had it not been for a dispute with the BMS over the operation of the Shansi mission and the proper deployment of new missionaries, he would doubtless have gone back to his evangelism. The dispute, and the ensuing sabbatical as a newspaper editor, moved him further along the thought path that the Great Famine had opened.

Richard had seen the helplessness of China in the face of famine and the horrors that followed famine; seen the paralysis of its institutions before natural disaster; seen an indigenous ethical system rendered incapable of application in time of the greatest need for it. But famine was not inevitable; it could be foreseen, and, with proper measures, prevented. Prevention involved scientific knowledge—for instance, of meteorology—and thus some understanding of the laws of nature. It involved economic foresight, with provision for prepurchase and storage of supplies. It assumed some flexibility in economic and fiscal policy—for instance, in tax remissions where suffering was greatest and incentives to move supplies to famine-affected areas. In the wake of the Great Famine, Richard used his newly forged relationships with officials to propagate these ideas; and indeed, most of them were already circulating among progressive Chinese thinkers of the period.[30] But what had these ideas to do with the work of a Christian missionary? If it was a Christian duty to extend the hand of mercy in time of disaster, was it not equally a Christian duty to use access to knowledge in order to prevent disaster happening? Could Christians conscientiously pray for the salvation of China and calmly acquiesce in the death by starvation of millions of the poorest Chinese people every year? Surely, the salvation of China must include its salvation from preventable hunger.

---

[29]On this, see Walls, *Missionary Movement*, ch. 16, "The Domestic Importance of the Nineteenth-Century Missionary Movement: The Heavy Artillery of the Missionary Army."

[30]See Bohr, *Famine in China*, ch. 5.

China was perishing for want of knowledge—not only knowledge of the salvation wrought by Christ, but the primary knowledge of the way God had ordered creation. Popular religion actually hindered that knowledge; the yin/yang principle and the idea of the five elements obstructed scientific understanding. These ideas did not belong to the Confucian ideal of good government; but many of the literati had found ways to accommodate them, and their hold on the public imagination was firm. Richard, who had once taken part in a student revolt to make science part of the training of ministers, began to give series of public lectures on science—physics, chemistry, biology—aimed especially at the literati. This he could hold to be entirely proper for a missionary—he was demonstrating the works of God. His own scientific education had been, of course, rudimentary, but he now applied himself to scientific literature, and had a whole crate of scientific instruments sent out to enable him to display to the local magistracy the capacities of the microscope and the telescope and even the bicycle.

This was quite an early development in Richard's thought. From there, it developed along two planes. One was the need for what would nowadays be called structural change in China if China was to feed its people. Structural change could finally be fully expected only at the highest, that is, the imperial level, and this long lay out of reach (though the time was to come when the influences Richard wished to promote began to operate even in the court). In the meantime, the attempt had to be made to reach the more accessible strata of government with ideas that could be disinterestedly recommended as being for the good of China. The second plane was theological. Structural change was a matter of the order of creation; the proper use of science and technology depended on the order established by God for the governance of the universe. It was ignorance of that order that held China back; the structural change that could save thousands of lives every year depended on a Christian view of nature.

The relation of these two planes is essential to the understanding of what Richard was about. He recognised and applauded the enlightened people at every level of Chinese administration who were working for structural improvement. But he was not a proponent of secular development; he saw no bright future that way. The mindset of China had to change if the desired scientific and technological changes were to occur without destruction. Religious change must underlie social and economic change.

These considerations led him to accept the newspaper editorship. In the columns of a progressive daily it was, Richard believed, possible to provide the outline of a coherent worldview. The establishment of sound religion was a good Confucian principle; there was no reason why a daily newspaper should not espouse that cause in a nonpartisan manner. When he moved from the editorship to the secretarial chair of the SDK, the opportunities were greater still. The Society's full title included the words "Christian" and "Useful" to indicate the types of literature that would be needed to promote the right form of structural change in China. In the twenty-five years that Richard served the Society, it published hundreds of books, some original, many translated. Some were about Christian doctrine and practice, others provided the "useful" information, whether geographical, historical, constitutional, or scientific, that was intended to open minds.

The special aim of the SDK in Richard's time was to reach the literati, the Chinese educated class that had proved the most rigorous opponents of Christianity. The "useful" literature of the SDK was meant to be useful above all to the younger literati such as crowded each year to the empire's two hundred examination centres for the competitive examinations from which administrators were chosen. Missionaries had long laid siege to these centres at examination time with their tracts; the SDK literature was aimed especially at those literati open to new ideas, ready to consider elements of modernisation, interested, perhaps, in Western political or economic thought. To such—"the worthy," as he might have described them—Richard sought to demonstrate that what they desired, or might desire, for China was inseparable from a Christian view of the world and of nature. Historically, natural science derived from Christian convictions about nature; the envied technological superiority of the West derived from its Christian inheritance. Such themes return endlessly in Richard's writings and in SDK publications.

At one point, Richard's annual report classified the publications of the SDK under four heads: those on the works of God, those on the ways of God, those on the laws of God, and those on the grace of God.[31] The first three categories covered the writings on science, history, political economy, law, and ethics; the last, those on Christian doctrine. The point is that *all* SDK publications, whether explicitly "Christian" or simply "useful,"

---

[31]Cf. *Missionary Herald* (1895): 209: "Our aim is to reach the higher and educated classes of China, men and women, so that the countless poor in China may be delivered, and to bring about a *renaissance* of a fourth of the human race. . . . Instead of selfish principles, which in the end only destroy nations as well as individuals, we intend to base all enlightenment on Christian principles of love and goodwill." Later he writes, "The Christian Church is not expected to fill every distant village of China with foreign missionaries, for the natives can do that part very much better than any foreigner, but the Church is expected to keep abreast of the times and to be co-workers with God, and to provide the Chinese reformers, who are looking to us for light, with Christian books of the first order to enable them to arrive at sound Christian principles of government in harmony with the will of God" (*Missionary Herald* [1899]: 239.). Later still: "The highest truths, whether found out by discovery or revelation, are the wonderful laws of God in nature, in human life and in God's own perfect character, and the highest inspirations to service, peace and progress are derived from the knowledge of these divine laws in all departments (2 Peter 1:2–3)" (*Missionary Herald* [1902]: 219f.).

were about God, even such as at first sight seemed to be of a "secular" nature. For Richard, this was more than an ingenious quibble about words. The SDK represented a further development in the paradigm of mission; it represented also an enlargement of the working theology of the missionary movement. A working theology focused on the work of redemption was now taking in the work of creation, with Christian witness to the Creator, and knowledge of the Creator's handiwork, as the key to right use of the creation and the sustaining of life.

Once again, Richard's experience represents a development that took place more widely in the missionary movement. Literacy grew with Protestant missions from their earliest time, and was taken for granted; literacy led to education, and education, or at least higher education, was not always seen as the proper work of missions.[32] From the beginning, Scottish missions, true heirs of the Scottish Enlightenment, argued that it was; by the early twentieth century, missions everywhere, often against their inclination or first desires, were engaged in education programmes. Those programmes were often justified along the lines that Richard and his colleagues argued on behalf of the work of the SDK. Mission began in christocentric, crucicentric terms, rooted in the doctrine of redemption. In the course of its exercise, it developed and expanded to take on a theocentric dimension, rooted in the doctrine of creation.

The SDK caught the tide of change in China. Richard believed that it helped to turn it but it is hard in such matters to assess causation. It is clear that many literati, including some who became very influential, did read SDK books, and numbers sought, in varying degrees, to apply ideas found there as the decaying empire tottered to its ruin. After the Boxer Rebellion, Richard persuaded the provincial government of Shansi to devote its indemnity to setting up a Western-style university, for which he would appoint the professors, all of them Christians. In later life he lamented that the missions had missed the opportunity to provide Christians to staff all the Chinese universities. It might have been possible to secure that the rapid process of modernisation that China entered with the fall of the empire would take place under Christian auspices.

But the argument, so dear to Richard, of the importance of the Christian heritage in explaining Western prosperity and success was, of course, double-edged. China had plenty to resent in its relation with the West, and in the last period of his life Richard became increasingly disillusioned with Western materialism and militarism. This strain becomes most noticeable following an unusually protracted period of residence in the West, and in the few years of his retirement. He was in Britain in 1904 when an imperial Chinese delegation arrived on a formal visit. He was disgusted to learn the

---

[32]See M. A. Laird, *Missionaries and Education in Bengal 1793–1897* (Oxford: Oxford University Press, 1972); cf. Walls, *Missionary Movement*, 203ff.

nature of the official programme arranged by the Foreign Office for the Chinese guests. It would have taken them to Woolwich arsenal, the royal dockyards, and steel mills and factories. Why not, thundered the Welsh Baptist, take them to Westminster Abbey? Why not to Oxford? What picture of British civilisation were His Majesty's ministers giving to China? The delegation already knew all its members needed to know about Western firepower and factory power. They would speak in polite admiration, and despise us in their hearts. So Richard wrote to the archbishop of Canterbury, suggesting that he invite the delegation to Lambeth, and ask the president of the Free Church Council to be present too. There was some ecclesiastical fuss about the latter point, but it all worked out in the end—and Richard came too.[33] The incident is a pointer to another feature of the missionary movement, which Richard's later years often exhibit: its capacity, sometimes richer in potential than in exercise, to provide a critique of the West and its ways, and to act for the enlightenment of the Western church.

It is necessary to make some reference, though the topic needs more consideration than can be given to it here, to a further development of Richard's thinking that proceeded in parallel with the aspects already described. We have seen how in the early phases of his work his pursuit of "the worthy" led him to identify the Buddhist sects as offering a particularly substantial concentration of them. This developed into an increasingly adventurous engagement with Chinese Buddhism, and an increasingly heightened appreciation of it. In general, Christian missionaries in China reacted against Buddhist practice, seeing it as corrupting and superstitious; a missionary scholar like James Legge, who rejoiced in the ancient religion of China and devoted his life to elucidating the Confucian tradition, hardly touches Buddhism when describing the religions of China[34]— presumably because he did not consider it as authentically Chinese. Richard, on the other hand, was fascinated by the particular development that Buddhism had followed in China. In China, he argues, Buddhism departed from the nontheistic assumptions of its founder, and developed a doctrine of grace and recognised a merciful Saviour. The outlines of a Trinitarian theism can be found in the Chinese Buddhist texts—a loving Father, a compassionate Saviour, and a life-giving Spirit. Indeed, Mahayana ought not strictly to be called Buddhist at all; it stood in relation to the Buddha's teachings as the Christian New Testament does to the Old.[35]

---

[33]Soothill, *Richard of China*, 286ff.

[34]See James Legge, *The Religions of China: Confucianism and Taoism Described and Compared with Christianity* (London: Hodder and Stoughton, 1880). Legge, missionary of the London Missionary Society in Hong Kong and later professor of Chinese at Oxford, was the outstanding British Sinologist of the nineteenth century.

[35]The argument is set out in Timothy Richard, *The New Testament of Higher Buddhism* (Edinburgh: Clark, 1910).

Richard and his wife translated into English the central sutras that, as he believed, proved this thesis. Neither the translations that appeared as *The Awakening of Faith*,[36] nor the more ambitious *New Testament of Higher Buddhism*, which comprehends both translation and commentary, brought overwhelming conviction either to Christians or to the growing corps of Western Buddhologists. Richard was neither an exact nor a profound scholar, and the manifest exaggerations and patent speculations in his work were unlikely to gain wide approval. The Western interpreters of Buddhism, products of the new interest in comparative religion, damned his translations as reading Christian meanings into texts that had a quite different significance. Richard countered that the interpretations he was giving were those of the Chinese monks with whom he talked, of sutras that were to be found on the lectern of every Chinese temple he had entered. He seems, however, to have convinced, or at least confirmed the convictions of, one crucially important person. The Norwegian Karl Ludwig Reichelt was to bring much more scholarly depth and a much surer grasp of the doctrine of grace at work within Chinese Buddhism, and of the quest there for the merciful Saviour in the West, a quest whose proper end was in Christ.[37]

Richard and Reichelt alike took inspiration from the thought of the divine Logos at work in the world, and recognised the operation of God in the pre-Christian past of Asia, God's activity in Asia many centuries before the arrival of the first Christian missionary. In his later years, Richard stressed this activity more and more, just as he stressed the present activity of the Holy Spirit as the critical factor in Chinese people becoming Christians.[38]

---

[36]*The Awakening of Faith in the Mahayana Doctrine: The New Buddhism by the Patriarch Ashvogosha*, trans. Timothy Richard (Shanghai: Christian Literature Society, 1907). A new edition, *Ashvoghosa, the Awakening of Faith*, ed. A. H. Watson, with a foreword by Aldous Huxley, appeared in 1961 (London: Skilton). Richard also produced *Ho Fo P'u: Guide to Buddhahood: Being a Standard Manual of Chinese Buddhism* (Shanghai: Christian Literature Society, 1907).

[37]See especially Karl Ludvig Reichelt, *Truth and Tradition in Chinese Buddhism: A Study of Chinese Mahayana Buddhism* (London: Lutterworth, 1961; repr., Taipei: SMC, 1990). The relation of Richard to Reichelt is explored by Eric J. Sharpe, *Karl Ludwig Reichelt, Missionary, Scholar and Pilgrim* (Hong Kong: Tao Fong Shan Ecumenical Centre, 1984), 53ff. Soothill, a more accomplished and more cautious scholar, devotes his penultimate chapter in *Richard of China* (311–19) to a cool, agnostic review of Richard's work on Buddhism. He concludes, "Richard's contribution to the study of Buddhism may be described as more valuable for its suggestiveness than for its literal accuracy. . . . To reveal a new point of view is the work of a prophet, and—to every man his gift!" (p. 319).

[38]E.g., in his evidence to Commission IV of the World Missionary Conference, cited below.

In his idiosyncratic way, Richard was once more demonstrating in his own person a significant development in the missionary movement. Among his contemporaries and successors, both in China and elsewhere, there are signs that, as Western Christians engaged at more fundamental levels with other religious traditions, they saw there the evidence of God's preparatory activity.[39] We have seen how, in Richard and more widely in the missionary movement, a conception of mission that was essentially focused in Christ expanded to comprehend the work of the Creator. In the same way, without in any way compromising its original christological base, the concept of mission, both in Richard and in the wider movement, expanded again to comprehend the special sphere of the Holy Spirit.

In 1910 Richard supplied a long memorandum to the compilers of the report of Commission IV of the World Missionary Conference at Edinburgh, the section that dealt with "the missionary message in relation to the non-Christian religions."[40] It is, like so much of his work, rambling and discursive, starting many hares without sustaining their pursuit. There is an analysis, called for by the Commission's questionnaire, of the features of Christianity that have proved particularly attractive in China. There is much about the divine activity in the religions of China and elsewhere, in response to the questionnaire's enquiry about "points of contact." But a substantial part of Richard's submission is taken up with his regular theme of the conversion of China. The rate of increase of the Protestant churches is only a fraction of the rate of increase of the Chinese population. Statistically therefore, the conversion of China is beyond the capacities of the four thousand Protestant missionaries currently serving there. It is a point Richard often made, and the conclusion he commonly drew from it was that the evangelisation of China would come only from Chinese people, and that missionary effort should be directed to the required preparatory change in the climate of thought. On this occasion, however, the argument follows a different line. The missionary failure has not been of the gospel, but of theology. Missionary theology, excellent in itself, has arisen out of the needs and situations of Western history; it has grown up in isolation and ignorance of the creeds of the East. Christian theology thus stands in need of revision: "We lose nothing, but gain immensely by following the latest revelations of God to man." But

---

[39]See Kenneth Cracknell, *Justice, Courtesy and Love: Theologians and Missionaries Encountering World Religions 1846–1914* (London: Epworth, 1995).

[40]The memorandum is included in a bound collection of typescripts compiled by the Commission's chairman, D. S. Cairns. There are copies in the archives of the University of Aberdeen; the Centre for the Study of Christianity in the Non-Western World, University of Edinburgh; and the archives of the Day Missions Library, Yale University Divinity School. Richard was present at the conference. There are hints that Richard was somewhat frustrated by the ground rules, which limited participants to seven minutes each (Richard, *Forty-five Years*, 332; Soothill, *Richard of China*, (29.)

what are those revelations? Rather surprisingly, the argument sharply changes direction to concentrate on the situation of the poor and oppressed—that "submerged tenth" who suffer equally under the corrupt governments of non-Christian nations (China?) and the tyrannical governments of Christendom with their "terrible armaments" (Britain?). He continues:

> If modern Christianity and other religions will not hearken to the cry of the poor and oppressed, God will call Socialists to listen to it and bid Revolutionists and Nihilists break the oppression.[41]

It is a remarkable statement for a missionary writing in 1910. But it represents a trend in the last phase of Richard's life, one that he had already hinted at in his heated response to the plans for entertaining the Chinese imperial delegation in London. What had begun as feeding the hungry led by natural steps to the processes by which the hungry could be fed and then to those that would eliminate the hunger. Now he could see the issues underlying these to be justice and peace issues embodied in the oppression manifest throughout Asia, the horror of the competitive buildup of armaments of the nations. The striking feature here is that the latter implicated Western nations, not least Britain itself. It is a critical move beyond the former argument that technological prowess was a sign of divine blessing, and arose from a worldview that acknowledged the laws of God. In 1914, the year in which he resigned the secretaryship of the SDK (though he stayed a further year at the Society's request), Richard wrote *Brotherhood vs. Militarism*. He had for some years been endeavouring to promote a Peace Society, and the idea of the ten leading nations undertaking to share a single army as a world police force. He had employed his public recognition in the Far East to seek the support of leading figures in Japan for his grand idea; he may have been used by them in furtherance of Japanese aims in Korea as a result. Richard was no more a practical operator in international politics than he was a great Buddhologist or historian of religions; but in each area he fixed on one great point with far-reaching implications, and signalled its relationship to the Christian gospel. In his retirement years, broken by ill-health and clouded by the Great War, he nursed hopes for the dawning idea of a League of Nations. But the commanding hope was the one he had set before the commission of the World Missionary Conference: an end to the sufferings of the poor and the crimes of their oppressors, and then as the sequel, the fulfillment of the vision that had first brought him to China so many years before, "Then the millions will follow the King of Kings as the rivers flow to the ocean."

---

[41]Commission IV Memorandum, 12 (volume marked "China").

The missionary movement was a great learning experience for Western Christianity. For those engaged in it it was a process of discovery. Beginning from the great evangelical certainty, witness to Christ as Saviour (and with that consciousness uppermost that recent Western Christianity knew best, that of the Saviour of individual sinners), the movement was led, step by step, to a steady enlargement of the scope of the task it had begun. Christian obedience demanded that preachers of the Saviour should respond to human suffering as he did; from there a further step led to identifying the causes of suffering and the means to remove them, looking beyond the divine Saviour to the divine Creator. Learning new languages as an instrument to communicate an already formulated message opened the way to a much more complex understanding of communication and context, and to the realisation that the Gospels themselves recognised this. As this led to steadily deeper engagment with other cultures, it followed that those cultures, including their religious aspects, were taken more and more seriously. Unremitting hostility was no longer possible; among all the other objects in view it was possible to discern divine footsteps. And that could only mean that God had been there before the missionary, and that meant a further enlargement of theology and of the concept of mission. Obedience to the evangelical imperative, christocentric and crucicentric of its nature, led to a widening response to the non-Western world, which in theological terms could be related to the consciousness of God as Father, Son, and Holy Spirit. Missio Dei was discovered in the process of following out the implications of preaching the gospel as beloved by evangelicals. It is no accident that one outcome of the process was a challenge to many of the assumptions that had originally undergirded the movement, assumptions about the nature of sin, assumptions about the values of Western society, and, eventually, about the adequacy of Western theology. Part of the story of the missionary movement as learning experience is the creation of an instrument for Western self-criticism.

The Western missionary movement was never uniform in its development and reactions; but the long-serving Timothy Richard reflects in his own lifetime all the developments just mentioned. His multiple conversions—from conventional evangelism to methods that took China seriously, to famine relief work, to prophet of structural reform, to theologian of religions, to worker for peace and champion of the submerged tenth—mark stages that marked the wider movement in different parts of the world and at different periods. Unsystematic, undisciplined thinker and rambling writer that he was, he never produced a convincing synthesis of his experience, and his attempts to do so were manifestly flawed and sometimes alarming. But his story is a paradigmatic one, of the instincts of the missionary movement at work: never abandoning its original position, but clearing space around it in response to developing perceptions.

14

The Scottish Missionary Diaspora

The missionary diaspora was geographically diffuse, and lacked the cross-generational dimension that was to produce permanent Scottish communities in various parts of the world—though in parentheses we may note that the missionary diaspora produced some remarkable cross-generational dynasties that allied with other Scottish diasporas, not least the overseas administrative and proconsular class. For instance, the East Lothian gardener Robert Moffat, who went to Southern Africa in 1816, produced a family that influenced church and state there into the twentieth century; his son John Smith Moffat, a notable missionary in his own right, became British commissioner in Bechuanaland. The India missionary Alexander Garden Fraser had a son who became a prominent Indian civilian, Sir Andrew Fraser; and a grandson (Alexander Garden once more) who became a missionary and helped to change the shape of education in Ceylon and West Africa and affected imperial education policies in the 1920s and 1930s.

But there are features of the missionary diaspora that make it well worth study in a setting that provides comparisons. For one thing, it sometimes developed features that were self-consciously Scottish. One of these was the Scottish form of Presbyterian church government, with its emphasis on the active participation of lay people. This did not inevitably produce situations where the missionary leadership could itself be challenged and defeated, but it always had the potential to do so, and on occasion had this outcome. For another, Scottish educational institutions, themselves the product of Scottish domestic influences, were transplanted by the missionary diaspora to Africa and Asia. And the combination of Scottish church government and education could give powerful self-expression to indigenous interests within colonial society. It was the very Scottishness of the Rev. Tiyo Soga, the first ordained Xhosa minister—

Presentation for a conference on the Scottish Diaspora, organized by the Research Institute for Irish and Scottish Studies, University of Aberdeen, 1999.

seven years of arts and divinity in Scotland, Scottish ordination, a Scottish wife, and a fluent pen—that meant the Cape newspapers could not ignore him or misrepresent his people unchallenged. Soga's sizable family, mostly educated in Scotland, included the first black medical doctor, in the Transkei, the first Xhosa historian, and South Africa's first veterinary surgeon. This illustrates how Scottish institutions interacted with the societies of Africa and Asia as well as with the colonial.

The Scottish missionary diaspora cannot be confined to the missions of the Scottish churches. Scots formed a significant part of the mission personnel of English, and sometimes American, mission societies. Until well into the twentieth century the English Presbyterian Mission was substantially staffed and funded by members of the Free Church of Scotland. Even more significant were the Scottish influences on the London Missionary Society (LMS), the main mission agency of the English Dissenters. I have identified some two hundred Scots among the first 1,300 missionaries; there are probably many more. And the incidence of Scots is heaviest in the early nineteenth century, when the total of serving missionaries is moderate; the Scottish contribution to the LMS dwindles to a trickle by the 1890s, when the British missionary movement as a whole reaches its highwater mark. Furthermore, in its early years from 1795, the LMS was often dominated by expatriate Scots, the committee weighted by the ministers of the Scots churches in London, and missionary preparation in the hands of the Scottish theologian David Bogue. Other societies, denominational and nondenominational, received an infusion of Scottish personnel. Anglican societies received Scots Presbyterians. One Scottish agency had such effect as to be worth an essay in itself: the Edinburgh Medical Missionary Society was established to enable suitable people who could not afford a medical education to acquire one to serve on the mission field. Many missionary doctors, of many missions, came this way, which gave access to the medical facilities and qualifications of Edinburgh. By this means, anesthesia was being practised in Kashmir in the 1860s, for young Dr. Elmslie from Aberdeen, who established the mission and the first hospital there, had attended Professor Simpson's lectures.

How far was the Scottish missionary diaspora distinctively Scottish? Do Scottish influences in the missionary movement constitute a distinct strand of it? This question, or some part of it, was addressed by the notable Aberdeen theologian David S. Cairns at a conference of Scottish students in 1911. The date is significant; just the previous year the World Missionary Conference held in Edinburgh had provided a glimpse of a Christian church spread over the whole world. It is against this background that Cairns argues that three elements of Scottish religious history are of special significance for the missionary movement.

The first of these elements is the kingdom of God—the central stream of Scottish religious life is theocratic. The aim of the preaching of the gospel ("the evangelization of the world in this generation" was a favourite phrase of the student Christian activists) was not simply saving souls or enlarging the church, but a Christian world society in which the legislative and economic order were brought into accordance with the mind of Christ. The second significant element Cairns identifies in Scottish religious life is the vital importance of the church. Grateful as we must be for the freelances of the Spirit, the conquest of the world for Christ will be by his regular army. The third element is strong theology, the tradition of strong thinking in religion, an element he saw as much needed in the contemporary flabby intellectual climate.

Cairns's second element, the organic connexion in Scottish experience of mission and church, is part of the conventional wisdom of the interpreters of Scottish missions. I believe it, however, to be questionable. Throughout its history the Western missionary movement was essentially entrepreneurial—the theatre of those whom Cairns describes as freelances of the Spirit—and Scotland was no exception. Detailed study of the history of Scottish missions suggests a kaleidoscope of initiatives by missionaries, concerned Indian army officers and civilians, Indian elite, overseas presbyteries, Glasgow merchants, and, not least, women's groups. The results were eventually digested by the Scottish church bodies with varying degrees of difficulty or reluctance. Overseas missions were seldom an active priority of the Scottish church except in its theology and its publicity; in practice, like the missions of other countries, they were the sphere of the enthusiasts.

But the other two themes identified by Cairns—the theocratic strain, with its Christian address to the structures of society, and what he calls strong thinking in religion—deserve more consideration. They raise the old debate about Scottish exceptionalism in education. I would argue that it is the patterns of Scottish education that make the Scottish missionary diaspora distinctive, at least from its English counterpart. (It may not have been so different from its continental counterparts, German, Scandinavian, and Dutch; and this too would be in line with other recent studies of Scottish education.) Time and space restrict the scope of investigation, so the immediate illustrations are drawn from India, the area that was the earliest and often the principal focus of Scottish church missions.

The former Missions Reference Library of the Church of Scotland now housed at the Centre for the Study of Christianity in the Non-Western World at Edinburgh University contains a large collection of bound volumes of pamphlets evidently assembled during Alexander Duff's convenership of the Free Church Foreign Missions Committee. One of the striking features of this collection is its miscellaneous character. There are, as one might expect, plenty of the productions of Scottish missionaries with a literary turn. There are endless expositions and vindications from Duff himself of the special nature of Scottish mission work, explaining why it is not a waste of time to concentrate on education. There is an equal flow from Duff's Bombay counterpart John Wilson, reflecting his wider range of intellectual concerns—cave temples and Buddhist monasteries, ancient coins presented to or exhibited at the Bombay branch of the Royal Asiatic Society, the Avesta (Wilson was probably its first English-speaking commentator), Jewish communities in western India, historical reconstructions from his journeys through Bible lands when going on home leave. Wilson's colleague Murray Mitchell contributes investigations in Zoroastrian literature, an early study of Tukaram, and improving tracts on mental and moral discipline. Kenneth Macdonald pens an affectionate celebration of the Hindu reformer Rammohun Roy ("a great religious reformer, far in advance of his time, and his name should be held in loving remembrance by his countrymen, and by all interested in the social and religious welfare of India"). There are writings by nineteenth-century Indian Christians—Dhanjabai Nauroji, G. R. Navalkar ("Thoughts on Idolatry Addressed to Educated Natives"), and others less known. There are writings by Hindu and Brahmo Samaj authors, including many by Keshub Chunder Sen. There are literary offerings, some of them curious; surely, it was not the relentlessly serious Duff who caused "A Tale for the Xmas Vacation" to be bound into one of the volumes. Or was it in illustration of his recurrent theme that literary trash was sent to India and reproduced there for children's reading? There is a "Legend of Harry and the Missionaries" in Hiawatha metre, and even the mighty John Wilson tries his hand at blank (sometimes very blank) verse. There is the entire catalogue of Calcutta Public Library. But the theme that appears again and again is that of education. There are discussions of English and vernacular education, analyses of government educational policy, examination papers, winning entries at school competitions, catalogues of educational materials and appliances, papers on medical education and on the place of the principles of agriculture in public education. There are papers from official, private, and missionary sources alike, on every aspect of education from the basic to the university.

The prominence of education in the collection is not accidental. The Scottish missions in South Asia invested a high proportion of their activity in education, and especially in higher education, and did so to an extent distinctive among the missions. Education was part of the identity of the Scottish missions. Scottish missions were frequently challenged on that ground, which explains that stream of vindications and explanations that flowed from Duff's pen. For many other missions, education was simply one branch of missionary activity, made necessary by the mission's other activities, or required as the price of its presence in the local setting. For the Scottish missions, at least for a substantial and determinative part of their existence, education *was* mission.

For Scots, education embraced the scientific, the mechanical, and the technological as well as the classically academic, and this was often evidenced in their missionary activity. Andrew Campbell, the leading figure in the Santal mission for forty years, was a mason by trade. He was certainly no slouch with the pen; he compiled a three-volume Santali dictionary that is also a compendium of Santal culture, and a collection of Santal stories that was plundered by Andrew Lang. But he was equally involved in designing buildings, planning irrigation schemes, and transforming the local economy. He introduced new cash crops (castor oil plant) and new industries (silk production), new export opportunities (gut for high-quality fishing lines), and promoted Santalia at the Indian and Colonial Exhibition of 1885 (he submitted seven hundred items) and judged that in agricultural skills and techniques, the West had nothing to teach the Santal farmer. In the early twentieth century the Glasgow printer Tom Dobson, vegetarian and socialist, went out to rescue the Pune printing works, an industrial scheme originally set up for famine relief, and went on to develop cooperative agricultural banks to reduce the debt burdens on what were then called untouchable groups. One is reminded of the impact of another Scottish Free Churchworker within an English mission; in the Church Missionary Society's early operations in Uganda, the engineering skills of Alexander Mackay, a man who could build and operate steamboats on the lake, were crucial. Yet Mackay was not an ancillary specialist; he *was* the missionary, the preacher, the negotiator, and the translator, as well as the technologist.

In India the Scottish churches early and consciously adopted education as their principal mode of activity. A higher proportion of their missionaries in India were engaged in higher education than was the case (so far as I have seen) in any other mission. This affected the profile of the Scottish missionary. For one thing—and this does not apply simply to India—the Scottish missionary tended to be rather better educated than the average English missionary. The Scottish missionary was in general recruited from the same sources as the home ministry, and had received the same academic training; for much of the nineteenth century this was a luxury beyond most English missionary societies. As a result of their training, Scottish missionaries were often intellectually curious; they read more and wrote more, and on more topics, and without the sense sometimes betrayed by their English colleagues that such activities were diversionary from the missionary vocation. To take an early example: Stephen Hislop was recruited to the Western India mission in 1845 because John Wilson thought that the mission needed teachers who could combine excellence in science with theology. Hislop was the architect of the Nagpur mission of the Free Church, with a heavy programme of itineration and vernacular preaching and the superintendence of Nagpur's only school. But he also studied and wrote on the local archaeology, botany, zoology, and, above all, geology. He built up a fossil collection that produced correspondence with geologists all over Europe, was the first to identify the region's coal seams, and discovered a mineral new to science. He was also responsible for the first ethnographic survey of the Gondh, and the designer of a Gondh orthography. His Nagpur colleague Robert Hunter had similar enthusiasms; after a severe breakdown induced his departure from India, he spent the rest of his life editing encyclopedias.

However, the most characteristically Scottish feature of this missionary group does not lie in such miscellaneous contributions to knowledge or journalism, but in the different constituency of the Scottish missions from that of most missionaries. The natural Scottish missionary habitat was not among those portions of India society that most readily responded to mission-related Christianity. The highest proportion of Indian Christians were drawn from people at the lower end of or outside the caste system, and the aboriginal or *adivasi* groups. Though there are important exceptions, the records of the Scottish missions do not usually give the best pictures of the toiling masses in the villages, and the Santal mission is exceptional in being addressed to a tribal constituency. The special form of Scottish mission issued in the Scots colleges, and these were designed to enter the Hindu intellectual heartland.

The reasons for this lie in the very origins of the Scottish missionary movement.

Scotland differed from England in a vital particular: while its Reformation had been more radical, it had left more of the country untouched. Consequently, at least in a Protestant view, Scotland was by the eighteenth century a primary mission field in a sense that England was not. Vast, unmanageable Highland parishes with a scattering of inaccessible parish schools offering instruction in English to a Gaelic-speaking population represented both a contrast with and a challenge to the central and southern belts of the country. There, Reformation and education had marched together, and the interdependence of those two factors became axiomatic in Scotland. Serious ecclesiastics, whether moderate or evangelical, could agree on that, and join in support of the Society in Scotland for Propagating Christian Knowledge (SSPCK). This body promoted Reformed teaching and Bible-based education in the Highlands, both in English and (against its original grain) in Gaelic. It needed no great policy shift (indeed, the provision was already in its foundation documents) to extend the Society's work from the Highlands to the Native Americans; David Brainerd, who became an icon of the Protestant missionary movement, was an agent of the SSPCK, though he never saw Scotland. The first Scottish writer to set out a comprehensive missionary programme, Robert Millar of Paisley, who wrote as early as 1723, foresees a new age of evangelization beginning with "the reviving of arts and sciences, knowledge and learning," just as happened at the Reformation itself. An early Scottish missionary in West Africa, Henry Brunton of the Scottish Missionary Society, writes in 1802 about the necessity for missions to lay a foundation of learning. Evangelical revival in Christendom, he argues, did not occur spontaneously; it was the fruit of long intellectual and literary preparation. Religious revival in Africa or Hindustan would come only after the steady dissemination of knowledge. As proof, it was necessary only to look at Highland experience. The SSPCK schools had taught children to read the Bible. Those children were now grown up and receiving the gospel gladly.

If there is a specifically Scottish philosophy of missions, its germ lies here. I would like in the rest of this chapter to illustrate it from a succession of four Scottish figures in South Asia whose careers cover the period from the beginning of Scottish church missions to the last years of the British Raj.

The first of the four, Alexander Duff (1806–78), arrived in India as the first missionary commissioned by the Church of Scotland in 1830, an evangelical through and through, but with a body of instructions drafted by the archetypal moderate, John Inglis. It was a prospectus on which moderate and evangelical could agree, the formula on which they were also in accord in the Highlands: education as the framework in which Christian teaching was set. Duff was far from being the first missionary to develop education in India; what was unusual was his deliberate relinquishing of other means. He announced that he would leave to the other missions the task of bazaar preaching and pastoring the resultant tiny communities of poor and leaderless adherents. He would aim directly at young high-caste Hindus, who might radically influence the whole of Indian society, and do so by means of what they most desired: access to education in English. He later described his activity thus:

> We thought not of individuals merely; we looked to the masses . . . we directed our view not merely to the present but to future generations. . . . While you [the other missions] engage individually separating as many precious items from the mass as the stubborn resistance to ordinary appliances can admit, we shall, with the blessing of God, devote our time and strength to the preparing of a mine, and the setting of a train which will one day explode and tear up the whole from its lowest depths.

In other words, Duff planned the intellectual renewal of Indian society by the propagation of a new worldview in which the whole encyclopedia of knowledge—philosophy, natural science, astronomy, history, political economy—was presented in the context of a Christian theology that harmonized them and had a place for them all. The God of creation, whose laws governed the structures of the world and the historical processes by which human affairs were resolved, was the same God who revealed his character and future plan for humanity in the Bible. It was very much the worldview that had been expounded in Duff's student days at St. Andrews by his moral philosophy professor, Thomas Chalmers: the rational Calvinism of the Scottish Enlightenment that united moderate and evangelical. It was not enough to create rebels against traditional Hinduism by exposing the incompatibility of traditional cosmology with empirical science; that was already done at the government's Hindu College. Duff held that secular learning—and British government educational policy was determinedly secular—simply corroded and destroyed. He sought a fresh implant with a new moral dynamic; he would teach moral philosophy in order to subvert the monist assumptions that reduced the essential mutual opposition of good and evil, and set forth an all-embracing view of learning that encouraged exploration by its very order, diversity and harmony. Rational enquiry was therefore to be encouraged, rote learning discouraged. Duff refused to dictate notes, lest his students memorize them and cease to think. One of those students, Lal Behari Day, describes the effect:

> The ideas of pupils were enlarged; their power of thinking was developed; they were encouraged to observe; they were taught to express their ideas in words; and as learning was made pleasant to them, their affections were drawn to the acquisition of learning.

Crucially, Duff early gained the support of Rammohun Roy, a leading Hindu whose own religious and social reformism acknowledged the inspiration of the New Testament and the Qur'an. Roy was able to persuade Hindu parents of the benefit to be gained from this style of education, and not to fear exposure to the Christian Scriptures, which he himself read devoutly. By this means the Scottish missions entered the trajectory of the Bengal renaissance and of Hindu reform.

For a time, Duff saw remarkable success. Some fifty young, educated, high-caste Hindus were baptised, and the religious and intellectual impact was wider still. Similar developments took place in the other centres of Scottish mission work in India. John Anderson in Madras operated on very similar lines; John Wilson and the other Bombay missionaries had originally no such idea, but found themselves drawn into it. In all three places a pattern developed: occasional conversions of individuals or small groups, leading to a crisis, threatening closure of the school or even civil disturbance. One outcome of this was that the converts, though few in number, made their Christian profession after a thorough intellectual grounding, and did so with firm intellectual commitment. Since baptism also generally involved a severe rift with family and society, converts consciously made a decision at great personal cost. These two factors meant that the convert group taken as a whole was of high mental and personal quality, with plenty of initiative and leadership potential. And the first generation of Indian Christians related to the Scottish missions included people of notable stature. Some, such as Krishna Mohun Banerjea, who argued that the Christian doctrines of the incarnation and atonement were foreshadowed in the Hindu scriptures, and that reform-minded Hindus could maintain the best in their heritage as Christians, joined other churches; the attributes that produced the early converts meant that they would not be passive clay in missionary hands. Others, like Lal Behari Day, already mentioned, or Rajagopal in Madras, or the Bombay Brahman Narayan Sheshadri, or the Parsi Dhanjabai Nauroji, became well-known figures in Scotland through their visits, or writings, or writings about them. Dhanjabai Nauroji, who was at New College, Edinburgh, in its early years, proudly points to the luminaries of the Free Church who were his classmates.

For a time, it seemed that Duff's mine might explode, as he had predicted. Then the flow of Calcutta converts subsided. Duff never abandoned his confidence, but as the sheer number of his published vindications show, the educational thrust of Scottish missions required continual defence. In the light of the 1857 war, the Scottish approach appeared discredited. In the eyes of critics in Scotland and of the missionary constituency at large, it pandered to high-caste pride (which, together with Islam, was often identified as the cause of the Mutiny). It also wasted scarce resources, and did not heed sufficiently the scriptural warning that the wisdom of this world is foolishness with God. Let missions leave the proud Brahmans to themselves and concentrate on vernacular evangelism among the most responsive groups in the lowest castes, or outside the caste system. At the Liverpool Conference on Missions in 1860, Thomas Smith, Duff's assistant and successor, had a hard time arguing that higher education was a form of mission, not just a service or a means of gaining a hearing. Smith's argument was that the intellectual preconditions of Christian faith are not present in Hindu society, and have, therefore, to be implanted. In effect, he sees the Scottish university arts curriculum as a natural preparation for Christianity. Logic and moral philosophy, properly taught, prepare the way for the gospel by creating a new set of intellectual conditions. But the greater number of his hearers—to judge from the published discussion—were inclined to judge this a waste of time and money. Their attitude might be summed up as "Never mind the intellectual conditions, preach the gospel to those who will listen." His most vigorous support came from the only Indian at the conference, Lal Behari. He, however, had another argument for Christian higher education: Christian leaders in India must be as skilled in the ancient biblical languages as Hindu and Muslim leaders were in Sanskrit and Arabic. Duff in fact contributed to the Bengal renaissance of Hinduism, and, both by direct effect and by reaction had become part of the story of Hindu reform. The progress of Hindu reform, and the adjustments to modernity it brought about, were no doubt major reasons for the drying up of the early stream of converts. When it was no longer obvious that eager young men must choose between Hindu tradition and modernity, angry young males ceased to be angry at the Hindu old men, and diverted their anger to the British. During the 1857–58 war, the Western-educated group by and large supported the British. After the war, their successors, including those educated in the Scots colleges, increasingly identified with their Indian heritage. Duff's mine train, it appeared, had burnt out.

One of the people who saw what was happening was William Miller (1838–1923), who became principal of the Madras school in 1863, when he was twenty-five years of age and it was in a state of virtual disintegration. He stayed for forty-four years, drove up the standards of the school until it could open a university department and affiliate to the University of Madras (he became, in due course, vice-chancellor of that university), and made it the nucleus of Madras Christian College.

Miller insisted that the Scottish educational institutions in India must do what they professed to do, and educate to the very highest standards. The time had passed when Christian institutions could expect to dominate the higher-educational scene; even in areas where the missions had led the way, such as women's education, there were now many other initiatives. The Christian institutions should concentrate on quality; and good standards involved opening minds. His predecessor, Duff's contemporary John Anderson, had insisted, "India must be brought to think." It was a theme to which Miller's educational policy was directed. Teaching people to think had a missionary function. Miller's analysis of the situation in the late 1860s was that all the missions, with the exception of the Scottish, had effectively given up the attempt to reach "true" Hindus. They were devoting their whole attention to the tribals and to the groups who were for practical purposes outside Hinduism. Converts from these groups could never influence "true" Hindus, and certainly not people of the sort who entered the colleges, whether of Christian, Hindu, or government foundation. Miller's remedy was to use the colleges "to influence the corporate thought of Hinduism." Hinduism had so successfully unified belief and practice that the individual impulse had virtually ceased. Individual action, deliberate choice, is virtually inconceivable, "swamped in the unconnected intensity of corporate life." This meant that conversion in the evangelical sense was virtually impossible; personal conviction of sin, for instance, had no way of entering. If conversions were to take place, therefore, the intellectual conditions must be created in which fresh decisions and new departures became possible.

This, of course, was basically what Duff and Anderson sought to do in earlier time; but they had been bringing in a new worldview from the outside in which modernity and Christian teaching were offered together. By Miller's time it was possible to take the first and reject the second. Miller sought, not the radical displacement of Hinduism as Duff had, not to blow Hinduism up with Duff's mine, but to influence its development, to make change possible, to create the conditions in which Christianity could grow in a Hindu setting. Hinduism, he argued, was no longer a *faith;* the earnest spirit of belief that once filled it had perished, leaving a connected living mass of custom and observance. The Christian colleges, therefore, must provide the sort of education that would "draw out and

revive those longings, yearnings and strivings for the good they comprehend not," to revive the implicit faith of Hinduism now ossified into a system. No longer are the colleges seen as a nursery for conversion-in-depth
(though Miller does claim that more direct conversions among "true Hindus" had occurred through the colleges than by all other methods put together); and indeed, numerous conversions (or at least, numerous bap-
tisms) would probably result in the closure of the colleges anyway. Their
task is not evangelistic, but preevangelistic: to awaken moral responsibility, the living apprehension of the spiritual world, the power of choice.
These elements were necessary to evangelical conversion; they were also
a function of a first-rate education.

Miller thus saw the Indian way to Christ as in one sense lying through
Hinduism, but in aspects of Hinduism now dead or dormant; and a prime
missionary function was therefore to influence Hinduism itself in order to
prepare for Christianity. The person who gave fullest expression to the
idea of Hinduism as a preparation for Christianity, of Hindu aspiration
fulfilled in Christ, was another Scot, John Nicol Farquhar (1861–1929), of
the London Missionary Society.

By 1900, when Farquhar had served his first decade in India, the situation of the Christian colleges was no longer what it was when Miller produced his new prospectus for them. As Miller had foreseen, they were no
longer the leaders of intellectual life, but only a small part of a huge educational sector. No longer were those of Western education contemptuous of
traditional Hinduism; traditional Hinduism was making terms with Western thought by absorbing it, indeed absorbing Christianity itself, into its
own body. Sri Ramakrishna had shown that Christ could be experienced
within Hinduism; if so, it could be held that all religions were true, and
conversion unnecessary. Indeed, the work of Swami Vivekananda appeared to show that the West was open to neo-Vedantic views of reality; if
conversions were to take place, they might well be of Westerners to Hinduism rather than of Indians to Christianity. The movements for political
self-rule were naturally strongest among those with the highest degree of
Western education. The combination of factors meant that the Hindu intellectual classes could no longer be seen as bound by the dead, faithless tra-
ditionalism of Miller's analysis. (How could one say that there was no faith
left in Hinduism in the light of the life of Sri Ramakrishna?) The educated
community, taken as a whole, was hostile to any form of Western domination, and to Christianity as a means of expressing that domination. The
hostility to Christianity was concentrated on the act of joining the church.
There was no need to reject the God of the Christian Scriptures, nor to reject Christ—Ramakrishna had met him in the garden; Keshub Chunder
Sen had seen him dancing with Chaitanya. But joining the church stood for
joining the enemy; baptism for breach of the community.

Miller had wanted the colleges to influence Hindu opinion by opening
minds; Farquhar decided that the task of intellectual engagement with

young Indians of the sort who committed themselves to the national movement could be best accomplished outside the classroom. His chance came in 1902 with an appointment to the YMCA in Calcutta with special responsibility for work with students.

The circumstances of the time, which made public meetings difficult and put interethnic friendships under strain, caused him to concentrate on literature. He wished to know what the young people were reading, and was led to the Bhagavad Gita. Clearly, neo-Krishnaism was being presented as the alternative to Christianity, an alternative suitable for good nationalists. The old-fashioned eclectic theism of the Brahmo Samaj was now outflanked; Krishnaism stood for Indianness, Christianity for foreignness. The way into this consciousness lay through the Bhagavad Gita. If Christianity was not really foreign to India, what had it to say about the Gita?

Duff had studied Sanskrit literature largely with a view to demonstrating its futility; on his assumptions it could have no permanent significance. Miller had seen it as a Christian task to revive instincts dormant in Hinduism. Farquhar found a Christian vocation in the study of Hindu literature by immersion in the language, and by seeking to understand its inwardness. First he essayed a Christian approach to the Gita, the loveliest flower, he believed, in the garden of Sanskrit literature. He feels its literary power, its religious sensibility, its moral aspiration. What it lacks is the historical foundation that Christians have in Jesus Christ. The Gita wants a personal saviour, and, not finding it, has to invent a myth. "The author of the Gita would have been a Christian had he known Jesus."

In other words, the phenomena of Hinduism reveal the existence of a need that cannot be satisfied by those phenomena, but can be satisfied through Jesus Christ. The rest of Farquhar's life was devoted to the examination on a wider basis of the theme that he had first enunciated in relation to the Gita: Christianity can be seen as the fulfilment of the Hindu scriptures, and of the whole Hindu religious quest.

In the process, Farquhar became an outstanding student of Indian religious literature. He produced his sympathetic general interpretations: the handy *Primer of Hinduism,* the more extensive *Crown of Hinduism,* an *Outline of the Religious Literature of India* that goes on being reprinted in India, and a study of *Modern Religious Movements in India* that despite its date has even now not been quite superseded. He stimulated others to study, and assisted their work. He formed a study circle of Christians, Hindus, and Brahmos, he initiated and edited three scholarly monograph series (The Religious Quest of India, The Heritage of India, and The Religious Life of India). Behind his work is the conviction that Christianity is not foreign to Indian religious aspirations, but a natural—that is, divinely directed—development of those aspirations. And the missionary task involves sympathetic and unremittingly scholarly study of the literature in which these aspirations are embodied.

Our final exemplar, Alfred George Hogg (1876–1954), was the child of a new era. He was the son of a missionary, but had had a hard road to faith, involving a major intellectual crisis and a nervous breakdown. He became a lay missionary in 1903, but was not ordained until many years later. He worked for thirty-six years at Madras Christian College, first as professor of philosophy, later as principal, and his considerable, if fragmented, oeuvre is best interpreted within a Hindu intellectual context. He was a philosopher by profession, teaching philosophy in an institution that was explicitly Christian while its student body was mostly Hindu. That is, Hogg's missionary activity in the presentation of Christian faith in India took as common ground between Christians and Hindus the practice of philosophy. His personal pilgrimage had included a shaking of the foundations of family and traditional beliefs. He thus saw the shaking of the foundations as a part of normal experience, and therefore expected and intended his teaching to produce opposition. He saw the real peril of the presentation of Christianity in India to be that it provoked so little opposition, except at baptism, when the threat to family and caste was imminent. The usual presentation of Christianity produced so little intellectual challenge that Hindus could meet it with indifference. Even Indian Christians were rarely *thinking* as Christians profoundly enough to provoke them.

The ready-made doctrinal formulations of the West, he argued, were of little help in the presentation of Christ in India, because they reflect matters that have interested the religious mind of the West and are set out in relation to Western ways of thinking. Some of the subjects they raise have never interested Hindus; some of the ways of thinking have never existed in India. "The doctrinal formulations which the missionary brings with him are largely useless . . . not because they are false but because they are irrelevant." The key to the relationship between Christianity and Hinduism was not to be found in fulfilment (Farquhar's regular theme), but in selective contrast. The Christian distinctives lie in the Christ of the Gospels, who, as Messiah, inaugurates the kingdom of God. For Hogg, the heart of the contrast between Christianity and Hinduism is the cosmic nature of Christian salvation. While acknowledging that a good deal of Christian preaching has concentrated on the salvation of the individual soul as much as Hindu tradition has concentrated on saving people out of the world, he insists to his very politically conscious audience that the Christ of the New Testament is the redeemer of the whole world order. We are back to the theocratic theme that David Cairns had indicated as characteristic of the Scottish religious vision.

From here, Hogg goes on to the exploration of the effect that India could have on Christian theology. The classical doctrine of the atonement, for instance, has been shaped by centuries of Western reflection on God as sovereign and judge. Those ideas belong to Europe; having no equivalent in Indian intellectual history, the classical doctrine has little impact in India. Accordingly, Hogg labours at a rethinking of atonement by way of the problem of pain and its unequal distribution—the theme that Indian thought has addressed by the doctrine of karma. From this attempt to develop Christian theology in terms of ideas that have exercised the religious mind of India, Hogg seeks to engage Indian thought with ideas that have not traditionally occupied it, but which might arise out of the restatement of Christian themes in Indian terms—for instance, the possibility of moral renewal. Perhaps, Hindu thought can recognize moral impotence as a problem more readily than guilt.

A. G. Hogg is still one of the most interesting theologians of the twentieth century writing in English. Long before most theologians for whom the classical Western formulations were a given, he realized the impact that the Christian encounter with the non-Western world was going to have on Christian theology. His theological starting point is still the Christ event and his working materials are still biblical. But he points towards a time when a non-Western Christianity expresses the Christian themes in categories arising from Christian interaction with the ancient cultures of Asia and Africa. And this comes from seeing his missionary vocation as teaching philosophy as a Christian in a college in which most of the students were, and would remain, Hindus. It may be noted in passing that one of his pupils, Professor Sir Sarvepalli Radhakrishnan of Oxford, would take the traffic in the other direction, and bring Indian categories into the Western philosophical discourse.

Hogg stands in a line that goes through Duff, Miller, and Farquhar, essentially Scottish figures who saw the task of the missionary diaspora in India as engagement at a fundamental level with the mainstream of the intellectual life and literature of India. The Scottish strand is only one small component in the missionary movement, but this may be one of its special contributions: a fruit of the rational Calvinism of the Scottish Enlightenment, and an aspect of the theocratic, society-orientated outlook and the desire for strong thinking in religion that David Cairns saw as hallmarks of Scottish religion. It is also a by-product of the traditional educational system of Scotland. Perhaps it is significant that it was a Scot—Alexander Duff, in fact—who developed the idea of a scientific study of missions, and that it was at New College, Edinburgh, that the first chair of what is now called missiology was established. (This Scottish initiative was not followed in England for over a century, and soon died in Scotland, but it took root in continental Europe and in the United States.)

When the missionary diaspora began, Christianity was a Western religion, whose adherents lived predominantly in Europe and North America. The Western missionary episode in Christian history is almost over, and Christianity is now predominantly a non-Western religion, with a steadily increasing majority of its adherents living in Africa, Asia, Latin and Caribbean America, and the Pacific. That is one good reason for studying the missionary diaspora and its influence, whatever we make of its Scottish dimension.

15

Missiologist of the Road

David Jacobus Bosch (1929–1992)

David Bosch was the most complete missiologist of our generation, perhaps of the whole century. There have been giants in the land, and some of them very great; but has anyone else explored, presented, and proclaimed mission with such manysidedness and variety? David Bosch combined comprehensiveness and originality of thought. He mastered the range of disciplines and cognate studies that the student of missions must lay under tribute. He presented his work in such a way as to bear on people of different traditions and nations and understandings of the Christian gospel. Not content with magisterial exposition, he spent much of his energy in steady, grinding labor, making tools by which the study of mission can be carried out. Not content with scholarly eminence, he devoted himself to bringing others together in common study and fruitful discussion. Not confining his labour to the study and the lecture room and the publishing house, he took it into the church, both locally and at large. And for all that, he is such a seminal figure in mission studies that the striking thing about him was his manifest personal, practical commitment to the Christian mission in its fullest reaches—to all, in other words, that is expressed in the charge "As the Father has sent me, so I send you."

David Bosch's completeness as a missiologist springs from the fact that he was not only a missiologist. There are missiologists who are content to play a specialist role in the theological arena and who make an ancillary contribution to a discourse of which other people provide the core. This means that at the theological banquet table, mission studies are roughly the equivalent of after-dinner mints. For Bosch, missiology was

Prepared for a conference of the British and Irish Association for Mission Studies devoted to the study of David Bosch's *Transforming Mission*. First published in the *Occasional Bulletin* of the British and Irish Association for Mission Studies (No. 2, New Series, 1994): 1–5.

theology, indeed *encylopaedic* theology. As is evident not just from his last great work, but from his writings as a whole, his missiology is biblical and systematic and historical and practical. All the classical theological disciplines are in constant use. For Bosch was brought up in classical theology. His doctorate was in classical theology, at Basel, done under Oscar Cullmann's direction, in Basel's classical period. Those days left their mark. I remember him saying once, apropos of his editorial labours, how he often found it necessary to check the sources of some enthusiastic collaborators because, "Yes, they know German, but *not enough* German." For many years he was dean—an innovative dean—of the largest theological faculty in the world, that of the University of South Africa. One of his last articles to appear during his lifetime is devoted to the nature of theological education.[1] It is a public activity, he argues, with three different domains to address. The academy is the first domain; the theology addresses both the academic and intellectual worlds as a whole; the church is the second; the wider society the third. Theology that does not address all three is either empty or sectarian. The three public domains represent three different dimensions of theology, which he denominates *theoria, poiesis,* and *praxis.* These are not alternatives but dimensions of the same reality, and theology involves the integration of intellectual rigour, particularly in the life of the church, and practical demonstration in the life of the world.

This attempt to integrate the domains of academy, church, and society, and life as a Christian participating in each was characteristic of his style and life. It brought him much discomfort, which those prepared to restrict their activity to one or two of the domains were able to avoid. It made him open and mobile, in settings where rigidity and predictability were often taken for granted. He was fond of the symbolism of the "road"—reflecting, no doubt, John A. Mackay's differentiation of the perspectives of the balcony and the road. The balcony is essentially the position of the spectator; the road means pursuit of a journey among people who are not all going in the same direction. One of Bosch's splendid little books, not as well known as it should be, is *A Spirituality of the Road.*[2] The things he talks about in his work were things that he himself practised and applied.

For Bosch, the road lay through South Africa. It is perhaps the most theologically active country in the world; for there, if anywhere, it is manifest that theology is a matter of life and death. (I remember a Desmond Tutu saying about theology in South Africa: "It's about being a Christian when you are hanging on by the skin of your teeth.") David spent his whole working life in South Africa. He did not have to. He had plenty of offers to go elsewhere, and the two most prestigious missiological chairs in North America were open to

---

[1]"The Nature of Theological Education," *Theologia Evangelica* 25, no. 1, (1992): 8–23.
[2]Scottdale, Pa.: Herald, 1979.

him. Either would have afforded him, when at the height of his powers, security and quiet independence and the opportunity to address a worldwide audience. He turned his back on these attractive prospects, because he concluded that his road still lay in South Africa, where it had begun.

David Bosch came from a conventional Afrikaner farming background, conventional in piety and lifestyle. He later would say that he grew up among Africans. But he would quickly add that in his youth, the Africans were simply figures in the background, part of the scenery, as the cows on the farm were. As human beings, they belonged to a world that did not impinge on his own. He never surrendered either his Afrikaner identity (he had, incidentally, a master's degree in Afrikaans language) or his Dutch Reformed Church loyalty. But both identities underwent profound reinterpretation through his experience as a missionary. He acquired an exceptional grasp of the Xhosa language. It is said that when he returned to speak in one parish after several years' absence, a blind man there, when told that the speaker was a white man, said, "It must be David Bosch. Only he speaks Xhosa like a Xhosa." The act of acquiring a language like this cannot take place without a high degree of wider sympathy, understanding, and identification.

As a missionary, David Bosch was responsible for a change in Dutch Reformed mission thinking that was symbolic of his whole life's work. The mission had only ordained workers as "real" missionaries. Medical missionaries and teachers were auxiliary in function—medical and educational work were considered ancillary to the church. A still young Bosch secured recognition of the fact that the healing and preaching mission were one. They were not, he insisted, primary and secondary operations, but one in the whole mission of Christ.

It was in his missionary days that his ecumenical activity began. "Ecumenical" has a different significance in South Africa from its common range elsewhere. It is costly. The factors that call Christians together call them across deep divides of historical memory and unequal power relations, divides reinforced by language and political structures. Ecumenism in South Africa is like ecumenism in the New Testament. It is about table fellowship. It belongs to the nature of the Christian church to practise it, but the emotional pressures against it are sometimes too much even for a Barnabas and Peter. That is why Africa's great ecumenical figure, the Afrikaner Beyers Naudé, is also such a symbol of the rejection of apartheid. Bosch—an Afrikaans-, Xhosa-, and German-speaker—also became completely at home in English. As a missionary, he began to enter other people's worlds. I am assured that he was the real architect of the Transkei Council of Churches, a marvelous accomplishment for an agent of the Dutch Reformed Church, considering that church's intransigent attitude toward the South African Council of Churches.

In time, the missionary came into theological teaching, then into the University of South Africa and its unique structure, where he became professor of missiology. This was the base for his best-known scholarly and literary work. It is not necessary to rehearse here the nature and extent of that missiological work. It is well known. One aspect, however, that is perhaps now forgotten is that he was one of the first mainline theologians to see the significance and abiding value of black theology. I vividly recall reading an early review by him of the original 1972 symposium on black theology in one of Beyers Naudé's creations, the splendidly brave journal *Pro Veritate*, itself later banned by the South African government. The volume of essays edited by Basil Brown had just been banned, which meant that no one could quote from it. Bosch solemnly produced a long review, full of quotations with brief comments. Of course, the quotations had to be omitted, leaving huge white spaces on every page. No more telling commentary could have been provided on the absurdity of government policy. It was about this time that I first met David Bosch, when he visited Europe to build relations with scholars seriously concerned with African Christianity; for his deep involvement with South Africa was always set in an African and an international context.

Meanwhile, South Africa's distresses intensified. Bosch's constant theme was reconciliation. The problem was that the word was a catchphrase used superficially by whites who had no idea of the extent of African hurt and no concept of repentance, and by others whose real desire was to gain consent for the existing power structures. Bosch, belonging to the Reformed tradition but also well read in the Anabaptist, was aware that both these positions were spurious. For Christians, reconciliation could be understood only in terms of the cross. I recall meeting him and his wife, Annemie, in their house near Pretoria at the time of the Soweto riots, and seeing the pain one feels when rejected by one's own community without being accepted by the other. I also noted his insistence that what he called the "masochistic agony" of many white liberals was not enough. Rejection by every party did not give one exemption from the task of steadily working for change. And so he continued on the dusty and turbulent South African road. He lived long enough to see the beginnings of change and to be convinced of its irreversibility. And he died in South Africa—literally and symbolically on the road—in a tragic accident, one with features that reflected the continuing contradictions of that land.

Bosch's devotion to South Africa was combined with a world Christian citizenship. On the world stage, as at home, he was a reconciler. It was impossible to put him in a theological box. He was at once thoroughly evangelical and essentially ecumenical. He insisted that both positions arose from the same premise. His searching theological critique ranged over both alike. I recall his sardonic commentary when he returned from a journey during which he had participated in the Commission on World Mission and Evangelism in Melbourne and the Lausanne meeting in Pattaya. Both appeared to be his clubs, and when he was in one, he felt like a member of the other. Yet his very discomfort arose from the fact that really he was an insider in both, affirming Christian verities, but seeing deeper than their conventional expressions. It was the same with the historic confessions. He was most throughly Reformed, and yet his ecclesial sense was thoroughly Catholic. The last time I saw him, he confessed that the Reformation figure with whom he most fully identified was Erasmus. I think that this feeling was merely an expression of his continuing quest to be simply and authentically Christian, rather than to be some particular sort of Christian.

He was an Erasmian in another sense, too. He was a comprehensive, encyclopaedic scholar, a scholar who honed the tools of scholarship for others. Had he done nothing else, the journal *Missionalia*, combining the features of a learned periodical and a missiological indexing and abstracting service, would be a monument to him. So would the Southern African Missiological Society, of which he was the first and, until his death, the only general secretary. It brought together southern Africa's theological and Christian polarities into missiological interaction. No wonder that when the Society honored him with a festschrift issue of *Missionalia* in 1990, they called it "Mission in Creative Tension: A Dialogue with David Bosch."[3]

David Bosch was an important contributor to the International Association for Mission Studies. Alas, the British and Irish Association for Mission Studies never quite succeeded in getting him to address one of its meetings.

When he left us, perhaps his work was done. He had worked for change and seen its dawn. He had brought many Christians to reexamine their mission and to find it more demanding than they had realised. And he had completed his own *Summa Missiologica*, entitled *Transforming Mission: Paradigm Shifts in Theology of Mission*.[4] Perhaps some words from that volume will form a fitting conclusion to this salute to the Missiologist of the Road:

> Such language boils down to an admission that we do not have all the answers and are prepared to live within the framework of penultimate knowledge, that we regard our involvement in dialogue and mission as an adventure, are prepared to take risks, and are anticipating surprises as the Spirit guides us into fuller understanding. This is not opting for agnosticism, but for humility. It is, however, a bold humility—or a humble boldness. We know only in part, but we do know. And we believe that the faith we profess is both true and just, and should be proclaimed. We do this, however, not as judges or lawyers, but as witnesses; not as soldiers, but as envoys of peace; not as high-pressure salespersons, but as ambassadors of the Servant Lord.[5]

---

[3]See *Missionalia* 18, no. 1 (1990). The collection is introduced by an article by Kevin Livingston entitled "David Bosch: An Interpretation of Some Main Themes in His Missiological Thought," pp. 20–23. Livingston's doctoral thesis, "A Missiology of the Road: The Theology of Mission and Evangelism in the Writings of David Bosch" (Ph.D. diss., University of Aberdeen, 1989), remains the fullest examination of Bosch's work.

[4]Maryknoll, N.Y.: Orbis, 1991.

[5]Bosch, *Transforming Mission*, 489.

Index